Global Queer Theologies

Global Queer Theologies

Intercontextual and Interreligious Perspectives

Lisa Isherwood
Hugo Córdova Quero

Registered Offices
John Wiley & Sons, Inc., 111 River Street, Hoboken, NJ 07030, USA
John Wiley & Sons Ltd, New Era House, 8 Oldlands Way, Bognor Regis, West Sussex, PO22 9NQ, UK

For details of our global editorial offices, customer services, and more information about Wiley products visit us at www.wiley.com.

The manufacturer's authorized representative according to the EU General Product Safety Regulation is Wiley-VCH GmbH, Boschstr. 12, 69469 Weinheim, Germany, e-mail: Product_Safety@wiley.com.

Wiley also publishes its books in a variety of electronic formats and by print-on-demand. Some content that appears in standard print versions of this book may not be available in other formats.

Limit of Liability/Disclaimer of Warranty
While the publisher and the authors have used their best efforts in preparing this work, including a review of the content of the work, neither the publisher nor the authors make any representations or warranties with respect to the accuracy or completeness of the contents of this work and specifically disclaim all warranties, including without limitation any implied warranties of merchantability or fitness for a particular purpose. No warranty may be created or extended by sales representatives, written sales materials or promotional statements for this work. The fact that an organization, website, or product is referred to in this work as a citation and/or potential source of further information does not mean that the publisher and authors endorse the information or services the organization, website, or product may provide or recommendations it may make. This work is sold with the understanding that the publisher is not engaged in rendering professional services. The advice and strategies contained herein may not be suitable for your situation. You should consult with a specialist where appropriate. Further, readers should be aware that websites listed in this work may have changed or disappeared between when this work was written and when it is read. Neither the publisher nor authors shall be liable for any loss of profit or any other commercial damages, including but not limited to special, incidental, consequential, or other damages.

Library of Congress Cataloging-in-Publication Data

Names: Isherwood, Lisa author | Quero, Hugo Córdova author
Title: Global queer theologies : intercontextual and interreligious
    perspectives / Lisa Isherwood and Hugo Córdova Quero.
Description: Hoboken, NJ : Wiley-Blackwell, 2026. | Includes
    bibliographical references and index.
Identifiers: LCCN 2025042222 (print) | LCCN 2025042223 (ebook) | ISBN
    9781394199228 paperback | ISBN 9781394199235 adobe pdf | ISBN
    9781394199242 epub
Subjects: LCSH: Queer theology
Classification: LCC BT83.65 .I84 2026 (print) | LCC BT83.65 (ebook)
LC record available at https://lccn.loc.gov/2025042222
LC ebook record available at https://lccn.loc.gov/2025042223

Cover Design: Wiley
Cover Image: © NishanDesigns/Shutterstock

Set in 9.5/12.5pt STIXTwoText by Straive, Pondicherry, India
Printed and bound by CPI Group (UK) Ltd, Croydon, CR0 4YY

C9781394199228_041125

Contents

Introduction

Why a Book on Global Queer Theologies?

This book serves as an initiation into the realms of queer theory and theologies, providing readers with a comprehensive overview. It meticulously traces the evolution and influence of queer theory within theological contexts, shedding light on its profound impact. By delving into the intersection of these disciplines, the text unveils a diverse panorama of theologies that have flourished worldwide across various faiths. This exploration highlights the transformative power of the amalgamation of queer theory and theology, showcasing the vibrant tapestry of beliefs and perspectives that have emerged as a result of this dynamic intersection.

The aim is to span different contexts in which we observe the agency of people and faith communities in deconstructing spirituality, sacred texts and beliefs. The volume makes the Divine's relationalities visible to all people in different spiritual paths and contexts. We will draw from various sources, experiences and realities to analyse how queer believers theologise and counter the discourses that seek to ostracise them from the faith communities. We will obtain an enriching global perspective beyond the traditional attention to Global North–rooted experiences.

In response to a growing imperative, this book directs attention to the unfolding landscape of queer theologies, particularly within Christianity, the pioneer of this discourse in the twentieth century. Recognising the expanding relevance across various religious traditions, the text extends its focus to encompass the diverse expressions of queer theologies within different faiths. By delving into Christianity's historical role and broadening the scope to include all religious bodies, the book seeks to illuminate the evolving narratives and perspectives within the context of diverse faith traditions. This approach underscores the necessity of understanding and engaging with the multifaceted dimensions of queer theologies as they manifest across the rich tapestry of religious beliefs and practices.

Most academic research has focused on the Global North for the last 30 years. The consequences are varied, ranging from the invisibility of religious experiences of queer believers in the global South to the Western ignorance of the development of literary and theological works in languages other than English. The authors' multilingual abilities can make much of this work known through this book. There is a lack of research into examining popular saint biographies, the statements of religious institutions regarding the relationship between faith and sexuality, and the creation of contextual spiritualities that takes into

Global Queer Theologies: Intercontextual and Interreligious Perspectives, First Edition. Lisa Isherwood and Hugo Córdova Quero.
© 2026 John Wiley & Sons Ltd. Published 2026 by John Wiley & Sons Ltd.

account the daily lived experiences of queer believers. Therefore, this book will provide various resources to foster this needed and much-awaited stage in current research from a global perspective.

Who Are We?

Lisa Isherwood was made Professor of Feminist Liberation Theologies at the University College of St Mark & St John in 2020, the first such chair in the United Kingdom. She is now Professor Emerita in Feminist Liberation Theologies at the University of Winchester and a research supervisor at the University of Wales, Trinity St David. As a feminist liberation theologian she believes theology to be a communal project fuelled by notions of radical equality and empowered by divine companionship. Her work explores the nature of incarnation within contemporary contexts and includes such areas as the body, gender, sexuality and eco-theology. She has written, co-authored or edited 3 books and written numerous book chapters and journal articles. She is a founder and Executive Editor of the international journal *Feminist Theology* [Sage] and sits on the international editorial board of the *Journal of Feminist Studies in Religion* (USA). She has lectured around the world and was honoured to be a visiting scholar at Garrett Evangelical Seminary, Evanston, in 1997; the Episcopal Divinity School, Cambridge Massachusetts, in 2000 and visiting professor in the University of Western Australia in 2004. In 2010 she was Vice President of the European Society of Women in Theological Research.

Lisa is a proud Welsh woman and feminist liberation theologian who employs queer theory to illuminate all areas of her work. Some context—The Welsh kingdoms were conquered by Edward 1 of England in 1284 and from that time onwards Wales became a colonised and reduced nation. There were a number of risings, but each was in time quelled and our royal houses never regained their power over our lands. Wales has continued to suffer from a colonial attitude imposed by the English most prominently in their efforts to stamp out our language by the use of the Welsh Not in schools. This was a piece of wood placed around the neck of children heard speaking Welsh, at the end of the day those with the Not would be punished. This practice carried on until the 1940s had a profound effect on the use of English particularly in the south of Wales. There were multiple 'reports' carried out by English government officials which caricatured the Welsh, particularly Welsh women, as immoral and lacking in any form of education and indeed dignity. It also goes without saying that any trace of indigenous Celtic religion was frowned on; every effort was made to imbed the Anglican faith in Wales. Take note of the Anglican which stands for anglicisation in many parts of the world. Thankfully, although not without its problems a large number of Welsh people opted for Methodism which did have a dire effect on certain parts of Welsh culture. However, the most insidious attack on culture often came from within the community itself, from those who aspired to be viewed as cultured and educated and subsequently looked down on what they often termed as 'too Welshy or taffy'. The latter being a term still used for the Welsh. A well-known ditty talks of Taffy as a thief and not too bright and deserving of murder. While our language is once again being heard and Welsh-speaking schools are popular with parents there is a legacy that still lingers in the psyche of my people, and it was not until 1999 that we had our own National Assembly which since 2006 has been known as the Senedd. However, the Senedd while being democratically elected by the people of Wales has limited powers granted by Westminster who also control the major budget that Wales receives.

Hugo Córdova Quero is an academic and theologian whose research focuses on the intersections of migration, gender, sexuality, and religion. He is known for his pioneering work in these fields, challenging conventional narratives and broadening the understanding of migration experiences from an interdisciplinary perspective. Córdova Quero was born in Argentina and received his education at various prestigious institutions in Latin America, the United States and Asia. He earned his doctorate at the Graduate Theological Union in Berkeley, California, and completed his post-doctoral studies at Sophia University in Tokyo, Japan. His academic training is characterised by a solid foundation in theology, cultural and ethnic studies, sociology and anthropology—especially his studies at the University of California, Berkeley—which has allowed him to approach his research from a holistic and integrative perspective. Throughout his career, he has collaborated with numerous scholars and participated in a wide range of international research projects.

One of Córdova Quero's most significant contributions is his analysis of the experience of queer immigrants and their relationship with religion. In his research, he explores how gender and sexuality identities influence the migration experience and how these intersections are mediated by religious institutions. He argues that migration and religion are not isolated phenomena but are intricately intertwined, profoundly affecting the lives of queer migrants. His work highlights the need to understand how power structures and gender and sexuality norms within religions impact individuals in migratory contexts.

Córdova Quero has also been influential in the study of religious and cultural diversity. His research encompasses various religious traditions, including Christianity, Islam, Hinduism and Buddhism, and how these religions interact with migrant communities. His inclusive approach and commitment to social justice have earned him recognition as a dedicated and respected scholar. In addition to his academic work, Córdova Quero has been actively involved in community and human rights initiatives. He has worked with organisations that support migrants and LGBTIQ+ communities, advocating for more inclusive and equitable policies. His dedication to research and activism demonstrates his commitment to creating a more just and understanding world.

What Are Our Aims With a Book Like This One?

In the realm of queer theology, numerous books address its multifaceted issues, yet our unique approach distinguishes this work. Positioned at a level suitable for introducing students to this discipline, our book stands as a pioneering resource for faculty members teaching theology courses. Unlike existing publications, our comprehensive approach not only demystifies the complexities of queer theology but also serves as a vital tool for educators to impart a nuanced understanding to students.

As envisioned, this book emerges as an indispensable resource in the hands of faculty members worldwide, providing a carefully crafted guide for teaching theology effectively. Its significance lies in bridging the gap, offering educators a comprehensive yet accessible tool that aligns with the dynamic landscape of contemporary theological studies. By adopting an engaging and thoughtful approach, we aim to break away from the stereotypical notions of theological texts as monotonous and dense. The intention is to present material that captivates students, making the exploration of queer theology an enriching and stimulating intellectual journey.

In essence, our book not only addresses the gap in literature concerning queer theology but also strives to redefine the pedagogical landscape by offering a resource that is both informative and engaging. Through this endeavour, we aspire to contribute meaningfully to theological education globally, fostering an inclusive and dynamic learning environment for both faculty and students alike.

How to Get the Best of This Book?

Consistent in its structure, each chapter unfolds through thematic sections, systematically developing the central topic. When exploring specific religions, we provide concise yet comprehensive information, offering insights into their origins, founders—when known—, sacred texts, places of worship and additional relevant details. Complementing the textual content, each chapter includes a visual aid, such as a graphic, elucidating the intricate organisational structures within the featured religion. By incorporating this visual element, we aim to enhance the reader's understanding of the various branches, schools, traditions and organisational intricacies that characterise each faith.

Recognising the inherent diversity within religious traditions, our approach explicitly emphasises this richness. We acknowledge that no religion exists as a monolithic entity, and our intent is to illuminate the multifaceted dimensions inherent in every faith. Through this comprehensive methodology, we strive to present an inclusive and nuanced portrayal of each religion, fostering a deeper appreciation for the intricate tapestry of beliefs, practices and structures that contribute to the diversity within the realm of queer theologies.

While unravelling the content in a narrative fashion, each chapter incorporates focused boxes highlighting specific terms, authors or schools of thought pertinent to the topic. These carefully placed boxes serve not to disrupt the narrative flow but to accentuate and centre key aspects, offering readers a nuanced understanding of the intricacies and highlighting focal points within the broader context of the chapter.

Concluding each chapter, we introduce a discussion section featuring thoughtfully crafted questions designed to encourage a conversational exploration of all facets covered. These questions are meticulously structured to engage both students and faculty in a comprehensive examination of the chapter's content. They facilitate individual reflection, allowing students to delve into personal insights, while also fostering a collaborative learning environment through class discussions, whether in-person or virtual. Emphasising intuitive inquiries over rote memorisation, these questions inspire critical thinking and encourage participants to synthesise and articulate their understanding. By promoting dynamic dialogue, our intention is to create an interactive and inclusive space where the diverse perspectives within each chapter can be thoroughly examined, enhancing the overall learning experience for readers at various levels of academic engagement.

We are aware of the impossibility of an exhaustive coverage of scholars within each religion; therefore, every chapter incorporates a curated list of selected works for further reading. This section serves as a gateway for readers, catering to both faculty and students, inviting them to delve deeper into the captivating subjects explored in each chapter. The aim is to provide additional avenues for intellectual exploration, enabling readers to broaden their understanding and engage with diverse perspectives. By offering this carefully curated collection, we aspire to facilitate continued scholarship and inquiry, encouraging a dynamic and ongoing dialogue on the multifaceted themes presented in the book.

Whenever feasible, our chapters feature images, graphics, maps and tables to visually augment the textual content. These visual aids serve to condense complex information into concise and accessible formats, providing readers with a graphic summary of nuanced topics. Carefully crafted by our team, these resources are thoughtfully integrated to enhance understanding and engagement with the material, unless otherwise specified.

Part I

Theoretical Section

A Brief Note About This Section

In this foundational section, we delve into the intricacies of essential concepts integral to understanding queer theologies. Functioning as a theoretical cornerstone, our exploration meticulously outlines the fundamental principles that serve as the bedrock of the book's overarching subject. This segment plays a pivotal role in establishing a robust conceptual framework, equipping readers with the indispensable tools needed to navigate the intricacies explored in subsequent chapters. By elucidating these key ideas with precision, we aim to cultivate a comprehensive understanding of the intricate tapestry that is queer theologies, fostering an enriched engagement with the broader discourse surrounding this nuanced field.

In this foundational section, our objective extends beyond mere introduction as we meticulously lay the groundwork for a profound exploration of the intricate interplay between theoretical constructs and the diverse traditions and spiritualities inherent in queer theologies. We aim to equip readers with a nuanced understanding, allowing them to navigate the complex web of ideas that characterise this field. As we unveil the theoretical lens, readers will gain insight into the rich tapestry of queer theologies, appreciating the subtleties and complexities that arise in their intersection with various religious and spiritual perspectives. This comprehensive approach ensures that readers not only comprehend the fundamental principles outlined but also grasp the dynamic relationships that unfold within the realm of queer theologies. By bridging theoretical concepts with diverse traditions, we pave the way for an enriched and meaningful exploration of the subject matter, fostering a deeper appreciation for the intricacies involved.

However, our focus in this initial section is not to delve into specific theologies or experiences, as that nuanced exploration is reserved for Sections 2, 3 and 4. Instead, our aim here is to provide readers with a comprehensive roadmap that will guide them through the intricate terrain of subsequent chapters. This foundational segment serves as a detailed orientation, elucidating the key principles and themes that will unfold in greater depth in the following sections. By adopting this approach, we establish a crucial foundation that prepares readers to delve into the particular theologies and experiences awaiting them in later chapters. Think of this section as the compass that points towards the cardinal directions of our inquiry, highlighting the theoretical landscape and essential concepts that will be

Global Queer Theologies: Intercontextual and Interreligious Perspectives, First Edition. Lisa Isherwood and Hugo Córdova Quero.
© 2026 John Wiley & Sons Ltd. Published 2026 by John Wiley & Sons Ltd.

explored in more detail. In doing so, we ensure that readers not only comprehend the overarching structure of the forthcoming content but also recognise the interconnectedness of ideas. This strategic approach not only facilitates a smooth transition between sections but also enhances the reader's ability to engage with the multifaceted dimensions of queer theologies presented throughout the book.

Glossary for Part I

BDSM:	An umbrella term encompassing Bondage, Discipline, Dominance, Submission, Sadism and Masochism, referring to consensual practices involving power dynamics, role-playing and erotic activities within a safe, sane and consensual framework.
Bisexual:	Attracted to both men and women.
Christology:	the meaning and significance of Jesus in Christianity.
Cis-heteronormativity:	The societal assumption that heterosexuality and cisgender identities are the norm, thereby marginalising and excluding non-heterosexual and gender non-conforming individuals.
Cis-heteropatriarchy:	A social system where cisgender heterosexual relationships are seen as the only 'normal' and 'natural' ones, reinforcing traditional male dominance and *machismo*.
Cis-Heterosexual:	Attracted to people of the opposite sex.
Gay:	A male attracted to other males.
Gender Dysphoria:	Clinically significant distress experienced when a person's assigned birth gender does not align with their gender identity.
Gender Identity:	Internal understanding of one's gender.
Heterosexism:	A belief system or worldview that categorises human sexuality according to stereotypes based on cis-heteropatriarchy.
Homophobia:	Fear, hatred, or prejudice toward homosexual people, often resulting in discrimination or hostility based on their sexual orientation.
Homosexual:	A term less used, refers to individuals attracted to people of the same sex.
Intersex:	Born with variations in sex characteristics either genitally or in chromosomes.
Lesbian:	A woman attracted to women.

Global Queer Theologies: Intercontextual and Interreligious Perspectives, First Edition. Lisa Isherwood and Hugo Córdova Quero.
© 2026 John Wiley & Sons Ltd. Published 2026 by John Wiley & Sons Ltd.

LGBT: Lesbian, gay, bisexual, transgender.

LGBTIQ+: Lesbian, gay, bisexual, transgender, intersex, queer and all questioning communities.

Oppression: Systematic exploitation where one social group benefits at the expense of another. It includes institutional control, ideological domination and the imposition of the dominant group's culture onto the oppressed group.

Queer: Term for anyone who does not identify as cisgender or heterosexual.

Racism: Systemic, cultural, institutional and individual beliefs and practices that favour and empower a particular ethnic group people while marginalising and discriminating against people of ethnic belonging.

Sex: Refers to biological attributes such as chromosomes, anatomy and reproductive organs that are typically categorised as male or female. This is distinct from gender, which encompasses social and cultural roles, behaviours and identities.

Sexism: Systemic, cultural, institutional and individual beliefs and practices that favour men while marginalising, discriminating against or stereotyping women.

Sexual Orientation: Sexual orientation refers to the emotional, romantic, sexual or affectional attraction towards other people.

Sexuality: A broad term encompassing a spectrum of behaviours, practices and identities related to intimate relationships, desire and sexual expression within social contexts.

They/Them/Theirs: Pronouns used by transgender, non-binary and gender non-conforming people.

Transgender: A person who identifies with a gender not assigned to them at birth.

1

Understanding Sex, Gender, Race and Capitalism in Queer Theologies

We live in a globalised world where terms do not mean the same for everyone due to culture, language and context. This chapter will aim to produce a common language from which to build the following chapters.

But What of Language?

Language is not without its baggage as it underpins the formation of consciousness yet is also a powerful tool in resistance to the formation of certain assumptions in society and religion. Language structures our reality and should not be seen as separate from other material conditions that embody our existence. How we use language and how it is used about us is a strong influence in how we see the world. In using language we participate in a consensus often unwittingly. While we continue to use the language that is common parlance around us, we do not disagree with the world view it carries. Our judgements and perceptions are directed by the values embedded in our language and in this way set limits on what we might imagine. Feminists pointed out that the concept woman is not a reflection of the lives of women in general but rather what counts as normal female behaviour.

The words homosexual, lesbian, gay, queer all fall into the same patterns; they tell us little to nothing about the people they are said to describe but a great deal about the behaviours attributed to those words. They also carry societal, cultural and contextual positioning. The spread of English as the universal language, in the opinion of the authors, has spread colonial, masculinist, white privilege through the use of language. We know that missionaries wrote down and categorised indigenous languages and infected native language with colonial concepts such as masculine deities replacing the wide range of genders on display in many indigenous religions. They also replaced the notion of sharing with ownership, a concept that was alien to many indigenous peoples. Colonisers also in many cases, as in Wales, beat the native language out of the indigenous inhabitants making it painful and even shameful to use. Language is powerful—please be careful how you use it! Indeed, be creative and follow in the footsteps of feminists and queer activists who have attempted to use language differently in order to create a new and more inclusive world. See for an example of different use of language and different ways of expressing the book, *Websters' First Intergalactic Wickedary of the English Language*, conjured by Mary Daly in cahoots with Jane Caputi (Beacon Press, 1987).

Global Queer Theologies: Intercontextual and Interreligious Perspectives, First Edition. Lisa Isherwood and Hugo Córdova Quero.
© 2026 John Wiley & Sons Ltd. Published 2026 by John Wiley & Sons Ltd.

While it may seem unnecessary we believe a basic grasp of what is meant by religion may be of help. Sometimes we take it for granted that religion is automatically a part of human life and that much that is said cannot be changed in any way. This of course is not true. Further, some scholars in the past gave the impression that religions developed along an ever-increasing trajectory of getting better, truer and more enlightened. This has led to prejudice and at times discrimination and even torture and murder. It certainly had a part to play in the colonial projects of past centuries when the brutality of conquest was over-laid with the notion that the West was civilising the parts of the world it overran and exploited. The same mindset was in play up to the 1970s in the Christian schools that took First Nations children in Canada from their families, removed their native names and forced them into a school system that was often brutal and never really gave them the education it promised but 'civilised' the children.

<table>
<tr>
<td>

Edward Said (1935–2003). Born in Jerusalem he was a Palestinian American scholar and was amongst the founders of postcolonial studies. He wrote a number of books including *Orientalism* (Pantheon Press, 1978) which examined Western attitudes to the east and in Culture and Imperialism (Knopf, 1993).

</td>
<td>

'none of us is completely free from the struggle over geography. That struggle is complex and interesting because it is not only about soldiers and canons but is also about ideas, about forms, about images and imaginings.' Edward Said (1993: 7).

</td>
</tr>
</table>

So What Is Religion?

The word 'religion' has become an academically contested ground (2008). What it means and what constitutes religion is by no means decided upon. Further, it is of course entirely possible that what was understood as religion has changed dramatically down the thousands of years of human evolution. And most importantly how we gain access to the long ago past and what we make of it is a tricky issue. This issue has become complicated by our own rapid development in terms of cultural change which as Eric Hobsbawn noted was threatening to cut us loose from our past altogether. In order to address this legitimate point of view some scholars have concentrated on what they term biological history, that is evolution which takes the human story all the way back and breaks with acknowledged conventions that history only begins approx. 5,000 years ago with texts. All the way back means for them back to the Big Bang; it also involves a rejection of distinctions such as prehistory and history—all is the human story (2008). We may have noticed that stating that all is the human story before there are actually any humans on earth is a radical thing to do—and will certainly have implications for how we might understand the evolution of religion in human history.

<table>
<tr>
<td>

Clifford Geertz defines religion as a system of symbols that when enacted establish powerful, pervasive and long lasting moods and motivations that make sense in terms of the general order of existence. He reflects that ritual is a way of creating another world since it is not just a belief but a set of actions that can place the actor in another sphere. The world as lived and the world as imagined fuse

</td>
<td>

Emile Durkheim 'Religion is a system of beliefs and practices relative to the sacred that unite those that adhere to them in a moral community.' (1995).

</td>
</tr>
</table>

There is no easy explanation of what religion is, but it does seem to have at its heart the idea that there is more to things than meets the eye. The German writer Rudolf Otto (1923) called this the idea of the *Numinous* which suggests that people feel that they can sense something bigger than themselves, but they still feel part of it. This in many cases leads not just to religious doctrine but also views of the world and the cosmos, for example, the Vatican took until 1951 to accept the notion that evolution is an innate part of the cosmos and the Big Bang as the beginning—this was because the Bible in the form of Genesis suggests that God made the world in six days and rested on the seventh. The Roman Catholic Church was not quite as literalist in this as many fundamentalist Protestant churches but still held the principle that God created the world and so still struggles, as many churches do, with the unfolding which is innate in the Big Bang Theory versus a once-and-for-all creation by a divine being.

Accepting a new world view comes slowly to many religions since their whole belief system is based on 'original ideas' of God(s) and the universe. It is often the case that theology, that is the academic study of notions of the divine, moves somewhat quicker than the established forms of religions themselves. This book sets out how based on the lived experience of people making sense of their lives and love queer theologies from around the globe demonstrates this very movement.

Religion of course comes in many different guises and has at its heart many different notions of God(s). So we suggest that you get to grips with the following definitions as they will come into play as the book unfolds:

- Monotheism is the belief that there is only one God. This is a belief held by Christianity, Judaism and Islam, although Islam challenges Christianity over the notion of Trinity which many Muslims suggest points to more than one God.
- Henotheism refers to a religious belief system where a person worships one specific deity while acknowledging the existence of other deities.
- Pantheism is the belief that the universe and God are identical and therefore that God is immanent in the world. This underpins the notion that everything in the world is alive with the divine.
- Panentheism considers God and the world to be interrelated, but some panentheists hold that God is greater than the universe and others suggest that the world is a manifestation of God.
- Polytheism is the belief in many gods who appear to have different functions in the world.
- Animism focuses on individual spirits and does not believe there is simply one god. Animists believe every being (human and non-human) has a soul which is connected with the spirit world.
- Atheism is not a religion but rather the rejection of any system of belief and the idea of a god or gods.
- Naturalism is a belief system that asserts that everything arises from natural properties and causes, and supernatural or spiritual explanations are excluded or discounted.

At this time in history, just like the concept of religion, sex and gender have become very contested terms, and there is confusion in the general public about the distinctions.

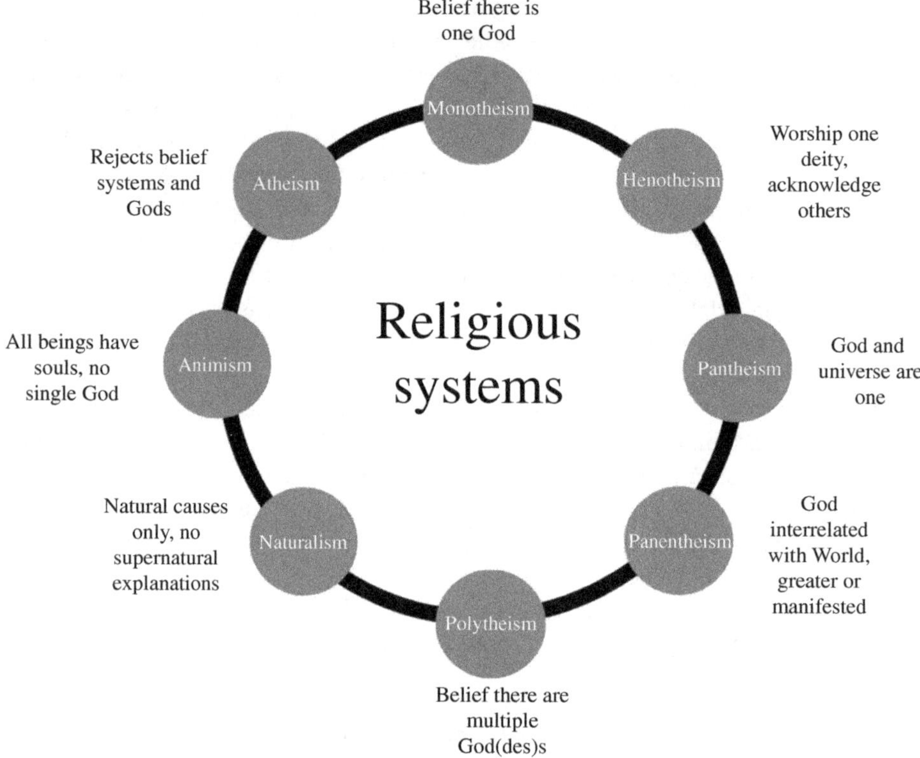

Graphic 1.1   Religious Systems

Sex

Sex has traditionally been connected to biology and hormones. When the midwife declares, 'Congratulations! It's a boy!' this is based purely on external genitalia, but there is more to it than that. An organism's reproductive cells are called gametes, and these have been used to define sex. A male produces smaller gametes, while a female produces relatively larger gametes for the purpose of reproduction. Should something like illness interfere with their production it does not mean that people are no longer defined as male and female. Added to this picture is the so-called chromosome account. The Y chromosome in a seven-week-old human child triggers gamete production. The human male has a Y chromosome, and so a standard distribution of chromosomes is XY for males and XX for females. There are rare disorders of sexual development which can cause this distribution to go astray, but it is the presence of a Y chromosome that is counted as defining the two groups as either male or female. While in the majority of humans this essentialist description is clear, in some people it is not so clear. One example is a person with XY chromosomes who also has Androgen Insensitivity Disorder which results in them having testicles which may be partially or fully descended and are male according to gametes and chromosomes. However, they are unable to respond to testosterone, so they develop a feminised body with breasts, vulva and clitoris. Some grow up thinking of themselves as female but are not according to their gametes and chromosomes. This is also true for those born XX who have a condition known as Congenital Adrenal Hyperplasia which results in a masculine appearance and even an enlarged clitoris and the appearance of an empty scrotum.

A further theory that has been proposed is the Homeostatic Property Cluster to account for sex in which sex was decided by possession of sufficient characteristics such as genitalia, facial characteristics, skeletal structure, muscle and fat distribution. For many this seems a good rule of thumb, but of course some people exhibit differences in sexual development. Anne Fausto-Sterling promotes the view that sex is not binary but rather lies across an infinitely malleable continuum. She is credited with introducing the term intersex, but her article claiming five sexes has been disputed from a chromosomal point of view. Even her definition of hermaphrodite (a person having both sets of characteristics and genitalia) has been discredited on the grounds that she seems to believe that people need to hold perfect balances of gametes, chromosomes, gonads and hormones in order to fit one category. It seems this is rarely the case.

In 1990 Thomas Lacquer published *Making Sex: Body and Gender from the Greeks to Freud* in which he argues that almost all claims about the differences between the sexes are culturally and historically relative. He says that before the eighteenth century most people had a one-sex model not two, and females were viewed as imperfect males where the differences were understood as in degree not kind. Thomas Aquinas believed that females were conceived if the east wind was blowing during sex!

Gender

Gender comes into play in most societies. Symbols identifying gender originated in alchemy and astrology where Mars came to symbolise male and Venus, female. In the present day these symbols have increased as we now acknowledge more than two genders and so many ways of situating oneself within gender categories.

In most societies gender acts to imprint 'appropriate' ways of acting on the young body, boys don't cry, girls are sugar and spice and all things nice. It is this imprinting that many societies consider to be crucial to the way they continue, while other societies feel more relaxed about the baby growing into itself.

Research has shown that in the Western world people play more roughly with boy babies, throwing them in the air and so on. They also speak louder and more directly to boys. Whereas for girls play is gentler they are spoken to in 'baby language' for longer and of course wear soft colours, pink being still the most chosen colour. Boys wear blue!

There are two terms that are still in use when people think of gender. They are 'essentialism' versus 'constructionism'. It is necessary to understand how these terms influence debates around gender.

Essentialism

The discussion about how one understands identities is complex in queer theory. The term 'essentialism' is a term that comes from philosophy, where it denotes either the possibility to know the 'essence' of something or the possibility to 'capture' that 'essence' through descriptions or definitions. There is an assumption that human beings, objects or texts possess underlying essences that define their 'true nature'. An 'essence' is fixed and unchanging, but has a double existence: as both the inherent or innate property of an individual object or being, and the abstract, external essence governing the type to which all examples conform.

In terms of sexual identity politics, this has been the traditional understanding of how queer folks 'are', implying a fixed, unchanging state, as Jagose states: '[...] [E]ssentialists regard identity as natural, fixed and innate. (...) Essentialists assume that homosexuality exists across time as a universal phenomenon which has a marginalised but continuous and coherent history of its own' (1996: 8–9).

Some theorists argue that gay and lesbian identity politics was built upon this concept in the 1970s and 1980s, which was challenged by queer theory from the 1990s.

Constructionism

It is the notion that culture is a human creation and that what we 'are' and 'do' is impacted by 'social influences'. This notion was taken by some feminists and philosophical theories about gender in order to explain the be/coming of human beings. Jagose suggests that:

> 'Constructionists assume identity is fluid, the effect of social conditioning and available cultural models for understanding oneself. (...) [They] assume that because same-sex sex acts have different cultural meaning in different historical contexts, they are not identical across time and space' (1996: 8–9).

As such, 'constructionism' opposes 'essentialism' in order to show that identity is fluid and that it can be modified or influenced by external forces, while at the same time people can re-enact that identity constantly.

> Gender theory is the study of male, female and queer behaviour in any community or society.

In 1955 the controversial sexologist John Mooney introduced the term *gender* to describe human characteristics related to men and women. This opened up a new field in sexology and led to what we have today, an idea of gender theory. There are four major theories relating to gender development which are social learning theory, neurophysiological theory, cognitive development theory and gender schema theory. Gender theories open up new ways in which to understand people in their different contexts. Judith Butler entered the debate and declared that gender is not in any way fixed to material identity but is purely a social construction that we learn to perform in order to support society and its patriarchal underpinnings. We can then unlearn and actually perform gender in any way we please, even from one day to the next, there is nothing fixed about it. Her theories have been taken up by other queer theorists to deconstruct the harshest understandings of queer sexuality and gender. Some feminist theorists are less enthusiastic about this level of flexibility believing that gender may play a significant role in how men and women see themselves and consequently how they view social reality which is believed to be crucial if society, as we have it, is to be refigured as more equal and relational.

Foucault said of gender theory that it is concerned with interrupting sexist systems and stereotypes in order to explore more fully new ways to be human in relation to any **gendered** performance of the self.

Michel Foucault (1926–1984) was a philosopher whose main idea was that we live under a codification of power relations across the whole social body. He wrote numerous works including '*The History of Sexuality*' Penguin Modern Classics, 2020, but first published in 1976. It is a four-volume examination of sexuality in the Western world.

Judith Butler, in her book *Gender Trouble* (2006), argued that gender is a performance, that is to say each society expects a set of behaviours from people who have been identified as male or female at birth. She argues that this has to be taught as it is not in any way natural since humans have a vast array of ways in which to sit in their bodies which may or may not fit with societal demands. In her most recent book *Who's Afraid of Gender?* (2024) she examines why societies find the flexibility of gender so alarming. Unsurprisingly, she concludes that this is because so much is placed on the role play associated with gender. People must know their place in society, and so much of that place relies on knowing and keeping within one's assigned gender roles. She systematically unpicks the claims by mostly right-wing thinkers that gender flexibility leads to child abuse and the general break down of family, society and of course church.

Judith Butler (1956–). Her groundbreaking book was '*Gender Trouble Feminism and the Subversion of Identity*',1990, London, Routledge.

So what is gender identity? This is a controversial question as you can see from the above. It depends whether you feel gender is a fundamental part of yourself, stable and integral to your personality. The medical model would give more credibility to this view since it suggests that gender identity is relatively permanent. Under this model many clinicians view a misaligned gender identity as a mental illness. As we have noted Judith Butler suggests that gender is nothing more than a performance coming from social constructionism and stereotypes around sex. The British sociologist Stuart Hall (1997) puts forward the so-called identification model of gender identity. Like Butler he argues that cultural identities, in which he included gender, are processes of active identification rather than stable facts about the self. This model involves a person consciously or subconsciously modelling themselves on another. This can range from wanting to be the other person or taking on the goals of the other right through the range of emotions to already seeing oneself in another. He suggests that recognition and the sense of belonging that accompanies it play a large part in this model. So according to Hall's theory a male who has 'misaligned gender identity' would strongly psychologically identify with one particular woman or with femaleness in general, while the reverse would be the case for a female. Hall's theory is based on the idea that representation is the process of using language to produce meaning, and that meanings are not fixed or real. He also argues that media texts often do not accurately represent people, places, events or history, because there is no single true meaning.

*Gender performance in action is its **ritualized repetition in the day-to-day**. This repetition gives gender its illusion of stability; the repeated performance of gender in accordance with the social norms of a given society.*

It has been argued that misaligned gender identity understood as identification fits well with the American medical model which acknowledges that some individuals have frequent and persistent feelings that they are really the opposite sex. The identification model also fits with gender dysphoria in which people say they are in a battle to make their external being fit with their internal feelings. These feelings can arise from strict stereotypes being imposed in family, church, society; one may not feel masculine enough or feminine enough according to these codes. Dysphoria and gender identity can be linked, and they may indeed trigger each other. The identification model does not posit that some absolute gender identity lies behind the feelings and convictions of similarity. In short then this model suggests that identifications may change throughout life. Importantly, this model does not suggest any form of mental illness involved in this process. It states that people are free to explore and express identification with the opposite sex or androgyny. The key being not to fix the identity realising it could change many times during a life time.

As we move to discussing race it is important to point out that gender and race are not unrelated topics. For example, within a Western Christian frame people who identify as transgendered are seen as part of the LGBTIQ+ community, whereas in Chile in the Mapoche people they are simply called third gender. Mapoche people do not work within a two-gendered world view based on sex assignment at birth as either male or female. This is because within that society gender identity is not based on sexual identity but rather on gender and spirituality. So within those societies a third gender person is within their gender/sex norm and so are not named as gay, bi, trans or queer – just simply third gendered. This ties in with their world view which is about balance embedded in a dualist understanding which blends opposing and complementary concepts such as earth/sky, masculine/feminine, good/evil. This is quite at odds with a Western mindset that views dualism as consisting of opposing views that may not be reconciled. As we shall see in Chapter 12 these third-gender individuals are considered to be spiritual leaders and healers within their communities.

Gloria Anzaldúa (1987) demonstrates how religious symbols, colonialism and gender intersect when she writes of the serpent-feathered goddess in Mexico, Coatlicue. This was a powerful, sexual female goddess, extremely fearsome and representing the dark earthy energy of creativity and life. Mexican women wore her on their skirts and called on her energy and creative power. Anzaldua says that the colonisers needed to reduce the power of women in society, and she shows how this vibrant goddess was changed into the virgin of Guadalupe. For her reclaiming indigenous religion is important as part of a journey of political becoming into multiple selves or the one-in-multiple as she calls it. Her work shows very clearly how coloniality sanctions a gendered and racialised world view through which power relations and social identities are constructed.

María Lugones (2008) agrees with Anzaldua and for her the production of social identities and the control of production and resources involve the biopolitical axis of sex and gender. Coloniality, she says, is an all-permeating system of signification and control of social relations. For many it is the liminal status of indigenous women who are marginalised because of race and often religion that makes them central in the multiple struggles of decolonisation. Sylvia Marcos (2006) finds the duality of the cosmovision in Mesoamerican women's religion a valuable resource. The Nahuatl have the understanding of duality as oppressed to dualism which points to a non-rigid reality characterised by plasticity and dynamism indicating a strong resistance to the modern Christian worldview imposed by Europe. This is a relational cosmovision declaring the immanence nature of the sacred and importantly declaring that the experiences of the body originate from the universe itself which is understood as the feminine divine. It also of course declares race to be an entirely manufactured concept.

Race

History

Race is a pseudoscientific construct developed in nineteenth-century Europe to justify the racist categorisation of human beings, with white being the pinnacle. Who gets to be seen as white has been rather fluid over time, but wherever the marker falls race still acts as a definitive social divider in many societies leading to the oppressions of those deemed to be non-white. Race is then a social, political and economic system in which whites have predominantly controlled power and material resources. The 'ideology of race' has a history.

Franz Fanon (1963) is an important thinker in the area of race, colonial politics and decolonial revolution. For Fanon the world view, based on a strict racial hierarchy, was not based on philosophical thinking alone. For Fanon this system stemmed from the Western world's metaphysical understanding. He observed that colonial governance cannot be administered by coercion only, although that is a powerful tool. Rather, it also requires a theological worldview that makes the colonised accept who they are and where they belong in the hierarchy. He also concludes that this theology needs a Manichean dualism which dictates the colonial reality and its values. That is to say one in which the white colonisers embody good, while the black colonised embody absolute evil. Further the native is understood to be impervious to ethics and only represents the negation of values (1963: 6). Fanon's work sheds light on what blackness came to signify under this worldview which of course was all the negative values of the colonising society. He makes an important point that colonial management of colonised people needed a sustained Manichean theology/theodicy.

Fanon presents Christian theology with a large problem as the duality inherent in so much of it has very negative consequences in the world. Sylvia Wynter (2003) develops Fannon's thought into a full-fledged critique of colonial political theology. She says that the figure of Man is based on the project of the modern secular–rational subject. Whereas the invention of the inferior race requires the transfer of the theological notion of Original Sin onto them so that they represent ontological lack.

> *Manichaeism is a form of religion that breaks everything down into good and evil. It has duality at its heart which means that everything is seen as black or white.*

When Christopher Columbus arrived in the Americas in 1492, not only did people from the other side of the ocean disembark with him, but they also brought with them ideas, conceptions of the world and of each other. One of these conceptions was how to understand themselves and others in racial terms. During the process of the unification of Spain, by the crowns of Castile and Aragon, the expulsion of Jews and Muslims from the Iberian Peninsula took place. This was part of a long process of compulsory conversion that took place between 1391 and 1415 CE, and then in the years leading up to 1492 CE. This ethnic cleansing was carried out based on the ideology of *limpieza de sangre* [cleansing of blood], also called *pureza de raza* [purity of race]. Basically, this ideology prevented Jewish and Muslim converts from accessing certain social spaces (Torres & Sebastián, 2003).

However, we owe its concretisation as an institutionalised ideology to the Archbishop of Toledo, Juan Martínez Silíceo, who clearly defined it in 1547 in what was called the 'statute of Toledo'. This document formed the basis for the subsequent 'statutes of purity of blood' that governed the public and religious institutions of the time (Torres & Sebastián, 2003).

The conquest of the Americas and the ideology of 'blood cleansing' permeated the relationship between conquerors and conquered. The Spanish conquistadors not only brought oppression in terms of political domination and slavery, but also imposed new categories for understanding the world and examining issues that were understood differently before Columbus' arrival in the Americas in 1492 (Dussel, 1994). Unlike their Anglo-Saxon counterparts, Spanish and Portuguese conquistadors generally married or procreated with people from the conquered native peoples, as well as from the African peoples who were subsequently enslaved. The descendants of these marriages were grouped under the category of *mestizxs*, in Spanish, or *mestiçxs*, in Portuguese. With the European conquest also came subordination to male power, often through violence, a factor that is evident in the multiple forced relationships (Vidart, 2000). Throughout the continent, the heritage of racial ideologies developed in European countries after 1400 was present in these relationships, with their own local characteristics. Thus, the emerging countries of the Spanish colonies have a strong imprint rejecting racial diversity (Vidart, 1968). This stems from the racial categories implanted in the Spanish colonies to form the racial stratification of the empire, which were even the motifs of what is known as *pinturas de casta* [caste paintings], that depicted daily life activities for different families and detailed the racial labels that every person would bear due to their ancestry (Carrera, 2003; Katzew, 2004).

The story did not end there. In 1758, the Swedish scientist Carl Linnaeus published his work *Systema Naturae*, thus establishing modern taxonomy on human races, which he characterised as follows:

- Americanus: 'reddish, choleric, upright posture, dark skin and black hair, straight and thick, with thick lips, large nose, chin almost without a beard, stubborn, content with his luck, lover of freedom, body painted with red lines combined in different ways' (Bitlooch, 1996).
- Europaeus: 'white, sanguine, muscular, light and abundant hair, inconsistent, inventive, completely covered with clothes, governed by laws' (Bitlooch, 1996).
- Asiaticus: 'yellow, melancholic, strict, black hair, brown eyes, severe, ostentatious, dressed in long tunics, governed by opinion' (Bitlooch, 1996).
- Afer: 'black, phlegmatic, with curly hair, wide nose, cunning, lazy, body rubbed with oil or grease, governed by arbitrary wills' (Bitlooch, 1996).

Linnaeus' studies adopted a predominantly geographical approach, aiming to contextualise peoples based on their places of residence. When he categorised humanity into these four groups, his intention was not to make judgements about the moral character of different peoples. Instead, he sought to describe his observations of how people lived and behaved across the known continents. While this does not negate the presence of Linnaeus's own prejudices, it underscores his aim to portray the world as he perceived it.

However, one of his disciples, Friedrich Blumenbach, coined and originated the term 'white race', which has significantly shaped racial relations in the Western world throughout modern and contemporary times. In 1795, Blumenbach introduced a different concept, no longer based on geography but on subjective valuations. By making this slight change, he laid the groundwork for the modern notions of race and racism. We believe it is important to understand how the white race became a category and occupied its place within the racial dynamics in the West. Blumenbach defined five racial categories:

- Caucasian or white.
- Mongoloid or yellow.

- American or red (Native American).
- Malayan or brown (from Southeast Asia).
- Ethiopian or black.

On top of the list was the 'White race'. The reason Blumenbach designated the Caucasian category was that, in his understanding, humans from this group possessed a 'superior beauty' compared to other inhabitants of the planet. In this manner, Blumenbach paved the way for other scientists to reinforce racial ideas of European superiority over the rest of the world, not based on scientific concepts, but on Blumenbach's subjective evaluation.

Critical Race Theory

Given that history, Critical Race Theory (CRT) emerged in the 1970s and 1980s, pioneered by Derrick A. Bell (1970, 1976) and Kimberlé Crenshaw (1988). Bell, a prominent civil rights attorney and scholar, critiqued the limitations of traditional civil rights strategies in addressing systemic inequality. He argued that racism is deeply ingrained in American society, beyond individual prejudice, and must be understood as a structural and enduring phenomenon (Bell, 1992). Kimberlé Crenshaw (1991) introduced the concept of intersectionality, emphasising how overlapping identities, such as race, gender and class, create unique experiences of oppression, particularly for women of colour.

CRT is a movement of scholars who try to understand the relationship between race, racism and power and through their analysis to dismantle the way race plays out in every society (Crenshaw, 2011). As explained earlier, race is a construction; there is no biological truth to the ideology of races except for the cooptation of phenotypes. A phenotype encompasses an individual's observable characteristics, including height, eye colour and blood type. The hereditary component influencing the phenotype is termed the genotype. While certain traits are predominantly influenced by the genotype, others are primarily shaped by environmental factors, highlighting the intricate interplay between genetics and the environment in determining an individual's observable traits (Smedley, 1998).

CRT challenges liberal approaches to racial equality, such as colour blindness and incrementalism, asserting that these frameworks fail to address the root causes of systemic racism (Williams, 1998). Instead, CRT seeks to uncover how laws, policies and institutions perpetuate racial inequalities, even under the guise of neutrality or fairness. Central to this critique is the concept of structural racism, which examines how historical and systemic factors maintain racial disparities (Khan, 2016).

In contemporary contexts, CRT has expanded beyond law into education and social justice activism. In education, CRT scholars analyse curricula, disciplinary practices and policies that sustain inequities for students of colour (Smith-Maddox & Solórzano, 2002). This framework inspires culturally relevant pedagogy and antiracist teaching practices. CRT also influences social justice movements like Black Lives Matter, providing language to address systemic injustice and strategies for challenging oppressive structures (Dixson, 2018).

Although CRT has gained traction, it faces resistance, especially in political and educational spheres. Critics often mischaracterise CRT as divisive, while proponents argue that its insights are essential for dismantling inequities (Crewe, 2021). By linking theory to practice, CRT continues to evolve, shaping discussions on race, power and justice across diverse fields. Its focus on the lived experiences of marginalised communities ensures that their voices remain central in the fight for equity and systemic transformation.

Capitalism

The term 'capitalist', meaning an owner of capital, appears earlier than the term 'capitalism' and dates to the mid-seventeenth century. 'Capitalism' is derived from capital, which evolved from *capitale*, a late Latin word based on *caput*, meaning 'head', which is also the origin of 'chattel' and 'cattle' in the sense of movable property, only much later to refer only to livestock (Merrill, 2014). *Capitale* emerged in the twelfth to thirteenth centuries to refer to funds, stock of merchandise, sum of money or money carrying interest.

Capitalism is driven by the desire for profit making and so constantly increases the productive capacity of everything from the earth's resources to human labour. In contrast pre-capitalist societies produced for the sake of satisfying the concrete needs of that society. With the domination of a capitalist system a world market is developed which requires transport systems, technologies and credit systems as well as developing artificial appetites in consumers. Critics argue that unchecked capitalism can lead to income inequality, environmental degradation and exploitation of labour (Brenner, 1991). Balancing the pursuit of profit with social responsibility remains a central challenge for capitalist societies. Additionally, globalisation has been a significant outcome of capitalism, intertwining economies and cultures across the globe, creating both opportunities and challenges for nations worldwide. The balance between humans and nature is altered beyond recognition with the result that capitalism is no longer productive but destructive and begins to threaten human existence (Meszaros, 1970).

The global reach of capitalism means it is always able to find new resources and new markets and shift the most negative consequences of its activities away from the Global North. In this way the Global South becomes the dumping ground for the waste capitalism produces and so suffers more than it should. Rosa Luxemburg (2015) developed the theory of the unequal relationship between capitalist centres of the world and those on the periphery. She criticised the destructive impact of capitalist development on non-capitalist societies and argued that capitalism from its inception was dependent on unequal exchange that provides cheap and often free labour and natural resources for the centre. This labour comes from the slaves, the indigenous, immigrants and women who are all viewed as a free gift to capitalism. Luxemburg notes that capitalism is the first form of economics that is propagandist, it needs to expand and eradicate all other forms of economic exchange, to be a universal system, but she noted it cannot be while it is dependent on non-capitalist systems. She was writing in 1913, and the situation today is very different with the Fall of the Berlin Wall and the spread of capitalism to larger parts of the world there are few non-capitalist systems left to challenge it. Capitalism faces a problem in the present since its exploitation of natural resources has brought the earth to the point where it can give no more, the externality as a precondition for capital accumulation is exhausted; however, it still continues to exploit people.

> 'We're here, we're queer, we're not going shopping'
> (Queer nation)

Why Is It Important to Understand the Interrelation Among Sex, Gender, Race and Capitalism in Queer Theologies?

Pellegrini (2002) argues that capitalism drives people into cis–heterosexual relations and attempts to keep them there but, on the other hand, capitalism undermines the family. The rise of wage labour transformed the structure of the family, the ideology of the family and the meaning of cis–heterosexual relations. As wage labour spread sexuality was released from the need to produce more and more children to help the economic status of the family. There was of course a diverse impact across class, gender, race, ethnicity and religion. While both men and women could work outside the home for wages, usually middle-class women stopped work once they married. Wage labour and the twentieth-century transformation of the sexual division of labour meant women had some independence from men, and this impacted queer women in a positive way. Throughout the twentieth century the family shifted from the site of production to the site of consumption. The nuclear family suits capitalism well as the products are created outside the home but belong to the owners of private property.

> **Ann Pelegrini (1964–).** In 1998, she founded the Sexual Cultures book series at NYU Press with Jose Munoz.

Pellegrini (2002: 137) asserts that gay identity exists within the contradictions inherent to the cis-heterosexual family structure. While wage labour offered a means to distance oneself from the heterosexual family dynamic, queer individuals often encountered discrimination in the workplace. This discrimination forced many to weigh the decision of revealing their sexuality against the risk of limiting their job opportunities. Over time, however, there has been notable progress. Some companies now extend benefits to same-sex partners, signalling a positive shift towards greater inclusivity and acceptance within the corporate world. Despite these advancements, challenges persist, highlighting the ongoing struggle for LGBTQ+ rights in the workplace.

There are major marketing campaigns targeting gay and to a lesser extent lesbian consumers. The emphasis on dual-income gay and lesbian homes is not without its problems, firstly that not all gay and lesbian people are in an income bracket to benefit from the consumables offered. Secondly and more importantly the willingness to chase the 'pink pound' or gay dollar does not signal that tolerance has won the day. Therefore inequality is not even an issue that crosses the mind of these corporations. Rather, corporations have calculated whether they would lose a conservative 'shopping base' if they reach for the pink pound. Evidence seems to suggest that this is more financially harmful in the United States than in the United Kingdom.

Corporations have also discovered that it is possible to sell a gay lifestyle, thus turning gay men particularly into capitalist consumers in a big way. Some theorists see this as the end of queer politics, but Pellegrini acknowledges that the queer community has never been free of capitalism and may still make a stand against the worst excesses of it. The contradictions persist and while this is the case the politicising of sex will also continue.

Theology

The word theology is made up of two parts *Theos* (God) and *logos* (word) which means that theology traditionally has been words about God. Too often it has been words *from* God and has dictated how the Christian Church and society should conduct themselves. These words have been conveyed through theology written almost exclusively by men for the best part of Christian history. We do not know a great deal about the sexual orientation of many of these men, but at fear of death they would have kept quiet about it, also not believing that who they were in their bodies could impact theology. Theology then has been a very top-down enterprise. With the twentieth century and the development of feminist and liberation theologies the emphasis on how theology should be conducted shifted considerably.

The question became 'What kind of world/society does this top-down, male-dominated mainly European theology produce?' This simple question, which questioned the power dynamics and gave voice to a wider group of people, has enabled the sexism, misogyny, heterosexism, racism and elitism of much Christian theology to be exposed. Queer theology is another step in this exposure demonstrating how certain groups of people have not simply been excluded but actively persecuted at times in Christian history. In addition to exposing discrimination in theology a number of theologians have claimed that the Christian faith has always been queer at its very heart which will be examined later in the book.

For Further Discussion

1   How does the evolving understanding of 'religion' challenge traditional historical and academic perspectives, especially when considering the entirety of human evolution and its impact on our interpretation of religious history?

2   In what ways has your religion or lack of it affected your understanding of sex and gender?

3   How does CRT challenge traditional understandings of race and its interplay with power and society?

4   Have you ever thought that capitalism is not a natural or inevitable system for global economics?

5   How has the development of feminist, liberation and queer theologies challenged traditional top-down, male-dominated Christian theology and its impact on society?

6   In what ways do you think Christianity is queer in its very nature?

References

Anzaldúa, Gloria (1987). *Borderlands/La Frontera: The New Mestiza*. San Francisco, CA: Aunt Lute Books.

Bell, Derrick A (1970). *Race, Racism, and American Law*. Cambridge, MA: Harvard Law School.

Bell, Derrick A (1976). "Serving Two Masters: Integration Ideals and Client Interests in School Desegregation Litigation." *The Yale Law Journal* 85, No. 4 (March): pp. 470–516.

Bell, Derrick A (1992). *Faces at the Bottom of the Well: The Permanence of Racism*. New York, NY: Basic Books.

Bitlooch, Eduardo (1996). "Ciencia, raza y racismo en el siglo XVIII." Ciencia Hoy 6, No. 33. Available at: <www.cienciahoy.org.ar/hoy33/raza01.htm>.

Brenner, Yehojachin S (1991). *The Rise and Fall of Capitalism*. Cheltenham: Edward Elgar Publishing.

Butler, Judith (2006). *Gender Trouble: Feminism and the Subversion of Identity*. London: Routledge.

Butler, Judith (2024). *Who's Afraid of Gender*. London: Allen Lane.

Carrera, Magali M (2003). *Imagining Identity in New Spain: Race, Lineage, and the Colonial Body in Portraiture and Casta Paintings*. Austin, TX: University of Texas Press.

Crenshaw, Kimberlé W (1988). "Race, Reform, and Retrenchment: Transformation and Legitimation in Antidiscrimination Law." *Harvard Law Review* 101, No. 7 (May): pp. 1331–1387.

Crenshaw, Kimberlé W (1991). "Mapping the Margins: Intersectionality, Identity Politics, and Violence against Women of Colour." *Stanford Law Review* 43, No. 6 (July): pp. 1241–1299.

Crenshaw, Kimberlé W (2011). "Twenty Years of Critical Race Theory: Looking back to Move Forward." *Connecticut Law Review* 43, No. 5 (July): pp. 1253–1352.

Crewe, Sandra E (2021). "Critical Race Theory—Uncomfortable but Necessary Tool for Change Agents." *Journal of Social Work Education* 57, No. 3: pp. 416–418.

Daly, Mary in cahoots with Jane Caputi (1987). *Websters First New Intergalactic Wickedary of the English Language*. Boston, MA: Beacon Press.

Dixson, Adrienne D (2018). "'What's Going On?': A Critical Race Theory Perspective on Black Lives Matter and Activism in Education." *Urban Education* 53, No. 2: pp. 231–247.

Durkheim, Emile (1995). *The Elementary Forms of Religious Life*, translated by Karen E Fields. New York, NY: Free Press.

Dussel, Enrique (1994). *1492. El encubrimiento del otro: Hacia el origen del "mito de la modernidad."* La Paz, Bolivia: Plural editores, Centro de Información para el Desarrollo, CID, and Facultad de Humanidades y Ciencias de la Educación, Universidad Mayor de San Andrés, UMSA.

Fanon, Franz (1963). *The Wretched of the Earth*, translated by Constance Farrington. New York, NY: Grove Press.

Hall, Stuart (1997). *Representation: Cultural Representation and Signifying Practices*. London: Sage Publications.

Jagose, Annamarie (1996). *Queer Theory: An Introduction*. Washington Square, NY: New York University Press.

Katzew, Ilona (2004). *La pintura de castas: Representaciones raciales en el México del siglo XVIII*. Madrid: Turner.

Khan, Anoosh W (2016). "Critical Race Theory: The Intersectionality of Race, Gender and Social Justice." *Putaj Humanities & Social Sciences* 23, No. 1: pp. 1–9.

Lugones, Maria (2008). "The Coloniality of Gender." *Words and Knowledge Otherwise* 2, No. Spring: pp. 742–759.

Luxemburg, Rosa (2015). "The Accumulation of Capital." In: *The Complete Works of Rosa Luxemburg, Vol 11: Economic Writings 2*, edited by Pter Hudis. London: Verso.

Marcos, Sylvia (2006). *Taken from the Lips: Gender and Eros in Mesoamerican Religions*. Leiden: Brill.

Merrill, Michael (2014). "How Capitalism Got Its Name." *Dissent* 61: pp. 87–92.

Meszaros, Isvain (1970). *Marx's Theory of Alienation*. London: Merlin Press.

Otto, Rudolf (1923). *The Idea of the Holy*. Oxford: Oxford University Press.

Pellegrini, Ann (2002). "Consuming Lifestyle: Commodity Capitalism and Transformations in Gay Identity." In: *Queer Globalizations. Citizenship and the Afterlife of Colonialism*, edited by Arnaldo Cruz-Malave and Martin F Manalansan IV. New York, NY: New York University Press, pp. 134–145.

Said, Edward (1978). *Orientalism*. New York: Pantheon Press.

Said, Edward (1993). *Culture and Imperialism*. New York: Knopf.

Smedley, Audrey (1998). "'Race' and the Construction of Human Identity." *American Anthropologist* (New Series) 100, No. 3 (September): pp. 690–702.

Smith-Maddox, Renée and Daniel G Solórzano (2002). "Using Critical Race Theory, Paulo Freire's Problem-Posing Method, and Case Study Research to Confront Race and Racism in Education." *Qualitative Inquiry* 8, No. 1: pp. 66–84.

Hering Torres, Max Sebastián (2003). "'Limpieza de sangre' ¿Racismo en la edad moderna?" *Tiempos Modernos: Revista electrónica de Historia Moderna* 4, No 9. Available at: <http:// www.tiemposmodernos.org/tm3/index.php/tm/article/viewArticle/26/48>.

Vidart, Daniel (1968). *Ideología y realidad de América*. Montevideo: Nueva America.

Vidart, Daniel (2000). *La trama de la identidad nacional: El espíritu criollo*. Montevideo: Ediciones de la Banda Oriental.

Williams, Patricia (1998). *Seeing a Color-Blind Future: The Paradox of Race*. New York, NY: Noonday Press.

Wynter, Sylvia (2003). "Unsettling Coloniality of Being/Power/Truth/Freedom: Towards the Human after Man, Its Overrepresentation-an Argument." *The New Centennial Review* 3, No. 3: pp. 257–337.

Further Reading

Christian, David (2008). *Maps of Time: An Introduction to Big History*. Berkeley, CA: University of California Press.

Foucault, Michel (2020a). *The History of Sexuality 1: The Will to Knowledge*. London: Penguin Books.

Foucault, Michel (2020b). *The History of Sexuality 2: The Use of Pleasure*. London: Penguin Books.

Smail, Daniel L (2008). *On Deep History and the Brain*. Berkeley, CA: University of California Press.

2

Origins of Queer Theologies

This chapter will analyse the origins of queer theologies. The guiding questions are: Where did queer theologies come from? Why is it not simply LGBTI? Who are the queers? We believe it is essential to trace a history of sexual theologies as a precursor to queer theologies:

> 'Queer is a continuing moment, movement, motive - recurrent, eddying, troublant. The word 'queer' itself means across - it comes from the Indo-European root - twerkw, which also yields the German quer (transverse). . .The immemorial current that queer represents is antiseparatist as it is antiassimilationist. Keenly, it is relational, and strange' (Sedgwick, 1990: xii).

Queer theory has three characteristics: the emphasis on the construction of sexuality, the element of plurality which needs to be present in any reflection and the idea of ambivalence or the fluidity of sexual identities (Butler, 1990). However, theology has been organised around a givenness, a monotheism and an exercise of the authority of the metanarratives of cis-heteronormativity. Therefore, Queer theory works as a new 'mediator science' in radical theologies. As Gustavo Gutierrez (2004) spoke of Liberation Theology as the irruption of the poor in theology so Queer theory has facilitated the irruption of the ultimately marginalised in Christianity those are people and institutional forms of organisation at the margins of cis-heteronormativity, gay, lesbians, transgenders, but also knowledge at the margin of cis-heterosexuality, too.

Queer theologies are an emerging discipline which takes as their starting point the radical, and as yet unexplored, nature of incarnation. That the divine left the heavens and moved into flesh once and for all is the queer ground that we inhabit. A ground from which we are also required to move, to transverse (Isherwood, 2006). Far from creating the same yesterday, today and tomorrow this dynamism is always propelling us forward into new curiosities and challenges. It does not shut us off from the world, rather it is the world drawing us into more of ourselves as we spiral in the human/divine dance. We are challenged to move beyond metaphysics and the comfortable world that they create. Queer theory, with its post-modern roots, asks us to distrust any master narrative, and there is no bigger one than metaphysics. Queer theology would like to take lives, including that of Jesus of Nazareth, in the raw and examine how we between us embody the transformative and spiralling reality of incarnation (Shore-Goss, 2002). There are no boundaries; all stories tell us of the incarnation we share and the redemptive space we strive for.

Queer theologies are, therefore, a deep questioning or an exercise of multiple and diverse hermeneutical suspicions. Theology has, for some time now, been reflecting on concerns for justice which have included class, race and gender becoming critical tools when thinking about God and human history. However, sexuality remains one of the most difficult and pervasive ideological areas of assumed understandings. Queering theology requires us to challenge the existent link between theology and sexual domestication and as such courage becomes a crucial tool in the theological kitbag. Theories of sexuality function as myths which organise a representation of history (Hennessy, 2000). Against that, other sexual thinking is rendered as deviant. However, the given coherence of certain social order and institutional life as the church also depends on the mythical cis-heteronormal matrix (Butler, 1990) which constitutes private and corporative identities. In theology, the question is how does the politics of cis-heteronormal identities (political and divine) pre-empt our representation of God and the reflection into the key themes of Christianity? (Althaus-Reid & Isherwood, 2004).

What has been lacking in much liberation theology is what Rosemary Hennessy (2000) calls 'the politics of profit and pleasure'. Queer theologies do not see capitalist expansion as separate from more personal embodied issues; it understands the destruction of the environment and the politics of exclusion to lie in the relation between capitalism and sexuality, between western economy thinking and cis-heterosexual thinking and ultimately to be rooted in the same cis-heterosexual binary thinking that underpins traditional theological ethics and narrow Christian praxis. To regulate sexuality in the name of divinities means to regulate the order of affectionate exchanges but also other human exchanges such as the political and economic systems (Isherwood, 2006). For this reason queer theologies do not take their place at the centre of theological discourses but at the margins. Queer theologies strive for differentiation and plurality in a sense for bio-diversity in theology, that is, life and love in all its diversity, which at the end, transforms and renews all its praxis.

Queer theologies are a political and sexually queering of theology which goes beyond the gender paradigms of the early years of feminist theology but also transcend the fixed assumptions of Lesbian and Gay theology. Queering theology, that is, questioning the cis-heterosexual underlying of theological reflections, exceeds the sphere of the private and also goes into the heart of the understanding of the exchange vision of the IMF and the understanding of what does it mean to be human in the Globalization philosophy. As Hennessy has pointed out, cis-heteronormativity has a labour division policy presupposed in gender hierarchies and the reification of sexual identities in our societies are linked to capitalism (Hennessy 2000). Queer theologies are political theologies.

As a genre, queer theologies partake of irony, humour and self-disclosure as does the Camp genre and Queer literature. The self-disclosure style means also that queer theologies are an 'I' theology. In this way, queer theologies are a form of autobiography because they imply an engagement and a disclosure of experiences which have been traditionally silenced in theology (Loughlin, 2007). For instance, issues of BDSM, transvestism, or even the denunciation of cis-heterosexuality as a construction which does not even properly apply to the real experiences of cis-heterosexual people.

As a subversive force, queer theologies focus on theological closets, in what has not been said or has been hidden (Guest et al., 2006). More than anything else, queer theologies are an incarnated, body theology which deals with desire, but also pleasure which has been ignored in theology for too long. Pleasure is after all, the incarnation of desires. Like post-modernism, queer theologies ask that we de-mystify, undo and subvert. Far from being seen as unhelpful this approach is viewed as crucial to our well being, but it has drawn concern from both feminist and liberation theologians who have long felt that some postmodern theology lacks a critical political/moral edge but as we have seen queer theologies operate on those edges.

Stages in the Development of Queer Theologies

Many scholars, notably Robert Shore-Goss (2002) and André Sidnei Musskopf (2012), have divided the history of queer theologies into three distinct stages. These stages, however, are not rigidly separate but exhibit significant overlaps and continuities, reflecting the evolving nature of queer theological thought. Later, Córdova Quero (2015) expanded on this framework, proposing two additional stages that further explore the historical development of queer theologies, offering a more comprehensive understanding of how these theological movements have emerged and evolved within diverse cultural and religious contexts.

First Stage: Homosexual Theologies

The emergence of homosexual theologies can be traced back to the 1950s, characterised by their apologetic tone. These theologies aimed to defend and legitimise the presence of homosexual individuals within Christian traditions, challenging widespread exclusion. The term 'homosexual' itself originated from the medicalisation of same-sex attraction in the eighteenth and nineteenth centuries, marking a shift from behaviour to identity classification. In contrast, during the Middle Ages, the term 'sodomy' was used to label specific acts as transgressions of cis-heteronormative expectations, without yet forming an identity-based categorisation of sexuality (Jordan, 1997). However, as Foucault (1990) states,

> The nineteenth-century homosexual became a personage, a past, a case history, and a childhood, in addition to being a type of life, a life form, and a morphology (. . .). [While] the sodomite had been a temporary aberration, the homosexual was now a species (1990: 43).

Homosexual theologies emerged in parallel with the demands of homosexual and homophile groups in mid-twentieth-century European and North American societies. Their focus was advocating for inclusion within Christian churches and challenging the discrimination and criminalisation faced by LGBTQ+ individuals. As Musskopf (2012: 126–127) highlights, these theologies presented a religious discourse 'about' homosexuality, questioning heteronormative interpretations of sacred texts.

For instance, Derrick Sherwin Bailey's *Homosexuality and the Western Christian Tradition* (1955) is a pioneering study of the Christian tradition's historical attitudes towards homosexuality. Bailey examines biblical, theological and legal texts, arguing that traditional condemnations are based on cultural and contextual interpretations rather than immutable doctrine. His scholarly approach—groundbreaking at the time—challenged dominant perspectives that condemned homosexuality as an inherent sin. The book significantly influenced theological and social debates, marking the beginning of a critical reconsideration of Christian positions towards same-sex relationships.

In the same tone, *Christ and the Homosexual* (1959), written by Robert W. Wood, is 'a work that called for a radical reappraisal of traditional Christian condemnations of homosexuality and an unapologetic acceptance of homosexuals in church and society' (Schlager, 2018: 161). He believed that the Church's disapprobation of (male) homosexuality was due to 'the connection between homosexuality and pagan religions and because the church insisted on maintaining a theology of marriage based on procreation' (Schlager, 2018: 168). Eager to defend the legitimacy of Christian gay men, Wood argued that same-sex attraction was part of a divine plan and is mirrored in the intimate relationship between Christ and the disciple John. Homosexual theologies boldly critiqued heteronormative scriptural interpretations that persecuted gay men.

Second Stage: Gay/LGBT Theologies

The second stage of queer theology development is closely tied to the revolutionary movements of the 1960s, which brought a heightened focus on liberation. Key events, such as the French 'May of 1968' protests and various revolutionary movements in Third World countries, played a significant role in shaping the emerging discourse around liberation within marginalised communities. These movements influenced the early gay liberation efforts in the 1970s, particularly in the aftermath of the Stonewall Riots in New York in 1969. The Stonewall Uprising, a pivotal moment in queer history, catalysed the growth of activist communities, shifting focus towards both social justice and the fight for LGBTQ+ rights. This period marked a significant transformation, where queer communities began to demand more than tolerance—they sought recognition, autonomy and liberation from societal oppression.

As a result, theologians began to explore the concept of liberation within the context of Christian churches. The formation of alliances with feminist theologies led to the development of new sexual theologies, which Musskopf (2012) and Shore-Goss (2002) identify as gay theologies. These theologies were also influenced by Latin American Liberation Theology, which emphasised social justice and the need for systemic change. The central aim of gay theologies was not only to challenge cis-heteronormative interpretations of sacred texts—building on the foundations of earlier homosexual theologies—but also to uncover the voices of gay individuals throughout Christian history. These theologies highlighted the long-standing oppression faced by gay people within the church, drawing attention to the marginalisation and persecution they have endured up to the present day. Through this critical examination, gay theologies sought to both reclaim space for queer believers and challenge the theological systems that have historically silenced their presence.

The focus of these theologies was shaped by the rise of identity politics, as they adopted the acronym LGBT to include gay, lesbian, bisexual and transgender identities. Influenced by seminal academic works such as John Boswell's *Christianity, Social Tolerance, and Homosexuality* (1980), the work of Gary David Comstock in *Gay Theology without Apology* (1993) clearly marks a shift from the apologetic tone found in earlier homosexual theologies to a more assertive and unapologetic stance in emerging gay/LGBT theologies. At the same time, gay theologies took on the task of reevaluating Christianity's doctrinal foundations from a gay perspective, examining the presence of gay and lesbian figures in biblical texts (e.g., the relationship between David and Jonathan as 'gay' lovers) and in Christian history (e.g., Hildegard von Bingen as a 'lesbian' saint). Important works by gay/LGBT theologians include J. Michael Clark's *Beyond Our Ghettos: Gay Theology in Ecological Perspective* (1993) and *Defying the Darkness: Gay Theology in the Shadows* (1997), as well as Richard Cleaver's *Know My Name: A Gay Liberation Theology* (1995), among others. These works collectively reflect a commitment to reinterpreting both scripture and history through a queer lens, while also confronting the traditional, cis-heteronormative doctrines of the church.

Third Stage: Queer Theologies

The third stage marks the development of queer theologies, which represent a significant departure from earlier homosexual and gay/LGBT theologies. It is important to recall that queer theory not only challenges cis-heteropatriarchal ideologies by subverting their norms and order, but also disrupts the rigid hetero/homo dichotomy that heavily shaped the lesbian and gay movements in the 1970s and 1980s. A key distinction in this shift is the destabilisation of identity politics, which was central to LGBT movements and often associated with assimilation into mainstream, heteronormative society. Many activists recognised that the identity politics around terms like 'gay' and 'lesbian' were dominated by white, middle-class perspectives. In contrast, queer movements have sought to highlight solidarity among all non-heteronormative sexualities, advocating for a broader, more inclusive approach.

Queer theologies emerged with a distinct approach, aligning with the broader tone of queer movements. While homosexual and gay/LGBT theologies often operated on the premise of assimilation into mainstream Christianity, queer theologies challenge the very authority of Christianity to question the religious experiences of queer individuals and communities. Rather than seeking legitimisation or acceptance, queer theologies assert the inherent diversity of humanity, highlighting the oppressive structures imposed by mainstream cis-heteronormative theologies that seek to preserve their privileges over sex- and gender-diverse groups. These theologies do not simply aim for inclusion within traditional Christian frameworks, but rather, they question the legitimacy of those frameworks themselves in their treatment of queer identities.

Rooted in the activism and solidarity that emerged from the 1980s onwards, queer theologies emphasise the need for alliances among all non-heteronormative sexual and gender identities. Such a perspective shifts the focus from seeking acceptance to challenging the very structures that have historically marginalised and oppressed queer individuals. By critiquing the power dynamics within both religious and social systems, queer theologies advocate for a more inclusive, equitable vision of human diversity, rejecting the privileges afforded by heteronormative interpretations of faith.

Works of queer theologians are represented by Marcella Althaus-Reid's *Indecent Theology* (2000) and *The Queer God* (2003), Robert Goss' *Queering Christ* (2002) and Ken Stone's *Practicing Safer Texts: Food, Sex and Bible in Queer Perspective* (2005), among others.

Fourth Stage: Ethnic and Regional Queer Theologies

It is important to recognise that categories such as ethnicity, nationality, race and social class are fluid and context-dependent, shaped by specific situations and societal expectations. As a result, discussions of ethnic queer theologies within the Global North differ significantly from those in other geographic contexts. Moreover, each pan-ethnic community within the Global North carries the distinct imprint of its own historical experiences and sociocultural dynamics. These unique histories influence how queer theologies are understood, articulated and practised, further emphasising the contextual nature of their development and expression.

Therefore, building on the three phases outlined by Shore-Goss (2002), Musskopf (2012) and Córdova Quero (2015) introduced a fourth stage in this periodisation. That phase highlights the developments at the turn of the twenty-first century, where queer theologies began to connect more deeply with racial, ethnic, social and geographic contexts. These dimensions are critical, as they shape the conditions and frameworks necessary for ethnic and regional queer theologies to take root. In deeply racialised societies like the United States, queer individuals and communities face challenges not only from the dominant hegemonic group—Caucasians—but also within their own ethnic communities, where cis-heteronormative understandings of gender and sexuality have been deeply entrenched for generations.

Regional queer theologies in Africa, Asia and Latin America, along with Asian-American, African-American, Latinx and Native (North) American queer theologies, represent a dynamic and evolving stage in the broader history of queer theological thought. These theologies bring diverse cultural, historical and social perspectives to the field, enriching its scope and depth. Notable theologians contributing to this development include Patrick S. Cheng, with works such as *Radical Love: An Introduction to Queer Theology* (2011), *From Sin to Amazing Grace: Discovering the Queer Christ* (2012) and *Rainbow Theology* (2013). EL Kornegay, Jr. also offers significant insights through his article 'Queering Black Homophobia: Black Theology as a Sexual Discourse of Transformation' (2004) and his book *A Queering of Black Theology* (2013).

Fifth Stage: Queer Theologies Within Global Religions

All religions contain elements that reflect the diversity with which issues such as gender, sexuality, couple and family formation, cis-heteronormative divisions of labour and culturally specific gender role expectations are constructed within particular times and contexts. Religions worldwide often engage with—and frequently legitimise—these constructs, often through transcendent frameworks. That is evident within all religious traditions, which include queer believers. While some of these individuals are more visible, others face greater oppression or acceptance. However, the presence of queer individuals across all societies underscores the need for religions to acknowledge and embrace their contributions. This remains an ongoing challenge.

Thus, Córdova Quero (2015) introduces a fifth stage, which focuses on the development and flourishing of queer theologies within global religions such as Judaism, Islam, Buddhism, Hinduism, Paganism and various regional spiritualities. In each of these religions, elements related to queer issues are already present, whether through the lenses of gay and lesbian concerns or queer theory critiques. It is particularly important for queer believers to challenge the validity of aspects of sacred scriptures that fail to promote freedom and respect. Furthermore, it is crucial to encourage reflection on the spirituality of queer believers, which expresses their relationship with the divine in everyday life. However, the personal experiences and life stories of queer individuals are not always valued or supported by the internal structures or interpretations of sacred scriptures. In this context, it is valid for queer believers to question and revise the role and interpretation of sacred texts within their faith tradition. This critical questioning is a vital step towards gaining a voice to subvert the homophobia, lesbophobia and transphobia that seem to be deeply embedded in many religious contexts.

A major obstacle to advancing these theologies is addressing the cultural dimensions of religion. Culture is fundamental to every religious tradition, shaping how individuals and communities express their faith or spirituality. Even when a religion is labelled a 'world religion', its practices and beliefs are always framed by the specific cultural contexts in which they emerge. Failing to acknowledge this reality leads to the mistaken assumption that what is effective in one cultural setting will automatically apply to another. Such an issue is particularly pressing when addressing queer matters, as they intersect with deeply ingrained cultural norms and values. Engaging with these cultural nuances is crucial for developing inclusive and contextually meaningful queer theologies across diverse religious contexts.

For Further Discussion

1 In what ways do you think queer theologies are different from LGBTIQ+ theologies?

2 Could it be argued that queer also needs to address cis-heterosexual sexual behaviour?

3 Althaus-Reid believed cis-heterosexuals need to come out about their understanding of sexuality. Do you agree?

4 In what ways do you think cultural differences affect the development of queer theologies?

5 In studying the different stages of the development of queer theologies, what elements stand out in your understanding of each stage?

References

Althaus-Reid, Marcella (2000). *Indecent Theology: Theological Perversions in Sex, Gender and Politics*. London: Routledge.

Althaus-Reid, Marcella (2003). *The queer God*. Routledge.

Althaus-Reid, Marcella and Lisa Isherwood (editors) (2004). *The Sexual Theologian, Essay on God, Sex & Politics*. London: T&T Clark.

Bailey, Derek S (1955). *Homosexuality and the Western Christian Tradition*. New York, NY: Longmanns Green and Co.

Boswell, John (1980). *Christianity, Social Tolerance, and Homosexuality: Gay People in Western Europe from the Beginning of the Christian Era to the Fourteenth Century*. Chicago, IL: The University of Chicago Press.

Butler, Judith (1990). *Gender Trouble: Feminism and the Subversion of Identity*. London: Routledge.

Cheng, Patrick S (2011). *Radical Love: An Introduction to Queer Theology*. New York, NY: Seabury Books.

Cheng, Patrick S (2012). *From Sin to Amazing Grace: Discovering the Queer Christ*. New York, NY: Seabury Books.

Cheng, Patrick S (2013). *Rainbow Theology: Bridging Race, Sexuality, and Spirit*. New York, NY: Seabury Books.

Clark, J Michael (1993). *Beyond Our Ghettos: Gay Theology in Ecological Perspective*. Cleveland, OH: Pilgrim Press.

Clark, J Michael (1997). *Defying the Darkness: Gay Theology in the Shadows*. Cleveland, OH: Pilgrim Press.

Cleaver, Richard (1995). *Know My Name: A Gay Liberation Theology*. Louisville, KY: Westminster John Knox Press.

Comstock, Gary D (1993). *Gay Theology Without Apology*. Cleveland, OH: Pilgrim Press.

Córdova Quero, Hugo (2015). "Queer Liberative Theologies." In: *Introducing Liberative Theologies*, edited by Miguel A De la Torre. New York, NY: Orbis Books, pp. 210–231.

Foucault, Michel (1990). *The History of Sexuality, Vol. 1: An Introduction*, translated by Robert Hurley. New York, NY: Vintage Books.

Guest, Deryn, Bob Shore-Goss, Mona West and Thomas Bohache (editors) (2006). *The Queer Bible Commentary*. London: SCM Press.

Gutierrez, Gustavo (2004). *The Power of the Poor in History*. Eugene, OR: Wipf and Stock.

Hennessy, Rosemary (2000). *Profit & Pleasure: Sexual Identities in Late Capitalism*. London: Routledge.

Isherwood, Lisa (2006). *The Power of Erotic Celibacy: Queering Heteropatriarchy*. London: T&T Clark.

Jordan, Mark D (1997). *The Invention of Sodomy in Christian Theology*. Chicago, IL: University of Chicago Press.

Kornegay, E L Jr (2004). "Queering Black Homophobia: Black Theology as a Sexual Discourse of Transformation." *Theology and Sexuality* 11, No. 1: pp. 29–51.

Kornegay, E L Jr (2013). *A Queering of Black Theology: James Baldwin's Blues Project and Gospel Prose*. New York, NY: Palgrave MacMillan.

Loughlin, Gerard (editor) (2007). *Queer Theology. Rethinking the Western Body*. Oxford: Blackwell.

Musskopf, André S (2012). *Via(da)gens teológicas: Itinerários para uma teologia queer no Brasil*. São Paulo, SP: Fonte Editorial.

Schlager, Bernard (2018). "Christ and the homosexual. An Early Manifesto for an Affirming Ministry to Homosexuals." *Theology & Sexuality* 21, No. 2: pp. 105–124.

Sedgwick, Eve K (1990). *Epistemology of the Closet*. Berkeley, CA: University of California Press.

Shore-Goss, Robert (2002). *Queering Christ: Beyond Jesus Acted Up*. Cleveland, OH: Pilgrim Press.

Stone, Ken (2005). *Practicing Safer Texts: Food, Sex and Bible in Queer Perspective*. London: T&T Clark.

Wood, Robert (1959). *Christ and the Homosexual*. New York, NY: Vantage Press.

3

Theologically Queer

In this chapter, we aim to explore the topics of theology from a queer theology perspective and connect them to the daily life impact on those who practice faith. Unlike other chapters—which present the most prominent people working in queer theologies—this chapter will demonstrate how queer theologies engage with the issues of life and decision-making: How ethics and moral perspective constitute the questions and concerns of queer believers and theologians. Therefore, we will present the creativity and audacity of queer theologians and believers as they investigate these topics outside the cis-heteronormative traditional pattern.

Theology

Theology has been called the queen of the sciences and is by definition the study of religions and the nature of the divine. Historically this has held a narrow focus with theologians usually employed by the church or academic institutions to 'prove' the correctness of doctrinal statements. This is best illustrated by the so-called five proofs for the existence of God laid out by Thomas Aquinas, all of which have been disproved by subsequent generations. It is only within the last 160 years or so that biblical criticism as we know it has been practised using literary techniques; before that time the Bible was considered literal and infallible. These days theology has moved a great distance from these early expressions; it still looks to religions and how they express God and even attempts to explore the deeper and almost unknowable questions such as the very nature of the divine. The great Harvard-based biblical scholar Elizabeth Schüssler Fioernza believes that one grasps something of the nature of the divine that individuals and societies worship by the complexion of that society or person.

As we will see throughout this book theology comes in many different forms throughout the world, and this for us is the richness of the subject. There are always many questions and what answers there maybe are always open to examination and change.

Theologising

Theologising refers to the act of engaging in theology, the study of the nature of the divine, religious beliefs and the practice of systematically developing, interpreting and critically analysing religious doctrines. It involves formulating doctrines and articulating religious beliefs and principles, as well as interpreting sacred texts to explain the meanings of scriptures and religious writings. Philosophical inquiry is also a part of theologising, where discussions about the nature of God, existence and morality take place. The historical study of religious beliefs and practices examines their context and development over time. Additionally, theologising explores the practical application of religious beliefs in daily life and practice. This process can occur within the context of a specific religious tradition or across religious traditions, looking at similarities and differences within various religions. It can be an academic endeavour or a more personal, devotional practice.

Christians theologise because they believe that theologising has practical consequences, specifically liberating ones. Christian theological methodologies and constructions reflect, in concrete forms of gender and sexuality, the very reference and source of why we engage in theology. In other words, we theologise in response to what we believe to be the queer/disruptive and liberating/salvific mystery of divine love. This is not about a manifest dysfunction of thought but an intentional deviation to theologise differently. It is a speculative theologising of a bodily relational moment that is always already theologised in itself.

However, while theologising is often associated with Christianity, it is a practice that extends to various religious traditions around the world, each with its unique approach and focus. The other two Abrahamic religions at some points run parallel to Christianity, while in other aspects they diverge. In Islam, theologising involves the study of the Quran, Hadith and other religious texts, as well as the development of Islamic jurisprudence (*fiqh*) and theology (*kalam*). It includes exploring the nature of Allah, the prophet and the principles of Sharia law. While theologising in Judaism is a multifaceted and evolving practice that seeks to harmonise ancient traditions with contemporary life, fostering a deep connection to the divine, the community and the ethical imperatives of the Jewish faith. This involves engaging deeply with the rich textual, philosophical and practical traditions that have developed over millennia. This process encompasses a variety of activities, including the study and interpretation of sacred texts, the formulation and articulation of theological ideas, and the application of these beliefs in everyday life.

Karmic religions also theologise in their own unique ways. In Hinduism, theologising encompasses the interpretation of ancient scriptures such as the Vedas, Upanishads and the Bhagavad Gita. It involves philosophical inquiries into concepts like dharma (duty/righteousness), karma (action/reaction) and moksha (liberation). In Buddhism, theologising focuses on the teachings of the Buddha, the interpretation of sutras and the development of various schools of thought such as Theravada, Mahayana and Vajrayana. It includes exploring the nature of suffering, the path to enlightenment and the nature of reality. Similarly, in other religious traditions such as Judaism, Sikhism and indigenous spiritualities, theologising involves the study and interpretation of sacred texts, the development of religious doctrines and the application of these beliefs in daily life and practice. Each tradition brings its own perspectives and methodologies, contributing to the diverse and rich landscape of global theological thought.

Theologising within Pagan religions involves a deep engagement with the spiritual practices, traditions and worldviews rooted in pre-Christian, polytheistic and animistic belief systems. Unlike organised religions with codified doctrines or centralised structures, Pagan religions are often decentralised, diverse and deeply connected to nature, seasonal cycles and ancestral wisdom. This diversity allows for a plurality of theological interpretations, as practitioners draw from ancient mythologies, oral traditions and personal spiritual experiences to articulate their understanding of the divine. Central to Pagan theologising is the emphasis on immanence, the belief that the sacred is present in all aspects of the natural world. This contrasts with many transcendent-focused theological frameworks, fostering a spirituality that honours the interconnectedness of all life. Pagan theology frequently involves reinterpreting ancient texts, symbols and rituals in light of contemporary spiritual needs and ecological concerns, creating a dynamic and evolving tradition. Additionally, Pagan theologians often challenge dominant narratives imposed by patriarchal and monotheistic systems, seeking to reclaim marginalised voices and practices, particularly those of women, queer individuals and indigenous communities. By embracing the multiplicity of deities, genders and cosmologies, Pagan theologising resists reductionist interpretations of the divine, instead celebrating diversity and complexity. Through its focus on lived experience, ecological ethics, and the revitalisation of ancestral practices, Pagan theologising offers a framework that connects spiritual insight with social justice, environmental stewardship and the honouring of ancient wisdom in a modern context.

Finally, theologising in ancestral spiritualities and belief systems that are not organised religions involves a deep engagement with the spiritual traditions, practices and worldviews passed down through generations. These belief systems often emphasise a profound connection to nature, ancestors and the cosmos, reflecting a holistic understanding of existence. In these contexts, theologising may include interpreting oral traditions, myths and stories that convey spiritual truths and moral lessons. It involves exploring the rituals, ceremonies and practices that connect individuals and communities with the sacred, the land and their ancestors. These practices often emphasise the cyclical nature of life, the interconnectedness of all beings and the importance of maintaining harmony and balance within the natural world. Theologising in ancestral spiritualities can also involve the embodiment of spiritual knowledge through art, dance, music and other forms of cultural expression. It is about understanding and living in accordance with the wisdom of the elders and the spiritual guides, who often play a crucial role in transmitting and interpreting the spiritual traditions. Moreover, this form of theologising recognises the sacred in everyday life and seeks to honour and preserve the spiritual heritage of the community. It is not only an intellectual pursuit but also a way of life that integrates spirituality into all aspects of existence, from relationships and community life to interactions with the environment. Overall, theologising in ancestral spiritualities is a dynamic and living process that adapts to the changing contexts and needs of the community while remaining rooted in the timeless wisdom of the ancestors.

Ethics

> 'We can probably say that moral questions have always arisen when moral norms of behaviour have ceased to be self-evident and unquestioned in the life of a community'. (Adorno, 2001: 9).

These words could well have been written for the LGBTIQ+ community but were not done so exclusively. What Adorno is saying is that the collective ethos of what we call morality is generally a conservative one which tries to suggest a false unity amongst the population at large and suppresses difficulties and discontinuity that exist within the generally accepted ethos. He is clear that there was never a unity in relation to morality but rather what he terms a nationalism of belief that is no longer credible. Therefore, a recourse to ethics in his view is a certain kind of violence and even a turn to violence. He says 'once the state of human consciousness and the state of social forces of production have abandoned these collective ideas, these ideas acquire repressive and violent qualities. It is this violence and evil that brings these customs into conflict with morality and not the decline in morals' (2001: 17).

Such violence attempts to maintain the appearance of collective agreement to the moral ethos, and while it has past in the general public it remains insistent that it is relevant to the present. Violence is the only way to impose it on the present. Adorno is clear about how this situation comes about he says it is when the 'universal' that is the accepted morality is in fact not universally accepted, does not take account of the individual and ignores the rights of individuals. The universal in his thinking has no substantial reality in the lives of human beings and he insists that any rules, morality, must be appropriated by individuals in a living way. (Adorno, 2001: 15). It is clear that this approach is helpful for LGBTIQ+ folk as it both exposes the assumption that morality is one thing shared by all and further that LGBTIQ+ folk by questioning received morality are in that way automatically living immoral lives. Further, of course it explains the violence that queer communities have endured over the years and still do.

Adorno is not however giving people a blank sheet and the green light to act as they will. He says we must pay attention to questions of right and wrong and always be self-critical realising our own fallibility in judgement making. He is of course clear that we can never know absolute good, but we can see the inhumanity that exists so he says, 'the place of moral philosophy today lies more in the concrete denunciation of the inhuman than in the vague and abstract attempts to situate man in his existence' (Adorno, 2001: 175) For him the question of what one ought to do is implicated in a social analysis of the world in which our doing takes place. Ethics cannot simply be accessed by judging the end and intention of one's action but in a rather bigger vista of the shaping of the world, and in this way the 'good life' merges into the right kind of politics which will give the best possible outcome in a world that is itself imperfect. He is signalling that individual action can only have limited impact if any at all it is community good will that is needed.

With the application of LGBTIQ lived experience and insights the stage for ethics has changed considerably, and an opening voice in this was Marvin Ellison (1996) who demonstrates how repression of sexual desire keeps people in doubt and uncertainty about their feelings and values making them open to control. He, like many gay theologians, believes that our sexuality embodies the injustice of our societies. He suggests that there are three dimensions to sexual injustice within the western Christian world that have to be overcome if we are to be free within our bodies and enabled to live justice seeking lives. These dimensions are sex negativity, cis-heterocentrism and the eroticisation of non-mutual relations.

For Ellison (1996), sex negativity takes several forms from the obvious viewing of the genitals and sex itself as unruly and dirty to creating a male hierarchy. The body is seen to be inferior and not part of who we essentially are; thus, it can be exploited, and it is here lies the heart of extended forms of capitalist exploitation, if the body is not important then it can be used for things that are important like money making. Desire of course threatens to disrupt everything and so has to be strictly monitored since it has the power to break down all boundaries. The dualism and distancing that such an approach encourages also lends itself to a male hierarchy as male and female are also divided into opposites and someone has to take the lead. The role of the women then becomes one of support and wifely duties ranging from sex to child rearing. Ellison denounces this as fundamentally non-Christian as he does the cis-heterocentrism that naturally follows from such a fundamental position of dualism as already described.

He points out that the injustice of heterocentrism is actually not simply theoretical but acted out in law with married couples getting tax benefits, social status and a range of partnership rights. Although some countries have extended partnership rights to gay and lesbian couples the situation is not consistent and the churches still oppose these measures. Ellison (1996) comments, 'heterosexual marriage is therefore far from being a free and voluntary choice; it is a political requirement for normative status in this culture' (1996: 27). It acts as the glue for a hierarchical system that is based on ownership and lends itself to the generation of wealth—just the kind of thing the Jesus movement seemed to disapprove of. One of the most pressing aspects of this arrangement for Ellison is the power that is eroticised in patriarchal sexual relations.

Ellison (1996) thinks that Christian sex ethics have failed to address the issue of power precisely because they have always concentrated on marriage, a system that is based on power. While 'compulsory coupling' as he calls marriage may fit the dominant capitalist ethos it does not lend itself to our full becoming as humans. It makes us dependent on one other for the fulfilment of our needs, limits our range and the importance that we place on friendship and weakens our ties with the wider community. It also tends to encourage us to think that our happiness depends on someone else.

Ellison (1996) wishes to move the debate away from the church councils and their desire to control and the dualistic philosophy which divides us within ourselves, and he does so by prioritising the Song of Songs when considering sexual ethics. Here he claims we see sex unencumbered by patriarchal considerations, the couple are not married, the woman is not required to bear children, she is independent and she is black just another upsetting of the social order which even in those days was based on colour and class. This couple show no shame and they love for love's sake, enjoying one another outside the procreative and familial bounds. Eroticism and not marriage become 'worship in the context of grace'. Some feminist critics may feel that Ellison is overstating the case, but his suggestion that this becomes the centre for the production of a sexual ethic is certainly a very positive first move.

Sexuality should be treated with special respect in times of great social stress. The world seems to be in that place today.

Monotheism

As you will see throughout this book not all religions are monotheistic, and it will be for you to judge whether this helps or hinders the development of queer theologies and the inclusion of queer lives in societies.

Not all queer theology challenges the notion of monotheism which is slightly surprising since the adherence to 'the One' is a problem for queers who lie beyond the strict boundaries of oneness. As we will see in chapter 16 questioning monotheism does not necessarily mean abandoning the notion of the divine but rather expanding it in the way that queer lives tend to expand notions of gender. Monotheism is not a belief shared by all religions but has been viewed as a superior belief by those who hold it (Roger, 2020). Perhaps the reason it has been seen in this way is because societies that flow from it are quite bounded and tightly regulated, categories of virtue and sin are easy to define across a range of issues, which in turn paves the way to violence against others (Schwartz, 1997). One reason for it being viewed as superior is embedded in the linear view of history; as societies develop they become more sophisticated and grasp more of what is real or so the story goes, especially in political terms (Assmann, 2005). This is not of course true and as we shall see later linear views of history, time and society are damaging to many parts of the world. In the name of the one True God colonisers took land, enslaved 'pagan people' and in the Christianising process carried out dehumanising abuse. For many who follow monotheistic religion there is still the idea that there are correct ways to be human, to rule society and to regulate global systems.

Monotheism is a late arrival on the religious scene and like all young things does see itself as superior. Often that has implied conflating monotheism with homogeneity, thus enhancing policing and controlling (Gnuse, 2007). Interestingly, many Islamic scholars do not see Christianity as monotheistic because of the belief in the Trinity, the three in One. For many contemporary theologians, amongst them queer theologians, taking the incarnation as the starting point for creating theology has also meant that monotheism as currently understood has been brought into question. This move from the death of Jesus as being the important aspect of Christianity, he died for our sins, to the birth of the divine in human flesh has given more space for queer people to enter the theological conversation and foster notions of plurality and multiplicity (Schneider, 2007). No longer viewed as only sinners but as bearers of the divine nature their voices as much as any may speak about God in the world.

An Example of Theologising: Christology

Feminist queer theologian Carter Heyward (1989) has stated:

> I have come to believe that an effort to do Christology in classic terms (Was Jesus divine? Was he human?) is much like trying to draw fresh milk from a very sick, tired, dry, sacred and as it turns out male goat. Christian feminists and others committed not only to the work of justice but also to holding our theologies and Christologies accountable to this work must set new terms for our faith, including and especially new terms for what we preach and teach about Jesus/Christ and for how we live in relation to the Jesus story and its Christic meaning (1989: 21).

In the 1980s, Episcopalian priest Carter Heyward (1982) made a close analysis of Mark's gospel in which she reread the meaning of, as she saw it, two significant words throughout the gospel.

These words were *exousia* and *dunamis*. *Exousia*, she noted, meant 'power over' and was routinely rejected by Jesus throughout the gospel. However, she concluded that *dunamis* is an inborn erotic energy, the birthright of us all that draws us to others and the world. Erotic in this sense may be sexual but is also that exuberant energy in all that lives. It propels us forward and is the energy of relationality, even across species, as we shall see later in the book. This human/divine energy makes us friends, not servants, of God and so enables Jesus to include us with him in what are traditionally understood as Trinitarian words, 'In that day you will know that I am in my Father and you in me and I in you' (John 14:20). The scholarly consensus that the gospel according to Mark did not originally include a resurrection narrative or any post-resurrection appearance narratives, further enables a greater understanding of dunamis as a birthright of us all. I suggest that it was no mistake by the author of the gospel according to Mark to alert us to our innate potential and then leave us standing at an empty tomb. The story continues with us in the human/divine nature we are now part of. We are pilgrim and resurrection people in the here and now, for all generations.

This approach highlights that we are part of a multi-dimensional divinity. The reality of the divine is not removed to another realm. Nor is it an outpouring from above. It is within and between us. For Heyward dunamis significantly destabilises dualistic metaphysics and yields new understanding. For her, transcendence carries a new understanding and has no hint of the 'above and beyond' within it. Rather it signals movement across and within, opening to new views and locations, among different companions all engaged in this dance of embodied transcendence. Heyward does hold on to a difference between our divine incarnation and that of Jesus, but this difference is nothing more than a breath, not the large chasm and the absolute model of purity and perfection that dualistic metaphysics produces.

Heyward's work enables the development of a queer theological method through her claiming of what she calls 'godding' as the birthright of all. 'Godding' is a process and it carries a spiralling element in it. While we have dunamis as a birthright, we grow towards greater fullness through life and experience, just as Jesus did. Heyward's insights have helped me to understand more acutely the flesh made word/s. Once we acknowledge the innate indwelling of dunamis as our birthright, then indeed our flesh and that of others does become the outpouring of incarnational possibilities. All bodies are now part of the divine becoming flesh with multiple outcomes and no one divine script. This is liberation for queer bodies who may no longer be excluded from the divine becoming.

Marcella Althaus-Reid (2000) also spoke of an obscene Christ, and by this she meant that obscenity uncovers what needs to be made visible. For example, she says that the black and feminist Christs are obscene as they uncover both the racism and sexism inherent in Christology. Even these images cause concern in some circles, where it is often claimed that the white male Christ does not lead to any exclusions or biases. Therefore, the entrance of queer bodies as the enfleshed realities 'of Christ' are no less alarming for some Christians, but this does not make them unnecessary for the inclusive church.

Speaking of the necessity of 'uncovering' Christ, Althaus-Reid says that any uncovering of Christ needs to follow that pattern of obscenity because Christ and his symbolic construction continue in our history, in relation to our own moment of historical consciousness. In our own time it is a matter of theological deceit and even falsehood if we continue to construct Christologies on the old knowledges.

It has to be said that lines are drawn around the body when the body gets too vocal in the creation of Christology. We can, perhaps, just about cope with a female Christ as long as we are not asked to look at questions of gender. Althaus-Reid is never afraid of these questions and gives us a kick-arse, leather clad-lesbian warrior as a Christ figure. This is Xena, lesbian warrior, who declares she will climb off the cross to save the woman she loves, who is hanging next to her, and to do so she will kill those who have put them there. This is no passive woman giving up her soul to a distant God. She is willing to fight, to be passionate and to change the narrative (Wagner et al., 1999–2000). Queer Christs are not simply sets of prepositions and internal relations of the divine with itself but rather a praxis, an ethical, embodied way of life. We no longer have to negotiate our being with the once and for all neat and tidy Christ of disembodied metaphysics but rather can engage in revolutionary living with a dynamic and changing multiplicity of Christ's whose core is ethical praxis. A praxis, far removed from ideas of mono sexual purity as a sign of holiness and deeply embedded in queers embracing and exploring their desire.

For Further Discussion

1   What part does an ethical system play in your life? Where did you develop this system, what influenced you?

2   How might we understand Ellis' assertion that sexual repression keeps people in doubt and does not allow them to embody justice?

3   Do you agree with Ellison that sexual ethics have failed to address the issue of power?

4   The obscene Christ gives space for diversity, while the universal Christ imposes sameness across time and place. What do you think an obscene Christ needs to uncover in this place and time?

5   Monotheism has been viewed as the pinnacle of religious development by many scholars through the ages. In your view is monotheism a world view fit for purpose in the contemporary world?

References

Adorno, Theodor (2001). *Problems of Moral Philosophy*, translated by Rodney Livingstone. Stanford, CA: Stanford University Press.

Althaus Reid, Marcella (2000). *Indecent Theology. Theological Perversions in Sex, Gender and Politics*. London: Routledge.

Assmann, Jn (2005). "Monotheism and Its Political Consequences." In: *Religion and Politics: Cultural Perspectives*, International Studies in Religion and Society # 3, edited by Bernhard Giesen and Daniel Šuber. Leiden: Brill, pp. 141–159.

Ellison, Marvin M (1996). *Erotic Justice: A Liberation Ethic of Sexuality*. Louisville, KY: Westminsiter John Knox Press.

Gnuse, Robert K (2007). "Breakthrough or Tyranny: Monotheism's Contested Implications." *Horizons* 34: pp. 78–95.

Heyward, Carter (1982). *The Redemption of God: A Theology of Mutual Relation*. New York, NY: University of America Press.

Heyward, Carter (1989). *Speaking of Christ: A Lesbian Feminist Voice*. Cleveland, OH: Pilgrim Press.

Roger, Trigg (2020). *Monotheism and Religious Diversity*, Elements in Religion and Monotheism Series. Cambridge: Cambridge University Press.

Schneider, Laurel C (2007). *Beyond Monotheism: A Theology of Multiplicity*. London: Routledge.

Schwartz, Regina M (1997). *The Curse of Cain: The Violent Legacy of Monotheism*. Chicago, IL: University of Chicago Press.

Wagner, John, Joyce Chin, Mike Deodato, Ivan Reis and Walden Wong (1999–2000). *Xena Warrior Princess*, 14 books. Milwaukee, WI: Dark Horse Comin Inc.

Further Reading

Isherwood, Lisa (1999). *Liberating Christ*. Cleveland, OH: Pilgrim Press.

Musskopf, André S (2012). *Via(da)gens teológicas: Itinerários para uma teologia queer no Brasil*. São Paulo, SP: Fonte Editorial.

Part II

Queer Theologies and Global Religions

A Brief Note About This Section

Within this section, our focus revolves around global religions, with a specific emphasis on unravelling the trajectory of queer theologies and their intricate connections with tangible, lived experiences. Recognising the potential pitfalls associated with categorising various theological reflections under the umbrella term 'theology', particularly in light of the presupposition of a Divine entity, our approach involves presenting the unique perspective of each religion through their distinct religious language. The primary objective is to probe and illuminate the captivating and avant-garde queer initiatives embedded within the fabric of these diverse religious traditions. By doing so, we hope to offer a nuanced understanding of the evolving landscape of queer perspectives within the broader context of global religions, highlighting the dynamic interplay between theology and the lived material reality of individuals identifying with diverse sexual orientations and gender identities.

Through a comprehensive exploration of how various theologies intersect with contemporary realities, our objective is to provide valuable insights into the ever-evolving landscape of queer perspectives within global religious frameworks. This methodological approach highlights the dynamic nature inherent in these discussions, shedding light on the multifaceted dimensions of the intersection between theology and the lived experiences of the LGBTIQ+ community. It underscores the significance of cultivating a nuanced understanding, emphasising the need to appreciate the subtle intricacies woven into the fabric of each religious tradition's engagement with queer narratives and experiences. As we delve into these complexities, we aim to foster a deeper awareness of the diverse ways in which global religions grapple with issues of sexuality and gender identity, ultimately contributing to a more inclusive and informed discourse surrounding the intersection of theology and queer perspectives.

The primary objective is to cast a spotlight on the progressive and transformative facets of queer initiatives across various global religious landscapes. Through the presentation of innovative and evolving dimensions of queer religious reflection, our overarching goal is to cultivate a profound understanding of the positive impacts and advancements taking place at the intersection of religious traditions and LGBTIQ+ narratives. This exploration seeks to highlight the dynamic and constructive contributions emerging from the interplay between religious contexts and diverse expressions of sexual orientation and gender identity, fostering a more inclusive and enlightened dialogue within the broader societal framework.

Glossary for Part II

Agni:	God of fire.
Androgynous:	A person who is partly male and partly female in appearance.
Autochthonous:	Indigenous person not descended from migrants.
BDSM:	Bondage, discipline (or domination), sadism and masochism as a sexual practice.
Bi-Christ:	Overcomes mono-relations in matters of sexuality and society.
Butch:	A masculine lesbian.
Christianity:	A monotheistic religion.
Christology:	doctrine about the significance of Jesus.
Cis-heterosexual Division of Labour:	Refers to the traditional arrangement where men and women adhere to economic roles and social structures within family and kinship groups.
Colonisation:	The process of establishing control over foreign territory and people.
Ecumenism:	The aim of promoting unity amongst Christian churches.
FTM:	Assigned female at birth but transitions to male.
Ganesha:	Remover of obstacles; God of wisdom.
Gender Bend(ing):	Go against expected gender performances.
Gender Expression:	Outward characteristics that show a person's identity to society.
Gender Fluid:	Not confined to a fixed gender performance.
Gender Role Expectations:	behaviour and roles of men and women according to social structures based on their socio-cultural and economic positions, considering the predominant division of labour between genders.
Gnosticism:	Salvation through knowledge not faith.
Guru Granth Sahib:	Sikh holy scripture.
Heterogenous:	Differing in kind.

Global Queer Theologies: Intercontextual and Interreligious Perspectives, First Edition. Lisa Isherwood and Hugo Córdova Quero.
© 2026 John Wiley & Sons Ltd. Published 2026 by John Wiley & Sons Ltd.

Kanda:	Symbol for Sikhism.
Karmic Faiths:	Those that believe in rebirth.
Kliba:	A word in Jainism for a person non-conforming to gender stereotypes.
Krishna:	God of love.
Male to Female:	Assigned male at birth and transitions.
Mariology:	Theology related to the Virgin Mary, mother of Jesus.
Matrilineal:	A kinship system in which lineage and inheritance are traced through the female line, with property and titles typically passed down from mother to child.
Midrash:	An ancient commentary on part of the Hebrew scriptures. The oldest midrash comes from the second century AD but contains parts that are much older.
Monotheism:	Worship of one God.
Neo-Platonism:	Third-century school of thought focussing on the teaching of Plato. It had a more religious leaning than that of Plato.
Noble Truths:	The central teachings of Buddhism.
Non-binary:	Gender identity open to a full range of gender expressions.
Orishas:	Spirits.
Outing:	Revealing someone's lesbian, gay, bisexual, transgender or gender non-binary identity to others without their permission. Outing can lead to significant consequences, including jeopardising employment, economic stability, personal safety and familial or religious relationships.
PA:	Polyamorous people.
Pantheism:	A doctrine which regards the world as manifesting the divine.
Patrilineal:	A kinship system where lineage and inheritance are traced through the male line, typically passing down property and titles from father to son.
Phet thi-sam:	A phrase for third-gender folk in Thailand.
Polygamy:	The practice of having multiple spouses simultaneously.
Santeria:	A syncretic religion whose literal meaning is union of saints.
Sheela na Gig:	Celtic female fertility image.
Sharia Law:	Muslim religious laws intended to promote human welfare and is based on five categories: obligatory actions, recommended actions, disliked actions, forbidden action and permitted action.
Shikhandi:	Transgendered hero in the Mahabharata.
Third Sex:	A category for people who do not fit into the traditional definitions of male or female, often recognised in various cultures and societies around the world.
Tonghzi:	The literal meaning is comrade but also used for queer people.
Transition/ing:	The process that some transgender individuals undertake to align their gender presentation and identity with their true gender.
Transsexual:	A person who identifies with a different sex from that assigned at birth.
Transvestite:	A term less used, referring to a person who is a cross-dresser.
Umbrella Revolution:	Street protests in Hong Kong in 2014 demanding transparent elections.

4

Christianity

Source: dimitrisvetsikas1969 / Pixabay

Christianity as a Religion

Christianity is offered first because its engagement with queer theory came earliest, not because of any priority given to Christian theology. This section centres on the vastly developed production of Christian queer theologies. This chapter will highlight the challenging work of queer scholars who examine the texts, doctrines and life of churches through the diverse experiences of queer folk.

Christianity is a religion with a 2,000 year history. It should be said that the roots of Christianity are deeply related to Judaism, as Jesus was a Jew who lived in Galilee in the first century CE, a place of huge political turmoil as it was under Roman occupation. The main historical record about Jesus can be found in the sacred texts, the Gospels, which were written almost 40 years after the death of Jesus. Even the Gospels have different information about him. While Matthew (1.18–24) and Luke (2.1–16) talk about his birth from Mary, the Virgin, the first Gospel written, Mark, describes the life of Jesus only after his baptism (Mk 1.9–11) and originally did not have a resurrection story. However, the Gospels and the rest of the Christian writings in the Christian Testament emphasise Jesus' teachings.

At first, Jesus' teachings were passed on through oral stories until the first letter of St. Paul, the First Epistle to the Thessalonians, written in c. 51–52 CE (Brown, 1997: 456). The first Gospel, Mark, was written c. 70 CE (Harris, 1985). Since then, Christians began to systematise Christian belief in both sacred scriptures and theological works. The Bible is made up of the Hebrew Bible, no longer named the Old Testament, and the Christian Bible, no longer known as the New Testament. Scholars have at last realised how dismissive and arrogant these terms were. There are Christian writings not included in the sacred canon of Scripture such as the Gospel of Mary Magdalene, the Gospel of Truth, or the Gospel of Judas. Contemporary scholars question why they were omitted; in some cases it was because they have only been found in fragments but in a push for theological orthodoxy it is undoubtedly true that a careful selection of scripture was made. There are other theological works such as Bible commentaries, devotional and spiritual writings that, although not considered 'sacred', have influenced the tradition for Christians. Amongst them perhaps the Summa Theologica of Thomas Aquinas, written between 1265 and 1274 has had the most abiding influence. His work was heavily influenced by the relatively newly discovered writings of Greek philosophers, predominately Aristotle. This has historically not been life giving for women, nature and queer people yet it remains the backbone of much theological work even in the present day.

Source: stux / Pixabay

Christianity summarises its beliefs in the Creeds: Apostles'(341 CE) produced in direct response to what was considered heresy, Nicene (325 CE and amended in 381 CE), and Athanasian (500 CE). To find a consensus for those Creeds involved many political controversies literally fought out between the many Christian churches during the second and the fourth centuries.

Despite the fights for uniformity Christianity has never been a unified religion nor a homogeneous movement. When the early followers of Jesus were forced to leave synagogue worship there developed different Christian communities, for example in Jerusalem, Antioch, or Samaria. Even within those communities, there were divisions and different groups. The situation became more complex when Paul and others preached the Gospel outside Hebrew communities. Churches in different parts of the Roman Empire disputed power and authority amongst themselves. There developed five episcopal sees: Rome, Constantinople, Antioch, Alexandria and Jerusalem.

In the second century, Gnosticism became prominent in Christianity, and churches were divided between Orthodox and Gnostics. In the year 451 CE, the Council of Chalcedon was convened, and it produced a major division between those who affirmed the 'human and divine' nature of Christ and those who considered that after the Incarnation, the nature of Christ was only divine. There are elements of this debate alive and well in queer theologies today. Centuries later, in 1054 CE, political struggles produced the great schism between the churches of the East and the West. The sixteenth century saw further division. The Protestant Reformation of Luther from 1517 CE which itself in time fragmented and the separation from Rome of the Church of England (Anglican) in 1540 CE None of this happened peacefully, and many people were tortured and killed for not believing the 'right' thing.

Branches of Christianity

Ecumenism developed in the twentieth century as an instrument to recover the relationality of those fragmented parts of Christianity. Technically, we can divide Christianity into four larger confessions. The term 'confession' comes from the Latin word confesare, which translates as 'to tell the faith'. Used in the denominational sense, 'confessionalism' embodies the reality of different forms expressed within the same faith (McGrath, 1999: 566–567). Christianity can therefore be grouped into four major confessions: (a) Catholicism (which also includes the Roman Catholic Church), (b) the Orthodox Churches, (c) the Anglican Communion and (d) Protestant/Evangelical churches. The following chart summarises the branches of Christianity:

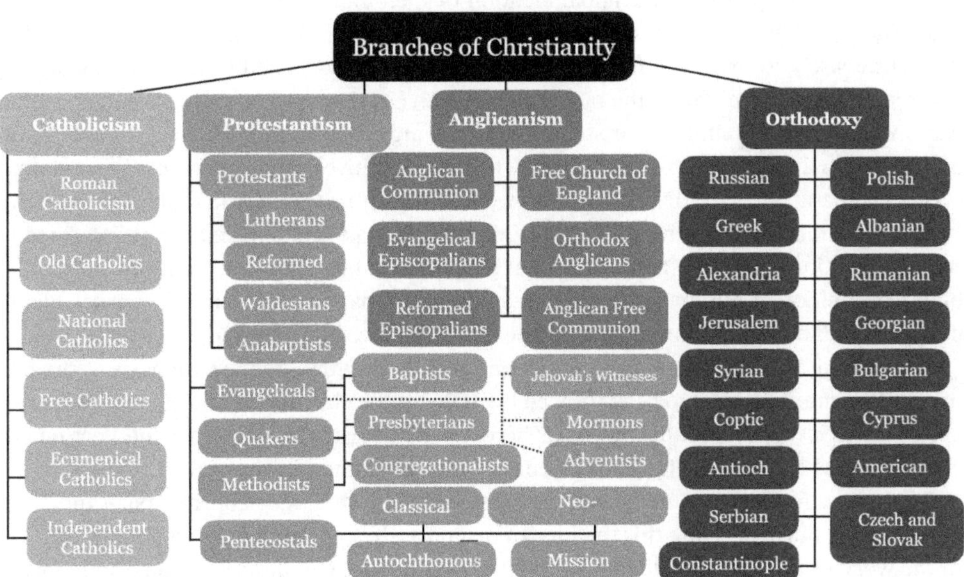

Graphic 4.1 Branches of Christianity

Sex in Paradise

Interestingly, theologians in late antiquity described Adam as sexually undifferentiated believing such a state reflected divine innocence and simplicity. This notion of primal androgeny took hold at the early part of the third century but there were critics of this idea; however, there was a strong embrace of the idea of nonbinary sex as the ideal. This idea developed from reflection on Genesis 1.27 which says 'male and female he created them' leading some to say that Adam may have housed the rib which was to be Eve so he, in that primal state, was sexually undifferentiated if not androgynous. Daniel Boyarin (1993: 42–43) notes that late Jewish midrash imagines Adam as a fused body containing two faces and two sets of genitals. The creation story in Genesis 2 is then understood to describe the splitting of the conjoined body into male and female. During the same period Gnostic texts declared God as a union of paternal and maternal elements who spoke in both male and female voices. Gnostic texts that held these ideas were copied throughout the third and fourth centuries which suggest they continued to hold interest for people.

Two influential Greek Christian Fathers, Origen of Alexandria (c. 185–254) and Gregory of Nyssa (c. 335–395), adopted the idea of an androgynous first human. Origen who worked in the Neo-Platonic tradition understood the first creation story as describing a human who was sexually undifferentiated and incorporeal. While, for Origen, the second creation story was about the infusion of the incorporeal soul into a body and thus the introduction of sexual difference but with no implication of sin. In the following century however, Gregory placed the theory in the context of the fall of man. Before the Fall he said the first humans lived in a serene undifferentiation as Adam and Eve were in his view angelic androgynes. It was sin that resulted in the division of the sexes and so binary sex was the result of the fallen state of humankind and was not the original way in which humans were created. They would, he said, regain this original angelic state after the resurrection at the end of time. Later theologians would link nonbinary sex with sin, but Gregory was sure it was differentiated sex that was sinful.

It was Augustine (354–430) who changed this view forwarded by Gregory and Origen. He said sexuality was part of the original creation of men and women who in paradise could enjoy the whole range of physical acts made possible by their complementary sexes. For Augustine sexuality was not at odds with the original innocence of Eden, it was later it became the cause of the fall of the race. Leah De Vun (2021) argues that Augustine's position was influenced by the shift of Christianity from a marginal movement to the official religion of the Roman Empire and so church leaders became sensitive to the laity whose lives centred on marriage and lineage (2021: 22). In case we feel Augustine was very liberal in his views we need to remember that his insistence that God created male and female from the start led to the rigid opinions of future theologians that only men and women as separate entities fit the biblical definition of human perfection. Despite this, in parts of his writing there seemed to be an understanding that some aspects of sexual difference lay outside rigid binaries.

Despite Augustine's insistence on male and female original creation the idea of the primal androgyne continued to be embraced by many in the church for a number of centuries even though it was eventually viewed as heresy. Unsurprisingly, mixed-sex intellectual circles found the idea appealing as did a community of women in the eighth century in the Rhine Valley. At this time texts containing such ideas were very controversial and were ordered to be burnt. Despite this the idea of primal androgyne appears in the ninth century in the work of the Irish theologian John Scotus Eriugena who described the original state of humanity before the Fall as one that is beyond the divisive categories of male and female. The idea can be seen in writing from the twelfth century, but by this time extreme caution was needed as sexual division and the hierarchy associated with it had been set firmly in place and the Church would not be challenged on what they saw as a fundamental reality.

Christian Queer Theologies

Source: K. B./Adobe Stock

Talk about sexuality from a theological point of view entails more than arguments for marriage; it involves interrogating the expectations of gender roles, the cis-heterosexual division of labour, the formation of couples and families, the concept of marriage and the performativity of affection, intimacy and eroticism produced within the context of each culture and determined beyond a cis-heteropatriarchal hegemony. Further, to do theology in the global context we also need to (re)consider how diversity and transnational movements complicate those elements in the life of queer individuals.

It requires queer theologians to think in multiple ways. Queer theologies should seek to be neither oppressive nor oppressed by hegemonic religious discourses constructed in the name of a God that often resembles an idol. Instead, queer theologies might think of themselves as more versatile theologies, altering the binaries that have led both classical theology and Christian denominations to take refuge in the absolutes of their traditions. Queer theologies share and exchange their contributions in a relationship with other disciplines as a way to embody justice and the reality of women and men who are left outside decent and orthodox theologies. We might even think of queer theologies, polyamory theologies, happily enjoying and honouring the many passions and commitments from where they lively exercise the gift of doing theologies deeply rooted in bodies, sexualities and genders.

Queer theologies invite us to highlight individuals as receivers of the love of God, that is, all people with their sexual stories, their hopes and their dreams. These experiences would allow its discourses to pass through our bodies and our senses, our daily experiences, and go with us from bed to the temple. At the same time, queer theologies take into account that daily-lived experiences are important to be remembered and that all individuals are shaped by their culture, their ethnicity and their various experiences of the divine, and that at those intersections lie within the richness and complexity of being human.

Christian Queer Theologies in the Latin American and Latinx Context

Marcella Althaus-Reid is one of the most prominent indecent and queer theologians. Her book *Indecent Theology: Theological Perversions in Sex, Gender, and Politics* (2000) marked a shift in the way that queer theologies have evolved within Christianity. Working in the United Kingdom but deeply rooted in Latin American liberation theology and her Argentinian background her work fully embraced queer theory in order to challenge classical theologies and address issues of gender and sexuality.

Althaus-Reid explains why indecent theology moves further than liberation theology. She explains:

> The paradigm is an indecent paradigm, because it undresses and uncovers sexuality and economy at the same time. Not only do we need an Indecent Theology which can reach the core of theological constructions, insofar as they are rooted in sexual constructions, for the sake of understanding our sexuality, we also need it because theological truths are currencies dispensed and acquired in theological economic markets (Althaus-Reid, 2004: 101).

Althaus-Reid (re)connected theology to the dignity of those under oppression, especially when that oppression is carried out against different gender identities and sexual orientations. Althaus-Reid's Indecent Theology showed how queer theology subverts the dictates of society and its concomitant alliance with legitimising religious institutions dating back to the Spanish colonial times, as in the case of Latin America. While her analysis was always connected with the reality of Argentina, her findings and conclusions definitely served other Latin American contexts and beyond.

The project of indecent theology is, in fact, a hermeneutic task that requires multiple deconstructions where sexuality is always a key element in understanding theological, political and ideological transactions. Althaus-Reid states:

> My purpose is (...) to explore the contextual hermeneutic circle of suspicion in depth by questioning the traditional liberationist context of doing theology. In this way the project of Indecent Theology represents both a continuation of Liberation Theology and a disruption of it (2000: 5).

For Althaus-Reid indecent theology is a critique of liberation theology as well as a way to continue its liberating tone. She seeks to actively liberate by outing liberation theology from the closets of tradition and power dominance. It is within this framework that its methodology and interpretation, through a queer hermeneutic circle, challenges indecent theology to incarnate those third spaces that would contest and challenge heteropatriarchal binaries. As Althaus-Reid showed queer theology disrupts and distorts the dictums of society and their counterpart in religious institutions while bringing into conversation sexual realities and their actors.

For Althaus-Reid, the stories of the daily lives of women and men in Latin America are predominant. These stories, when told, are often skewed by moral judgements, especially when their stories intersect sexuality and religion (Córdova Quero, 2010). Somehow, society segregates those stories and only some stories of privilege come out (Althaus-Reid, 2000: 135). Althaus Reid stresses repeatedly that queer theologies must comprise theological reflection that does not negate or gloss over the sexuality and sexual activity of those who formulate it (Althaus-Reid, 2000: 28). To compartmentalise sex out of the rest of one's life, she says, is to remain closeted, and risk 'duplicity between the realms of a public and a private theology' (Althaus-Reid, 2000: 88). So to do theology which seeks a Queer God, then, is also to 'do sex in public'. The introduction to Indecent Theology spells out what underpins all her work, the significance of 'selling lemons whilst not wearing underwear': in other words, allowing our literal and metaphorical bodily odours and sited locations, to intermingle with 'issues of theology and economy' (Althaus-Reid, 2000: 2). A Queer God is not scandalised by sexual smells, and is not affronted by indigenous customs such as not wearing undergarments, or selling sex if the lemons do not make enough money to feed the family. This God exists in contradistinction to the grand narratives which suggest that 'underwear' is necessary and decent.

Rather than forcing people to come out and tell their sexual stories, Althaus-Reid focused her criticism on the fact that Christianity through heteropatriarchal oppressive theologies contributed largely to maintain cultural closets in the West (Althaus-Reid, 2000: 173). However, indecent theology necessarily claimed sexual stories as revelation (Althaus-Reid, 2000: 148). By doing so, indecent theology becomes a vehicle for doing theology while listening to the experience of people as a theological act. In following Althaus-Reid we see that liberation theology was not free from the 'Christian' duty of monitoring and censoring the morality of the Christian 'poor'. In fact, the absence of a critical analysis on this matter due to a heavy leaning towards economic and socio-political aspects of society has created a vacuum that can no longer be tolerated.

The work of Althaus-Reid is very diverse and her work about Salvation shows how diverse she can be. She not only examines the notion from a sexual standpoint, but specifically, from a BDSM perspective. Her initially short article was later expanded to be included in Althaus-Reid's second book, *The Queer God* (2003). By bringing BDSM as a lens for her analysis, Althaus-Reid challenges us to ever expand the boundaries of what is 'acceptable' or 'permitted' in Christianity. She states:

> Fetishism has a way of understanding objectives and a projected eschatology which may differ from other ways of knowing. A Queer theology can make a contribution to our theological project by showing alternative ways of action and reflection based on a different way of knowing sexually to the current accepted models in theology (Althaus-Reid, 2001: 242).

This 'different way of knowing sexually' provides a theological standpoint and self-affirmation of sexual diversity. Althaus-Reid continues by assuring that:

> The concept of Christian salvation has served totalitarian theological synthesis well, whenever controlling, defining and organising people's sexuality was the objective of dogmatics. Truth, manifested in a desire for harmonious and orderly forms denied the chaos of sexuality, and the chaotic God which emerged from it. However, there is a sexual supplement in salvation which may show us that the road to untidiness and indecency is worth the effort. This supplement of Sexual Salvation is a dangerous surplus within Christianity. Its power is the power of the per/verted options that bring the possibility of alternative imaginaries to current versions of power in order to produce rupture as a counter-discourse to the symbolic violence of totality (2001: 243).

Althaus-Reid points to the disruption of the binaries that have policed and censored sexuality within Christianity for millennia. Nevertheless, these third spaces are not always welcome, as seen in the case of bisexuals who cannot be pushed into either/or identities, or drag queens who embrace and disrupt the binary by hyper-performing it. Nevertheless, queer theology does not only challenge dominant theo(ideo)logical discourses, but also aids the recovery of the discourses of those who have been ostracised. In bringing the voice of BDSM people into the core beliefs of Christianity, Althaus-Reid is finally achieving liberation and points to salvation from the totalitarian classical systematic theology that as oppressed believers across the centuries. Salvation can take many turns. Salvation, for example, could be felt while in horizontal suspension, engulfed by the touch of spandex over one's skin, the rush and ecstasy by being surrounded by a community of believers invested in the same praxis of liberation. This shibari-like coming-home may signal a way to be true to oneself at the heart of the dungeon while embracing and enjoying the diversity of pleasure that humanity has been denied for millennia by hegemonic vanilla theo(ideo)logies.

Althaus Reid is just one of the people who called theologians to face the full reality of people's lives when expounding doctrine. It was her development of the Bi-Christ (2003) which contributed to furthering queer Christology. The Bi-Christ is a figure who is not bi in the sense of sexual preference but rather in terms of thought and life, is one who is fluid and full of contradictions and therefore enables the destabilization which she saw as crucial. She argued that the Bi-Christ is, in fact, a gospel image pointing out that the gospels present us with the Prince of Peace and the one who whips the traders from the temple, the one who talked to the women at the well and could not change the impurity laws regarding menstruation. When we take these stories as starting points we go in contradictory directions but far from wishing to harmonise these points of tension Althaus-Reid wants us to embrace them as the fluid movements of Christology. Taking the evidence before us and asking the challenging questions allows the false harmonising to be stripped away and a new and exciting rupture to emerge. The Bi-Christ is beyond the hetero, the Christ who is deeply engrained in clear and limited boundaries; the Christ of power over and hierarchies, the Christ of deadening dualism. The Bi-Christ is beyond either/or.

As a theological category the Bi-Christ overcomes mono-relations, and this has an impact in sexuality and beyond. Althaus-Reid shows how the mono-relational pattern works. Firstly the hetero-Christ even defines sexual relations that are not heterosexual, the gay man is seen as effeminate and the lesbian as either butch or femme. These are heteronormative categories that prohibit naming the diverse range of sexual identities that are actually operational within people's lives. Heteronormativity stabilises categories and colonises experience in order to keep some control. The second example is of how mono-relations lead to economic oppression. Using the colonization of Africa as an example, Althaus-Reid pointed out that the relationship under one [mono] heavenly Father could never be equal. The exclusion of 'otherness' meant that the needs, desires of the other do not enter the equation and are replaced by exploitation. Althaus-Reid argued that the Bi-Christ dismantles the mono-relations of naming, organising, exploiting and owning that underpin economic, racial and sexual exclusions and the worlds this leads to. Bi-Christ allows other ways to think. But perhaps even the Bi-Christ is not queer enough unless we hold on to the not either or of its construction.

Althaus Reid (2004: 30–43) also addressed the issue of the worship of the Virgin Mary in Latin America. While this is a widespread custom Althaus Reid tells us it is not helpful to women as the Virgin is a white woman who does not walk. Furthermore she is an imposed image coming from a medieval concept of how women should be, originating in the colonisers' religion not the indigenous understanding. This white woman replaced the original deities of Latin America such as *the woman* who was widely worshiped and gave agency to women in their everyday lives, including their sexual lives. What has replaced her is an image of passive virginal sexuality linked to marriage and motherhood, a model used harshly against women during the dictatorships in Latin America. It was not only the image of passivity that came with the Virgin Mary but also one male God. In Mexico, deity was understood as changing between male and female, the female was not a passive figure but a fierce serpent who fought for her children. She was an agrarian deity and as such took care of people's economic lives, good harvest meant good finances, she also enabled women in childbirth and held them when they lost their children. This god was one of passion and compassion not of passivity. The imposition of the western, white Virgin Mary reduced the lives of indigenous women and held them in a form of femininity they had not previously known. Can the image of the Virgin Mary be freed from this colonial cis-heteropatriarchy and become a liberating image for women? Latin American scholars have declared that reclaiming the virgin womb within themselves and for all women is a sign that they will not be dominated or oppressed by the systems under which they live. They may no longer be physical virgins, but they will remain free of cis-heteropatriarchy. Further, the role of Mary in raising a son concerned with social justice, as we see in the words of the Magnificat, should not be overlooked. Perhaps it has been a theological oversight to regard the Song of Mary as simply something from her heritage rather than a blueprint for her approach to radical child rearing (Isherwood, 2024).

Brazilian Anglican theologian Mario Ribas (2006) analyses the case of Nossa Senhora de Aparecida [Our Lady of Apparition], the national Marian symbol in Brazil, and he states:

> On the other hand, in Latin America the iconography of saints is not confined to churches or religious environments. Such icons are often found in public places, schools, government offices, courts of justice and homes. They can also be found in bars, cabarets and brothels as well as in garages, displayed alongside pictures of naked women. The icons, therefore, in popular religion are part of daily life, mixed with the profanity of every aspects of human life. There is also the syncretism of Latin American popular religiosity as the icons of the saints are often placed alongside Afro-Brazilian representations of spiritual entities. Sacred and profane are mixed up in popular expressions: the statue of the Virgin Mary or a crucifix can be placed on the wall above the same bed where sexual activities take place. But the statue of the Virgin can also be there as a reminder of the pure example of ideal womanhood (2006: 126).

This queering of the Virgin by sex workers is important in order to acknowledge not only the blurring of the 'sacred/profane' divide, but also points out the agency and malleability of beliefs among the faithful.

In the work of Chicana academic Irena Lara (2008) we find her addressing the issue of the Virgin in Latin America. Saying this, we should be aware that while the Virgin of Guadalupe is important in understanding the situation of Mariology in Mexico, it cannot be extended to the whole continent. That would be to overlook other Marian expression in different countries. Lara's work is important as it shows how Mariology is a key characteristic of Latin American religious life and, therefore, a powerful device for heteronormativity. The careful delimitations of the sexual division of labour in Latin American societies reflect the heteropatriarchal tone embedded in Christianity. Therefore, a symbol that proclaims liberation and resistance as Mary did in the Magnificat (Lk 1.46–55) can be co-opted as its opposite. In popular religiosity, the image of the Virgin has commonly embraced the Christian ideal of womanhood and motherhood. Moreover, she has traditionally represented a clear-cut exemplar of what is decent as opposed to what is indecent. For centuries, the lives of women in Christian contexts have been judged, condemned or approved by their conformity or their lack of conformity to the image of the Virgin Mary.

Ribas points out how some women try to reclaim their power he says:

> Placing icons of Mary in brothels is the way in which prostitutes tend to symbolise
> their re-claiming of their faith in God and in Mary. It is at the same time a way to
> undermine the current theological assumption that procreation is the only purpose
> of sex, rather than pleasure, or the result of economic exclusion. In this way, placing
> an icon of the Virgin in a brothel illustrates to some extent a theological contrast, as
> was pointed out by Ruth Adams, in her essay 'Idol Curiosity—Andy Warhol and the
> Art of Secular Iconography' [...]. She presents Marilyn Monroe as an antithesis of
> Mary. Mary in this case represents the one who reproduces without sex, while
> Monroe is the one who has sex without reproducing. The same antithesis applies to
> prostitutes, who find in their job a way to survive. In their case, they cannot procre-
> ate, although some of them do, accidentally. So it is that the situation of the children
> of a prostitute can be even worse, as shown in the popular expression filho da puta
> (son of a whore). Such an expression, often used in moments of anger, is applied to
> anyone who has been a source of annoyance: it symbolizes one of the lowest categories
> of people within society. On the other hand, Jesus himself might have been called
> filho da puta, either by his contemporaries, or even perhaps unconsciously by the
> current theological tradition that denies to Joseph the biological fatherhood of Jesus
> and by the current iconography that routinely portrays Mary alone with a child in
> her arms (2006: 126).

The heteropatriarchal tone assigned to the Virgin is contested by feminists as well as by
Queer activists and believers of other religions such as Santería or Umbanda. Terry
Rey writes:

> In the African-based religion of Santeria, homosexual men find acceptance by cer-
> tain orishas (spirits) (namely Ochun, Yemaya, and Ogun) [orishas that are friendly
> to gay men] and rejection by others [...]. The Virgin Mary's assimilation in Cuban
> Santeria with Ochun (as Caridad del Cobre) and Yemaya (as Our Lady of the Regla)
> opens a discursive locus of legitimacy for homosexual men in popular Cuban
> Mariology (1999: 969).

However, cis-heteropatriarchalism is constantly present, reminding us that it is impossible to live outside the matrix. Nonetheless, it is possible, exactly by living within the
matrix, to disrupt its mandates and to produce performances that counter their assumptions and dictums. I bring two examples.

Giuseppe Campuzano, scholar and drag queen created in 2007 the Museo Travesti del
Peru [Transvestite Museum of Peru], which is a mobile exhibition of transgender issues in
the country since Pre-Columbian times. One of his most famous performances is that of
the Virgin Mary. The performance of the Virgin Mary by a drag queen is not new in
Christian history or in Latin America. In fact, by inhabiting the place of the Virgin Mary
by a drag queen, there is a tone of resistance and deconstruction of the place in which
women have also been confined. In describing the performance, Campuzano is reported
as saying:

> There exists a confessional relationship between the Virgin Mary and Peruvian
> transvestites and, subsequently, a conceptual relationship between the Virgin and
> the transvestite that transcends the catholic clichés of unity, apparitions, and

idolatries as cultural mestizajes (and poverty). The Virgin is the transvestite par excellence with her magnificent trousseau and her performative apparitions. I am not the first transvestite to dress as the Virgin--this was done in theatre during the Middle Ages. But it was in 2007, in the context of the publication of the transvestite book, that I decided to exchange the image of the whore for that of the virgin, as a metaphor of transvestism as ritual and mestizaje- moving from the triangulated, sacred, stable composition of the Renaissance to the transposition of bodies and cultures that destabilized it' (La Fountain-Stokes, 2010).

By recovering the connection of the Virgin Mary and transvestites, Campuzano undresses the reality of gender and sexuality in one of the most sacred icons of Latin America, which has been used to categorised any woman who does not conform to its heteropatriarchal depiction as a whore.

A fascinating queer reading of the Virgin of Guadalupe by Los Angeles-based Chicana artist Alma López is one in which she depicts the religious icon as inscribed within homo-eroticism. Of López' depiction of the Virgin Mary, Clara Roman-Odio says:

In Lopez's image, Our Lady does not wear the maternity band that marks the original icon. This new turn in meaning points to a body that goes beyond the cultural mandate of sexual reproduction to become a site of beauty and truth, meanings that are encoded by both the Aztec and the Christian symbols of the rose. As Lopez has stated, for her, the rose signals that which is real or the evidence of being real. Hence, in Our Lady the roses covering the body can be interpreted as a synecdochic expression of the real beauty and truth of Latina bodies. Also important, the bare-breasted young Latina angel emerging from a Viceroy butterfly serves as a synecdoche for queer identity (2011: 141).

While queering Mary, López brings into daily life the experiences of lesbian women who dare to keep their faith alive against the regulations of their churches. The dichotomy 'saint/prostitute' reinforces heteropatriachalism, thus oppressing everyone who does not conform to a narrow understandings of femininity or heterosexualism. Many lesbian women such as López, transgender folks like Campusano, or theologians such as Ribas affirm the same critique that Lara does in her image by contra-posing the Christian Virgin Mary with the Nahua Goddess Tonantzin.

Venezuelan Otto Maduro points out that oppressed people, because of categories of 'indecency', used to be degraded which tended to be harsher against queer people than the elites in power. Maduro states:

Maybe that is why those who resist economic, political and cultural oppression are often more scrupulous than their own oppressors precisely in that dimension of sexual and gender relations. In order to show the falsity of the stereotypes used against them and in order to claim a higher moral ground than the elites, the oppressed often adopt, exacerbating them, the dominant criteria of morality and decency, thus reducing morality to the strict observance of certain traditional, dominant patterns regarding sexual relationships, sexual identity, and gender construction (2006: 27).

This quotation of Maduro helps to understand why in some revolutions in Latin America, queer people also suffered the heavy hand of the new powers. An emblematic case is the one of Cuba and Fidel's revolution, which imprisoned queer people as criminals or sent them to concentration camps to work and 'rehabilitate'. José Quiroga in his book *Tropics of Desire: Interventions from Queer Latino America* (2000) analyses the political situation of Cuba's queer folks in the light of the film *Strawberry and Chocolate* (1994). In the film, the subversive artist Diego attempts to seduce the straight communist militant David who plays along with Diego's attempts in order to spy on his activities and report him to the communist party. Quiroga reflects on the paradox of the Left and queer rights shown in this film:

> These would be simply matters of social history were it not for the fact that the post-Stonewall gay intellectual was a creation of the New Left, and that the Cuban revolution, as the most visible Third World liberation struggles, mobilised minority revolts in Europe and the United States as the time when those same minorities were being excluded from participation in Cuba itself. The paradox of this situation is clear, at a thirty-year distance. The revolution was the litmus test for a revolutionary Latin America society, and at a time of external and internal threats it has to count on the support of disaffected communities outside Cuba that included, but were not limited to, feminists, gays, and lesbians—communities that also constituted segments of the New Left (2000: 127).

Vincent D. Cervantes (2014) aims to build a theology for Mexican and Mexican-American/Chicana/o queer believers. The term joto could roughly be translated as 'faggot' although this is an Anglo-Saxon category which does not exist in Mexico.

The one aspect that Cervantes brings into the analysis is that of the racial/cultural assumptions and expectations that many people in the Global North have about people in the Global South. He narrates his experience as follows:

> When I told mentors and colleagues that I wanted to study theology, I consistently met with the response, "You must want to study liberation theology, then." Because of my Chicano identity, it was expected that I would work within the frameworks of liberation theology and Latin American religion. It is an expectation I resented, because while I worked within the context of queer Latin America, I did not think I needed to be categorized as a "liberationist" in order to be considered a Latin American theologian (Cervantes, 2014: 199).

This is a very (neo)colonial mentality; an anthropologist from France is not expected to study French people or culture either in France or in the Diaspora. We simply do not assume that the interests of people in research are related to their place of origin, class, race. But this (neo)colonial mentality does and often diminishes the work and value of the research of those from the Two-Third world.

However, Cervantes is able to start carving a place for Latina/o queers to voice and develop their own understanding of their faith beliefs and practices. He uses jotería studies in order to mediate between religious beliefs and ethno-racial and sexual identity formations. Cervantes asserts:

> Queer theology today remains dedicated to naturalizing homosexuality and sanctifying same-sex marriage. Queer theology has become redundant over the past decades in its attempts to make sense of same-sex orientations through a relationship to the divine. However, while these issues are important from the standpoint of equal human rights, they do not always have much to do with the racialized and class conflicts that shape our experiences as queer Chicana/os. The ways in which I relate

to the divine and my own theological understandings of how we experience God's love are heavily influenced by my queerness and chicanidad. I cannot separate the two, because they also influence each other. Jotería studies offers a language and space to talk about the interconnectedness of identities that we embody and how those identities affect other ways of thinking (2014: 204–205).

As an emerging queer theology, Jotería theology offers a much-needed ground for Mexican/Mexican-American/Chicana/o queer believers to further expand their presence in the world of queer theologies. This is necessary in order to foster a Global South conversation that is constantly being resisted in the Global North due to ethno-nationalist assumptions. In this sense, queer theologies in the Global South not only need to face the pressure of cis-heteropatriarchy, of (neo)colonial heritages, of class discriminations, but also of ethno-nationalism already ingrained in the culture of many queer theologians in the Global North.

Christian Queer Theologies in the African and the African Diasporic Context

Turning to Africa we hear Adriaan Van Klinken (2014) focus on the role that Christianity plays in the lives of believers of any religion in Zambia. The declaration of Zambia as a Christian country has produced terrible consequences for queer Zambians. The connection with religion, especially the Christian right-wing in this case, is very visible. However, its roots reside in cross-continental situations. For example, Lovemore Togarasei and Ezra Chitando, two prominent theologians from Africa, offer a contribution that helps us to see the issue of the Bible and same-sex desire and relationships in the context of Africa. In their article 'Beyond the Bible: Critical Reflections on the Contributions of Cultural and Postcolonial Studies on Same-sex Relationships in Africa' (2011) they describe the two major sectors of proponents and opponents to same-sex desire and its relation with the Biblical texts. What is common to both sectors is the issue of the Bible as a key topic in terms of censoring/accepting the lives and experiences of queer individuals and communities. However, the Bible is also co-opted for political gains, and that is when the West also comes on board. The sanctions and pressures that Western governments exercise over African countries do not make the situation easier. Togarasei and Chitando affirm:

> It is our opinion that as long as there is a perception that Africa is being "civilized" or talked down to accept same sex sexuality, it will remain extremely difficult to make headway in changing attitudes towards same-sex relationships (2011: 122).

This is an important issue because it shows the colonial mentality of the West knowing what is best for non-Western contexts. It is important to recognise that the situations that many queer folks face in countries such as Uganda are difficult and dangerous. However, external intervention may only continue to damage and hurt queer individuals and communities, who are living amidst those situations. The same is true of theological discourses, which is why it is so important that theologians such as Togarasei and Chitando raise their own voices.

Van Klinken demonstrates that Pentecostalism is the basis for constitutional rights and the declaration of Zambia as a Christian country. Pentecostalism is a branch of Christianity rooted in a literal, and yet selective, interpretation of Sacred Scriptures from a theo(ideo)logical point of view (Córdova Quero, 2015). The influence of Pentecostalism, which started in 1901, is increasing worldwide as more churches experience a process of charismatisation. This has led Pentecostal churches to actively create political parties and to influence politics and create lobbies in many countries. Much of this work is with the economic support of organisations based in the United States and so is not free of western political influence.

The contribution of Van Klinken resides in the fact that he uncovers not only the presence of Pentecostal leaders in the political decisions of Zambia but also in naming the many voices who opposed this joining of religion and politics. In the midst of this, the lives of queer individuals and communities are decided upon without their consent or consultation. This totalitarian/fascist way of intersecting religion and politics is noxious to those who seek to recognise sexual and gender diversity among the faithful. In fact, this fictitious clear-cut divide between 'Christian and Homosexuals' prevents the recognition of third spaces by individuals and communities who are simultaneously Christian and queer.

We include African American theologians here not because we think Africans and African Americans are the same but because the theological field is plagued with absences that African American engagement may highlight. Queer African-American theologians critique Black Liberation Theology claiming it failed to address the issues of queer believers. They also add an extra aspect within their critique namely religions connection with a colonial past. In a clear postcolonial analysis, Horace Griffin writes in his book *Their Own Receive Them Not* (2006) that the negative views on homosexuality in black churches can be traced back to the colonial times when African slaves were converted to conservative Christianity by white Christians. In a similar vein, EL Kornegay, Jr., in his article 'Queering Black Homophobia' (2004) deconstructs the assumption of a black archetypical identity that seems to be disrupted by the presence of queer individuals, thus, leading to the emergence of black homophobia. For Kornegay, Black Liberation Theology was never interested in sexual liberation, and the task for queer theologians today is to focus in forming a Black theology as a sexual discourse of transformation, whose proposals he sets in his book *A Queering of Black Theology* (2013).

However, despite the fact that many African-American queer theologians are denouncing the effects of colonialism and the racial heritage in the United States, they still seem to contribute to the absence of attention towards Black lesbian spirituality. This is precisely what Elana C. Betts (2012) addresses by exploring how race, gender, sexual orientation and spirituality unfolds and intersect in the personal stories of African-American lesbians. Specifically, Betts affirms that fluidity not only applied to the sexuality of lesbian believers who she interviewed but also to their spirituality, priorities in life and forms of expressing faith. These elements were conclusive for the African-American lesbians in her study to achieve spiritual wholeness but integrating faith and sexuality. Betts explains that in her study:

> All participants mentioned that spirituality is a fluid process. The expectation of fluidity and being open to that fluctuation is essential in maintaining a sense of spirituality. Some of the factors that participants considered fluid is how they defined their sexuality, their competing priorities in life, the form of how they express their spirituality and how others interpret their own spirituality (2012: 37).

This fluid process towards spiritual wholeness is not free from adversities. In fact, Betts (2012) reports that 'All [participants] also found the mixed messages from religious outlets as being highly disturbing. Most faiths preach loving all people, but many continue to discriminate against those who identify as a sexual minority' (2012: 37).

It is important to acknowledge that the life of believers is cut across by the racial divide and that this influences not only their opportunities in society but also their development as persons. The contribution of Betts is important to make visible the voice of lesbian Christian believers struggling to hold both their faith as well as their same-sex desire. One of such outspoken and visible voices is Bishop Yvette Flunder. She is the founder of City of Refuge, a United Church of Christ church originally located in San Francisco, and now in Oakland. Her prophetic voice has led her to create the Ark of Refuge, a non-profit organisation providing housing, direct services and education for those affected by HIV/AIDS.

LeRhonda S. Manigualt-Bryant (2015) addresses issues of religion in the African diaspora to North America and the Caribe. Manigault-Bryant does an excellent job in mapping several key aspects of African religion in the diaspora. Please note how geography, culture, language, ethnicity, gender and sexuality intersect in every example that Manigault-Bryant brings into the discussion, especially in her use of W. E. B. DuBois book *The Souls of Black Folks* (1996), a classic in Postcolonial/Ethnic Studies.

One key aspect is that the African heritage is present in different religions as well as denominations within Christianity, such as the African American Episcopal Church. Although the author uses the term 'syncretism', many authors are now using the term 'religious hybridity'. The former term has been loaded as something that is negative, that is untrustable, while the latter term aims to point to the positive aspect of negotiation and creation of third spaces that happen in the hybrid space.

Sylvia Tamale (2014) brings a key analysis intersecting aspects that not all the time are considered as being together: religion, culture, law and sexuality. It makes sense that the lives of individuals and communities would be conditioned by these areas, but very few scholars bring them together into a single analysis. Many scholars just dissect individuals and communities into more 'objective' topics, thus diminishing the deepness of the situation.

By 'religions,' Tamale not only considers the role that both Islam and Christianity have played in (re)shaping the African continent, but also how African Traditional Religions have also influenced that (re)shaping. At the same time, by 'law' she not only considers the enacted legislations but also the sometimes more subtle religious regulations and dictums that modelled daily-lived experiences along with de facto traditions and customs that rule over the lives of people.

Why is this so important? Because the intersection of religion, culture, law and sexuality is an unavoidable aspect necessary to understand how in Africa sexuality is constructed. Tamale states:

> Contrary to popular belief, sexuality is not exclusively driven by biology; a very significant part of it is socially constructed through legal, cultural and religious forces driven by a politico-economic agenda. Sexuality is very much a socio-cultural invention that is closely linked to power and to the processes of subjugation. As Africans, how we 'do' and experience sexuality is heavily influenced by society and culture. How and with whom we have sex, what we desire, what we take pleasure in, how we express that pleasure, why, under what circumstances and with what outcomes, are all forms of learned behaviour communicated inter alia through the institutions of culture, religion and law (...). It is through these social institutions and social relationships that sexuality is reified or given meaning (2014: 155).

If, in the pre-colonial period, people's lives were heavily influenced by the social dicta, this situation was dramatically changed during the Europeanisation of Africa by the colonial powers. This colonisation deprived the continent of its resources for centuries and even enslaved its populations. The consequences are still visible and will last for a long time in the future. Tamale affirms:

> In Africa, the process of separating the public-private spheres preceded colonisation but was precipitated, consolidated and reinforced by colonial policies and practices. Where there had been a blurred distinction between public and private life, colonial structures (law, religion) and policies (for example, educational) focused on delineating a clear distinction guided by an ideology that perceived men as public actors and women as private performers. Where domestic work had co-existed with commercial work in pre-colonial satellite households, a new form of domesticity, existing outside production, took over. Where land had been communally owned in pre-colonial societies, a tenure system that allowed for absolute and individual ownership in land took over. At the same time, politics and power were formalised and institutionalised with male public actors. The Western capitalist, political ideology (that is, liberal democratic theory) that was imposed on the African people focused on the individual, submerging the African tradition that valued the collective (2014: 161).

We can observe that gender and the cis-heterosexual division of labour played a key role in marking the boundaries of what is private and public as well as what is allowed or forbidden for both women and men. All this, according to Tamale (2014: 161), was done on a religious and heteropatriarchal basis.

It may seem logical from a Western perspective that one is free to pursue one's sexuality and gender performance as one wishes, but this may not apply in the African context. The high stratification in which society as whole constructs the very roots of gender and sexuality may prevent this 'one size fits all' Western ideology from being suitable for the African continent. Tamale (2014: 166) cites the work of Kaoma, a researcher at a think-tank called Political Resource Associates in the United States. In a paper that he wrote in 2009, Kaoma researches the role that right-wing Christians from the United States have played in Africa, especially in the homophobic legislations such as those of Uganda in 2011. The marriage of religion and politics is undeniable. Because of that legislation, activist and 'father of the Ugandan LGBT rights movement'. David Kato, was murdered. Kato was among the 100 people whose names and photographs were published in October 2010 by the Ugandan newspaper *Rolling Stone* in an article that called for their 'execution' as 'homosexuals' (Xan, 2010). On January 26, 2011, at around 2 p.m., Kato was assaulted in his home in Bukusa, Mukono Town, by a man who hit him twice in the head with a hammer. Katy died in the ambulance that was taking him to a hospital (Xan, 2011).

The situation in Uganda and other parts of Africa is complex and cannot be explained in a few sentences. This is a very difficult topic and so much needs to be solved for queer people across Africa. The connection that Tamale, and her citing of Kaoma's work as well as the work that Onziema is doing in Uganda, points to the fact that religion is an intrinsic marker of the boundaries of gender and sexuality. Dismissing this connection risks to colonise the situation in Africa and misses the point in understanding the realities of believers and societies in general about these topics.

Christian Queer Theologies in the Asian and the Asian Diasporic Context

Asian queer theologies develop in a region marked by a multi-religious environment in which Christianity is one among other religions such as Islam, Buddhism, Hinduism and local religions as well as its interaction with Confucianism, the Chinese ethical and philosophical system.

Since the beginning of the twenty-first century the emerging Tongzhi theology in Hong Kong and Taiwan has become an important contribution. The purpose of tongzhi theology lies in paying attention to both the stories of oppression of individuals and communities as well as the mechanisms that reify that oppression. To this, Boon Ling Ngeo adds that, 'Tongzhi Theology is not only a queer theology, which attempts to justify the inclusion of LGBTI people, it also seeks to formulate the doctrine of God in queer theology' (2013: 132).

One approach to reformulate Christian classical theological topics from a queer theology perspective has been to embrace the very heart of the doctrine of the incarnation, which is relationality, as Chin Pang Ng states:

> (...) in order to seek a theology which truly reflects God's incarnation among all of God's people and to reaffirm God's erotic power in relation, we must reconnect sexuality to spirituality. In doing so, I propose that we first have to recognize God's incarnation in a relational manner. God and God's Creation cannot be separated because 'in the beginning is the relation (2000: 44).

Ng is a Tongzhi theologian from Hong Kong and is the first to write about this theology. Ng was instrumental in the creation and growth of Blessed Minority Christian Fellowship in Hong Kong, a queer church with steady commitment for activism in favour of Tongzhi individuals and communities in the city. For him, Tonghzi theology is aligned with other queer theologies in order to embrace the core of the Christian tradition, which is incarnation, and, from there, subvert/per-vert constructions that have distorted that core through the centuries (Ng, 2001). Boon Lin Ngeo uses process theology, especially the contribution of Whitehead, in order to explain his position about Tongzhi theology:

> The significance of Tongzhi Theology is twofold. First, its a theology of God; second, it is relational philosophy of reality. According to Tongzhi Theology, God does not possess absolute power. God's power is not authoritative or coercive, but it is persuasive. God calls us to do what is possible and what is the best in God's vision in our moment-to-moment activities. God does not and cannot make us do anything we do not want to do. God does not determine our future. God can only call, lure, persuade, and influence us to embrace God's "initial aim" or God's will in every context in our moment-to-moment activities. We, as human beings, are free in Tongzhi Theology. We freely make our decisions in every context and God is always working with us by providing guidance for what is the best in every circumstance, but God does not impose God's will on us nor does God determine our paths or decisions. God does have "primordial vision" for us, that is God sees all the possibilities that promote beauty and truth. But God does not make decisions on behalf of us. We are responsible for our lives and for every decision we make in every circumstance (2013: 170–171).

Another example is Hong Kong Roman Catholic theologian Lai-Shan Yip (2012), who focuses particularly on the experience of oppression of nu-tongzhi (female tonghzi) both within the Roman Catholic Church's moral teachings on sexuality as well as Hong Kong's tongzhi movement which is strongly oriented towards male's experiences. Yip interrogates the daily-lived experience of the nu-tongzhi in Hong Kong particularly in the context of Chinese societies, marked by Confucian moral philosophy. The reality of Roman Catholic nu-tongzhi in Hong Kong is in itself a hybrid experience. Yet, the Roman Catholic nu-tongzhi in Hong Kong are able to resist the two mainstream traditions through a creative re-synthesis of the traditions, fostering an understanding of their religious experiences and their sexuality that blends and opens up for flexible spaces of agency and negotiation that liberate them (Yip, 2010).

Hong Kong Protestant theologian Rose Wu (2000) agrees with Yip for the need to make more visibly the experiences of nu-tongzhi in the spectrum of the tongzhi movement in Hong Kong. However, in order to carry out her work as a theologian, Wu looks for sources beyond those experiences and particularly reaches a dialogue with other experiences for example in liberation theologies in Latin America. In her book *Liberating the Church from Fear* (2000), Wu examines the recent background of British colonialism in Hong Kong. It was only in July 1, 1997, that Hong Kong was returned to Chinese administration, and it is still considered a Special Administrative Region (SAR) of China, a situation that adds another layer to the oppression of Tongzhi people in Hong Kong.

Wu recovers classical liberationist topics such as the story of the 'Exodus' (2000: 100–103) as well as that of 'Re/Membering' (2000: 103–107) in order to construct her tongzhi theology. However, she also recovers classical contributions from feminism such as Schüssler-Fiorenza's notion of the Discipleship of Equals and the Basilea. This alternative vision of God for the world is opposed to the male-oriented notion of the Kingdom of God (2000: 107–111) and helps craft a community of tongzhi believers. Finally, she recovers the conception of Eucharist as hospitality and solidarity (2000: 111–115), which is a concept that traces its roots back as early as the second century CE. All these topics nurture and foster Wu's vision of an inclusive community where tongzhi folks are at the centre of the liberated and dynamic life of the faithful's assembly. Her task and her call is to be truly an *ev-angello*, that is, someone who 'proclaims good news'. Her commitment has led her to be involved in the Umbrella Revolution in 2014.

Wu understood that queer people need to belong and so in 2009 she founded the Queer Theology Academy (QTA) which provides a theological home for those who feel marginalised or rejected by their churches. The QTA invites oppressed sexual minorities to narrate their own stories theologically and in so doing to find mutual empowerment and often life transformations. The work of the QTA theologises from the position of triple marginalisation, as queer and Christian they stand on the outside of Chinese society, as Chinese and queer they are on the outside of the global Christian community and as Chinese and Christian they stand on the margin of global queer communities. The theology emerging from this organisation is praxis based and offers a pioneering model of community among Christian and Asian queer Christians. By offering theological resources in Chinese it nurtures young queers in Christian leadership and provides a clear voice in local and regional queer movements. It also and importantly offers a strong voice against the Chinese Christian Right which is so strongly influenced by its American counterparts and their network of evangelical churches.

The QTA engages in three main activities in the theological arena. They queer mainstream Chinese Christian ethics, they contextualise worldwide queer theologies into Chinese contexts and they theologise Chinese queer bodies and social experiences. It is believed that Chinese Christian ethics are oppressive as they uphold heteronormativity which springs from both Chinese Confucian culture and conservative Western Christian ethical traditions. They focus mainly on sexuality and gender and the concept of sin as their cultures see anything outside cis-heteropatriarchy in relation to these notions as sinful. Interestingly, they have been able to turn the concept of sin on its head seeing the queer community as a community sinned against and the idea that queer folk should be celibate as disrespectful to a God who planted love and the ability to love in humans. As part of their contextualising of worldwide queer theologies they translate important works into Chinese and then pair them with local contexts, experiences and reflections. Importantly the QTA is not uncritical of western scholarship even when they translate them. They are sure to make local experiences the starting point for their theological reflections. They ask local questions and develop local theology. The questions they ask are of course personal but also communal, and this is reflected in their theological and liturgical outputs.

It is not surprising that the QTA began in Hong Kong since it had a more progressive attitude and used to enjoy freedom of speech in a society well connected internationally. Since the hand back to China this is no longer the case, and a number of members of QTA have left Hong Kong, so the QTA has a diasporic quality now. Plans for the development of QTA include spreading from beyond Christianity and being more religiously inclusive.

Other theologians in Asia seek to address the role of religions in promoting discriminative actions. Juswantori Ichwan, a theologian in Indonesia, in his essay 'The Influence of Religion on the Development of Heterosexism in Indonesia' (2014) embarks on the project of de-coupling homophobia from heterosexism in order to expose its pervasive influences amidst civil society. For him, while homophobia is based on the fear of sexual diversity, and while heterosexism is an ideological system that favours heterosexuality over other sexual orientations, it will be empowered and dominant in societal structures. Ichwan investigates the distinctive forms through which Hinduism, Buddhism, Islam and Christianity have all contributed to ingrain heterosexism in Indonesian society.

In a similar vein, Yuri Horie brings to light the situation of lesbians in the Christian churches in Japan. In her essay 'Possibilities and Limitations of 'Lesbian Continuum': The Case of a Protestant Church in Japan' (2006) she analyses the invisibility of lesbians in a Protestant Christian denomination amidst a non-Christian society. She affirms that the exclusion of gay and lesbian individuals from the Christian communities is not only rooted in religious teachings but also in the way in which those teachings fit with ideologies of society. However, she points out that this situation could be overcome through the activism of queer individuals and their straight allies who, together, can debunk these pervasive ideo(theo)logies.

For Further Discussion

1   In your experience, whether in a religious community, religious organisation or place of activism, how common is it to talk about issues of sexuality? Do you observe that there are people who are ashamed of talking about their own bodies?

2   When queer folks enter into a conversation with you, do they consider theological topics to be of importance for them? What are those topics? Could you offer some examples?

3   How do you understand the daily lived experiences of Asian queer believers? Does their particular case resonate with our own experience?

4   In your own faith tradition, which are the 'institutional' images of God? How do queer faithful interact with these images? Could you offer examples?

References

Althaus Reid, Marcella (2000). *Indecent Theology. Theological Perversions in Sex, Gender and Politics*. London: Routledge.

Althaus-Reid, Marcella (2001). "Sexual Salvation: The Theological Grammar of Voyeurism and Permutations." *Literature & Theology* 15, No. 3 (September): pp. 241–248.

Althaus-Reid, Marcella (2003). *The Queer God.* New York, NY: Routledge.

Althaus-Reid, Marcella (2004). "Queer I Stand: Lifting the Skirts of God." In: *The Sexual Theologian: Essays on Sex, God and Politics,* edited by Marcella Althaus-Reid and Lisa Isherwood. London: T&T Clark, pp. 99–109.

Betts, Elana C. (2012). "Black Lesbian Spirituality: Hearing Our Stories." Proceedings of the 53rd Adult Education Research Conference. Manhattan, KS: New Prairie Press, pp. 32–40.

Boyarin, Daniel (1993). *Carnal Israel-Reading Sex in Talmudic Centuries: 25.* California: University of California.

Brown, Raymond E (1997). *An Introduction to the New Testament.* New York, NY: Doubleday, pp. 456–466.

Cervantes, Vincent D (2014). "Traces of Transgressive Traditions Shifting Liberation Theologies through Jotería Studies." *Aztlán: A Journal of Chicano Studies* 39, No. 1 (Spring): pp. 195–206.

Córdova Quero, Hugo (2015). "Saintly Journeys: Intersections of Gender, Race, Sexuality, and Faith in Alejandro Springall's Santitos." *God's Image* 42, No. 2 (December): pp. 71–82.

DeVun, Leah (2021). *The Shape of Sex. Nonbinary Gender from Genesis to the Renaissance.* New York: Columbia University Press.

DuBois, W E B (1996). *The Souls of Black Folk.* New York, NY: Random House.

Griffin, Horace (2006). *Their Own Receive Them Not: African American Lesbians and Gays in Black Churches.* Eugene, OR: Wipf & Stock Publishers.

Harris, Stephen L (1985). *Understanding the Bible.* Palo Alto, CA: Mayfield.

Horie, Yurie (2006). "Possibilities and Limitations of 'Lesbian Continuum': The Case of a Protestant Church in Japan." *Journal of Lesbian Studies* 10, No. 3/4: pp. 145–159.

Ichwan, Juswantori (2014). "The Influence of Religion on the Development of Heterosexism in Indonesia." *Religión e Incidencia Pública: Revista de Investigación de GEMRIP* 2: pp. 197–223.

Isherwood, Lisa (2024). "Nothing Queer Here: The Straight Family and Ministry of Jesus." In: *The Bible and Sexualities: A Handbook,* edited by Chris Greenough and Caroline Blyth. London: SCM Press. (in press)

Kornegay, E L Jr (2004). "Queering Black Homophobia: Black Theology as a Sexual Discourse of Transformation." *Theology and Sexuality* 11, No. 1: pp. 29–51.

La Fountain-Stokes, Lawrence (2010). "Giuseppe Campuzano and the Museo Travesti del Perú. Interview with Lawrence La fountain-Stokes (University of Michigan, Ann Arbor)." *E-misférica* 6, No. 2. Available at: <http://hemisphericinstitute.org/hemi/en/campuzano-interview>.

Lara, Irene (2008). "Goddess of the Américas in the Decolonial Imaginary: Beyond the Virtuous Virgen/Pagan Puta Dichotomy." *Feminist Studies* 34, No. 1/2 (Spring–Summer): pp. 99–127.

Maduro, Otto (2006). "Once Again Liberating Theology? Towards a Latin American Liberation Theological Self-Criticism." In: *Liberation Theology and Sexuality,* edited by Marcella Althaus-Reid. Aldershot, Hampshire: Ashgate, pp. 19–31.

Manigault-Bryant, Le Rhonda S (2015). "African and African Diaspora Traditions: Religious Syncretism, Erotic Encounter, and Sacred Transformation." In: *Religion: Embodied Religion,* edited by Kent L Brintnall. Farmington Hills. MI: Macmillan Reference USA, pp. 183–201.

McGrath, Alister E (1999). *Teologia Cristiana.* Torino: Claudiana.

Ng, Chin P. (2000). "Breaking the Silence: A Post-Colonial Discourse on Sexual Desire in Christian Community." Master's Thesis. Hong Kong, SAR: The Graduate School, Chinese University of Hong Kong.

Ng, Chin P (2001). "Breaking the Silence." *God's Image* 20, No. 2: pp. 50–55.

Ngeo, Boon L. (2013). "We Are Comrades!—Tongzhi (Comrade) Theology (同志神学) and Its Contribution to Christian Theologies of God in the New Millennium." Doctoral Dissertation. Boston, MA: School of Theology, Boston University.

Córdova Quero, Hugo (2010). "Risky Affairs: Marcella Althaus-Reid Indecently Queering Juan Luis Segundo's Hermeneutic Circle Propositions." In: *Dancing Theology in Fetish Boots: Essays in Honour of Marcella Althaus-Reid*, edited by Lisa Isherwood and Mark D Jordan. London: SCM Press, pp. 207–218.

Quiroga, José (2000). *Tropics of Desire: Interventions from Queer Latino America*. New York, NY: New York University Press.

Rey, Terry (1999). *Our Lady of Class Struggle. The Cult of the Virgin Mary in Haiti*. Trenton, New Jersey: Africa World Press.

Ribas, Mario (2006). "Liberating Mary, Liberating the Poor." En: Liberation Theology and Sexuality, editado por Marcella Althaus-Reid. Aldershot: Ashgate, pp. 123–135.

Roman-Odio, Clara (2011). "Queering the Sacred: Love as Oppositional Consciousness in Alma Lopez's Visual Art." In: *Our Lady of Controversy. Alma Lopez's "Irreverent Apparition"*, edited by Alicia Gaspar de Alba and Alma López. Austin, TX: University of Texas Press, pp. 121–147.

Tamale, Sylvia (2014). "Exploring the Contours of African Sexualities: Religion, Law and Power." *African Human Rights Law Journal* 14: pp. 150–177.

Togarasei, Lovemore and Ezra Chitando (2011). "'Beyond the Bible': Critical Reflections on the Contributions of Cultural and Postcolonial Studies on Same-sex Relationships in Africa." *Journal of Gender and Religion in Africa* 17, No. 2 (December): pp. 109–125.

Van Klinken, Adriaan (2014). "Homosexuality, Politics and Pentecostal Nationalism in Zambia." *Studies in World Christianity* 20, No. 3: pp. 259–281.

Wu, Rose (2000). *Liberating the Church from Fear: The Story of Hong Kong's Sexual Minorities*. Hong Kong, SAR: Hong Kong Women Christian Council.

Xan, Rice (2010). "Ugandan Paper Calls for Gay People to Be Hanged." *The Guardian* (London), October 21. Available at: <https://www.theguardian.com/world/2010/oct/21/ugandan-paper-gay-people-hanged>.

Xan, Rice (2011). "Ugandan Gay Rights Activist David Kato Found Murdered." *The Guardian* (London), January 27. Available at: <https://www.theguardian.com/world/2011/jan/27/ugandan-gay-rights-activist-murdered>.

Yip, Lai Shan (2010). "A Proposal for Catholic Lesbian Feminist Theology in Hong Kong." *God's Image* 29, No. 3 (september): pp. 21–32.

Yip, Lai-Shan (2012). "Listening to the Passion of Catholic Nü-Tongzhi: Developing a Catholic Lesbian Feminist Theology in Hong Kong." In: *Queer Religion: Homosexuality in Modern Religious History*, edited by Donald L Boisvert and Jay Emerson Johnson. Santa Barbara, CA: Praeger, pp. 63–80.

Further Reading

Althaus-Reid, Marcella (2008). "The Bi/girl Writings: From Feminist Theology to Queer Theologies." In: *Post-Christian Feminisms: A Critical Approach*, edited by Lisa Isherwood and Kathleen McPhillips. London: Routledge, pp. 105–116.

Butler, Judith (1993). *Bodies that Matter: On the Discursive Limits of Sex*. New York, NY: Routledge.

5

Judaism

Source: Julija/Adobe Stock Photos.

The Star of David is the symbol of Judaism and is thought to represent the shield of King David. Others see the interlocked triangles as representing the relationship between God and man.

This chapter features an examination of how queer theologies emerged and continue to unfold in Judaism. First, we explore queer issues in Judaism through the lenses of Jewish

Global Queer Theologies: Intercontextual and Interreligious Perspectives, First Edition. Lisa Isherwood and Hugo Córdova Quero.
© 2026 John Wiley & Sons Ltd. Published 2026 by John Wiley & Sons Ltd.

Queer Theologies. We will investigate: How are the sacred texts of the Hebrew Bible, taken by Christians to condemn queer folks, read by Jewish religious scholars? Can we challenge 'old' assumptions by embracing Jewish theology? Do queer folks in Judaism face the same situations as their counterparts in Christianity?

Judaism as a Religion

Judaism, a monotheistic religion, traces its origins to the ancient Israelites and the covenant established with YHWH [Adonai] through Moses, as embodied in the 10 Commandments. Some scholars believe Judaism as an established monotheistic religion did not come into force until after the Fall of the Temple, although the word was known. For example, Asphodel Long (1988: 120) argues that Jewish women baked cakes for the Queen of Heaven and offered them in the temple not a monotheistic form of worship. She acknowledges that the prophets argued against such practices and even viewed it as paganism, Long suggests that in fact it was part of the way in which the Hebrew people took part in rituals that were practised by their neighbours in the Middle East. Further of course as part of Hebrew women's history it shows they were more involved in the religious life of their people than has previously been thought. She argues that the disapproval from the prophets was what the rabbis after the fall of the temple in the first century CE preserved, and it continues to form part of contemporary Judaism. However, she says they preserved only one part of a very flexible and inclusive tradition. As an example she points to Jeremiah 7: 17–18 where the women are accused of pagan worship and held to be the cause of the exile that has befallen them. Their response is that it is because they stopped baking cakes for the Queen of Heaven and burning incense to her that the calamity has befallen them (1988: 121). This highlights that there is more than one way to read history.

Judaism is one of the three major Abrahamic/monotheistic religions, alongside Christianity and Islam. However, the term 'Judaism' refers specifically to 'the religion of the Jews, an ethnic, cultural, and religious group with roots in the ancient Near East' (Swartz, 2005: 4868). This designation gained prominence during the Hellenistic period of Israel (302–383 BCE). Swartz says:

> The term Judaism first appears in Hellenistic Jewish literature, most prominently 2 Maccabees (a narration of the Judean revolt against the Seleucid Greeks in the second century BCE), where the word Ioudaïsmos seems to identify the ways and practices of the Jews in contradistinction with those of the "barbarians" (which in 2 Mc. 2:21 actually means Greeks). There Ioudaïsmos is contrasted with Hellenismos, the ways and practices of the Greeks that the Maccabees' Jewish opponents wished to follow. Thus the term Judaism began as a way of distinguishing itself from the other (2005: 496).

Judaism exhibits a complex and multifaceted religious landscape characterised by various branches that often maintain distinct theological interpretations and practices, reflecting its diverse historical and geographical trajectories. This diversity is not unique to Judaism but is a common characteristic across many religious traditions. The plurality within Judaism can be attributed to several factors: (a) its extensive history spanning millennia, encompassing numerous theological developments and interpretations; (b) the diasporic movements of the Jewish people over centuries, resulting in their settlement across diverse global regions; and (c) the encounters with varied cultures, languages and power dynamics throughout this migratory process. For instance, the expression of Jewish faith in Argentina may differ significantly from its practice in the United States or Israel, underscoring the influence of local cultural contexts on religious observance and identity formation within Judaism.

Branches of Judaism

All branches of Judaism share a foundational text, the Torah, which comprises the first five books of the Hebrew Bible: Genesis, Exodus, Leviticus, Numbers and Deuteronomy. The term *Torah* translates to 'teaching' (Swartz, 2005: 4969), serving as a central religious and ethical guide within the Jewish tradition. Alongside the *Torah*, the *Nevi'im,* meaning 'prophets', and the *Ketuvim,* meaning 'writings', collectively form the Tanakh, or Hebrew Bible. This tripartite structure of the Tanakh represents a comprehensive repository of Jewish religious thought, narrative and law, serving as a foundational text across diverse Jewish denominations.

The sacred scriptures of Judaism encompass a rich and diverse textual tradition, prominently featuring the Tanakh, the Talmud and the Midrash. The Tanakh serves as the foundational text of Jewish religious thought and narrative. The Talmud comprises oral rabbinical interpretations and discussions of the Torah, compiled between the second and fifth centuries BCE, while the Midrash consists of rabbinical sermons and commentaries, predominantly compiled between the fourth and sixth centuries CE.

Beyond these core texts, various branches of Judaism also accord significant importance to other writings, including (a) Halakhic literature, which pertains to religious law; (b) Kabbalah, encompassing esoteric teachings and (c) Hasidic works, representing Orthodox Jewish mysticism. These diverse religious and ethical writings were composed across different periods, reflecting the evolving theological, cultural and historical contexts of Judaism. The attached image illustrates the distinct branches and their respective textual traditions within Judaism, highlighting the multifaceted nature of Jewish religious scholarship and practice.

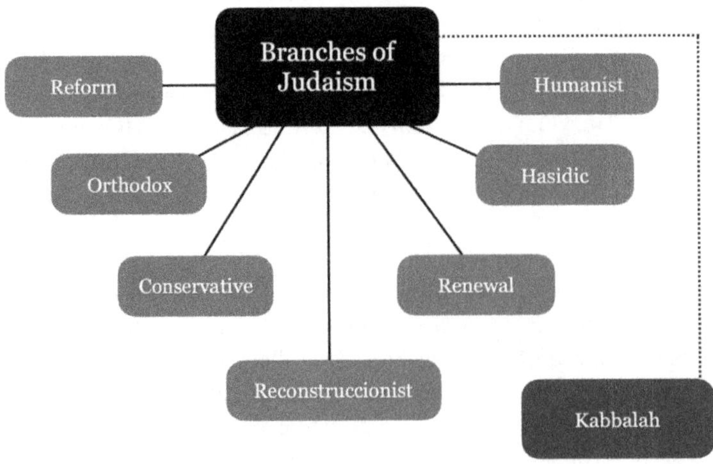

Graphic 5.1 Branches of Judaism

Midrash

Midrashim has the root 'drash' which means to inquire and clearly shows how the Jewish community engages with sacred texts. It is the duty of the community to examine texts and to fill the gaps left by those texts. For example, the Torah prohibits work on the Sabbath but does not state what is prohibited. Legal Midrashim lays out the categories of work prohibited by expanding the understanding of the original texts. There is also Narrative Midrashim which expands and interprets biblical stories. For example Adam's first wife Lillith, who is not mentioned in the Torah, becomes a focus of midrashim and a story is told about her thus giving her real presence in the religion. The earliest midrashim found is from the second century CE.

The rabbis of centuries ago told the tales as if those being spoken about were contemporaries of theirs which had implications for the telling of the story. For example one midrashim mentions Jacob studying Torah with this father Isaac as if they were students in a Talmudic academy. This is clearly impossible since the Torah would not be given until generations later and Talmudic academies did not exist of course at the time of Jacob and Isaac. This did not stop the development of the story. It also gives a way that queer scholars may enter into this practice, telling their own stories set in time and place that acknowledge the reality of queer life and challenge the anti-queer thrust of some of the texts. These texts may now be re-read through queer eyes rather than being discarded where they remain as anti-queer in the same way as if they were accepted.

Jewish Queer Theologies

It is essential to recognise that there is no singular 'Jewish Queer Theology' due to the inherent diversity within Judaism. Judaism comprises various branches, each with its unique emphases and interpretations. Consequently, this diversity naturally gives rise to a range of theological reflections concerning gender, sexuality, identity and queer issues across different Jewish branches.

Moreover, Judaism's extensive history spanning over 3,000 years, coupled with its diasporic experiences across diverse geographical locations, has contributed to evolving interpretations and practices of the faith over time. These historical and geographical variations further underscore the complexity and multiplicity of Jewish perspectives on queer theology. Therefore, any examination of Jewish Queer Theology must consider this rich tapestry of diversity, historical context and evolving interpretations to provide a comprehensive understanding of the intersections between Judaism and queer identities.

A common focal point in Jewish Queer theology involves engaging with biblical texts, notably Leviticus 18 and 20, which have historically been central to discussions around sexuality and morality. Similar to other queer theological frameworks, Jewish Queer theology grapples with the heteronormative perspectives embedded within these sacred scriptures. One of the principal objectives of Queer theology across religious traditions is to critically engage with and challenge the normative and foundational texts that underpin religious beliefs.

In this context, Jewish Queer theology assumes a particularly nuanced role, given the broader appropriation and selective interpretation of Hebrew Bible texts by right-wing Christian factions in the twentieth century. Additionally, as the oldest among the three Abrahamic religions, Judaism has significantly influenced the theological and scriptural interpretations within Christianity and Islam. Therefore, Jewish Queer theology not only navigates the complexities of Jewish textual traditions but also engages with the broader Abrahamic religious landscape, reflecting its multifaceted and dynamic nature.

Judaism is a global religion, and, as such, it is also cut across colonial situations. Political contexts do shape religion, and industrialised countries shape not only the economies of the world but also the way that religions understand their beliefs. It is unsurprising that the major theological elaborations for Jewish Queer theologies happen in industrialised countries, where economic resources and political global dynamics interact in particular ways. We also need to keep this in mind to examine how queer theologies, in general, may be coopted for legitimisations that exceed the boundaries of queer issues.

Judaism, which is inherently tied to the Jewish ethnic group, often presents challenges in distinguishing religious beliefs from culturally ingrained traditions. This complexity parallels the internal power dynamics observed within the diverse branches of Christianity. Jewish Queer theologies, operating within this intricate framework, are not immune to these dynamics. Faced with this multifaceted interplay, Jewish Queer theologians navigate a complex intersectionality, striving to develop a theology that honours both Jewish beliefs and the significance of queer issues. This endeavour places Jewish Queer theology at the confluence of religious tradition, cultural heritage and contemporary socio-cultural challenges, highlighting its unique position within the broader landscape of religious and queer studies.

The emergence of Jewish Queer theologies has been relatively delayed compared to other religious traditions, prompting two plausible hypotheses to explain this phenomenon. Firstly, within Judaism, there exists a nuanced understanding of gender and sexuality that does not necessarily compartmentalise the two, potentially obviating the need for a distinct sexual theology. Secondly, the decentralised nature of Judaism, characterised by congregational autonomy and limited centralised political decision-making, may have resulted in a less stringent emphasis on regulating the private lives of queer individuals beyond the confines of worship spaces.

These hypotheses warrant rigorous academic investigation, currently being pursued by Jewish Queer scholars such as Jay Michaelson (2009). Through scholarly inquiry, these theories can be critically examined to highlight the intricate intersections between Jewish theology, cultural practices and queer identities. Such research endeavours contribute to a deeper understanding of the complexities inherent in Jewish Queer theologies, shedding light on their unique historical, cultural and theological contexts within the broader landscape of religious studies.

While pinpointing distinct stages in the development of Jewish Queer theology may pose challenges, it is feasible to identify various trends or thematic areas that warrant attention within Jewish Queer Theologies. These focal points offer valuable avenues for scholarly exploration and contribute to a nuanced understanding of the intersections between Judaism, queer identities and theological discourse.

Biblical Studies

Similar to other Queer theological frameworks, Jewish Queer theology must grapple with the heteronormative perspectives embedded within their sacred scriptures. Daniel Boyarin (2007) offers valuable insights into this complex interplay, demonstrating the ways in which Jewish Queer theology seeks to reinterpret and reclaim these foundational texts to challenge and expand traditional understandings of gender, sexuality and religious identity:

> Both biblical and Talmudic texts confirm rather than refute Foucault's general hypothesis of the "history of sexuality." Neither of them divides sexual practices from the general categories of forbidden and permitted. Precisely because there is no separate realm of sexuality with all its definitional fraughtness for self-identification

and that of others, there is also no separate realm of the sexually forbidden. (...) [T]he taboos and tolerances of the culture vis-à-vis same-sex genital practice were tied precisely to structures of maleness and femaleness, to gender and not to a putative sexuality (2007: 141–142).

Jewish Queer theologies face a heightened responsibility when engaging with Hebrew Bible texts, which have been appropriated and reinterpreted by right-wing Christian factions throughout the twentieth century. These interpretations have become deeply ingrained in Western cultural frameworks, complicating efforts to disentangle these texts from their Christian-centric interpretations. Additionally, the 'Judeo-Christian' construct has often subsumed Judaism within a broader Christian narrative, further obscuring the distinctiveness of Jewish theological perspectives. Thus, Jewish Queer theologians navigate a complex landscape, seeking to reclaim and reinterpret Hebrew Bible texts in ways that challenge prevailing Christian interpretations while asserting the unique theological contributions of Judaism within the broader Western religious discourse.

Boyarin argues that what distinguishes the Jewish approach to theology is the absence of a clear demarcation between systematic and biblical theology, as well as between dogmatic and narrative theology. Within Jewish tradition, theology is predominantly conducted through the reading and interpretation of narratives, leading to the production of new narratives based on existing ones. He contends that, from a dogmatic standpoint, Jewish theology necessitates philological engagement; it requires meticulous textual analysis and reasoned interpretation. According to Boyarin, this emphasis on close reading and textual reasoning is integral to the development and understanding of Jewish theology. Therefore, for a theology to be authentically Jewish, it must be deeply rooted in philological exploration and rigorous textual analysis, reflecting the interconnectedness of narrative interpretation and theological reflection within Jewish intellectual traditions.

Daniel Boyarin deals with two major theses in his writing. One could be named as 'the prohibition thesis' and according to this thesis, the Hebrew bible, especially Leviticus, is framed in a binary 'prohibiting/allowing', actions that people can or cannot do. Boyarin states:

> I suggest that the interdiction on male–male anal intercourse enters, in the biblical cultural system, into the sub-system of such violations of the symbolic realm. In its immediate literary context, the verse just cited that prohibits male anal intercourse follows immediately on the verse that prohibits "bestiality" within which the word "confusion" [of kinds] is emphasized, hinting that there may be a connection between the two prohibitions on this level as well (2007: 135–136).

These prohibitions are given in order not to 'mix different species', whether they be animals, plants, garments or sexual acts. In this sense, he affirms that only 'male-to-male anal intercourse' is forbidden in the Leviticus.

The previous thesis is tied to a second thesis proposed by him, namely, the notion that there are sexual acts named in the Hebrew Bible, but we can neither talk about 'sexuality' nor 'sexual identity.' Boyarin says:

> It is only after the production of a category of sexuality per se, of a sexual identity determined by object choice, that any form of physical intimacy between men, and indeed almost any form of intimacy at all, becomes so problematic for our culture (2007: 143).

While this second thesis seems to support the Foucauldian understanding of 'sexual identities' only developing from the eighteenth century onwards, the first thesis is debatable. Boyarin states that

> the final conclusion is that there is no evidence in the Hebrew Bible for a category of homosexuals or homosexuality at all, and whatever explanation be adopted for the prohibition of male anal intercourse, there is as little reason to believe that it extended to other forms of homoerotic practice (2007: 141).

In the analysis, Boyarin mentions an important term: *Cinaedus*. This is a word to describe a certain male behaviour namely those who do not enact the expected social norms of maleness. In Koine Greek, the one in which the Christian Scriptures were written, the word *kinaidos* also referred to 'effeminate male', something that was not accepted in the Roman Empire. David M. Halperin states:

> The prospect of losing one's masculine gender status and being reduced to the social ranks of women therefore represented a universal possibility for all men. In such a context, the figure of the kinaidos stands as a warning to men of what can happen to them if they give up the internal struggle to master their desires and if they surrender, in womanly fashion, to the lure of pleasure. [...] The kinaidos, in this view, is not someone who has a different sexual orientation from other men, or who belongs to some autonomous sexual species. Rather, he is someone who represents what every man would be like if he were so shameless as to sacrifice his dignity and masculine gender status for the sake of gratifying the most odious and disgraceful, though no doubt voluptuous, bodily appetites (2002: 50).

We need to remember that in the Roman Empire, that a man would have sex with another man was not a problem, if that man adhered to the strict codes of conduct required from the Roman citizens. First of all, Roman citizens have the 'right of body' over their slaves, that is, they could have sexual relations with both women and men. However, Roman citizens should always be the one penetrating, as a way to exert their power over 'lesser beings', as slaves were deemed in Roman society. The semen of Roman citizens was part of the political as well as bodily realms of these men, and could not be 'wasted' by indulging in excessive sexual activities (Brown, 1988).

Although we cannot equate Cinaedus with 'homosexual' as explained by Michel Foucault, some scholars do consider that they may be considered a 'socially deviant' person due to their desire to be penetrated, a negatively socially sanctioned activity for Roman male citizens but this did not prevent them seeking penetrative sexual relations with women (Williams, 1999: 210). This is why modern categories cannot be applied easily.

Therefore, according to Boyarin, the Hebrew Bible's concerns are not explicitly focused on 'homosexual prohibitions' but rather on the disruption of distinct boundaries delineating gender and species. He draws a parallel between the act of one man treating another man as a female and the agricultural practice of planting two different species together. In both instances, there is a transgression of boundaries that traditionally separate male from female and distinct species from one another. This perspective suggests that the Hebrew Bible is primarily concerned with maintaining clear demarcations between different categories, highlighting the significance of preserving these boundaries as integral to the biblical worldview.

From Boyarin's viewpoint, the biblical texts address the consequences of blurring these boundaries, emphasising the importance of maintaining distinct categories and the inherent order they represent. This nuanced interpretation invites a deeper exploration of biblical texts, challenging traditional understandings and prompting reconsideration of the complex interplay between identity, boundaries and transgression within biblical narratives.

David Shneer (2009) argues that Jewish communities have undertaken a critical reevaluation and reinterpretation of the Bible to incorporate the experiences and identities of gay, lesbian and bisexual Jews. This transformative effort emerges as a pivotal social justice initiative, echoing the momentum generated by the feminist revolution within Judaism. Such endeavours have profound implications, necessitating a rigorous and reflective engagement with biblical texts and established interpretative frameworks. This ongoing process not only challenges traditional theological perspectives but also fosters a more inclusive and equitable religious discourse, highlighting the dynamic interplay between tradition, identity and social justice within Jewish theological scholarship.

Moreover, as transgender Jews increasingly advocate for greater inclusivity and recognition of diverse gender expressions within Judaism, there has been a renewed scrutiny of Judaism's historical relationship with gender. Shneer (2009) observes that those engaging in nuanced explorations of gender complexities often discover that the Talmudic rabbis, frequently criticised for establishing rigid gender frameworks, actually possessed a more multifaceted understanding of gender than contemporary perspectives often acknowledge. Thus, the efforts to challenge and expand traditional understandings of gender within Jewish theology not only contribute to a more inclusive religious discourse but also invite a reevaluation of historical Jewish perspectives on gender and identity.

Theological Reflection

The conceptualisation of the Divine and its interrelation with humanity necessitates the inclusion of discussions on gender and sexuality. Furthermore, considerations of bodies, desire and pleasure emerge as essential components in this theological discourse. Jay Michaelson also works on Jewish Queer Theologies and the way that he writes is very queer, interweaving academic and daily-lived experiences gives his writing an authentic flavour. A key argument in Michaelson's work is his critique of the 'prohibition thesis' in the Hebrew bible that seem to condemn homosexuality. Michaelson states:

> My purpose in this chapter, however, is (...) to argue that the entire focus on prohibition is unfortunate. First, it tends to reduce homosexuality, and queer sexuality more broadly, to questions of permission and prohibition, as if that were the sum total of its religious significance. Second, and relatedly, it implies that gays and lesbians (and mutatis mutandis bisexuals and transgendered persons) will essentially fall into preexisting religious and/or theological categories, with nothing new or distinctive about them: they/we are either kosher or treif, with no disruption of those categories and assumptions and nothing religiously significant about sexual variance. Indeed, it is generally only the opponents of inclusion who argue that GLBT (...) people in some way challenge existing structures; there is often an implicit claim among advocates that they do not (2009: 212–213).

His point is to move beyond the 'prohibition thesis' to include the experience of queer individuals. He is correct in pointing to the many binaries behind the 'prohibition thesis' argument. As in many theological discussions, the debate is not resolved in a unique way, and given that Judaism is a complex and heterogeneous religion, we may never have just one answer. Michaelson concludes that

> God/dess is not only male, not only transcendent; S/he is not only female, not only immanent; there is a unity of sames as well as opposites. This is perhaps the great contribution of the mythic theosophical Kabbalah: not the unity of the Divine but its manifestation as multiplicity—itself an important dimorphism but one replicated on the planes of emanation, creation, formation, and action in countless ways (2009: 219).

As Michaelson (2005) shows, these elements play a pivotal role in shaping our understanding of the Divine–human relationship, challenging traditional theological frameworks and prompting a more nuanced exploration of spirituality, identity and embodiment within religious thought:

> Within Judaism, we are warned against speculating why God creates or manifests in a particular way; to do so can lead to a dehumanizing reductivism and a dangerous claim to know the will of the Divine. But we can approach the question of homosexuality by observing some distinctive, theologically- relevant experiences of gay and lesbian people. The yield is abundant (2005: 11).

This quotation sheds light on the distinctive approach Judaism adopts towards theologising. A primary emphasis lies in the caution against presuming or defining God's actions or words, a tendency often observed in Christian theological traditions. Such presumptions risk violating the second commandment, potentially leading to the creation of an idol rather than engaging with the true essence of the Divine. Contrary to this caution, Jewish theologians possess the capacity to engage in a form of 'queering' Judaism, challenging and expanding traditional understandings. As Michaelson points out this process allows for a dynamic reinterpretation and exploration of Jewish theology, fostering a more inclusive and multifaceted understanding of the Divine, human identity and the interplay between tradition and contemporary perspectives within Judaism:

> [T]o "queer" (i.e., as rejecting the notion that binary gender and normative sexuality are natural categories) theology helps to undermine normative tendencies in theological thinking. Removing assumptions of Divine gender, speaking of permutations of gender fluidity that are quite removed from most of our experiences, denying that categories of gender even exist ultimately at all—all these are moves closer to the Infinity and Oneness of the Divine. The farther we get from our preconceived notions of what "identity" is supposed to be, the closer we are to realization (2009: 223).

In following Michaelson's (2009) argument, we realise that engaging with non-binary and fluid conceptions of gender within theology serves to challenge and disrupt conventional norms entrenched in theological discourse. By eschewing established frameworks that assign fixed gender attributes to the Divine, theologians open up avenues for exploring the boundless nature of the Divine's essence and unity. This approach encourages a deeper exploration of identity beyond conventional boundaries, pushing theological inquiry towards a more expansive understanding of existence and interconnectedness. Embracing diverse and fluid understandings of gender not only fosters inclusivity within religious frameworks but also facilitates a richer, more nuanced exploration of spirituality that transcends traditional limitations and fosters a deeper connection with the infinite facets of the Divine.

Michaelson's argument presents a refreshing and liberating perspective, offering believers the opportunity to pursue understanding beyond the confines of cis-heteronormativity. This approach encourages a more inclusive and expansive theological exploration, challenging traditional boundaries and fostering a space for diverse identities and experiences within religious discourse. By embracing a broader spectrum of gender identities and expressions, individuals are empowered to engage with spirituality in ways that resonate with their unique experiences, promoting a more inclusive and enriching religious dialogue.

Liturgy and Pastoral Care

The inquiry into the practical manifestation of theological principles is often imperative for embodying theological precepts. Within queer theological discourse, including Jewish Queer Theologies, a pivotal concern revolves around the application of these principles during communal religious observances. As posited by Michaelson (2005), the significance lies in the congregational gatherings for religious services. This underscores the necessity for a nuanced examination of how theological concepts intersect with the lived experiences of LGBTIQ+ individuals within the context of Jewish religious practice. Hence, elucidating the integration of queer perspectives within religious rites and rituals becomes a crucial endeavour in contemporary theological discourse:

> The process of relating to sacred text, liturgy, and teshuvah is indelibly coloured by the same process of "coming out" morally, intellectually, and spiritually. At first, the religious lesbian or gay man loves religion and thus hates him/herself. Then, s/he may either affirm the self and hate religion, continue to repress the self and "love" religion, or, somehow, reconcile religion with the reality of love and sexual expression. Even if the third option is chosen, though, gay religious consciousness is necessarily distrustful, because it has seen—and more importantly, felt—how rules, codes, and even the operation of conscience itself can actually be tools of oppression and self-repression (Michaelson, 2005: 12).

Liturgy and rites play integral roles in shaping the individual and communal identities of queer individuals. The efficacy of these rituals hinges upon the power dynamics that dictate their interpretation, whether they serve as agents of liberation or oppression. The emancipatory potential inherent in the enactment of liturgical practices parallels the compassionate pastoral care extended to queer communities. Regrettably, a dearth of pastoral competence exists among religious leaders when navigating the complexities of queer lived experiences. Rabbi Stephen Greenberg underscores this challenge, emphasising the pressing need for clergy to develop pastoral sensitivity and efficacy in addressing the concerns of LGBTIQ+ individuals within religious contexts:

> Rabbis desperately need help. Most of my colleagues admit that they have no idea what to do or say when a young man or woman comes out to them and asks for their understanding and direction. While the risks of coming out are so much more personal for the gay person, the risks of empathetic listening on the part of rabbis should not be minimized (2004: 219).

This is an important aspect to keep in mind as many of the religious institutions that train and form future religious leaders do not have in their curricula elements to deal with gender and sexuality. The pastoral care of queer folks still remains one of the most invisible areas of religious formation.

Rabbi Greenberg is the first Orthodox Rabbi to be out, and his book *Wrestling with God and Men: Homosexuality in the Jewish Tradition* (2004) was written in a non-academic way and is a fascinating examination of the relation between Judaism and queer studies. Rabbi Greenberg navigates the complex relationship between Jewish law, tradition and homosexuality. Greenberg explores how traditional Jewish texts address homosexual behaviour and identity, challenging conventional interpretations. He argues for a more nuanced understanding of scriptural references and rabbinic commentary, advocating for an inclusive approach that reconciles faith with sexual orientation. The book is a significant example of Jewish queer theology, integrating theological analysis with personal narrative to reflect Greenberg's journey of faith and identity. By examining historical and contemporary Jewish perspectives, Greenberg demonstrates how Jewish tradition can evolve to embrace diverse sexual identities without compromising its core principles. This work contributes to the broader discourse on theology, sexuality and inclusivity within Jewish contexts.

Finally, Andrea Moraes Alves addresses female homosexuality in Judaism. Alves states:

> The "invisibility" of female homosexuality is not a trait exclusive to the Jewish worldview. Various scholars of female homosexuality have already pointed to the difficulty of examining the theme and the predominance of male over female homosexuality. In academic analyses of the latter, the activity/passivity antinomy is argued to be inadequate for the analysis of sexual relations between women (...). Produced to conceptualize a hierarchical view of male homosexuality, this opposition reflects the idea that homosexuality is related to the passivity pole, the person who is penetrated being labeled a bicha, 'queer,' and occupying the relationship's female position (2010: 97).

Her work is a great contribution to the academy, especially since it is based on fieldwork. The article basically features the life stories of Natalia and Wagner, aliases for two Jewish Brazilian individuals who agreed to be interviewed by the author.

In her analysis, Moraes Alves (2010) delves into the intricate nuances surrounding female homosexuality within the framework of Jewish tradition's conceptualisation of human sexuality. Drawing from interviews with esteemed rabbinical figures, Alves sets out a prevailing viewpoint among these scholars which is the contention that female homosexuality is essentially non-existent within Jewish orthodoxy due to its perceived lack of efficacy as a penetrative sexual act. Central to this perspective is the absence of a phallic component, synonymous with masculinity and penetrative capacity, thereby precluding its classification as a genuine expression of sexuality. Consequently, female sexuality is construed solely within the context of male–female relations, wherein the male assumes a dominant role as the defining agent of sexual expression. This delineation underscores a broader pattern within Jewish thought regarding gender dynamics, wherein women are relegated to a separate yet complementary sphere distinct from that of men. The prescribed gender relations are imbued with notions of reverence towards women and their association with the sacred, while men are tasked with the responsibility of upholding the boundaries delineating this separation and fostering an environment of mutual respect.

The incorporation of authentic voices as exemplified in interviews serves as a crucial methodology for discerning individuals' positions within the intersection of sexuality and faith. Noteworthy in this regard is the documentary *Trembling Before G-d* (2001) directed by Sandra DuBowoski, which provides a platform for the candid expression of diverse perspectives. DuBowski (2013) succinctly encapsulates the essence of the film, highlighting its exploration of the complexities inherent in navigating the tensions between religious convictions and personal sexual identity:

> *Trembling Before G-d* shatters assumptions about faith, sexuality, and religious fundamentalism. Built around intimately-told personal stories of Hasidic and Orthodox Jews who are gay or lesbian, the film portrays a group of people who face a profound dilemma – how to reconcile their passionate love of Judaism and the Divine with the drastic Biblical prohibitions that forbid homosexuality. As the film unfolds, we meet a range of complex individuals – some hidden, some out – from the world's first openly gay Orthodox rabbi to closeted, married Hasidic gays and lesbians to those abandoned by religious families to Orthodox lesbian high-school sweethearts. Many have been tragically rejected and their pain is raw, yet with irony, humor, and resilience, they love, care, struggle, and debate with a thousands-year old tradition.

Therefore, *Trembling before G-d* emerges as a seminal contribution to the ongoing discourse surrounding Judaism and sexuality. By amplifying the voices of individuals grappling with the intricate interplay between religious orthodoxy and personal sexual orientation, the documentary enriches our comprehension of this complex terrain. Through its nuanced portrayal of lived experiences and the multifaceted nature of faith, the film serves as a catalyst for deeper exploration and introspection within both religious and secular communities. In essence, *Trembling before G-d* transcends the realm of mere documentary filmmaking to become a pivotal resource in fostering greater understanding and dialogue regarding issues of profound significance.

For Further Discussion

1 In what ways have the readings shaped your understanding of how Judaism perceives queer issues? How significant do you consider the engagement with sacred texts in Judaism in addressing these concerns?

2 Given the crucial teachings within Judaism on queer issues, how do these principles align with or challenge your personal religious faith, tradition, or philosophical beliefs? Can you provide specific examples to illustrate this connection?

3 In exploring the intersections of Jewish teachings and LGBTIQ+ acceptance, how might cultural factors contribute to varying perspectives within diverse Jewish societies?

4 Building on the understanding of Judaism, how do interpretations of Jewish sacred texts contribute to or hinder discussions on sexual diversity, and how might these dynamics impact contemporary debates on LGBTIQ+ rights within Jewish contexts?

5 How does the examination of female homosexuality within Jewish tradition challenge traditional views on gender dynamics and sexual expression, and what implications does it have for understanding the intersection of sexuality and religious orthodoxy?

References

Boyarin, Daniel (2007). "Against Rabbinic Sexuality: Textual Reasoning and the Jewish Theology of Sex." In: *Queer Theology: Rethinking the Western Body*, edited by Gerard Loughlin. Malden, MA: Blackwell, pp. 131–146.

Brown, Peter (1988). *The Body and Society: Men, Women, and Sexual Renunciation in Early Christianity*. New York, NY: Columbia University Press.

DuBowski, Sandi S, dir. (2001). *Trembling Before G-d*, 84 minutes. US/Israel/France: New Yorker Films, DVD.

DuBowski, Sandi S., Dir. (2013). "Trembling Before G-d: Turning A Movie Into A Movement." *The Huffington Post*, January 8. Available at: <http://www.huffingtonpost.com/sandi-dubowski/trembling-before-gd-turni_b_2428257.html>.

Greenberg, Steven (2004). *Wrestling with God and Men: Homosexuality in the Jewish Tradition*. Madison, WI: University of Wisconsin Press, pp. 217–261.

Halperin, David M (2002). "Forgetting Foucault: Acts, Identities, and the History of Sexuality." In: *Sexualities in History: A Reader*, edited by Kim M Phillips and Barry Reay. New York, NY: Routledge, pp. 42–68.

Long, Asphodel (1988). *In a Chariot Drawn by Lions. Exploding the Myth that God is Male*. London: The Women's Press.

Michaelson, Jay (2005). "Toward a Queer Jewish Theology." *Shma* (December): pp. 10–12.

Michaelson, Jay (2009). "On the Religious Significance of Homosexuality; or, Queering God, Torah, and Israel." In: *The Passionate Torah: Sex and Judaism*, edited by Danya Ruttenberg. New York: New York University Press, pp. 212–224.

Moraes Alves, Andrea (2010). "Identity, Judaism and Homosexuality: Two Stories About Belonging." *Vibrant* 7, No. 1: pp. 78–102.

Shneer, David (2009). "Introduction: Interpreting the Bible through a Bent Lens." In: *Torah Queeries: Weekly Commentaries on the Hebrew Bible*, edited by Gregg Drinkwater, Joshua Lesser and David Shneer. New York, NY: New York University Press, pp. 1–8.

Swartz, Michael D (2005). "Judaism: An Overview." In: *Encyclopedia of Religion*, edited by Lindsay Jones, volume 7. New York, NY: Macmillan, pp. 4968–4988.

Williams, Craig A (1999). *Roman Homosexuality: Ideologies of Masculinity in Classical Antiquity*. Oxford: Oxford University Press.

6

Islam

Islam, as a global religion, encompasses a diverse array of societies with varying economic statuses, cultural norms and religious interpretations. The term 'Islamic world' is not monolithic but rather a mosaic of different communities shaped by their unique historical, cultural and geographical contexts. The lived experiences of Muslim believers, like those of adherents to any faith, are influenced by a complex interplay of factors, including religious interpretations of sacred texts, linguistic traditions, cultural practices and regional influences.

In this diverse landscape, some Islamic societies lean towards conservatism, while others exhibit more liberal tendencies. This diversity underscores the multifaceted nature of Islam and highlights the need for nuanced approaches to understanding and interpreting the faith. Queer theologians within Islam face the challenge of navigating this complex terrain, reconciling their identities and experiences with traditional religious teachings. Their work involves exploring and interpreting sacred texts, engaging with cultural norms and addressing the socio-political realities of their respective communities.

By engaging with these multiple dimensions—culture, sacred texts, faith and context—queer theologians in Islam strive to foster inclusive and liberating theologies that resonate with the lived experiences of Muslim queer believers. Their efforts contribute to a richer, more inclusive understanding of Islam that honours diversity, promotes acceptance and champions the dignity and rights of all individuals, regardless of their sexual orientation or gender identity.

Islam as a Religion

Islam, along with Judaism and Christianity, is one of the three major monotheistic religions, often referred to as the Abrahamic faiths due to their shared roots tracing back to Abraham. Central to Islam are the teachings of the Quran, the holy book revealed to the Prophet Muhammad, peace be upon him, often abbreviated as 'pbuh', between 610 and 632 CE. in the city of Medina. Muslims believe the Quran to be the literal word of God, serving as a divine guide and source of spiritual wisdom. Its teachings encompass a wide range of topics, from moral and ethical principles to guidance on personal conduct

Global Queer Theologies: Intercontextual and Interreligious Perspectives, First Edition. Lisa Isherwood and Hugo Córdova Quero.
© 2026 John Wiley & Sons Ltd. Published 2026 by John Wiley & Sons Ltd.

and societal norms, shaping the beliefs and practices of over a billion followers worldwide. In fact,

> the Quran [is] regarded as 'uncreated', hence coextensive with God. As Wilfred Cantwell-Smith observes, it occupies for believing Muslims the position Christ has for Christians. A Muslim should not handle the text unless he or she is in a state of ritual purity (Ruthven, 1997: 23).

Islam recognises that there is one God, Allah, of whom Muhammad is his last and main prophet. Allah, usually translated as 'God', comes from the Arabic word al-ilah, which means 'the [one] God' (Soon, 2010: 2); and is one of the 99 names by which the followers of Islam call God. The city of Mecca in Saudi Arabia, along with Medina and the Al-Aqsa Mosque in Jerusalem, are Islam's three holy sites.

Branches of Islam

Islam has three main branches and one spirituality path: (a) Sunni, (b) Shia, (c) Sufi and (d) Khawarij. The following chart illustrates the schools and different groups in each of those branches:

While the Quran is the sacred text of Islam, the Ḥadīth constitute a second source of authority after the Quran, the Ḥadīth are the sayings of the Prophet (pbuh). Ian Richard Netton explains this term in a very helpful way:

> This Arabic word has a large number of meanings including 'speech', 'report' and 'narrative'. It also has the very important specialist sense of tradition, i.e. A record of the sayings and doings of the Prophet MuḤammad and his companions, and as such is regarded by Muslims as a source of Islamic law, dogma and ritual second only in importance to the Quer'an itself (1992: 90).

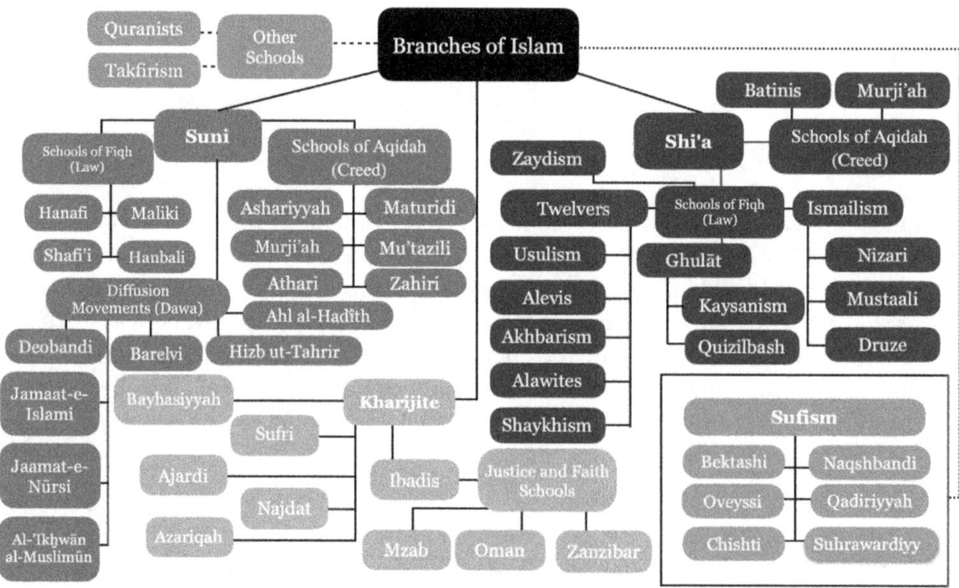

Graphic 6.1 Branches of Islam

In the history of Islam, the compilation of these sayings has endured the scholarly work of legal experts, and it is now a form of moral code.

It is important to highlight that the guidelines governing social life in Islam are referred to as *Fatwā*. A *Fatwā* is a juristic ruling or interpretation of Islamic law issued by Islamic scholars known as *Muftīs*. As noted by Netton (1992: 82), a *Fatwā* serves as a 'living bridge from pure Islamic jurisprudence to everyday Islamic life' (1992: 174). While a *Fatwā* is technically intended only for its author, in practice, conservative factions often attempt to impose these rulings as universally obligatory for all Muslims. This dynamic underscores the ongoing tension within Islamic communities between traditional interpretations and the diverse lived experiences of believers, including those who identify as queer.

Five Pillars of Islam

Regardless of the differences among the many branches of Islam, all of them do agree in practising and honouring what is known as 'the five pillars of Islam', which are:

1) Shahadah: declaring there is no god except Allah, and Muhammad is Allah's Messenger
2) Salat: ritual prayer five times a day
3) Sawm: fasting and self-control during the blessed month of Ramadan
4) Zakat: giving charity to the poor and needy
5) Hajj: the pilgrimage to Mecca at least once in a lifetime (Newby, 2002: 5).

Islamic Queer Theologies

For centuries, the Western world has often portrayed the Islamic world as 'backward' or 'lagging behind'. Such a perspective overlooks the significant contributions of Muslim scholars to the preservation and advancement of knowledge. It's worth noting that much of what the West knows about Greek philosophy today is thanks to the efforts of these scholars. They translated the works of ancient Greek philosophers and poets into Arabic, which were later translated into Latin and eventually reached Western scholars. Much of the scientific knowledge the West values also came from Muslim scientists well before most of the West even engaged in those areas of research. For example, Ibn Sina (980–1037 CE), known as Avicenna in the West, was a polymath who engaged with philosophy, science, medicine, mathematics and astronomy. His most famous work was the *Canon of Medicine* which was used in most medieval European universities.

Furthermore, the West's dominant Christian ideology has historically clashed with Islam on matters of theology and religious practice. Given this historical context, it is understandable that many in the West might assume that Islam and queer identities are incompatible. However, there is a strand of Islamic Queer theologies as well as historical instances within the religion where same-sex love was acknowledged and even celebrated. In revisiting these narratives, we can challenge the oversimplified and often biased views that have shaped perceptions of Islam and queer identities in the West.

For instance, the Islamic tradition has rich examples of queer theologies found in the works of Jalāl al-Dīn Muḥammad Rumi (1207–1273), one of Islam's most celebrated scholars, poets and mystics. Rumi frequently explored themes of divine love and human affection, including his profound love for God and other men. One poignant example is a poem believed to have been written upon the mysterious disappearance, and some speculate murder, of his beloved Shams al-Din Muhammad, also known as Shams Tabrizi. In this poem, Rumi's deep emotional connection and spiritual devotion to Shams are palpably expressed, challenging conventional perceptions and offering a more inclusive understanding of love within Islamic theology:

> From my first breath I have longed for Him—
> This longing has become my life.
> This longing has seen me grow old. ...
> But one mention of Shams-e Tabriz
> and all my youth comes back to me (Star, 2008: 17).

In the depths of his grief over the loss of Shams, Rumi channelled his profound emotions into his poetry. So intense was his sorrow that upon completing these poetic expressions, he attributed authorship to his beloved Shams, honouring their deep spiritual and emotional connection. One such poignant poem stands as a testament to their bond, capturing the essence of Rumi's love and the transformative power of his grief:

> No one has ever escaped from hardship
> without something worse happening in return.
> Don't take the bait!—
> It will only lead to disaster.
> Don't give in to your doubts!—
> It will shake you from your ground.
> Now Shams has shown us his mercy— He went away
> and left us with nothing but ourselves (Star, 2008: 135).

It can be argued that Islamic Queer Theologies trace their roots back to the thirteenth century, emerging from the heartfelt expressions of one of Islam's renowned believers, Jalāl al-Dīn Muḥammad Rumi. Yet, in contemporary times, the discourse surrounding these theologies is marked by heightened tension and debate. Scholars Scott Kugle and Stephen Hunt underscore this complexity, highlighting the challenges and nuances involved in navigating the intersection of Islam and queer identities in today's sociocultural landscape:

> Contemporary Muslim communities are displaying heightened tension over issues of homophobia and patriarchy as Islamic feminists, constitutionalists (progressives), and human rights activists question traditional norms within their communities. Western domination and the demise of post-colonial authoritarian regimes have added force to these reformist critiques of patriarchal power structures. In reaction, some Muslim authorities voice a 'Neo-traditional' Islamic ideology, seeking to 'defend' Islam against these challenges. Neo-traditionalists seek popular support via discourses of conventional masculinity deemed natural, traditional, moral, and politically necessary to protect Muslim communities against Western domination (2012: 255).

Islamic Queer Theologies have emerged within a complex cultural and religious landscape, seeking to encompass and affirm the religious experiences of queer individuals within the Islamic faith. While this field is relatively new and lacks a well-documented historical trajectory in contemporary times, it presents a vital opportunity for queer Muslims to engage in self-reflection and scholarly exploration. As an emerging area within Islam, the history and development of Islamic Queer Theologies remains largely unwritten, making it imperative for queer Muslims to take the lead in documenting and shaping this discourse.

In navigating this uncharted territory, there are three key areas where queer Muslim theologians and scholars can channel their energies. First, there is a need to reinterpret Islamic texts and traditions through an inclusive lens, challenging traditional interpretations that may marginalise or exclude queer individuals. Second, fostering dialogue and building bridges between queer communities and mainstream Islamic institutions can help facilitate greater understanding and acceptance. Lastly, promoting advocacy and activism within both religious and secular spaces can drive social change and foster greater inclusivity for queer Muslims.

Queering Quranic Interpretations

In every religious tradition, there exists a critical need to revisit and reassess the 'classical' interpretations of sacred texts, many of which have been historically influenced by deeply ingrained prejudices, including homophobia. Queer theologians and scholars endeavour to reconcile these interpretations with the lived experiences of LGBTIQ+ individuals, striving to affirm the spirituality and religious practices of queer communities as valid in the eyes of the Divine. This endeavour is particularly challenging within Islam, where orthodox positions often marginalise and dehumanise queer individuals, labelling them as 'deviant sinful' and accusing them of 'violating Islamic precepts' (Goh, 2012). Imam Muhsin Hendricks underscores the complexities of this task, highlighting the need for a more inclusive and compassionate approach to understanding and embracing diversity within Islamic teachings.

> Orthodox Muslims who justify their condemnation of homosexuals often use verses from the Quran and hadith to support their position. While Islam, through the word's very meaning, promotes peace in all spheres of life, many queer Muslims struggle to find peace with a representation of Islam that does not include them. This often instills feelings of alienation from their communities and rejection by God, friends, and families (2010: 31–32).

It is important to distinguish between the actual words of the sacred texts and the diverse interpretations that believers derive from them. While not disputing or undermining Islam's assertion that the Holy Qur'an is the 'speech of Allah', believers, following the insights of Paul Ricoeur, engage with and interpret the text from various perspectives. As Imam Hendricks asserts, each individual approaches and interacts with the sacred text from their unique vantage point, shaping their understanding and relationship with the Divine through personal reflection and interpretation. This acknowledgement underscores the richness and complexity of religious interpretation, highlighting the diversity of thought and belief within Islamic communities:

> The poetic nature of the Quran is such that it can be interpreted in many ways. It depends on the personality and disposition of the interpreter. However, the liberty of interpretation that this noble book affords us was never intended to disregard diversity or to exploit its subject's freedom of choice, right to life and freedom to co-create (2010: 27).

Interpretation is integral to Islam, not confined to scholarly study but permeating everyday practices. This is particularly evident when considering the translation of the Qur'an's original Arabic text into the languages spoken by its diverse global community of believers.

Rusmir Musić offers a compelling example of this interplay between language, interpretation and practice, highlighting the complexities and nuances involved in conveying the Divine message across cultural and linguistic boundaries:

> The Original Arabic of the sacred texts unlocks itself to multiple interpretations, accentuating ambiguity at the core of multiple Islams responding to needs of its diverse constituents. For example, Ahmed Ali's (1988) translation of Surah Al-A'râf ayet 81: for ye practice your lusts On men in preference To women
> in Muhammad Behbudi and Colin Turner's (1993) version becomes
> In order to satisfy your lust, you sleep with men rather than women. Man's innate opposition is towards the opposite gender; by lying with those of the same sex [sic] you have corrupted your own souls and denied your womenfolk their rights (to sexual satisfaction).
> [...] Even a quick glance at the differences between these translations reveals the translator's ideological orientations, calling into question why scholar historically choose certain meanings when other, radically different ones, are also possible (2003: 7–8).

Musić (2003) underscores the inherent challenges and nuances that come with translating the sacred text of the Qur'an. He emphasises that the process of interpretation transcends mere linguistic translation, evolving into a profound spiritual journey. As believers delve into translated versions of the Qur'an, they navigate the intricate interplay of language and meaning. Their aim is to capture the essence of the Divine message, adapting it to resonate authentically within their unique cultural and linguistic contexts. This ongoing process of interpretation exemplifies the dynamic and evolving nature of Islamic tradition, showcasing its adaptability and enduring relevance across diverse cultural landscapes.

Queer theologians and scholars within Islam, along with those in other religious traditions, confront the crucial challenge of interpreting sacred texts through a queer lens. This demands a nuanced and thoughtful approach that goes beyond traditional interpretations. It involves reevaluating cis-heteronormative readings of religious texts and exploring alternative interpretations that resonate with and affirm the lived experiences of LGBTQ+ individuals within their religious frameworks. This transformative engagement with sacred texts seeks to foster greater inclusivity and understanding, challenging long-standing norms and advocating for a more compassionate and accepting religious discourse.

Carving a Niche for the Presence of Queer Muslims

In relation to the previous point, the existence of queer Muslims is often jeopardised by dehumanising attitudes and prejudices directed towards them. This presents a significant challenge, as there exists a prevailing rigidity that fails to recognise sexual diversity as an inherent aspect of the human experience, which can be harmoniously integrated with the Muslim faith. Challenging this conventional understanding, Imam Hendricks claims that:

> Islam, at its very core, does not condemn non-heterosexual sexual intimacy. Instead, it is embraced as part of a divine plan. Islam, in its true meaning of peace and justice, accommodates the individual's sexual orientation as an intrinsic part of their biological and psychological makeup (2010: 32).

Moreover, the notion that queer individuals are incompatible with Islam is viewed by some scholars as an inconsistency within a monotheistic faith like Islam.

Momin Rahman (2010) positions the presence of queer individuals within Islam outside the framework of the 'clash of civilizations' (Huntington, 1996). Rather than viewing Western and Eastern cultures as inherently conflicting or mutually exclusive, he argues that queer Muslims challenge these oversimplified dichotomies. Their intersectional identity sheds light on the complex interplay of sexuality and desire within Muslim communities. Rahman contends that the 'East/West' divide is a fictitious construct, as human experiences continually defy the rigid cultural boundaries imposed by such categorisations. I would further argue that this East–West dichotomy stems from a skewed colonial perspective that portrays the East negatively in relation to the West. Gender, sexuality, desire and bodily experiences are all influenced by this power dynamic, perpetuating stereotypes that label queer individuals in the East as 'backward', while positioning those in the West as 'progressive'. Such a narrative mirrors aspects of (neo)colonialism. Fernando Revelo La Rotta (2013) concludes that Queer Muslim intersectional subjectivity challenges and redefines the conventional discourse rooted in the outdated binaries of East versus West and modernity versus tradition.

Queering Pastoral Care in Dialogue with Activism

Scholar Susannah Cornwall concludes that 'Queer Muslim theology and interpretation are shifting from apologetics to proactive queer readings, grounded in activism' (2011: 4). We view this transition as a crucial step towards prioritising the pastoral care of queer Muslims. Activism has historically been instrumental in challenging and expanding the boundaries within various faith traditions. In Islam, activism plays a pivotal role not only in reinterpreting sacred texts but also in supporting and advocating for queer believers. In recent decades, Queer Muslim activism has gained unprecedented visibility, particularly at the grassroots level (Habib, 2013).

However, Muslim activists face challenges from both conservative Muslims and Islamophobic non-Muslims, as noted by Junaid Jahangir (2013) from MacEwan University. He warns that people who generalise and stereotype the Muslim position on queer issues end up being strange bedfellows with extremists. Because by downplaying progressive Muslim efforts, they create divisiveness between Muslims and society at large. Despite these obstacles, queer Muslim activists have been instrumental in advancing new Quranic interpretations, queer theological discourses and innovative pastoral-care approaches for queer believers. This underscores the importance of ongoing collaboration between queer Muslim scholars, theologians and activists in this critical area.

For instance, Australian researcher Carolyn Poljski (2011) explores the complexities faced by female Muslim migrants when navigating the concept of 'coming out' while in same-sex relationships in host countries, especially when they have families or extended family who could be affected. She proposes that terms like 'coming home' and 'inviting people in' might better capture the essence of navigating personal situations without risking one's safety by 'coming out'. Therefore, it is essential to exercise caution when judging individuals from different societies or cultures who may not have the material means, despite their personal desires, to come out. In many respects, 'coming out' is more a matter of privilege than possibility.

Imam Muhsin Hendricks delves deeply into the realm of queer theology with his groundbreaking work. As the first openly gay Muslim Imam, he leads the 'Inner Circle', a centre for Muslim queers in South Africa. In his writings, Hendricks introduces and elaborates on key terms that are crucial for a comprehensive understanding of his arguments. He presents the concept of 'political Islam' as a central thesis, challenging traditional interpretations and inviting readers to reconsider the intersections of faith, identity and activism. Hendricks (2010) asserts:

> It can only be concluded that there is another face of Islam, other than the one propounded through the Quran, that has taken power through the employment of secondary Islamic sources. The Islam we are engaging with today seems to be an Islam that has usurped religious power for political gain. This has a huge impact on the lives of Muslims who are afraid to utter their discomfort with certain issues pertaining to Islam, as the religion itself teaches blind-following and obedience to authority (2010: 46).

Dervla Sara Shannahan (2010) poses critical questions that warrant thoughtful consideration. She raises concerns about the tendency to associate queer theologies exclusively with specific religions such as Christianity, Islam or Judaism, or to particular cultural contexts, predominantly those of the Northern Hemisphere. Shannahan questions the limitations imposed by such associations, particularly in terms of imposing mandates like 'coming-out narratives'. She urges for a broader, more inclusive approach to queer theology that transcends these boundaries. Shannahan articulates:

> Queer theology/ies have sought to underline, undermine, and undress much of the emotional baggage of heteronormative interpretations of religion and provide a significant departure from queer theory's presumption of atheism. They have successfully disrobed the 'theological closets, in what has not been said or has been hidden', offering instead a 'theology which denounces the domestic sexual violence of theology on its dissidents' (...). The astounding contributions of such theorists have altered the terrain of queer theory and further troubled the underlying assumptions of a spiritless queer subject. However, the theoretical ambiance that Christian (and to a large extent Jewish) theologies share with queer theory and Northern queer culture are evident. It remains 'an anti- identity based theology' (...) in contention with a distinct theoretical identity, and it takes the need for a coming-out narrative as a given (2010: 675).

Her insights are crucial as they highlight the fundamental challenges faced by queer Muslims within their specific contexts. In regions where coming out may not be a viable option, the lived experiences of individuals differ significantly from those in the United States, Canada or Europe. This disparity is not solely rooted in legal restrictions, such as prohibitions on same-sex relationships, but also encompasses cultural worldviews that shape community belonging. It's essential to recognise that imposing a 'coming out' narrative can, in certain contexts, pose life-threatening risks rather than offering liberation. Shannahan's exploration of these complex issues adds significant depth to the discourse on queer theologies.

Minwalla, Rosser, Feldman and Varga's study serves as a significant case study of Al-Fatiha, an international organisation for LGBTIQ Muslims. The authors conducted ethnographic research, amplifying the voices of believers who often remain marginalised in academic discourse. In their article, the authors note the absence of academic studies exploring the intersection of gay identity and Muslim identity, stating that they 'could find no academic studies addressing the experience of integrating a gay identity with a Muslim identity' (Minwalla et al., 2005: 114). While they reference various studies, poems and materials, there is a noticeable lack of academic research specifically addressing the intersection of sexuality and Islam. It is worth noting that this article was written in 2005, and since then, some studies have emerged in academia. However, many of these studies focus on Scriptural analysis rather than centring the lived experiences and concerns of queer Muslims.

The findings of this study are remarkably insightful, offering a nuanced understanding of the complex interplay between faith and sexuality among the participants. The individuals interviewed navigated the intersections of their religious beliefs and sexual identities in diverse ways, revealing profound perspectives on the subject matter. For instance, one participant eloquently articulated the intricate relationships between sexuality, power dynamics and race, shedding light on the multifaceted nature of these intersections within the context of their lived experiences. Such contributions enrich the academic discourse and deepen our understanding of the complexities inherent in queer theology and identity:

> A former roommate had told me that he had a crush on me ... I was 22 and he was 40, and I was really offended by it. It made me feel like I do not really want to be your South Asian boy-toy. I really do not want to be in a position where you have complete power over me. You're White, you are relatively well off economically, and you are older than me. You command a lot more authority in society in general and in the queer community. I do not want to be with somebody who has that much power, where there's that much of a power differential between myself and my partner. When I told him, he was totally shocked. He was offended that I could think of our friendship in terms of power structures instead of being in a friend ship (sic.) based on love that could blossom into a relationship. I was like, I have to think that way, I cannot think otherwise (Minwalla et al., 2005: 123).

The inclusion of such voices is imperative within academic discourse to gain a comprehensive understanding of the multifaceted challenges faced by individuals navigating intersecting identities. As we all grapple with various complexities in our daily lives, these narratives offer invaluable insights into the lived experiences of those contending with multiple issues, including faith and sexuality. A critical factor to consider is the influence of culture, which can significantly shape the experiences of migrants, particularly those relocating to the Northern Hemisphere. The cultural parameters in these new environments may starkly contrast with the cultural norms of their countries of origin, presenting unique challenges for queer individuals. As highlighted by Minwalla et al.:

> Participants described their Eastern cultures as more permissive of homo-sociality, particularly expressions of physical intimacy and emotional closeness. In many Eastern cultures, intimate expressions between men are not constructed as sexual or feminine. Therefore, these behaviors are not internalized or perceived in a context of homosexuality, shame or stigma as they are in the West. Instead they are often internalized as part of cultural brotherhood, deep friendship and masculinity, similar to the Mediterranean pedagogical-Socratic love ideal (Khan 1997a). Notably, in our study, Muslim men from Eastern cultures appeared to have a heightened awareness that the process of constructing of a gay identity that is, constructing homo-social expression into an internal and social identity-is more of a Western process. This may be why some respondents seemed to struggle with and resist the construct of gay, perceiving it as a confining label or a box-a resistance to cultural assimilation (2005: 124).

Simultaneously, scholar Ibrahim Abraham delves into the concept of 'Queer space', offering a thought-provoking metaphorical framework to comprehend the intersection of queer identity within Islam: that of the veil. Abraham's analysis serves as a critique of homonormativity, a theme previously explored in our discussions, as well as challenges the West's role as a neo-colonial agent imposing a singular understanding of culture, sexuality, gender and identity globally. By interrogating these dominant narratives, Abraham asserts:

> Against the neo-assimilationism of (...) homonormativity, the very notion of a queer public space as much as a Muslim public space, is something that challenges supine assimilation, and resists a recourse to notions of liberal tolerance that amount to an ethic of 'do what you like, but don't do it here'. The corollary of which is not just the limitation on tolerance – which itself is a rather limited notion – but a disavowal of the public reality of possibly dysfunctional aspects of minority communities. (...) Leaving aside the vexed question of ideology in western Marxist thought, we see echoes of this in the calls for assimilation within the ethics of homonormativity and the liberalism of so-called 'boutique multiculturalists', who delight in limited, essentially superficial forms of difference, but cannot or will not accept difference at the more fundamental level, including the notion of spatial difference or exclusion (2007: 4).

Abraham's analysis is pivotal in elucidating the intricate dynamics of power and identity within the contemporary world-system, particularly for queer Muslims navigating these complex terrains. Similarly, Nicole Kligerman (2007) engages with Quranic scriptures, examining their perceived references to homosexuality. She further enriches the discourse by tracing the historical nuances of homosexuality within Islam, particularly during the Middle Ages. Kligerman's exploration offers valuable insights into the evolving interpretations and understandings of homosexuality within the Islamic tradition. Reflecting on this historical context, Kligerman asserts:

> homosexual relationships reinforced dominant and subordinated roles already present in society. Homosexual relationships followed traditional gender and power patterns; boys played the passive role (emulating the woman), while adult males asserted their power by receiving sexual pleasure through domination. Egalitarian sexual roles, however, were seen as "inexplicable and unacceptable" (2007: 55).

Similar to many Mediterranean, Latin American, African and Asian societies, Kligerman says that homosexual activities are often permissible within Muslim-majority societies without necessarily attributing a gay identity to the individuals involved: 'In the Muslim world, it is common to engage in homosexual activity without being considered gay if one is the active partner in the act' (2007: 57). Such a nuanced understanding diverges from the Western conceptualisation where sexual acts are frequently tied to specific identities. Indeed, the West's influence has contributed to exacerbating challenges faced by queer individuals within Islamic societies:

> The rise in Western colonialism in the Middle East and larger Muslim world correlated with the increasing stigma against homosexuality. The destruction of the kinship-based community, stemming from the rise of capitalism and the male wage-work force reinforced the patriarchal, heterosexual family unit. As state governments fostered such a change, the stigma against homosexuality increased (Kligerman, 2007: 59).

Kligerman's contribution underscores her critique of human rights violations perpetrated against queer individuals. While private same-sex activities may occur discreetly behind closed doors, the public disclosure of such engagements often exposes individuals to legal repercussions, including severe penalties up to and including death. This stark disparity between private freedoms and public consequences highlights the precarious and often perilous position of queer individuals within these societies. Furthermore, Kligerman highlights the complicit role of Western influence in perpetuating these abuses, thus emphasising the global implications and responsibilities inherent in addressing such human rights violations:

> An obstacle that a potential gay rights movement will encounter in combating these human rights abuses is the prevailing view that the movement is not indigenous, but rather a Western-imposed ideal that is not in line with traditional societies. Joseph Massad, a Palestinian born professor of Arab politics at Columbia University, argues that it is the work of organizations like the International Lesbian and Gay Association (ILGA) and the International Gay and Lesbian Human Rights Commission (IGLHRC) —which he dubs the "Gay International"— that inadvertently causes these humans rights violations by projecting their Western notions of sexuality on the Muslim world. Like gay and feminist theorists, Massad claims that gay rights are not universal, and by attempting to assert the human rights of supposed "homosexuals" who do not self-identify as such, the Gay International puts Muslims who engage in homosexual activity in the position of defending themselves to their increasingly repressive governments (2007: 62).

It is imperative to heed Kligerman's insights, as they illuminate the neo-colonial undertones inherent in certain gay politics. Such approaches often lack the cultural sensitivity required to recognise that queer individuals in Third World countries bear the brunt of the repercussions stemming from international advocacy campaigns. A non-colonial response would entail acknowledging the existing socio-cultural negotiations within these societies and striving to amplify them in a manner that genuinely fosters liberation. This underscores the significance of Kligerman's article, which prompts a critical reevaluation of how advocacy efforts can be more culturally attuned and empowering for marginalised communities.

While academic writing constitutes a significant medium for exploring queer theologies within Islam, it is not the sole format employed for this purpose. Parvez Sharma's documentary *A Jihad for Love* (2007) stands as a seminal contribution in this realm, elucidating the intricate challenges and experiences encountered by Queer Muslims in their daily lives. The documentary serves as a pivotal platform for shedding light on the multifaceted realities and narratives of Queer Muslims, thereby enriching our understanding of their lived experiences beyond academic discourse:

> Fourteen centuries after the revelation of the holy Qur'an to the Prophet Muhammad, Islam today is the world's second largest and fastest growing religion. Muslim gay filmmaker Parvez Sharma travels the many worlds of this dynamic faith, discovering the stories of its most unlikely storytellers: lesbian and gay Muslims (Media Diversity Institute, 2009).

Co-produced by Sandi DuBowski—director of 'Trembling Before G-d'—and Sharma, 'A Jihad for Love' is a documentary that spans 12 countries and is presented in nine languages, emanating from the core of Islamic culture. Rather than focusing solely on a hostile and conflict-ridden present, the film seeks to reclaim the Islamic notion of a greater *Jihād*. This concept, deeply rooted in the faith, is understood as 'an inner struggle' or 'striving in the path of God', allowing its diverse subjects to transcend the narrow interpretation of Jihad as merely a holy war. The documentary employs the term *jihād*, a term fraught with controversy due to its frequent misinterpretation as a 'terrorist term'. Indeed, as Netton asserts:

> The word derives from an Arabic root meaning basically 'to strive'. Jihād is sometimes considered by some groups to be a sixth pillar of Islam, for example by the Khārajites and the Ibāḍīs. Of course, all Muslims are obliged to wage a spiritual jihād in the sense of striving against sin and sinful inclinations within themselves: this is the other major sense of jihād. It is interesting, albeit ultimately superficial, to compare the concept of jihād with that which underpinned the Crusades (1992: 136–137).

Netton makes a very important point: while the West has demonised the sense of duty of Muslims in relation to the term *jihad*, Christianity for 2,000 years has often recursed to a notion of 'holy war' as the one pointed out by Netton in his example of the Crusades. The difference is that the West has erased all guilt from the Crusades and has charged radical Muslims as the only 'guilty' ones, thus (re)producing and reifying the same colonialism that has been displayed since the sixteenth century.

Transgender Spirituality

Yuenmei Wong's (2012) scholarly contributions focus on the intricate interplay between sexuality and Islam within the Malaysian context. She critically examines the challenging landscape shaped by Islamic conservatives who exert significant influence over societal norms and individual lives. Wong's research specifically delves into female-to-female relationships and the lived experiences of individuals in Malaysia. She rigorously interrogates the confluence of gender, sexuality, class, ethnicity and religion, shedding light on the multifaceted nature of oppression faced by *Pengkid*, a term believed to have originated from a mispronunciation of 'Punk Kids'. Through her work, Wong offers nuanced insights into the complex socio-cultural dynamics shaping contemporary Malaysian society.

Wong interrogates the presumed marginalisation of transgender practices and same-sex desires within societal frameworks, offering a nuanced exploration of the intricate intersections of identity, gender, sexuality and religion in a Muslim-majority context. In Malaysia, where Muslim-Malay sexual minorities confront escalating threats of moral policing, the concept of *Pengkid* emerges as a distinct identity marker. This term encapsulates the experiences of marginalised sexual subjects, framed within the Islamic discourse prevalent in Malaysia. Wong's analysis challenges monolithic understandings of sexuality and gender, highlighting the complex negotiations and contestations that characterise the lived experiences of sexual minorities within religious and cultural contexts. By delving into the multifaceted dynamics at play, Wong's work enriches our comprehension of the intricate interplay between religious doctrine, cultural norms and individual identities, particularly within the specific socio-political landscape of Malaysia. This nuanced examination underscores the imperative for a more inclusive and empathetic approach to understanding and addressing the complexities faced by sexual minorities in diverse cultural settings.

Wong's scholarly analysis provides a nuanced critique of the prevailing criticisms directed towards female masculinity, particularly within the context of the masculine–feminine coupling pattern observed in female same-sex relationships. Rather than accepting these criticisms uncritically, Wong's work embraces the opportunity to validate and affirm the diverse gendered bodies and subjectivities that exist beyond conventional norms. Drawing upon oral accounts, narratives and lived experiences of the *Pengkids* and their partners, this study advocates for the recognition of an alternative perspective on transgender practices and women's same-sex desires. By doing so, it seeks to intervene in and challenge the dominant discourse surrounding lesbianism among Malaysian girls and women. This alternative perspective not only enriches our understanding of gender diversity and sexual identities but also serves as a catalyst for reevaluating and reshaping the discourse on sexuality, gender and identity within the Malaysian cultural context. Thus, Wong's work contributes significantly to ongoing academic discussions on gender, sexuality and cultural representation.

Joseph N. Goh has directed his scholarly inquiry towards the experiences of male-to-female transgender individuals in Kuala Lumpur. His research is informed by personal engagement; between 2010 and 2012 when Goh volunteered with PT Foundation, a community-based non-profit organisation dedicated to promoting HIV/AIDS awareness and empowerment among Malaysians.

During his tenure as the coordinator of counselling and HIV/AIDS prevention at PT Foundation, Goh gained extensive firsthand experience with the realities faced by transgender individuals, known in Bahasa Malaysia, the official language of Malaysia, as *Mak Nyahs*. Drawing from this immersive experience, his work delves into the spirituality of transgender Muslims, offering valuable insights into the intersectionality of gender identity, religion and cultural context within the Malaysian setting. Goh's research contributes meaningfully to the academic discourse on transgender studies, particularly highlighting the nuanced experiences of transgender Muslims navigating their faith and identity in contemporary Malaysia.

The term *Mak Nyah* can be loosely translated as 'transsexual', although it is worth noting that queer communities in Malaysia often refrain from using this term due to its implications. The intertwining of Malaysian government and legal frameworks with Islamic principles, particularly through the Sharia or Islamic code of conduct, has resulted in significant persecution and discrimination against transgender individuals.

Indeed, the Syaria Courts in Malaysia are state-sanctioned institutions tasked with enforcing Sharia law. Consequently, Malaysia operates under a dual judicial system, one civil, governed by the Constitution and Judicial law, and another religious, guided by Islamic tenets. Given their state-sanctioned status, the Syariah Courts' rulings exhibit variability across regions. Presently, Malaysia hosts 13 Syariah Courts. Violations of Shariah law can result in penalties ranging from imprisonment for up to two years, fines, to corporal punishment in the form of up to six canings (Nawi, 2007). This legal landscape underscores the challenges faced by transgender individuals in navigating both their gender identity and religious–cultural norms within Malaysian society.

Amidst this complex socio-religious landscape, there exists a diverse group of individuals unwilling to renounce their faith or succumb to false dichotomies. Instead, they actively seek avenues for reconciling and authentically living out their faith, gender and sexuality in harmony. Goh's theological scholarship contributes significantly to the affirmation of human dignity and the inherent right of individuals to pursue their spiritual quest, even when confronted with religious institutional structures that may deny such rights. For Goh (2012), this pursuit is not merely a personal choice but a sacred imperative. His work underscores the importance of recognising and respecting the spiritual journeys of transgender individuals, advocating for a more inclusive understanding of faith that accommodates diverse expressions of gender and sexuality. Through his scholarship, Goh challenges traditional religious norms and encourages a broader discourse that honours the complexity of human identity within the context of religious belief systems:

> In uncovering the spiritualities of mak nyahs in "mostly Muslim Malaysia", and being aware of the struggles of the Muslim mak nyahs in the face of institutional Islam, I found myself with a sacred imperative to focus on the unique methods with which they practised Islam (2012: 33).

The tension between individual spiritual beliefs and institutional interpretations of Islam is a persistent challenge faced by queer individuals in Malaysia. They are often labelled as 'recalcitrant' sinners, with their bodily modifications viewed as 'violations of Islam and transgressions against God' (Goh, 2012: 36). Such perceptions highlight what some consider to be inconsistencies within the monotheistic framework of Islam. That observation is echoed by Ugandan-Canadian author Irshad Manji, who states:

> [Going] back to the Quran, everybody is a deliberate act of creation on God's part. So even gays and lesbians have been created by God (...). For those who say that they are somehow misfits or abominations, what they are really therefore saying is that 'Allah made mistakes' (Malaysiakini, 2012).

Acknowledging the diverse creative expressions inherent in all individuals, Goh (2012) underscores the profound spiritual and creative experiences of Mak Nyahs. He posits that these experiences not only affirm their unique identities but also highlight the intricate interplay between spirituality, creativity and personal expression within the context of their lived realities:

> There are two important considerations that I wish to highlight from my interviews with the mak nyahs on the subject of God and religion: the idea of an accepting God vis-à-vis organized religion, and the role of God and organized religion in considerations of G[enital] R[econstruction] S[urgery]. I postulate that although concepts of a personal God are initially conflated with institutionalized religion, mak nyahs demonstrate an ability to construct and maintain personalized belief systems when they are able to transgress religiopolitical rigidities and distinguish the concept of a Divine Entity from hierarchical constructs. (...) Here is an acknowledgment of the persecuting prowess of organized religion that yields serious disparities between the idea of an accommodating, merciful Deity with an intolerant, tyrannical, official representation of that Deity. The evidence suggests that while a personal God is important for the mak nyahs, if the institutional representation of such a God condemns them, the mak nyahs explicitly resist the institution in favor of personalized belief systems (2014: 135).

Goh's choice to term this theology 'Nyah-Islam' rather than simply renaming it as 'transgender spirituality' reflects specific contextual perceptions of queer individuals in Malaysia. For instance, Jaylanee, whom Goh interviewed during his fieldwork, asserts: 'I am a mak nyah (...) but I don't agree with the term "transgender." I already have my gender, my femaleness. Only my sex, my genitals need "trans." ' (Goh, 2014: 134). Furthermore, in exploring the spirituality of the Mak Nyah, Goh (2014) highlights the significance of this transformative process, emphasising its crucial role in redefining and affirming diverse gender identities within religious contexts:

> I engage in a queering of their spiritualities in order to reveal the multiple, migratory movements of their gender identities. (...) My queering project argues that the interminable resistance and transgression of oppressive sexual and gender normativities form a migratory praxis of power shifts, which generate empowerment for the mak nyahs of PT Foundation, and that this empowerment serves as the wellspring of their multiplex spiritualities.The objective of such an exploration is to reveal and name in a more articulate fashion the passion and alacrity with which they not only perform their designated tasks but also live and flourish as human persons who take great pride in who they are becoming (2014: 124).

Goh illuminates a multifaceted reality faced by queer individuals in Malaysia, characterised by intersecting factors such as nationality, ethnicity, religious affiliation, social class and the region's (post)colonial history. His theology embodies what Muslim theologian Ibrahim Abdurrahman Farajajé (2000: 20–21) terms 'Queer-in-Intersection'. This concept captures the intricate interplay and intermingling of various categories in the constitution, formation and deconstruction of bodies and identities. Goh's work underscores the complexity of queer experiences, highlighting the need for an intersectional approach that acknowledges the diverse factors shaping individual and collective identities within specific cultural and historical contexts.

Thus, Nyah-Islam spirituality accompanies the journey of Malaysian Mak-Nyahs in their self-understanding of the Muslim faith and in challenging the institutional Islam that oppresses through its 'instrument[s] of the regulatory regime' (Butler 1993: 308). Goh's work is pivotal, as it not only amplifies a distinctive queer theology within the Muslim context but also introduces these voices into academic discourse, illuminating their complexity and fostering dialogue with Christian and queer theologies. This scholarly engagement is further exemplified by the contributions of Sharon Bong (2009, 2011) in both the Malaysian and Singaporean contexts.

For Further Discussion

1   How might challenging 'political Islam' in favour of a more 'religious Islam' be beneficial for queer Muslims?

2   What role does the interpretation of religious texts play in shaping attitudes towards homosexuality within the Islamic community?

3   How do queer Muslims navigate the intersectionality of their religious identity and sexual orientation, particularly in societies where homosexuality may face societal or legal challenges?

4   Are there instances of progressive or inclusive interpretations of Islam that accept and support the LGBTQ+ community, and how are these perspectives received within the broader Islamic discourse?

5   How do Muslim-majority countries vary in their legal and societal treatment of homosexuality, and what factors contribute to these differences?

References

Abraham, Ibrahim (2007). "The Veil and the Closet: Islam and the Production of Queer Space." Proceedings of the Conference "Queer Space: Centres and Peripheries," University of Technology Sydney (UTS), Sydney, Australia, February 20–21, pp. 1–6.

Bong, Sharon A (2009). "Not 'For the Sake of Peace': Towards an Epistemology of the Sacred Body." *Asian Christian Review* 3, No. 1 (Spring): pp. 50–68.

Bong, Sharon A (2011). "Negotiating Resistance/Resilience through the Nexus of Spirituality-Sexuality of Same-Sex Partnerships in Malaysia and Singapore." *Marriage and Family Review* 47, No. 8 (December): pp. 648–665.

Butler, Judith (1993). *Bodies that Matter: On the Discursive Limits of Sex*. New York, NY: Routledge.

Cornwall, Susannah (2011). *Controversies in Queer Theology*, Controversies in Contextual Theology Series. London: SCM Press.

Farajajé, Ibrahim A (2000). "Loving 'Queer': We Are All a Big Mix of Possibilities of Desire Just Waiting to Happen." *The Family* 6, No. 1 (Summer): pp. 15–21.

Goh, Joseph N (2012). "Nyah–Islam: The Reconstruction of God and Institutional Islam by Malaysian Male-to-Female Transsexuals." *God's Image* 31, No. 2 (December): pp. 33–44.

Goh, Joseph N (2014). "Transgressive Empowerment: Queering the Spiritualities of the Mak Nyahs of PT Foundation." In: *Queering Migrations Towards, From, and Beyond Asia*, edited by Hugo Córdova Quero, Joseph N. Goh, and Michael Sepidoza Campos. New York, NY: Palgrave MacMilland, pp. 123–137.

Habib, Samar (2013). "Sexualities and Queer Studies." In: *Women and Islamic Cultures: Disciplinary Paradigms and Approaches: 2003–2013*, edited by Suad Joseph, Marilyn L Booth, Bahar Davary, Hoda El Sadda, Sarah Gualtieri, Vriginia Hooker, Therese Saliba and Elora Shehabuddin. Leiden: Brill, pp. 325–338.

Hendricks, Muhsin (2010). "Islamic Texts: A Source for Acceptance of Queer Individuals into Mainstream Muslim Society." *The Equal Rights Review* 5: pp. 31–51.

Huntington, Samuel P (1996). *The Clash of Civilizations and the Remaking of World Order*. New York, NY: Simon & Schuster.

Jahangir, Junaid (2013). "Why All Muslims Are Talking About Queer Sexuality." *The Huffington Post*, March 13. Available at: <http://www.huffingtonpost.ca/junaid-jahangir/queer-muslims_b_2855300.html>.

Kligerman, Nicole (2007). "Homosexuality in Islam: A Difficult Paradox." *Macalester Islam Journal* 2, No. 3: pp. 52–64.

Kugle, Scott and Stephen Hunt (2012). "Masculinity, Homosexuality and the Defence of Islam: A Case Study of Yusuf al-Qaradawi's Media Fatwa." *Religion and Gender* 2, No. 2: pp. 254–279.

La Rotta, Fernando R (2013). "Queer Ijtihad: Queer Muslim Intersectionality and a Close Reading of Islamic Texts." *Juhood: The Journal of Middle Eastern and North African Affairs* 3, No. 1. (Fall). Available at: <http://juhood.wixsite.com/juhood/queer-ijtihad-queer-muslim-intersection

Malaysiakini (May 22, 2012). "Manji: Allah Made Gays and Lesbians, Too." Available at: <http://www.malaysiakini.com/news/198652>.

Media Diversity Institute (2009). "A Jihad for Love," September 23. Available at: <https://www.media-diversity.org/a-jihad-for-love>.

Minwalla, Omar, B R Simon Rosser, Jamie Feldman and Christine Varga (2005). "Identity Experience among Progressive Gay Muslims in North America: A Qualitative Study within Al-Fatiha." *Culture, Health and Sexuality* 7, No. 2 (March): pp. 113–128.

Musić, Rusmir (2003). "Queer Visions of Islam." Master's Thesis in the John W. Draper Master's Program in Humanities and Social Thought. New York, NY: Graduate School of Arts and Science, New York University.

Nawi, Nor F (2007). *Principles of Public Administration: An Introduction.* Kuala Lumpur: Karisma Publications.

Netton, Ian R (1992). *A Popular Dictionary of Islam.* London: Curzon Press.

Newby, Gordon D (2002). *A Concise Encyclopedia of Islam.* Oxford: Oneworld.

Poljski, Carolyn (2011). *Coming Out, Coming Home or Inviting People in? Supporting Same-Sex Attracted Women from Immigrant and Refugee Communities.* Melbourne: Multicultural Centre for Women's Health.

Rahman, Momin (2010). "Queer as INtersectionalityL Theorizing Gay Muslim Identities." *Sociology* 44, No. 5: pp. 944–961.

Ruthven, Malise (1997). *Islam: A Very Short Introduction.* Oxford: Oxford University Press.

Sharma, Parvez, Dir. (2007). *A Jihad for Love*, 81 minutes. New York: NY, First Run Features, DVD.

Shannahan, Dervla S (2010). "Some Queer Questions from a Muslim Faith Perspective." *Sexualities* 13, No. 6: pp. 671–684.

Soon, Tamara (2010). *Islam: A Brief Introduction.* Chichester, West Sussex: Wiley-Blackwell.

Star, Jonathan, tr. (2008). *Jalal al-Din Rumi, Maulana, 1207–1273. [Selections] Rumi: In the Arms of the Beloved.* New York, NY: Penguin Books.

Wong, Yuenmei (2012). "Islam, Sexuality, and the Marginal Positioning of Pengkids and Their Girlfriends in Malaysia." *Journal of Lesbian Studies* 16: pp. 1–14.

Further Reading

Yip, Andrew K T (2003). "The Self as the Basis of Religious Faith: Spirituality of Gay, Lesbian, and Bisexual Christians." In: *Predicting Religion: Mainstream and Margins in the West*, edited by Grace Davie, Linda Woodhead and Paul Heelas. London: Ashgate, pp. 135–146.

Yip, Andrew K T (2004). "Negotiating Space with Family and Kin in Identity Construction: The Narratives of British Non-Heterosexual Muslims." *Sociological Review* 52, No. 3: pp. 336–350.

Yip, Andrew K T (2005). "Queering Religious Texts: An Exploration of British Non-Heterosexual Christians' and Muslims' Strategy of Constructing Sexuality-Affirming Hermeneutics." *Sociology* 39, No. 1: pp. 47–65.

About Karmic (Dharmic) Faiths: Buddhism, Hinduism, Jainism and Sikhism

Karmic faiths have been misunderstood as they have for generations been seen through the eyes of Abrahamic faiths. Karmic faiths view the idea of queer very differently as they do not understand the question as based in laws and commandments. These faiths are based on the idea of rebirth and so do not hold that there is only one life followed by an eternal afterlife, nor do they hold to damnation or salvation according to whether one keeps the commandments.

Belief in rebirth means that each entity is viewed as unique according to its(their) karmic burden. This accounts for the diversity in the world and also creates the idea that there is no blame for one's situation in life. Abrahamic faiths hold to the doctrine of equality, while karmic faiths have a doctrine of diversity and see society and people as ever changing. They are highly contextual and thrive on fluidity and are comfortable with heterogeneity.

They place greater emphasis on ritual practice than on scriptures and also place emphasis on experience. For example while Hindus have always valued their sacred books they see them as communicating an idea through chants, stories, song and music rather than containing a rigid code of life to be studied. The general belief is that rules need to be adapted to place, time and quality of community because the world is fluid and flexible going through many changes. The aim of rules in karmic faiths is to facilitate community living not to create good people.

Karmic faiths are often confused with tribal and Oriental faiths, but this is incorrect as is the putting together of the tribal religions of India under the heading Hinduism.

How do karmic faiths understand queers? There are no scriptures which condemn queers, and so one has to look to stories to get any sort of answer to this question. Hinduism has stories of gods becoming goddesses, but at the same time while there are stories of same-sex friendship there is no overt reference to same-sex sexuality. Many have argued that this shows Hindus more comfortable with gender than sexuality. A case in point may be that India acknowledges and gives rights to 'third gender' people but not homosexuals.

However, despite no obvious condemnation of sexuality within the hermit traditions in these faiths there is a distrust of sexuality which is seen as polluting. Nevertheless despite outlining purification rituals for those involved in non-vaginal sex these rituals are more severe for heterosexuals who commit adultery or rape. Karmic faiths believe the living owe a debt to their ancestors which is repaid by marrying and having children which may seem to preclude same-sex marriage. However, as marriage is viewed as between souls not bodies some karmic scholars do not indeed preclude same-sex marriage.

Karmic Faiths Can Affirm Queer Dignity

There is no such thing as Judgement Day in karmic religions, and so God is not seen as a judge and eternal damnation is not a concept. Karmic faiths believe that the divine is infinite and infinity has no boundaries but is fluid and so includes everything and everyone. This is contrasted with the human mind which is limited and does not understand the complexities of existence so should just accept even what we do not understand. Karmic faiths understand our bodies and personalities as outcomes of karmic burden, and therefore they are as they should be and wisdom lies in accepting them as they are in us and in others. Condemnation would come from the limited human mind not the essence of the divine.

Karmic faith encourages people to develop knowledge which helps us understand and accommodate the wide variety of people in the world. Prejudices that were once acceptable are no longer so and people need to change with the times. This includes thinking very practically about matters such as families including queer people and addressing matters such as care for old queer people. As karmic religions view marriage as between souls they do not prohibit gay marriage. Further, as they affirm that God is within us and that we realise the infinite divine through the other they encourage openness to queer people who also carry the divine within them. One discovers God within by being more open hearted to others.

Of course it has to be taken into account that karmic faiths are not homogeneous as they contain many sects and communities, but the overarching fundamental wisdom that they hold in common makes it possible to accept queer people. This understanding may not be evident in the countries and states in which these religions are practised, but that does not change the fundamental precepts that allow for inclusion of queer people.

7

Hinduism

The Om/aum is one of the symbols of Hinduism and is understood to be the sacred sound symbol that represents the universe.

Of all these religions, Hinduism because of its multilayer composite offers many non-heteronormative examples already present in the sacred texts as well as the praxis of the believers. This is because religion is a conglomerate of many different spiritual paths. At the same time, it is not easy to disconnect Hinduism from its place of origin. However, we need to remember that Hinduism is a global religion, with followers in many regions of the modern World-System and therefore take faith and sacred texts related to gender and sexuality in multiple ways due to the different contexts. We may need to consider the possibility that Hinduism has already created 'queer theologies' due to the character of its teachings. However, those theologies are not named as such.

Hinduism as a Religion

India is sometimes called a sub-continent; this is because it is so large and gathers so many nations and cultures that the contrast is impossible to be avoided from region to region. This is translated not only in different languages or cultural values but also in different religions.

Therefore, Hinduism is an umbrella term to gather under one label the many different religions that express the local beliefs of villages and even social classes, which in India are organised into a caste system. Many of these religions indeed have common denominators, which can be traced as early as the twelfth century CE (Nicholson, 2010: 2), but they have particular distinctiveness from each other.

The term Hindu is the result of several transformations. It comes from the Sanskrit term Shindu, the Indo-Aryan term for the Indus River which runs across Tibet, Pakistan and India. The Aryans were the main inhabitants of the region (Tewari & Tewari, 2009: 35) and constitute the base for the Brahmin caste, which originally was the priestly caste and located at the top of the caste system. There are three other castes in lower progression: *Kshatriyas,* military caste, *Vaishyas,* merchants, landowners and peasants caste and *Shudras,* the servants subordinated to the other three castes. There is another group called *Dalits* which literally means 'oppressed' in Sanskrit or 'the untouchables', who are the cobblers, street sweepers and latrine cleaners. They are technically outside the caste system and are at the lowest of the lowest caste, the Shudras. The term *Shindu* evolved in Persian as *Hindū* to designate the 'people who live across the Indus river' (Flood, 1996: 6). Later the Arabic transformed the term into Al-Hind which means literally across the Indus river (Thapar, 1993: 77), from which the European language took the term as *Hindu.* In the thirteenth century, the region was named as Hindustan, that is 'land of the Hindus' (Thompson Platts, 1884).

It was British colonialism in the nineteenth century that extended the notion of a 'Hindu religion' or 'Hinduism' as a single religion (King, 1999a: 2). When the British colonisers took India, they relied on information about society from the perspective of the privileged caste, the Brahmin (King, 1999b: 171). In fact, Richard King (1999a) states that 'British scholars closely aligned with Britain's imperial project looked for an Indian analogue to the Western Religions that they already knew' (1999a: 1). Therefore, it was based on the information provided by the Brahmin, the British colonisers fixed the term Hinduism for this new religion that they created.

In fact, in order to reach this goal, the British colonisers took the writings of the Brahmin—representing only 3% of the immense amount of sacred scriptures—for translation, thus dismissing the writings of the other castes, which represented 97% of the sacred scriptures as Paola Bacchetta affirms:

> Orientalism was a completely European enterprise, embedded in colonial relations of power, from its inception. Orientalist, which began in 1757, operated to reconstruct "knowledge" of India. While this reconstruction was multifaceted, what concerns us here is the fact that orientalist operated to condemn or marginalise what now are designated as dissident genders and sexualities, as it reconstituted and redefined the Hindu symbolic. To make sense out of the multitude of Hindu sacred texts, oral traditions, and practices, orientalist divided them into two categories that are still operative today in some circles: a "Great Tradition" (comprised of texts of the Brahmin elite, or 3 percent of the Hindu population) and a "Little Tradition" (Hinduism of the masses). Orientalist selectively translated "Great Tradition" works and left "Little Tradition" works by the wayside (1999: 146).

The moral views of the British colonisers could not stand sacred writings that openly and without the shame which was so ingrained in the Western world depicted gender and sexuality related to religion in a positive way. Although the British coined Hinduism as a religion, the caste system continues to be an important aspect of the religions now grouped as a new religion.

Branches of Hinduism

Hinduism can be classified either by philosophies or by deities. The classification by deities offers us better ways to identify the different branches of Hinduism. The following chart illustrates branches of Hinduism:

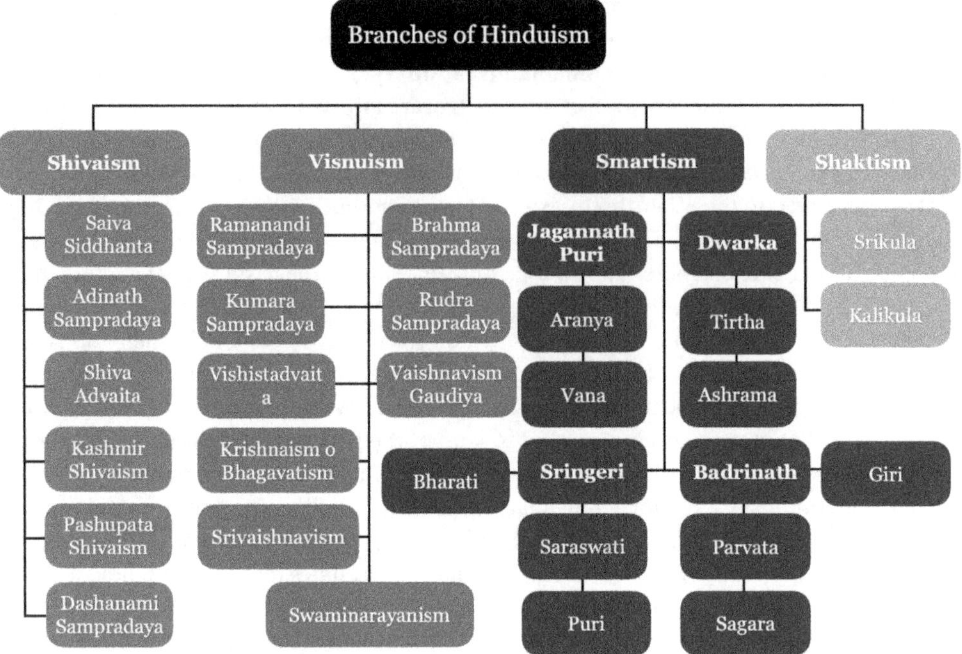

Graphic 7.1   Branches of Hinduism

Hindu Queer Theologies

It may seem that no other religion has elements for the development of queer theologies in the same way that Hinduism has. Acknowledging that 'theology' is a Western term, we employ it as a heuristic tool to comprehend the intricacies of Hinduism. Simultaneously, three intersecting aspects warrant consideration in the formulation of what could be termed as 'Hindu Queer Theologies'. First, an exploration of Hindu scriptures, rituals and historical perspectives is imperative. Second, an examination of the diverse expressions of gender and sexuality within Hindu culture is essential. Lastly, an analysis of contemporary reinterpretations and inclusive movements within Hinduism must be undertaken. By delving into these facets, a nuanced understanding of Hinduism's potential for embracing queer theologies emerges, enriching the discourse on spirituality and inclusivity. Ruth Vanita states that in Hinduism 'principles of attraction and fusion take primacy over gender. This happens not just in written texts but also in some social practices, where same-sex marriage between a God and a human is institutionalized' (2009: 75).

Box 7.1

Sanskirt is the language of Hindu scriptures and is a standardised dialect of old Indo-Aryan originating in the Vedic scriptures as early as 1700 BCE. *It has three words for gender masculine, feminine and gender neutral.*

As a karmic faith Hinduism believes that the actions of a previous life affect the way in which one will incarnate in the next. This could be as human or non-human or even not entirely human. The physical body is understood to be endowed with a pre-provided set of psycho-sexual traits that remain manifest in its lifetime. Gender is one such trait. Hindus believe that the immortal soul has no gender and no orientation, while the psycho-sexual body is the seat of emotions, desires and moral agency. Therefore, a psycho-sexual woman could be stuck in a male body or vice versa as well as holding a variety of orientations that the body inherits from its karmic past. The Hindi scripture the Bhagavad Gita declares: In every body resides the divine who witnesses, guides, supports and enjoys all that the body experiences (Bhagavad Gita, chapter13, verse 22).

Box 7.2

The Bhagavad Gita is a 700-verse poem which is part of the Mahabharata.

Box 7.3

The Mahabharata is the longest poem in the world and was written by Vyasa. It contains hundreds of smaller stories within it. Believed to have been written between 1,500 and 2,000 BCE.

Even the gods and goddess in Hindu mythology exhibit gender fluidity and queer orientations.

Queer Deities

Hinduism has multiple manifestations of the divine many of which would within the language of the West be called queer.

Agni is one example who is the god of fire, wealth and creativity who rides on a ram, has two heads, multiple arms and tongues and flaming red skin. While he is married to the goddess Svaha he is often shown as having a relationship with Soma the god of the moon and delighting in swallowing his semen. Another major story about him says he volunteers to accept the semen of Shiva who in the myth is not allowed to ejaculate into his wife Parvati due to the fear of the other gods that such an event would result in an extremely powerful deity. Agni is therefore eagerly standing by to swallow Shiva's semen.

A further example is Ganesha who is the god of wisdom and remover of obstacles. He is seen as a chubby deity with four arms and an elephant's head. As he is overweight he is usually depicted with enlarged breasts that are believed by followers to lactate. Although his trunk is seen as phallic it is always flaccid and his appearance is understood as androgynous not least because of an elephant's head and a human body. Ganesha is also the

Source: Katikam/Adobe Stock Photos.

Source: Bardel, Louis Thomas (1804-p.1841) / Wikimedia Commons / Public domain.

Source: Cavan/Adobe Stock Photos.

deity of the root chakra which is located between the genitals and the anus and as such presides over ritualistic anal sex practised amongst certain sects in an effort to release kundalini energy.

Krishna is the god of love, beauty, knowledge and divinity. He is shown with blue skin and is eternally beautiful. He is represented in many myths and is often shown as changing gender and being sexually fluid seducing anyone regardless of gender. In one myth he is even shown as seducing himself. Many of his followers understand him to be the model of a man embracing his femininity, and they too strive to find a balance of gentle femininity and sexualised masculinity.

Shikhandi is a female-to-male transgendered hero in the Mahabharata. In a past life she was female and swore to avenge herself after the warrior Bhishma rejected her and said she was unmarriageable. She killed herself after Krishna promised she would be reincarnated as male and therefore able to avenge her honour. Sadly she was reborn as a female but was brought up by King Drupada as a boy who married her to a princess. However, the princess discovered her true gender and complained to her father that they had been deceived. Shikhandi fled to the forest where a sympathetic nature spirit swapped sexes with her making her biologically male as Krishna had promised. He finds himself in the epic battle of Mahabharat where he played a significant role in killing Bhishma.

Brihanalla is a man who loses his manhood for a year and lives as a woman. There are many more examples of gods who change gender, for example, Bhagashavava is a woman who lives part of her life as a man, husband and father and the rest as a woman, wife and mother. Amazingly, another myth speaks of Yuvanashva who drinks a magic potion and becomes pregnant and delivers a baby from his thigh. Aruna, the god of the dawn, is of intermediate gender and chooses to become a woman. All these descriptions of inherent gender fluidity and diversity demonstrate how at ease with queer manifestations the ancients were. They should be read as metaphorical vehicles to communicate complex ideas about metaphysics, sexuality, diversity and human nature. For example, the image of Ardha-Nareshwara the half-woman god can either indicate a queer form like the hijra or indicate the union of the mind(god) with matter(goddess) creating a complete whole. In this way suggesting the holistic unity of the universe or the incompleteness of the masculine principle without the animating force of the feminine.

Moving forward from the age of myths to 2016 we see that a place of worship was founded by transgender priests during the Ujjain Kumbha Mela and was headed by a well-known transgender activist Lakshmi Narayan Tripathi. At the ceremony Tripathi was anointed by various Hindu leaders demonstrating a gradual mainstreaming of the hijra community. It has been noted that this venture also helped bridge the gap between LGB and transgender folk. Interestingly, transgender folk have been viewed as the more traditional expression of Indian culture, while LGB are seen as a modern manifestation. However, the idea of homosexuality as a sin does not fit into the Hindu religious frame as it does not conceptually fit with an idea of karma and infinite birth. This has meant that within Hindu cultures homosexuality has never been punished. Fascinatingly the Caraka Samhita which is an ancient Vedic medical text lists eight types of men who are unable to have sex with women. Of the eight two are particularly interesting for our present purpose, the first Dviretas explains that a person is born with male and female seed, while the third Samskaravahi says that the man can only be aroused according to previous life impressions. Here we see a medical 'explanation' with religious roots and no condemnation.

Box 7.4

The Kurukshetra War is described in the Hindu epic poem Mahabharata. The battle was between Kauravas and Pandavas which lasted for 18 days and was won by the Pandavas.

Autochthonous 'Hindu Queer Theologies'

It is plausible to contemplate that Hinduism has, perhaps inadvertently, given rise to 'queer theologies' through the inherent nature of its teachings. Though these theologies may not have been explicitly labelled as such, this lack of nomenclature is inconsequential considering the affirming stance towards gender, sexuality, desire and pleasure prevalent in sacred texts over millennia. The absence of explicit nomenclature does not diminish the potential richness of queer theologies within Hinduism, which can be discerned through an exploration of its teachings and their inclusive perspectives on diverse aspects of human experience. Notably, pleasure holds a pivotal role in Hindu spirituality, as emphasised by Anantanand Rambachan:

> Krishna's teaching in the Bhagavadgītā about the transient nature of pleasure follows logically from his statement that experiences with a beginning inevitably come to an end. As a subjective experience, pleasure is associated with our own classifications of objects and persons as desirable, undesirable, or neutral and the consequent development of likes (rāga) and dislikes (dveṣa) that condition our responses. In the gain of that which we regard as desirable and which conforms to our likes, we experience pleasure. The opposite occurs in the case of the undesirable object or person. Likes and dislikes are constantly shifting, objects and

persons change, and, as Naciketas observed, the instruments of enjoyment decline and wane. Pleasures turn out to be capricious, leaving us wanting and incomplete. Understanding the fickle nature of pleasures leads to the state of informed detachment, quite different from a self-denial that is based on fear or the rejection of pleasures (2015: 22).

For Hinduism, the challenge lies not in pleasure itself but in understanding its intricate connections with other facets of existence. Simultaneously, one's sexual orientation is not a source of concern. Rambachan says:

> In Advaita [Vedānta], persons are not valued for their procreative abilities or sex. Human work is the outcome of the immense of brahman, and the discerning of this truth is equated with liberation (mokṣa). The equal and identical presence of brahman in all is the ground for human dignity and equal justice. the tradition emphasizes the inclusivity of divine love and the accessibility of liberation. The significance of sexual identity, homosexual or heterosexual, has to be seen in relation to the teaching that the self (ātmā) is not bound or limited by sexual specifications (2015: 130).

In numerous Hindu traditions, the theological framework has inherently positioned bodies, desires, sexuality, pleasure and sexual diversity in a manner that advocates and rejoices in what can be termed as 'Hindu Queer Theologies'. It is important to approach this concept cautiously, recognising that urging Hinduism to explicitly label its theologies in this manner might inadvertently perpetuate colonial influences. Such imposition could be detrimental, particularly in light of our next consideration. Emphasising the sensitivity of terminology, we strive to avoid imposing Western constructs on the diverse and nuanced landscape of Hindu thought. That cautious approach ensures a respectful engagement with Hinduism's inherent inclusivity and allows for a more authentic exploration of the rich tapestry of theological perspectives within the tradition.

Colonialism and Homophobia

Until the arrival of colonialism, the situation regarding gender and sexuality may have been very different from what is today in countries that follow Hinduism such as India. In order to queer Hinduism we need to acknowledge that homophobia was exported from the West by British missionaries. That was coupled with the anti-sodomy law enacted by the British rulers in 1860, who introduced section 337 in their attempts to 'moralize' India. The section reads:

> 377. Unnatural offences: Whoever voluntarily has carnal intercourse against the order of nature with any man, woman or animal, shall be punished with imprisonment for life, or with imprisonment of either description for term which may extend to ten years, and shall also be liable to fine.
>
> Explanation: Penetration is sufficient to constitute the carnal intercourse necessary to the offense described in this section (India Code, n.d.).

This legislation significantly disrupted the established norms within Indian society concerning sexuality, impacting groups such as the Hijras.

Box 7.5

Hijras are born male but dress and act as female. Many undergo castration ceremonies as an offering to the goddess Bahuchara Mata. They tend to live in communities that follow a kinship system known as the guru–chela system.

The legal intervention had far-reaching consequences, reshaping societal agreements and challenging the traditional understanding of sexual diversity and identity. Therefore, as Ruth Vanita states:

> Most Indian nationalists internalized this homophobia and came to view homosexuality as an unspeakable crime, even as they also attacked polygamy, courtesan culture, matriliny, polyandry, and other institutions that were seen as opposed to heterosexual monogamous marriage. Prior to this, homosexuality had never been considered unspeakable in Indian texts or r̥eligions. [...] Homophobia is thus only one aspect of their larger opposition to all forms of erotic love outside marriage, which they view as products of globalization, Western neo-imperialism, and market forces that commercialize sex (2009: 2).

Box 7.6

Hijras appear in Hindu mythology. When Lord Rama was banished to the forest he ordered all men and women to leave and return to the city so the people training with him were the hijra. He was so moved by their loyalty that he conferred the power to offer blessings at marriages and child birth.

While it is true that queer individuals often bear the brunt of cis-heteropatriarchalism, it is imperative to scrutinise the underlying structures perpetuating these consequences. A deeper examination allows for a more nuanced understanding of the complex dynamics at play and facilitates targeted efforts towards dismantling oppressive systems:

> While the stigmatisation of homosexuals in Hindu society seems particularly connected with the value of male progeny, this desire is explicable in the context of labor needs in an agricultural economy and high infant mortality rates. The need for a male child to perform postmortem rituals that avert the suffering of the parent belies the core Hindu teaching about the doctrine of karma. Today, we need to put more emphasis on personal responsibility (Rambachan, 2015: 129).

Box 7.7

Ila is a rare case of female-to-male transition. Her parents wanted a son and their prayers were answered; however, through the course of her/his life he transitioned back and forwards even marrying a man while in a female phase. He remained male in the end due to the blessing of Shiva.

The material consequences of colonialism joined the previous social organisation and stratification with its concomitant cis-heterosexual division of labour and the gender role expectations in Hindu society. That is a key element that may enlighten the discussions about the negative views of same-sex desire in itself or about the perception that same-sex relations have within the complex and interrelated social stratification. In this latter case, for example, the Western 'coming out' narrative may produce negative consequences over the lives of people who have to manage to negotiate their desire and the expected duties within the cis-heterosexual division of labour in that society.

Arvind Sharma highlights a very thorough analysis of the dilemmas faced by Hinduism when confronted with the topic of 'homosexuality'. As Sharma cleverly asserts 'The discussion of homosexuality in Hinduism is therefore beset with difficulties. First, there is the terminological problem [...]. Then there is the problem of the limited nature of the evidence available' (1993: 49). In other words, terms such as 'homosexuality', 'gay' or 'queer' did not exist prior to the nineteenth century. Therefore, expecting them to appear in history, sacred texts or religious teachings as such is impossible. At the same time, the evidence of same-sex relations and activities may be present in those realms, but also made invisible by cultural and political agendas.

The way that he addresses the topic of same-sex features in Hinduism and its relation to culture is certainly innovative. By taking the Puruṣārthas or four ends of humans, Sharma explores the aspects of *dharma, artha, kāma* and *mokṣa*. The meaning of these concepts is as follows:

a) *Dharma*: Righteousness
b) *Artha*: Wealth
c) *Kāma*: Pleasure of the flesh and
d) *Mokṣa*: Release from transmigratory existence, or liberation (Swami Harshananda, 2008).

While the first three concepts, *dharma, artha* and *kāma,* are developed in the Vedas, the concept of *mokṣa* is only developed in the Upaniṣads (Hiltebeitel, 2002: 17). If we focus only in the concepts from the Vedas, they are called *trivarga* [three categories], while the four concepts are known as *caturvarga* [four categories]. Rajendra Prasad (2008: 360) expounds on the trivarga's emphasis on social spheres, asserting that while it delineates societal duties, the distinct recognition of *Mokṣa* underscores the personal realm. This elucidates the intricate interplay between communal responsibilities and individual spiritual aspirations within Hindu philosophical discourse. The *trivarga,* comprising *dharma, artha* and *kama,* delineates societal norms, while *mokṣa* represents the ultimate pursuit of liberation from worldly attachments. Prasar's insight sheds light on the nuanced understanding of Hindu ethics, where societal obligations coexist with the pursuit of personal enlightenment, thus offering a holistic perspective on the human experience within the Hindu tradition.

It is interesting at the end of the chapter how Sharma states:

> The influence of the Ghandhian idealism that imparted a puritanical tone to Indian nationalism, of the Independence Movement, of Gandhi himself [...], and of the depiction of the struggle for independence as between virtue and vice [...] has injected a stronger dimension into the assessment of homosexuality than might have been the case otherwise (1993: 70).

One may think that those fighting for some liberation would support other liberations, but the case often is that in the midst of some struggles, others are made invisible or even condemned in order to achieve a good outcome in what is seen as the main struggle. It seems that in India, this was the case with homosexuality. Sharma states that 'We should, however, distinguish between Hindu religious attitudes and Hindu cultural attitudes. As a religion, Hinduism is perhaps more tolerant of homosexuality than it is as a culture, and the underlying reason seems to be historical' (1993: 68).

On the other hand, Jeffrey S. Lidke repeats a line of argument that was also present in Sharma's piece (1993: 68–69), namely, the role that Muslims played in making visible same-sex acts in Indian society. Lidke states:

> The institutionalization of the antisodomy act instilled in Hindu India a homopho-bic reaction that has yet to be purged or understood. Hindu apologetics were quick to claim that homosexuality and its variants were foreign to Hinduism, that they entered the subcontinent with the Muslims and later with the British, thus ignoring the multiple themes and descriptions of same-sex love in their classical textual and cultural traditions (2003: 127).

It is interesting that Hindu people and Hinduism often blame Muslim people for the presence of homosexuality in India. This perspective appears to be an excuse to obscure and deny the existence of sexual diversity within the subcontinent, which has been present long before the arrival of any foreign religion. By attributing homosexuality to external influences, this viewpoint attempts to erase the rich and varied history of same-sex love and relationships in India's autochthonous cultural and religious traditions.

In the same vein, it is noteworthy to point out that Vanita's edited anthology is a signifi-cant contribution to the study of sexuality in India, exploring the diverse expressions of same-sex love and desire within Indian history, literature, religion and culture. The book brings together essays from various scholars, offering a comprehensive examination of how same-sex relationships and eroticism have been understood and represented in Indian society. The collection includes analyses of historical texts, contemporary literature, film and popular culture, illustrating the presence and significance of queer identities and rela-tionships in India. By challenging cis-heteronormative assumptions and highlighting the fluidity of gender and sexual identities, *Queering India* opens up new avenues for under-standing the complexities of Indian society and its engagement with issues of sexuality and eroticism. Ruth Vanita's work is notable for its interdisciplinary approach and its effort to place Indian experiences within a global context of queer studies.

Decolonising Sacred Texts

A third aspect that impacts negatively in the way that gender and sexuality is perceived in society is the cis-heterosexualisation of the 'entire literary canons and genres (such as the Urdu ghazal, or love poem, which gendered both lover and beloved as male)' (Vanita, 2009: 2) carried out by the British colonial power. Again, even when the sacred texts supported what we could now call as 'Hindu Queer Theologies', much damage has been done inten-tionally based on a narrow understanding of Western scholars. On this Vanita says:

> Unlike some other religions, Hinduism has not one but thousands of sacred texts. If a line disapproving of same-sex unions can be found in one text, a story celebrating it can be found in another. Modern Hindu right-wing organizations are attempting to stamp out this diversity by imposing a uniform authoritarian version, with little scriptural backing, from above (2009: 7).

In the same line, Rambachan declares that:

> The homophobia that is now discernible in sections of the Hindu community is absent in the ancient texts. While there are certain legal penalties for homosexual conduct mentioned in the law codes, these are really mild in nature, and there is no evidence on medical treatises of attempts to convert or cure homosexuals. [...] We need to remember also that the term "homosexuality," like "heterosexuality," should not be narrowly equated with sex. The issue, as with heterosexuality, is about preferences in relationships and the values of love, justice, loyalty, trust, caring and friendship that are at the heart of all good relationships. We need to emphasise the importance of these values in relationships (2015: 129–130).

Beyond the ostensibly Western-centric and cis-heteronormative lens through which Rambachan portrays relationships, the significance of his scholarship, alongside that of his peers, lies in its critique of the prevalent absence of condemnatory homophobia within sacred texts. This observation underscores a colonial endeavour to impose foreign interpretations onto these texts, thereby desacralising their intrinsic meaning. Rambachan's work highlights the imperative of revisiting and recontextualising religious narratives to reveal their inherent diversity and inclusivity, countering prevailing biases. Such scholarly efforts contribute to a more nuanced understanding of religious traditions, fostering dialogue and fostering greater acceptance within diverse communities.

The accepting tone of the Hindu sacred regards gender and sexuality can be observed in the case of the 'third sex'. The Vedas, for example, recognise a 'third sex', embracing individuals whose sexuality is not procreative due to factors like impotence or a lack of desire for the opposite sex. Notably, members of this third sex are not ostracised but are occasionally acknowledged for possessing divine powers or unique insights. Such an inclusive stance reflects a nuanced understanding of sexuality within Hinduism, challenging stereotypes and promoting a more accepting approach towards diverse expressions of human sexuality within the cultural and spiritual context of Hindu traditions.

For example, the Hijras are considered a 'third-sex/gender' in India. Every society with a rigid system like India with the caste and arranged marriages systems, needs a way for some folks to escape from this situation. One way has been to separate between the social mandate, to marry and procreate, and the search for pleasure with the same or the opposite sex. The situation is very complex as it entails public discourses and private practices, social mandates and personal leeway, and not all heterosexual males are able to pursue this. However, there are some individuals who have been granted the possibility to do so.

The Hijras have been able to bend the social mandate to marry and procreate and live a different life. They are free to pursue their lives and it is considered 'lucky' to have a Hijra at one's wedding and they received monetary compensation for this 'presence', although this is an unspoken rule. As mentioned above they may also offer blessings at weddings. Hijras also exist in other parts of South Asia. The situation of the Hijras in Pakistan and Bangladesh is not that different from their counterparts in India, and in both areas many of them work as sex workers. Not all Hijras pursue a sexual life as some have chosen celibate lives.

Further insights into Hindu perspectives on sexuality are found in the Kamasutra, a revered text that delves into the art and pleasures of sexuality. Particularly, it advocates for the enjoyment of same-sex experiences:

> Even young men, servants who wear polished earrings, indulge in oral sex only with certain men And, in the same way, certain men-about-town who care for one another's welfare and have established trust do this service for one another (Kamasutra II, 9.35–36).

That perspective underscores a broader acceptance of diverse expressions of human sexuality within the cultural and spiritual framework of Hinduism. Hugh B. Urban (2010) is part of an interesting book that focuses on Tantra. Tantra is an esoteric tradition closely related to Shaktism, although there are followers in Shaivism and Vaishnavism (Flood, 2005). Gavin D. Flood (2005: 158) affirms that the earliest Tantra texts in which Tantric practices were described dates from 600 CE, although the term 'Tantra' appears about 500 BCE. Regarding Tantra in Hinduism, Georg Feuerstein explains that unfortunately,

> Tantra gradually fell into disrepute because of the radical antinomian practices of some of its adherents. During the Victorian colonization of India, puritanism drove Tantric practitioners underground. Today Tantra survives mainly in the conservative (samaya) holds of the Shrī-Vidyā tradition of South Indian and the Buddhist tradition of Tibet, though both heritages also have their more radical practitioners who understandably prefer to stay out of the public limelight (1998: x).

As a long tradition, Tantra was appropriated in the West. One of the consequences of this was the development of Tantra massage through the hand of the neotantric movement (Stubbs and Saulnier, 1999). Tantra in the West may be very different from what it has been across the history of Hinduism. On this Urban states:

> Tantra as we know it is to a large degree a complex creation of what Mary Louise Pratt calls the "contact zone," that is, "the space of colonial encounters ... in which peoples geographically and historically separated come into contact with each other ... involving conditions of coercion, radical inequality and conflict." To reiterate, however: this is surely not to say that Tantra is simply a colonialist fabrication or Orientalist projection onto the colonised Other. Rather, it is to say that the colonial era witnessed a clear "trend toward conceiving of a new entity called Tantrism as a specific modality of Indian religions experience," as the diverse body of texts known as āgamas, nigamas, saṃhitās, tantras, and so on, and the vast body of traditions known as Kāpālika, Pāñcarātra, Kula, Krama, Śākta, Śrīvidyā, and others, were gradually assimilates into a singular universal entity (2008: 44–45).

It is important to remember that colonialism has left lasting consequences. Nevertheless, these ancient texts challenge contemporary assumptions and highlight the historical existence of a more inclusive and accepting attitude towards sexual diversity within Hindu traditions. This rich tapestry of perspectives contributes to the ongoing discourse on the intersection of spirituality and sexuality, urging a reevaluation of societal norms and fostering greater understanding.

Hindu scholars cover a wide range of aspects related to gender, sexuality, desire, bodies and passion within the context of Hinduism. However, their work cannot always be regarded as 'theological' texts in light of the Western expectations of the term. They cover aspects of beliefs in connection to their cultural and societal context. Ruth Vanita (2005) is perhaps one of the most renowned scholars in the field of Hinduism and sexuality. In her work, Vanita details various ways in which marriage or weddings relate to the divinities and the believers within Hinduism. She examines the sacred rituals and ceremonies that connect marital unions to divine blessings, emphasising the spiritual significance of these traditions. One interesting aspect of this piece is how Vanita maintains a dialogue with Plato and his famous work *Symposium*, drawing parallels and contrasts between Platonic and Hindu notions of love and union. Additionally, she engages with the Judeo-Christian background in the West to unpack these topics in the Indian context, highlighting both commonalities and distinctions. By doing so, Vanita bridges Eastern and Western philosophies, offering a comparative theological perspective. Her approach can be seen as 'theologizing' in the broad sense of 'God(s)/(esses)-talk', as she explores divine–human relationships and their implications for understanding marriage across different cultural and religious landscapes. Such interdisciplinary method enriches the discourse on theology and religious studies, providing deeper insights into the universal aspects of spiritual and marital bonds, thus enriching further theologising.

For Further Discussion

1   In considering the assertion about a differentiation between religion and culture in their varying attitudes towards homosexuality, how do you perceive this dynamic within Hinduism, and do you think similar distinctions exist in other religions?

2   Reflecting on the content of this chapter, how has it influenced your comprehension of the intersection between queer studies and Hinduism? Furthermore, how do you reconcile this with the coexistence of evidence indicating the prohibition of homosexuality in certain sacred texts?

3   Given the complexities explored in the chapter regarding Hinduism and homosexuality, what insights does it provide into the broader dialogue on the relationship between religious doctrines and LGBTQ+ acceptance? How might these insights be applicable to understanding similar dynamics in other religious traditions?

4   How do you interpret the historical perspectives on sexual diversity within Hinduism, and in what ways do these interpretations influence contemporary discussions on LGBTQ+ rights and acceptance in Hindu communities?

5   Considering the acknowledgment of a 'third sex' and the nuanced perspectives on sexuality in Hindu texts, how might these ancient insights inform discussions on modern LGBTQ+ identities and contribute to fostering greater inclusivity within Hindu societies?

References

Bacchetta, Paola (1999). "When the (Hindu) Nation Exiles Its Queers." *Social Text* 61 (Winter): pp. 141–166.

Feuerstein, Georg (1998). *Tantra: The Path of Ecstasy*. Boston, MA: Shambhala.

Flood, Gavin D (1996). *An Introduction to Hinduism*. Cambridge: Cambridge University Press.

Flood, Gavin D (2005). *The Tantric Body: The Secret Tradition of Hindu Religion*. Hampshire: I.B Taurus.

Harshananda, Swami (2008). *The Concise Encyclopedia of Hinduism, Vol. 1*. Bangalore: Ram Krishna Math.

Hiltebeitel, Alf (2002). "Hinduism." In: *The Religious Traditions of Asia: Religion, History and Culture*, edited by M Joseph. Kitagawa. London: Routledge, pp. 3–40.

India Code (1836). "Section 377. Unnatural offences." Available at: <https://www.indiacode. nic.in/show-data?actid=AC_CEN_5_23_00037_186045_1523266765688&orderno=434>.

King, Richard (1999a). *Orientalism and Religion: Post-Colonial Theory, India and "The Mystic East"*. London: Routledge.

King, Richard (1999b). "Orientalism and the Modern Myth of 'Hinduism'." *Numen* 46: pp. 146–185.

Lidke, Jeffrey S (2003). "A Union of Fire and Water: Sexuality and Spirituality in Hinduism." In: *Sexuality and World's Religions*, edited by David W Machacek and Melissa M Wilcox. Santa Barbara, CA: ABC CLIO, pp. 101–132.

Nicholson, Andrew J (2010). *Unifying Hinduism: Philosophy and Identity in Indian Intellectual History*, South Asia Across the Disciplines Series. New York, NY: Columbia University Press.

Prasad, Rajendra (2008). *A Conceptual-Analytical Study of Classical Indian Philosophy of Morals*, History of Science, Philosophy, and Culture in Indian Civilisation Vol. 12, part 1. New Delhi: Concept/Centre for Studies in Civilizations.

Rambachan, Anantanand (2015). *A Hindu Theology of Liberation: Not-Two Is Not One*. Albany, NY: State University of New York Press.

Sharma, Arvind (1993). "Homosexuality and Hinduism." In: *Homosexuality and World Religions*, edited by Arlene Swidler. Valley Forge, PA: Trinity Press International, pp. 47–80.

Stubbs, Kenneth Ray and Louise-Andrée Saulnier (1999). *Tantric Massage: The Erotic Touch of Love*. London: Rider.

Tewari, Babita and Sanjay Tewari (2009). "The History of Indian Women: Hinduism at Crossroads with Gender." *Politics and Religion* 1, No. 3: pp. 25–47.

Thapar, Romila (1993). *Interpreting Early India*. Delhi: Oxford University Press.

Thompson Platts, John (1884). *A Dictionary of Urdu, Classical Hindī, and English*. Oxford: W. H. Allen & Co.

Urban, Hugh B (2008). *Tantra: Sex, Secrecy, Politics, and Power in the Study of Religion*. Delhi: Motilal Banarsidass Publisher.

Urban, Hugh B (2010). *The Power of Tantra: Religion, Sexuality, and the Politics of South Asian Studies*. London: I. B. Tauris.

Vanita, Ruth (2005). *Love's Rite: Same-Sex Marriage in India and the West*. New York, NY: Palgrave MacMillan.

Vanita, Ruth (2009). "Same-Sex Weddings, Hindu Traditions, and Modern India." *Feminist Review* 91: pp. 47–60.

Further Reading

Vanita, Ruth (editor) (2002). *Queering India: Same Sex Love and Eroticism in Indian Culture and Society*. New York, NY: Routledge.

Vatsyayana, Mallanaga (2009). *Kamasutra*, translated by Wendy Doniger and Sudhir Kakar, Oxford World's Classics Series. Oxford: Oxford University Press.

8

Buddhism

The Dharmachakra or eight-spoked wheel represents the Buddha and Buddhism.

As one of the oldest religions, Buddhism has taken root throughout Asia and other continents. As with any other global religion, many branches, interpretations, emphasis and culturally based decisions affect the faithful's daily-lived experiences. Talking about Buddhist Queer Dharmologies refers to an area of Buddhism that is still emerging. However, significant precedents of works and praxis uphold the inclusiveness of several traditions and schools of Buddhism.

Buddhism as a Religion

Buddhism is a pantheistic religion believing there is a divine force in everything that exists, and, although it is a non-theistic religion, it has deities, including female deities. Buddhist philosophy is based on the Vedas of Hinduism, and originated from the teachings of Siddhārta Gautama, who became the Buddha [enlightened] in India in the fifth–fourth century BCE.

Global Queer Theologies: Intercontextual and Interreligious Perspectives, First Edition. Lisa Isherwood and Hugo Córdova Quero.
© 2026 John Wiley & Sons Ltd. Published 2026 by John Wiley & Sons Ltd.

Siddhārta Gautama 'was born into the Śākya family, which belonged to the kṣatriya (noble) caste, considered by Buddhists to be the highest caste' (Bechert, 2004: 83). He lived in Kapilavastu, in the current border between India and Nepal. Siddhārta married YaŚodharā and the couple have only one son, Rāhula. At the age of 29 years, Siddhārta abandoned his home as he was not happy with the rich life he was leading and that, eventually, would lead him like any other mortal to age, get sick and die. Bechert (2004: 83) tells us that Siddhārta decided, after procuring monk garments and shaving his head, to go into the streets in order to live an ascetic life as a homeless monk. Siddhartā wandered from master to master in order to obtain salvation, but he was not reassured of it neither by the teachings of those masters nor by his ascetic life. Bechert concludes that:

> when he finally understood that this extreme austerity would not lead to salvation, that it was fruitless, he ended these efforts, ate a substantial meal, took a bath in the river, and sat down under a tree of the botanical species ficus religiosa, which Buddhists thereafter called the bodhi tree. It was here, seven years after he had left home, that he obtained Bodhi (awakening), perfect enlightenment, and thereby became a samyaksam-buddha, or "fully enlightened one" (2004: 83).

After his awakening under a pipal tree, now known as the Bodhi tree, in Bodh Gaya, India, the Buddha met Taphussa and Bhallika, two merchant brothers from the city of Balkh in what is currently Afghanistan who became his first lay disciples. He then travelled to the Deer Park near Varanasi (Benares) in northern India, where he set in motion what Buddhists call the Wheel of Dharma by delivering his first sermon to the five companions with whom he had sought enlightenment. Together with him, they formed the first saṅgha: the company of Buddhist monks (Huntington, 1986).

For the remaining 45 years of his life, the Buddha is said to have travelled in the Gangetic Plain in what is now Uttar Pradesh, Bihar and southern Nepal teaching a diverse range of people. According to Buddhist tradition, the Buddha died at Kuśinārā in present-day Kushinagar, India, which became a pilgrimage centre (Huntington, 1986).

As with any other religion, the teachings of the Buddha spread orally until they were written down. In Buddhism there is no single holy book, but there are several compilations of the teachings of Buddha followed by the many schools of Buddhism in the different countries that took root. The following map shows the predominance of Buddhism in Asia across its history:

Branches of Buddhism

There are three main schools of Buddhism: Mahāyāna, Theravāda and Vajrayāna, as shown in the following graphic.

Theravada Buddhism

Theravada, meaning 'Teaching of the Elders', is the oldest and most conservative school of Buddhism, focusing on the original teachings of the Buddha as preserved in the Pali Canon. It emphasises individual enlightenment (nirvana) through meditation, moral conduct and wisdom. Theravada is dominant in countries such as Sri Lanka, Thailand, Laos, Cambodia and Myanmar. Practitioners follow a strict monastic lifestyle, with monks and nuns playing a central role in preserving teachings and guiding laypeople. The path to enlightenment is seen as a gradual and disciplined journey, with a strong emphasis on mindfulness (sati) and insight (vipassana) meditation.

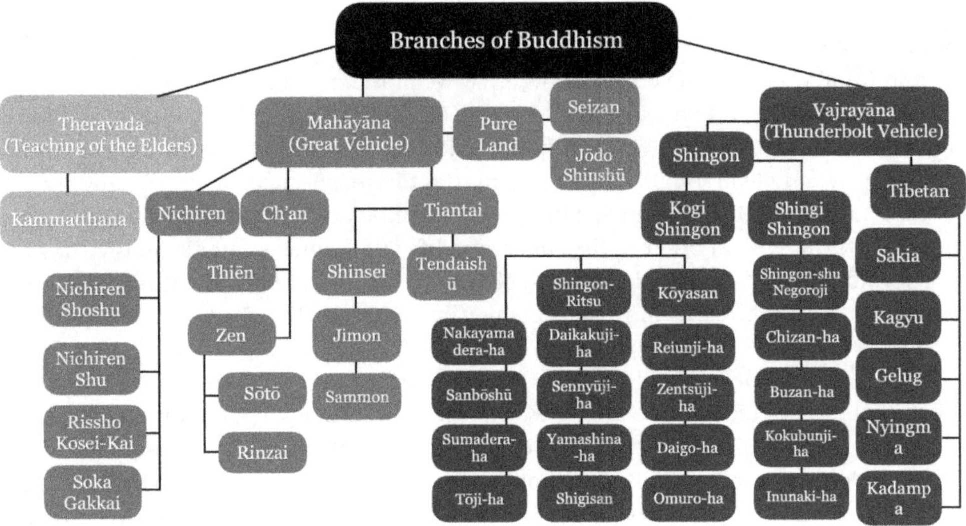

Graphic 8.1 Branches of Buddhism

Mahayana Buddhism

Mahayana, meaning 'Great Vehicle', is the largest and most diverse branch of Buddhism, encompassing various traditions and schools, such as Zen, Pure Land and Tibetan Buddhism. It focuses on the ideal of the Bodhisattva, a being who seeks enlightenment not only for themselves but for all sentient beings. The Bodhisattva vow encourages compassion and altruism, stressing that enlightenment is achievable by anyone, not just monks or spiritual elites. Mahayana texts include the Mahayana Sutras, which expand on the teachings found in the Pali Canon. Mahayana Buddhism is practised widely in East Asia, including China, Japan, Korea and Vietnam, and emphasises practices like chanting, devotion to bodhisattvas and ritual.

Source: Gordon Dylan Johnson (GDJ) / Wikimedia Commons / Public domain.

Vajrayana Buddhism

Vajrayana, or 'Diamond Vehicle', is considered an esoteric and tantric form of Buddhism, closely associated with Tibetan Buddhism, though it also exists in parts of Nepal, Bhutan and Mongolia. It incorporates rituals, mantras, meditation techniques and visualisation practices aimed at accelerating the path to enlightenment. Vajrayana emphasises the use of symbolic tools and tantric practices, such as the deity yoga and the guru–disciple relationship, to transform ordinary experiences into opportunities for spiritual growth. A key concept is the belief that enlightenment can be attained within a single lifetime, and thus practices are often intense and highly structured. It involves deep meditation, the use of mandalas and various forms of devotion.

Four Noble Truths

They are a central teaching to all Buddhists and aim to offer a framework for understanding suffering (*dukkha*), one of the main concerns of the Buddha which inspired him to search for truth, knowledge and enlightenment. These truths are the summary of the Four Noble Truths Sutra, one of the earliest recordings of the teachings of the Buddha. Geshe Tashi Tsering (2005) enunciates them as follows:

1) The noble truth of suffering
2) The noble truth of the origin of suffering
3) The noble truth of the cessation of suffering and the origin of suffering
4) The noble truth of the path that leads to the cessation of suffering and the origin of suffering (2005: 2).

Noble Eightfold Path

The fourth noble truth is usually also known as the 'Noble Eightfold Path', with enunciates the 'factors' to achieve the actual cessation of suffering the end of the origin of suffering: 'right view, right intention, right speech, right action, right livelihood, right effort, right mindfulness, and right concentration' (Bodhi, 2006: 12).

The Five Precepts

The 'Five Precepts' are usually considered to be oriented to cis-heterosexual followers, which is inaccurate. By 'Five Precepts' we understand the basic code of ethics required to lay Buddhist believers in both Mahāyāna and Theravāda Buddhism. The precepts are the following:

- Do not destroy life.
- Do not steal.
- Do not commit sexual misconduct.
- Do not lie.
- Do not become intoxicated (Kozak, 2011: 54).

These precepts are extended into the 'Eight Precepts' for those who want to follow Buddhism in a more strict way and to the 'Ten Precepts' for those who become monks and nuns. These latter precepts overlap with the 'Five Precepts'.

Jōdo Shinshū Buddhism

Jōdo Shinshū Buddhism is also known as Shin Buddhism and has its roots in Mahāyāna Buddhism. It is part of the Pure Land Buddhism which traces its roots to India as early as the second century CE. In these traditions, entering the Pure Land is popularly perceived as equivalent to the attainment of enlightenment. Pure Land Buddhism follows Amithābha Buddha. In 1175 CE Hōnen, a Tendai Buddhist monk, founded his own sect, Jōdo shū or 'Pure Land School', of whom Shinran became a disciple after leaving his life as a Tendai monk in Mt. Hiei (Keel, 1995: 32). Tendai is a branch of Japanese Mahāyāna Buddhism which originated in the Chinese Tiantai or Lotus Sutra school.

In 1205, Hōnen's critics persuaded Emperor Go-Toba to prohibit Hōnen and his teachings after two of his mistresses converted to Hōnen's new faith. Hōnen and six of his followers, including Shinran, were forced into exile while four of his disciples, including Anraku and Jūren, were sentenced to death (Machida, 1999: 17). Shinran was exiled for four years in Echigo Province, currently Niigata Prefecture under the criminal name of Fujii Yoshizane (Keel, 1995: 43). However, in 1211 Shinran was pardoned and he resettled in Kantō, where current Tokyo is located. While living there, in 1224, Shinran wrote the Kyogyoshinsho, an abbreviation of the Japanese title Kenjōdo Shinjitsu Kyōgyōshō Monrui, or 'The True Teaching, Practice, Faith and Attainment of the Pure Land'. This constitutes Shinran's most important work and where he laid down his doctrine of Jōdo Shinshū. The main practice of Jōdo Shinshū Buddhism is the recitation of the nembutsu—or the repetition of the name of Amitābha Buddha—which in Japanese is *Namu Amida Butsu*, as a way to express gratitude to Amitābha Buddha (Dessi, 2013: 71). It was Hōnen who fought for the nembutsu-exclusive practice in Pure Land Buddhism, a radical doctrine that shocked societal foundations of the time by subverting political power from traditional Buddhist temples (Machida, 1999: 7).

When Jōdo Shinshū Buddhism migrated to the United States and the Kingdom of Hawai'i, before its colonisation by the United States, through Japanese migrants working either in the plantations in Hawai'i or farming in the West coast of the United States, especially in California. Jōdo Shinshū Buddhism did not spread in Hawai'i and the United States from missionary initiatives but by the request of the migrants themselves. Arthur Nishimura (2008) explains that: 'In 1889, the Rev Soryu Kagai arrived in Honolulu and began to establish Buddhist groups among the Japanese workers on the plantations' (2008: 93). This resulted in the formation of the Honpa Hongwanji Mission of Hawaii (HHMH) within the Buddhist Church of America (BCA).

On the other hand, in 1898, Rev Eryu Honda and Rev Ejun Miyamoto established the 'Young Men's Buddhist Association', which in 1899 with the aid of Dr Shuye Sonoda and Rev Kakuryo Nishijima formally organised the group into the *Bukkyo Seinen Kai* or 'Young Men's Buddhist Association' (YMBA) in San Francisco, a formal branch of Japanese Jōdo Shinshū in the United States (Nishimura, 2008: 94). In 1905, the San Francisco association changed its name to the Buddhist Church of San Francisco (Nishimura, 2008: 95). By 1923 there were 33 Buddhist churches in the United States organised under the North American Buddhist Mission (NABM) (Morgan, 2004: 115). This name was changed in 1944 to its actual stand: Buddhist Churches of America (BCA) (Morgan, 2004: 115–116).

Buddhist Queer Theologies

Buddhism and Transgender Issues

The Buddhist canon does not presume a world of only two genders, male and female. It refers to many genders such as man like woman (*vepurisika*), the sexually ambiguous (*sambhinna*) and the androgyne (*ubhatovyanjanaka*) which shows an awareness of the existence of 'queer' people at the time of writing these texts. Further Buddhist texts include several stories about transgenderism. In the Dhammapada written in the fifth century there is a story of a man called Soreyya who was so entranced by a monk's complexion that he transitioned into a woman and later married and had children. In the Lotus Sutra the young daughter of the Naga king transformed into a male while teaching the Buddhist dharma. This sutra has been interpreted as confirming that all genders can have wisdom and enlightenment and all living beings possess the world of Buddhahood.

Further, in Tibetan Buddhism the Mahakala Ma Ning is a transgendered yet genderless deity who is understood to be the defender of the dharma. It was written that Ma Ning signified a balance between maleness and femaleness which echoed the preference for the middle path favoured by early Buddhist teachings. The Buddha himself was said to believe that transgenderism is a result of behaviours or karmic seeds (*vasasa*) spread across lives and is not an innate truth or more importantly, a moral fault.

It seems fair to say that Buddhist discomfort with sex as desire which entraps the person is not more rigid when considering same-sex relations as all relations can trap the person and stop their journey of enlightenment. The current Dalai Lama has affirmed the full human rights of all people but also said same-sex marriage was not according to nature, but was in the end a personal matter since we all bear our own karmic debt. This implied there was no condemnation in relation to human sexuality but rather concern that relationships should be responsible. Some contemporary commentators have suggested that the Buddha's words 'Be a light unto yourself' imply that a fundamental duty is to be true to the self.

To talk about Buddhist Queer Theologies is to make reference to an area of Buddhism that is still emerging. As explained in previous pages, Buddhism is divided into three major schools and hundreds of groups within those three traditions. Neither a single authoritative body nor a single sacred scripture would forbid or permit same-sex love, relationships and practices. Therefore, talking about Buddhist Queer Theologies implies considering the tradition in which the theological reflection is based upon.

Fluid Understanding of Sexuality

In order to talk about Buddhist Queer Theologies, we need to consider the cultural, social and historical context of Buddhism in every country where it has, and continues to exercise influence. In many societies, same-sex desire and homosociabilisation were not only permitted but also encouraged, such as in China and Japan, which in turn influenced Buddhism. For example, in Japan the Chigo Monogatari, or stories of love between monks and their chigo, who were teenagers living in the temple, were quite common in the Feudal era (Childs, 1992: 1–5). At the same time, Kuan Yin, the Asian Goddess of Compassion, is sometimes depicted as male, giving fluidity to the gender-bending of this deity. Patrick S. Cheng (2013) states:

> Kuan Yin is characterized by gender fluidity at the very core of her being. In her study, Dr. Chun-Fang Yu traces the evolution of Kuan Yin from the male Bodhisattva Avalokitesvara in India to the female goddess in China. According to Yu, Kuan Yin was initially depicted as male – complete with moustache – until the tenth century. Yu's hypothesis is that the feminization of Kuan Yin in China was a response to the "patriarchal stance of institutional Buddhism and Neo-Confucianism," both of which lacked "feminine symbols and female practitioners." Kuan Yin has also taken on various genders in her incarnations as Kannon (Japan), Kwan Um (Korea), and Chenrezig (Tibet) (2013: 146).

Some have also pointed out that several masters of Buddhism have been queer. For example, some have attributed the introduction of monastic homosexuality to Japan to Shingon founder Kukai, a fact that has been disputed lately by some scholars (Schalow, 1992: 215). Other scholars affirm that Buddhism did not forbid same-sex desires because those desires were not always made explicit (Coleman, 2002: 146).

In all these contexts, gender fluidity and same-sex attraction are not seen as negative aspects of the human experience, but as positive aspects of humanity. On this, José Ignacio Cabezón states:

> Buddhism has been for the most part neutral on the question of homosexuality. The principle question for Buddhism has not been one of heterosexuality vs. homosexuality but one of sexuality vs. celibacy [...]. The fact that Buddhism has been essentially neutral in this regard does not imply that the cultures in which Buddhism arose and flourished have always been neutral. Some, at certain times, have been tolerant of same-sex relations; others have not. However, because of the essential neutrality of the Buddhist tradition in this regard, it has adapted to particular socio-cultural norms, so that throughout its history we find a wide gamut of opinions concerning homosexual activity, ranging from condemnation (never to the point of active persecution) to praise (1998: 30).

Furthermore, the case for the fluid understanding of sexuality in Buddhism is ultimately related to the value that sexuality has in its teachings, as Vajra Karuna (2010) affirms:

> I came to realize the major problem that Buddhism has with sex is that having originated in a monastic environment it never had any way of validating the sexual lives of the laity. The best it could do was to tolerate sex in the lay community. This, in turn made me understand that no religious tradition, Eastern or Western, can be genuinely gay-friendly, unless it can accept sex, in and of itself, as having value. If sex is only valued as a means to an en, for example, reproduction, then sex can never really be viewed as inherently good.

This is an important aspect that queer Buddhists need to keep in mind when doing a queer reading of the sacred texts or of the Buddhist teachings.

The Issue of Colonialism in the Encounter of East and West

We also should remember that the contact of Asia with the West, heavily influenced by Christianity and its negative vision of same-sex desire and activities, certainly produced negative views in Buddhism. In present times, because in the West there are Buddhist converts who are queer, they are pressing Buddhism as a global religion to develop a different view. The presence of Buddhist converts in the West as well as the assimilation of Asian Buddhists into Western societies have impacted Buddhism. In 1997, a visit of the Dalai Lama Tenzin Gyatso to San Francisco was met with resistance and criticism as the leader stated: 'We have to make a distinction between believers and unbelievers [...]. From a Buddhist point of view, men-to-men and women-to-women [relationships are] [...] generally considered sexual misconduct' (Lattin, 1997).

Although the Dalai Lama's statement generated a certain level of rejection from the queer Buddhists in the San Francisco Bay Area, it is not an out-of-place comment if we take into account the words of Karuna (2010) in the previous section. Monasticism has greatly influenced Buddhism, but the religion is not completely impervious to the fluctuations of societies. Furthermore, what in the West, from an eminently Christian perspective, could be considered as negative, in Asian societies may not be seen as such.

This is an important reminder as Buddhist converts in the West are already socialised into the mindset of a Western puritanical worldview. This can be negative or positive depending on how queer Buddhists reflect on their spirituality. We are mentioning this because it has been seen primarily among Western converts that Queer Buddhist Theologies have begun to emerge, and it needs to avoid the 'orientalist gaze' (Said, 1979) as a way to let the subaltern speak (Spivak, 1988) its own queer understanding of Buddhism.

A special moment in this development of Queer Buddhist Theologies was the publication of *Queer Dharma*, two volumes edited by Winston Leyland (1998, 2000). These volumes largely contributed to bridge gender, sexuality, queer experiences and Buddhism. The materials below show different aspects of the emerging Buddhist Queer Theologies. They are written by scholars in the West and they offer important insights. Robert Shore-Goss, who is an expert in Comparative Religion, which is part of an ambitious two-volume collection of essays edited by Donald L. Boisvert and Jay Emerson Emerson (2011). Shore-Goss (2011) emphasises the cultural context of Buddhism and its views on queer issues when he notes that there have been 'disparate Buddhist views on homoerotic sexuality: from mild acceptance to mild rejection, and sometimes to vehement rejection. Acceptance and rejection were often the result of the host culture' (2011: 26). One of the concerns examined by Shore-Goss is the issue of same-sex marriage. This has already begun in Buddhism, such as the first wedding in Taiwan of Fish Huang and You Ha-Ting in 2012. In the same line, Jeff Wilson focuses on the question about same-sex marriage in the United States within Jōdo Shinshū Buddhism. It is surprising that this branch of Buddhism began performing same-sex marriages in the early 1970s (Wilson, 2012: 37).

Burkhard Scherer (2006) is one of the most renowned scholars of Comparative Religion, Gender and Sexuality in Buddhism and Indian Literature. He explores gender-crossing in Mahāyāna and Tibetan Buddhism, which includes Hindu deities. Scherer (2006) focuses on transgender issues by reinterpreting a teaching of the Buddha and concludes that 'By incorporating the modern Western distinctions between sex, gender and sexualities into a Buddhist discourse, the Buddha's approach to his followers' needs and capacities can be applied towards e.g. transgenderism and homosexuality in a truly humane way' (2006: 74).

An example of this is the presence of the Kathoey in Thailand. Traditionally, Kathoey have been considered as a third sex in Thai society, as Peter A. Jackson explains:

> Before the 1960s, only three forms of phet [gendered/sex being] were recognised in public discourses, namely, normatively masculine 'men' (phu-chai, ...), normatively feminine 'women' (phu-ying, ...) and an intermediate category called kathoey (...). Kathoey variously denoted a person, male or female, who exhibited hermaphroditic features or expressed behaviour considered inappropriate for their gender, and have long been called a 'third gender/sex' (phet thi-sam, ...) within both popular and academic discourses (2000: 409).

Although a term popular in Thailand, it could also be pejorative, and the closest meaning to English terms would be 'fairy' or 'queen'. Their activities are explained by Heinz Duthel as follows:

> Kathoey work in predominantly female occupations, such as in shops, restaurants and beauty salons, but also in factories (a reflection of Thailand's high proportion of female industrial workers). Kathoey also work in entertainment and tourist centres, in cabarets and as sex workers. (...) Kathoeys are more visible and more accepted in

Thai culture than transgender or transsexual people are in Western countries or the Indian subcontinent. Several Thai models, singers and movie stars are kathoeys, and Thai newspapers often print photos of the winner of female and kathoey beauty contests side by side (2013: 9).

One could argue that Kathoey occupy a specific role within the cis-heterosexual division of labor. However, this role can sometimes be perceived through an essentialised lens, which reduces their complex identities to a singular, often stereotyped, representation rather than recognising their diverse and multifaceted experiences. In practice, the attitudes of Buddhists towards Kathoey can vary. Some monks and practitioners might view being Kathoey as a result of past karma or see it through the lens of non-attachment and compassion. There are also instances where Kathoey are involved in religious ceremonies and practices.

While some Kathoey may find acceptance within Buddhist communities, they generally face barriers if they wish to be ordained as monks. Nonetheless, Kathoey participate in many traditional Thai cultural and religious activities. Some festivals and local traditions may even have specific roles for Kathoey, integrating them into the community. However, despite their visibility and relative acceptance, Kathoey often face societal prejudice and discrimination. Their status can sometimes be complex, with public attitudes ranging from acceptance and admiration to marginalisation and stigma.

Colleen Maher takes Buddhism as a monolithic religion rather than a conglomerate of schools, organisations, masters' teachings and spiritual paths. With that understanding Maher suggests that: 'Perhaps one day, Buddhism will be the first major faith tradition to openly accept homosexual practice' (Maher, 2010: 25) which seems to indicate that somebody or some part of the religion will declare a rule of acceptance for all Buddhists in the world. That would be impossible, in the same way that it would be impossible in any other religion. We can talk about major organisations/branches within a religion, such as Roman Catholicism in Christianity, or Sunni Islam, but even if those organisations/branches would enact a rule that could not lead to a global compliance by all followers of the given religion. Even the Dalai Lama, who speaks for Tibetan Buddhism, is not the leading authority for all Buddhists. We believe the value of this study is to pose the questions that Western Buddhism is having at the moment that may or may not be the same questions that Buddhist followers have in other contexts different from the West.

For Further Discussion

1   To what extent does this chapter align with your pre-existing knowledge or personal experiences of Buddhism? Were you previously aware of the diverse perspectives on queer issues within the Buddhist context?

2   In the context of ancient texts and contemporary categorisations, how do you perceive the analysis of queer Buddhist dharmologies? Do you find yourself in agreement or disagreement? Can you provide a more in-depth exploration of your stance?

3   How have cultural and historical factors influenced the varying attitudes towards homosexuality within different Buddhist traditions?

4 Are there examples of Buddhist communities or leaders actively advocating for LGBTQ+ inclusivity and acceptance, and how has this been received within the broader Buddhist community?

5 In what ways do Buddhist teachings on compassion and acceptance intersect with or challenge societal attitudes towards homosexuality, and how do practitioners reconcile these aspects within their personal beliefs and practices?

References

Bechert, Heinz (2004). "Buddha, Life of the." In: *Encyclopedia of Buddhism, Vol. 1*, edited by Robert E Buswell Jr. New York, NY: Macmillan Reference USA, pp. 82–88.

Bodhi, Bhikkhu (2006). *The Noble Eightfold Path: The Way to the End of Suffering*. Kandy, Sri Lanka: Buddhist Publication Society.

Boisvert, Donald L and Jay Emerson Johnson (editors) (2011). *Queer Religion: Homosexuality in Modern Religious History, Volume 1*. Santa Barbara, CA: Praeger.

Cabezón, José I (1998). "Homosexuality and Buddhism." In: *Queer Dharma: Voices of Gay Buddhists, Volume 1*, edited by Winston Leyland. San Francisco, CA: Gay Sunshine Press, pp. 29–44.

Cheng, Patrick S (2013). "Kuan Yin: espejo del Cristo queer asiático," translated by Hugo Córdova Quero." *Religión e Incidencia Pública. Revista de Investigación de GEMRIP* 1: pp. 129–148.

Childs, Margaret H (1992). "Chigo Monogatari: Love Stories or Buddhist Sermons? In: *Asian Homosexuality*, edited by Wayne R Dynes and Stephen Donaldson. New York, NY: Garland Publishing, pp. 1–5.

Coleman, James W (2002). *The New Buddhism: The Western Transformation of an Ancient Tradition*. Oxford: Oxford University Press.

Dessi, Ugo (2013). *Japanese Religions and Globalization*. New York, NY: Routledge.

Duthel, Heinz (2013). *Kathoey Ladyboy: Thailand's Got Talent*. Norderstedt: Books on Demand.

Huntington, John C (1986). "Sowing the Seeds of the Lotus: A Journey to the Great Pilgrimages Sites of Buddhism, Part V." *Orientations* (December): pp. 46–58.

Jackson, Peter A (2000). "An Explosion of Thai Identities: Global Queering and Re-Imagining Queer Theory." *Culture, Health & Sexuality* 2, No. 4 (October–December): pp. 405–424.

Karuna, Vajra (2010). "Zen & Sexuality." Available at: <http://members.efn.org/~sybilnatawa/zensexual.html>.

Keel, Hee-Sung (1995). *Understanding Shinran: A Dialogical Approach*. Fremont, CA: Asian Humanities Press.

Kozak, Arnie (2011). *The Everything Buddhism Book: A Complete Introduction to the History, Traditions, and Beliefs of Buddhism, Past and Present*. Avon, MA: Adam Media.

Lattin, Don (1997). "Dalai Lama Speaks on Gay Sex / He Says It's Wrong for Buddhists But Not for Society." *San Francisco Chronicle*, June 11. Available at: <http://www.sfgate.com/news/article/Dalai-Lama-Speaks-on-Gay-Sex-He-says-it-s-wrong-2836591.php>.

Leyland, Winston (editor) (1998). *Queer Dharma: Voices of Gay Buddhists, Volume 1*. San Francisco: Gay Sunshine Press.

Leyland, Winston (editor) (2000). *Queer Dharma: Voices of Gay Buddhists, Volume 2*. San Francisco: Gay Sunshine Press.

Machida, Sōhō (1999). *Renegade Monk: Hōnen and Japanese Pure Land Buddhism.* Berkeley, CA: University of California Press.

Maher, Colleen (2010). "Unanswered Questions Buddhism and Homosexuality." *Voices* 1 (Spring): pp. 19–26.

Morgan, Diane (2004). *The Buddhist Experience in America.* Westport, CT: Greenwood Press.

Nishimura, Arthur (2008). "The Buddhist Mission of North America 1898–1942: Religion and its Social Functions in an Ethnic Community." In: *North American Buddhists in Social Context*, edited by Paul David Numrich. Leiden: Brill, pp. 87–105.

Said, Edward (1979). *Orientalism.* New York, NY: Vintage Books.

Schalow, Paul G (1992). "Kukai and the Tradition of Male Love in Japanese Buddhism." In: *Buddhism, Sexuality & Gender*, edited by Jose Ignacio Cabezon. New York, NY: State University of New York, pp. 215–230.

Scherer, Burkhard (2006). "Gender Transformed and Meta-gendered Enlightenment: Reading Buddhist Narratives as Paradigms of Inclusiveness." *REVER: Revista de Estudos da Religião* 3: pp. 65–76.

Shore-Goss, Robert (2011). "Queer Buddhists: Re-visiting Sexual Gender Fluidity." In: *Queer Religion: Homosexuality in Modern Religious History*, edited by Donald L Boisvert and Jay Emerson Johnson. Santa Barbara, CA: Praeger, pp. 25–50.

Spivak, Gayatri C (1988). "Can the Subaltern Speak?" In: *Colonial Discourse and Postcolonial Theory*, edited by Patrick Williams and Laura Chrisman. New York, NY: Columbia University Press, pp. 66–111.

Tsering, Geshe T (2005). *The Foundation of Buddhist Thought, Vol. 1.* Foreword by Lama Zopa Rampoche. Somerville, MA: Wisdom Publications.

Wilson, Jeff (2012). "'All Beings are Equally Embraced by Amida Buddha': Jodo Shinshu Buddhism and Same-Sex Marriage in the United States." *Journal of Global Buddhism* 13: pp. 31–59.

9

Jainism and Sikhism

Jainism is the third religion of India that comes from ancient times and has been practised continuously in India since the middle of the first millennium BCE. On the other hand, Sikhism is a modern religion that emerged in the sixteenth century. Exploring the questions that believers of these two faiths have regarding gender, sexuality and the embryonic development of queer theologies is vital to expand the comprehension of the global phenomena of queer theologies.

Jainism as a Religion

The Ahisma, a hand with a wheel on the palm, symbolises the Jain principle of nonviolence.

The name Jainism derives from the Sanskrit word *Jina*, meaning 'liberator' or 'conqueror', in reference to spiritual conquest (Vallely, 2009: 325). The goal of faith is to free oneself from karma and attain nirvana.

Box 9.1

Nirvana refers to the state of enlightenment and according to Jainism can be achieved by any human soul without rituals or fasting but by human effort. Once achieved the soul is released from karma.

To help them achieve this goal, Jains venerate a group of 24 liberated souls called Jinas or Tīrthaṅkaras, i.e., 'those who ford the river' between the material and spiritual worlds, who act as teachers and role models for those who practice the religion (Long, 2009: 2).

Box 9.2

The human soul can follow the so-called three jewels or Tri Ratna which bring about enlightenment. These are samyagdarshana or right faith, samyagjnana or right knowledge and samyakcharitra or right conduct.

Table 9.1 Sikh Gurus and Years as Guru

	Name	Years		Name	Years
1	Guru Nanak Dev	1469–1539	6	Guru Har Gobind Sahib	1606–1644
2	Guru Angad Dev	1529–1552	7	Guru Har Rai Sahib	1644–1661
3	Guru Amardas Sahib	1552–1574	8	Guru Har Krishan Sahib	1661–1664
4	Guru Ram Das	1574–1581	9	Guru Tegh Bahadur Sahib	1665–1675
5	Guru Arjan Dev	1581–1606	10	Guru Gobind Singh	1675–1708

Like many religions, Jainism has a founder: Vardhamana Mahāvīra, who was born in 599 BCE in the city of Kundagrama (Singh, 2016: 313). Jeffery D. Long states:

> Mahāvīra, the 'Great Hero,' lived at about the same time and in the same region as the Buddha: approximately 2500 years ago in the northeastern region of India that recent studies have designated 'Greater Magadha'. One might call Mahāvīra the founder of the Jain community as it exists today (2009: 2).

Jainism—along with Buddhism—emerged in a social context in which those seeking a new way to understand the religion renounced their lives as householders to become wandering mendicants. Mahāvīra was a mendicant (Shah, 2004: 30) and is considered the 24th Tīrthaṅkara (Long, 2009: 29).

The following table shows the 24 Tīrthaṅkaras along with the symbol that identifies them:

These people questioned the dominant Vedic Brahmanic orthodoxy which considered Brahman as a supreme being and its stratified caste system with Brahmins [priests] occupying the upper caste as mediators between the divinities and mankind. Based on that monopoly, they began elaborate rituals with animal sacrifices (Shah, 2004: 28).

The followers of Parsva, the Tīrthaṅkara 23 rejected animal sacrifice. Jains wear masks across their faces in order not to inhale any insects thus killing them. They also use a brush to sweep away any small creatures such as ants that might be in their path so as not to tread on them.

The three symbols below symbolise good omens that come from Hindu culture, and are shared by Buddhism, Hinduism and Jainism. These symbols are as follows:

While these symbols are shared by all three religions, their meaning varies. Jainism understands them as follows:

First, we find the Srivatsa, which often marks the chest of the Tīrthaṅkara. It is one of the Ashtamangala—eight auspicious symbols—found in Jainism (Von Glasenapp, 1999: 427).

Secondly, there is the Nandyavaata, which is used for worship and can be prepared with rice grains (Shah, 2004: 31).

Finally, there is the symbol of the svāstika or swastika. The svāstika represents the community in its four dimensions: male and female, laity and ascetics. It is an auspicious and non-violent symbol. For Jains in particular, a central tenet of their faith was the renunciation of violence in all its forms and concern for all forms of life. Unfortunately, the religious symbol of the svastika has been distorted and associated with Nazism in the West by taking it completely out of its original context (Long, 2009: 209, note 21). Here we see an example of the ideological co-optation of elements that are then re-signified and removed from their original meaning. This is a dynamic that the West has carried out with all religions, many times changing the tone of those religions.

Branches of Jainism

One of the characteristics of those who converted to Jainism was the renunciation of everything, including clothes. They went about naked in the streets, begging for food and sleeping in squares, sheds or streets. When the followers of Bhadrahābu returned, there was a dispute among them regarding the authenticity of the Aṅgas. Moreover, those who remained in Magadha began to wear white clothes, which was unacceptable to those others who remained naked. The question of clothing was viewed in two different ways.

On the one hand, those who remained naked assumed that those who began to wear clothes had abandoned the teachings of the faith. Those who affirmed nudity as an intrinsic part of the faith began to be called Digambaras, meaning 'those clothed by the air'. On the other hand, those who were in Magadha and had begun to wear white robes considered the returnees to be radical fanatics who had misinterpreted the teachings of the faith. Therefore, they began to be called Śvetāmbaras, meaning 'those dressed in white'.

Helmuth von Glasenapp (1999: 46) proposes the theory that since Jain nuns were forbidden to be naked, the precept about complete nudity for all people following the faith was not universal. Thus, from its inception, both ways of living the tradition existed, and that the reason behind it was actually the survival of the faith in all the places where Jainism spread accentuated the differences of each group.

The following chart illustrates the branches of Jainism:

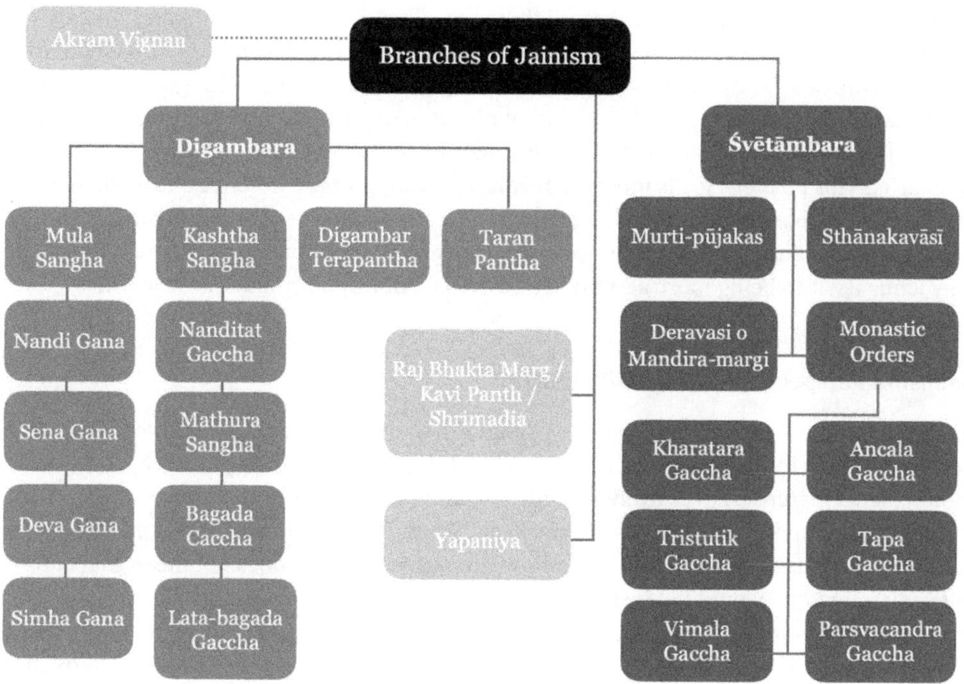

Graphic 9.1 Branches of Jainism

Sexuality and Gender in Jainism

All sexuality is problematic for Jains who regard it as a distraction from attaining *moksha,* or liberation from the cycle of life and death as the body becomes trapped in the endless cycles of birth and death. Sex for procreation within marriage is tolerated but not celebrated. Jains see homosexual sex and heterosexual sex in the same way as distractions and indulgences which disturb the balance of life and keep one tied to the material world. Within Jainism there is no greater condemnation of homosexual sex than of non-procreative cis-heterosexual sex.

Interestingly, the ancient Jain texts acknowledge three genders, masculine, feminine and neuter. The Tattvaartha Sutra explains these and the accompanying sexual characteristics in detail. It also describes the external physical signs of these characteristics as well as the internal motivations of desire. In modern terms we may understand this as the difference between physiological sex, psychosocial gender and sexual attraction or orientation. The Sutra goes on to describe the Jain attitude to gender as understood in three worlds: the upper world in which heavenly beings display either male or female characteristics; the lower world of hellish beings who are neuter gendered and have mixed sexual characteristics and the middle world of humans and animals who may be male, female or neuter.

The gender one is born in is a consequence of karmic actions from previous births, but the sexual characteristics and desires are a consequence of mental unease. The Digambara Jains believe women are capable of enlightenment but not in their female form, so they need to be reborn into a male body. However, the Shwetambara Jains believe liberation is attainable for men and women in their current physical form, the relevant factor being the will, not the gender. In Shwetambara lore the nineteenth-century Tirthankara Malli-natha was born into a female body but became a Jain Tirthankara and is regarded as male but his name which translates as Lord Jasmine and his symbol of a pot both allude to his femininity. Today we may understand this as an example of trans personhood.

Unlike Greek logic Jains do not regard things as either absolutely existent or non-existent Judgements are relative and never absolute; thus, the concept of pure identity whether in race, religion or sexual orientation is dismissed as it denies plurality. Things having infinite qualities, modes of expression, forms and relations to other things are not exclusive or universal. They are a combination of both with their identity embedded in both difference and similarity. This ideology feeds into an ethical framework of non-violence and as such when considering all possibilities and viewpoints conflict and oppression is eliminated. This posture of non-violence takes precedence over certainty and authority, and thus Jain philosophy lends itself to being more accepting of diversity, multiplicity and queer realities.

Jainism's Perspective on Sexuality Issues

In Jainism, like in many other ancient religious traditions, views on homosexuality are influenced by cultural, historical and interpretative factors. Jainism primarily emphasises non-violence (*Ahimsa*), truthfulness (*Satya*) and non-attachment (*Aparigraha*) as central tenets of its ethical and spiritual framework. Therefore, homophobia would not be an acceptable way in which to think of a fellow human being. That does not mean that culturally any individual would not be influenced by societal views.

It is important to note that interpretations of Jain teachings on sexuality can vary among different branches and individuals within the Jain community. Some modern Jains may adopt more liberal views on homosexuality, emphasising compassion, acceptance and non-judgement as essential virtues in line with Jain principles.

As with many religious traditions, contemporary perspectives on homosexuality in Jainism may evolve over time, influenced by cultural shifts, individual interpretations and dialogues within the community. Thus, while traditional Jain teachings may not explicitly address homosexuality, the broader principles of Jainism can be interpreted to encourage understanding, compassion and respect towards all individuals, regardless of their sexual orientation.

However, the discussion about same-sex desire is not new in Jainism. Michael Anderson (2017) argues that prior to the current discussions on the topic, Jains have already set some precedents through their standpoints on gender, sexuality and bodies. In the context of Jainism, there are three terms often used to describe individuals who may not fit traditional binary understandings of gender and sexuality. Jainism shares these terms with other traditions.

The first term is *kliba*, which refers to individuals who do not conform to conventional male or female gender roles. They are often described as having ambiguous or non-normative gender characteristics. The understanding and treatment of *kliba* individuals varied across different texts and cultural contexts, but they were generally considered to occupy a unique social and religious status. While the exact treatment and acceptance of *kliba* individuals in Jain communities may have varied, the overarching Jain philosophy of non-violence and compassion would suggest a respectful and compassionate approach towards all individuals, regardless of their gender identity or expression.

The second term is *Sandha(ka)*, which is used in ancient Indian literature to describe a eunuch or a person who has been castrated. Eunuchs played various roles in Indian society, including serving in royal courts, religious ceremonies and as part of certain social communities. They often occupied a distinct social and cultural space, with their own customs, traditions and forms of social organisation. Within Jain communities, *Sandha(ka)* might have been involved in religious ceremonies, serving as attendants to Jain monks and nuns, or participating in various social and cultural activities.

Finally, the third term is Napumsaka, which refers to individuals who do not belong strictly to either male or female categories. It can be translated as 'neuter' or 'impotent' and is used to describe individuals with non-binary gender identities or sexual characteristics, usually inscribed within a third sex. In religious and philosophical texts, 'napumsaka' individuals are sometimes portrayed in symbolic or allegorical contexts, reflecting broader cosmological and metaphysical ideas. In Jainism, this term has been the one upon which the discussions on homosexuality have happened.

In Jainism, homosexual activity among monks was historically perceived as a challenge to monastic discipline. The concept of third-sex sexuality was viewed with ambiguity, and individuals identified with a third sex were often equated with women. This equivalence arose from the perception that both groups posed potential threats to the monks' chastity. Michael J. Sweet and Leonard Zwilling note that Jains made a nuanced distinction between 'the masculine napumsaka (purusanapumsaka) and the effeminate napumsaka (pandaga or kliba)' sering (1993: 373). This differentiation was significant as it influenced the eligibility of individuals for ordination, with third-sex persons often being suspected of lacking the ability to uphold their vows.

Over time, attitudes towards the ordination of third-sex individuals began to evolve, reflecting changing societal perspectives and interpretations of Jain teachings. The emphasis in Jainism on purity and the observance of vows applies universally, requiring the control of both homosexual and heterosexual urges and passions. Thus, the regulation of sexuality within Jain monastic life is guided by principles of self-discipline, restraint and commitment to spiritual purity, rather than strict adherence to conventional gender norms or sexual orientations.

Sikhism as a Religion

The Kanda is the symbol for Sikhism and represents three swords, a khanda, a chakram and two kirpans which represent the warrior code. Sikhs are considered the warrior class who defend the weak.

The name *Sikhism* comes from the word *Sikh* in the Punjabi language which means 'disciple' or 'apprentice'. This word is related to *sishya* in Sanskrit, which also means 'disciple' (Kalsi, 2005: 3). A Sikh person is a follower of a Guru (Nesbitt, 2005: 2) and while a *guru* is a teacher of any doctrine in the Indian context, for Sikhism a Guru written with capital letters, is one who not only teaches but also one who 'removes the darkness' and refers to the 10 spiritual leaders who originated the religion (Nesbitt, 2005: 3). These 10 human Gurus are detailed below:

Sikhism emerged in the Punjabi region in the northern part of India towards the end of the fifteenth century CE. Its founder is Guru Nanak Nev, who lived between 1469 and 1529 CE. According to Eleanor Nesbitt (2005: 13), we should remember that while Martin Luther was carrying out the reformation of Christianity in modern Europe, Guru Nanak was developing a new religion in India.

While it has roots in Hinduism and Islam, Sikhism is a monotheistic religion that has evolved as a particular religion over the centuries. This is explained by Nesbitt:

> Sikhism has become a separate religion in terms of the self-definition of Sikhs, and because Sikhism has all the marks of a religion. These include a separate scripture and calendar, separate life-cycle rites, places of worship, and a sense of shared history. At the same time, like other religions, Sikhism cannot be understood completely in isolation from its religious, social and historical context (2005: 4).

Table 9.2   Twenty-four Jain Tīrthaṅkaras and Their Symbols

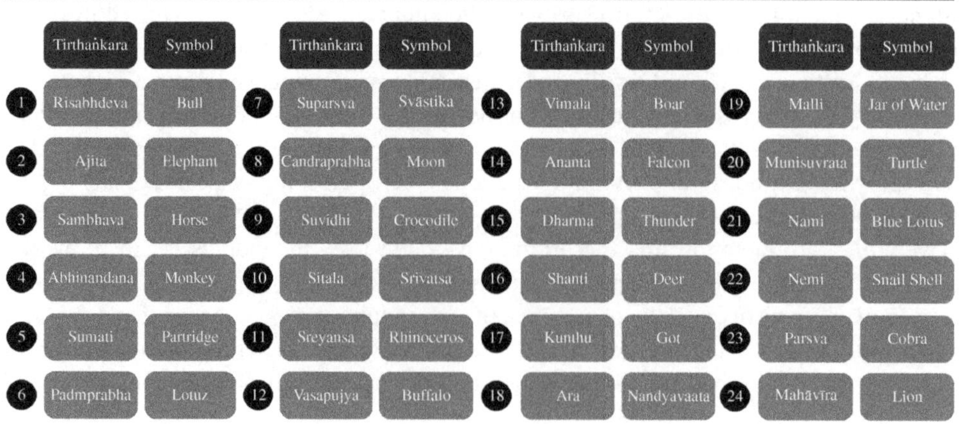

Tirthaṅkara	Symbol		Tirthaṅkara	Symbol		Tirthaṅkara	Symbol		Tirthaṅkara	Symbol
1 Risabhdeva	Bull	7	Suparsva	Svāstika	13	Vimala	Boar	19	Malli	Jar of Water
2 Ajita	Elephant	8	Candraprabha	Moon	14	Ananta	Falcon	20	Munisuvrata	Turtle
3 Sambhava	Horse	9	Suvidhi	Crocodile	15	Dharma	Thunder	21	Nami	Blue Lotus
4 Abhinandana	Monkey	10	Sitala	Srivatsa	16	Shanti	Deer	22	Nemi	Snail Shell
5 Sumati	Partridge	11	Sreyansa	Rhinoceros	17	Kunthu	Got	23	Parsva	Cobra
6 Padmprabha	Lotuz	12	Vasapujya	Buffalo	18	Ara	Nandyavaata	24	Mahāvīra	Lion

People who are part of the religion are called Sikhs, although they are divided into two categories.

On the one hand, those who have not yet been initiated into the religion are called *Kesdhari Sikhs*, people who comply with all the regulations of the religion but have not gone through the rite of initiation (Kalsi, 2005: 5).

On the other hand, those who have already passed the *Amrit* or initiation rite are called *Amritdhari Sikhs*. But accessing *Amrit* requires displaying the five emblems of the *Khalsa*, the radical institution founded by Guru Gobind Singh in 1669 CE. The term *Khalsa* comes from the Arabic word *Khalis*, meaning 'pure', and refers to groups of Sikhs who maintain their loyalty to the Guru (Nesbitt, 2005: 58). Along with the creation of the Khalsa, Guru Gobind Singh instituted a new style of the *Amrit* ceremony that includes the water of immortality, the creation of the so-called *Panj Pyarey*, the five beloveds and the titles of *Singh* for males and *Kaur* for females (Kalsi, 2005: 5). The term *Singh* means 'lion' and the term *Kaur* means 'princess' and 'lioness'; both titles act

The first guru of Sikhism: Guru Nanak. *Source:* Amritpal Singh Mann. Painted by Jaimal Singh Naqqash (1860–1916), Mehtab Singh Naqqash (1871–1940), and Hukum Singh / Wikimedia Commons / CC BY-SA 4.0.

as middle names. As surnames in India are related to caste, Guru Gobind Singh broke with the imposition of caste by making his community free of this requirement (Singh and Rai, 1984: 42). Thus, many people stop using the family name and opt for these titles as their surname.

Sewa Singh Kalsi lists the five emblems of Sikhism, or the five 'K's' as follows:

1) kes (uncut hair)
2) kangha (a small wooden comb worn in the hair)
3) kirpan (a sword; today, initiated Sikhs wear a small sword)
4) kachha/kachhahira (a pair of knee-length pants)
5) kara (a steel bracelet/ring worn on the right wrist) (2005: 5).

These emblems thus distinguish those who have been initiated into the faith and those who are yet to be initiated. There is, however, a sixth element for males: the turban.

Sikhs worship in 'Gurdwaras', but it must be accompanied by the langar which is a communal refectory which provides food every day for those who attend, Sikh or not. Both the worship and the providing of food are considered to be the essence of the Sikh religion.

The holy scriptures are the Guru Granth Sahib which are made up of poems, wisdom sayings, prayers and writings from different scholars as well as 5,867 hymns. Sikhs never turn their backs on the holy book when in worship and often place offerings near it. A *granthi* is the person who reads from the Holy Scriptures, and this can be a man or a woman in line with Sikh teachings of equality. The first version of the Holy Scriptures was compiled by the fifth guru Arjun at Amritsar. He included his hymns and sayings and those of the gurus who came before him.

Golden Temple of Amritsar.

The major religious holidays of the Sikhs are Vaisakhi, which celebrates the creation of the Khalsa who are the warrior saints, Bandi Chhor Divas that celebrates the release of Guru Hargobind from prison and Maghi which celebrates and remembers the Sikhs who died in battle against the Mughals.

Branches of Sikhism

Branches of Sikhism evolved from the faithful believing in an alternative lineage of gurus, a different interpretation of the Sikh scriptures or by following either a living guru or other concepts that differ from the orthodox (Takhar, 2014). The following four illustrate the different branches of Sikhism:

Sexuality and Gender in Sikhism

A key tenet of Sikhism is equality, diversity and inclusion. This is not just in terms of caste or religion but also gender, beliefs, practices and identity. This had profound effects for women who were seen as equal and treated accordingly, but it also had implications for understanding how a state should be run. It should be one of peace and equality where no one is harassed by others for any reason which should be reassuring for queers living under this tenet.

According to Sikhism every living being has a soul and like God the soul is formless and genderless. Sikh gurus primarily advocate for the union of two souls in married life, emphasising the genderless nature of the soul. In Sikhism, the focus is on the spiritual connection and unity between individuals rather than their gender identities. This perspective underscores the belief that all souls are equal and formless, transcending gender distinctions, highlighting the inclusive and egalitarian ethos of Sikh teachings. As in all karmic faiths rebirth leads a soul to unity with the divine having gone through many manifestations.

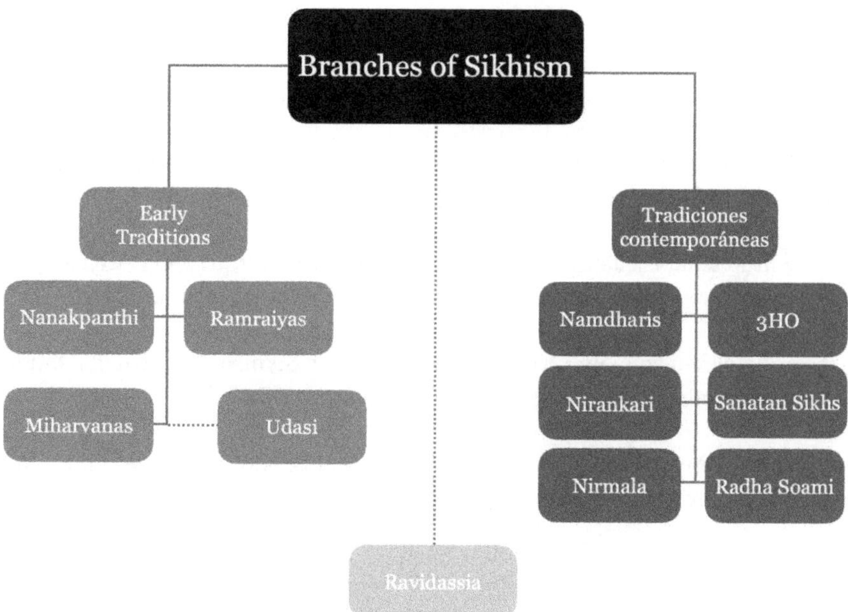

Graphic 9.2 Branches of Sikhism

Since the soul (*atman*) is the same in all living things a trans person is regarded as metaphysically no different from other individuals. Interestingly, Sikhism affirms that diversity in nature and of course in humans is intentional on the part of God. This diversity could be in race, gender, colour or sexual orientation, and so no condemnation can be found for any of these characteristics as they simply show the diverse glory of God.

Unlike Hinduism which has multiple stories of queer encounters and gender fluidity Sikhism does not have many. However, there is one story in which Guru Nanak meets a Sufi saint who has crossdressed and apart from asking the Sufi why he did it there is no condemnation in the story and they are reported to continue their conversations about the divine. Many Sikh scholars take this to mean that due to the comfort and acceptance of Guru Nanak there should be acceptance in the Sikh community.

Sikhism teaches that self-acceptance is of the highest importance since sexual and gender identities are God-ordained matters of human reality. One must honour God through self-acceptance. This is not to say that Sikhism accepts the idea of same-sex marriage, but Sikhs in the West are changing attitudes about this and pointing out there are no scriptures that condemn homosexuality. There is however a tradition of fighting for the rights of minorities which is the basic calling of any Sikh man or woman. It could be argued that the willingness to combat oppression could be applied to standing for the dignity and equality of queer people.

While Sikh scriptures do not explicitly address homosexuality, many Sikh scholars and leaders emphasise the importance of love, understanding and non-judgement in interactions with LGBTIQ+ individuals. There is a growing recognition within the Sikh community, especially in Western contexts, that LGBTIQ+ rights should be respected and upheld. Sikhism's emphasis on social justice and fighting against oppression can be interpreted as support for the rights and dignity of queer individuals. While traditional views on same-sex marriage may vary, there is a movement towards greater acceptance and understanding, driven by the core Sikh values of equality, compassion and human rights.

For Further Discussion

1   How do Jains perceive sexuality in relation to the attainment of *moksa*?

2   According to the Tattvaartha Sutra, how are genders classified in the Jain tradition and what is the attitude of Jains towards gender in relation to enlightenment?

3   How do the central tenets of Jainism, such as nonviolence (*Ahimsa*) and truth (*Satya*), relate to modern perspectives on homosexuality within the Jain community?

4   How are the principles of equality, diversity and inclusion in Sikhism reflected in relation to perspectives on gender identity and sexual orientation within the Sikh community?

5   How does Sikhism approach the concepts of self-acceptance and LGBTIQ+ rights, and how are these views evolving, particularly in Western contexts?

References

Anderson, Michael (2017). "Homosexuality (Jainism)." In: *Buddhism and Jainisim*, Encyclopedia of Indian Religions vol. 5, edited by K T S Sarao and Jeffery D Long. Dordrecht: Springer, pp. 565–568.

Kalsi, Sewa S (2005). *Sikhism*, Religions of the World Series. Philadelphia, PA: Chelsea House Publishers.

Long, Jeffery D (2009). *Jainism: An Introduction*. London: I. B. Tauris.

Nesbitt, Eleanor (2005). *Sikhism: A Very Short Introduction*. Oxford: Oxford University Press.

Shah, Natubhai (2004). *Jainism: The World of Conquerors, Volume 1*. Delhi: Motilal Banarsidass Publishers.

Singh, Upinder (2016). *A History of Ancient and Early Medieval India: From the Stone Age to the 12th Century*. Uttar Pradesh: Pearson.

Singh, Khushwant and Raghu Rai (1984). *The Sikhs*. New Delhi: Lustre Press.

Sweet, Michael J and Leonard Zwilling (1993). "The First Medicalization: The Taxonomy and Etiology of Queerness in Classical Indian Medicine." *Journal of the History of Sexuality* 3, No. 4 (April): pp. 590–607.

Takhar, Opinderjit K (2014). "Sikh Sects." In: *The Oxford Handbook of Sikh Studies*, edited by Pashaura Singh and Louis E Fenech. Oxford: Oxford University Press, pp. 350–360.

Vallely, Anne (2009). "Jainism." In: *The World's Religions: Continuities and Transformations*, edited by Peter B Clarke. New York, NY: Routledge, pp. 325–337.

Von Glasenapp, Helmuth (1999). *Jainism: An Indian Religion of Salvation*, translated by Shridhar B. Shrotri. Delhi: Motilal Banarsidass Publishers.

Further Reading

IAS Parliament (2017). "History of Ten Sikh Gurus," January 8. Available at <https://www.iasparliament.com/current-affairs/history-of-ten-sikh-gurus>.

10

Pagan Spiritualities

In this chapter, we will delve into the diverse world of Paganism and unpack how this fascinating religion relates to the different groups of sexual diversity. We will learn from a religion that engages with diversity in ways other faiths can only dream about. This religion has been disrespected and sidelined in religious studies because it failed to adhere to the norms or expectations of world religions. At the level of practice, Paganism does not exclude any believer, and this all-embracing acceptance of believers is beneficial for queer believers. Therefore, we will explore some aspects of the manifold richness of Paganism at the intersection of gender and sexuality. They represent different perspectives, and each author/branch of Paganism prioritises one central aspect.

Paganism as a Religion

The term 'Paganism' comes from the Latin word paganus, which means 'country dweller'. Although originally paganus was only used as a geographical descriptor, that is, to indicate those who live in the countryside as opposed to the city dwellers, it soon changed its meaning. From the fourth century CE onwards, the term shifted from its geographical tone to a religious one, and began to designate individuals and communities whose beliefs and rituals fell outside of the Christian boundaries (Cameron, 2011: 14–15). The term also was pejorative as the Christian Fathers believed that the country dwellers were not as educated (Hehn, 2000: 1) or sophisticated as the city's inhabitants. Peter Brown says:

> The adoption of paganus by the Latin Christians as an all-embracing, pejorative term for polytheists represents an unforeseen and singularly long-lasting victory, within a religious group, of a word of Latin slang originally devoid of religious meaning. The evolution occurred only in the Latin west, and in connection with the Latin church. Elsewhere, "Hellene" or "gentile" (ethnikos) remained the word for "pagan"; and paganos continued as a purely secular term, with overtones of the inferior and the commonplace. [...] The use of pagans in Latin Christianity echoed a widespread need to see the world in strictly religious categories (2000: 625).

The problem with making 'Paganism' a religious term resides in the fact that it was used to describe non-Christian religions within the Roman Empire and, later, to catalogue new religions encountered by Christians during their conquests on other continents. It was in many ways Christians who 'created' Paganism by including under an umbrella term very different religions that were simply not Christians, as John North says:

> It is perhaps misleading even to say that there was such a religion as paganism at the beginning of [the Common Era] ... It might be less confusing to say that the pagans, before their competition with Christianity, had no religion at all in the sense in which that word is normally used today. They had no tradition of discourse about ritual or religious matters (apart from philosophical debate or antiquarian treatise), no organized system of beliefs to which they were asked to commit themselves, no authority-structure peculiar to the religious area, above all no commitment to a particular group of people or set of ideas other than their family and political context. If this is the right view of pagan life, it follows that we should look on paganism quite simply as a religion invented in the course of the second to third centuries CE, in competition and interaction with Christians, Jews and others (1992: 187–188).

The religions that were grouped under the term Paganism were very different. Many of them related to nature and the natural world and many involved rites celebrating sexuality, the cycles of crops, or the harmony of the earth and the stars. What we today know as 'Paganism' is in fact the sum of differently rooted religions in Greece (Campbell, 2000), Egypt (Scott-Moncrieff, 1913), Germany (Winterbourne, 2004), Spain (McKenna, 1938), England (Carver et al., 2010; Stanley, 2000), Ireland (Butler, 2005), the Balkans (Rybakov, 1981), Russia (Aitamurto, 2016), Ukraine (Lesiv, 2013) or Scandinavia (Clements, 2005), as well as Europe as a region in which ancestral religions have been almost obliterated (Blain, 2005; Dowden, 2000; Petts, 2011). These authors based their research both in the historical past, in early and medieval European history, as well as Modern times.

Prudence Jones and Nigel Pennick have written the most comprehensive history of Pagan Europe. In their work, these authors acknowledge that, despite the divergences in time and geography, Pagan religions have some commonalities:

> They are polytheistic, recognising a plurality of divine beings, which may or many not be avatars or other aspects of an underlying unity/duality/trinity etc. They view Nature as a theophany, a manifestation of divinity, not as a 'fallen' creation of the latter. They recognise the female divine principle, called the Goddess (with a capital 'G', to distinguish her from the many particular goddesses), as well as, or instead of, the male divine principle, the God (Jones and Pennick, 1995: 2).

Although Christianity made many efforts to eradicate these religions it never succeeded. Naturalist religions survived even hidden in the architectural constructions of cathedrals and basilicas. As religions based in oral cultures it can be very difficult to make direct links to the distant past. However, as we know stories do travel well down the generations and so along with images found in castles and churches we do have the memory of the local communities.

One such image that is on many churches and castles through the United Kingdom and Ireland is the Sheela na Gig. Of course, when found on these buildings it is claimed that the image originated as a Christian symbol in the tenth century; however, the stories that accompany it suggest a much earlier origin and one more suited to pagan religion than Christian. This is an image of a woman, whose face is very much in the Celtic style, with large prominent eyes, a head rather too large for the body and exaggerated genitals. She is in a squatting position and holding open her vulva. This image is found under pews and on entrances to churches and believed to be an image that protects people from harm as well as being a fertility image.

Sheela in Kilbeck Church, Hereford, United Kingdom. *Sources:* Graham-H / Pixabay; Jononmac46 / Wikimedia Commons / CC BY-SA 4.0.

What one wonders is such an image doing on and in churches? The only answer seems to be that it is an image that was important to the pre-Christian people of these areas and was co-opted into Christianity. Remarkably creation of these images lasted until the seventeenth century as they were held in such reverence by the people. Their disappearance has been put down to the taking hold of the Reformation and the final disappearance of practices from the Celtic Church. It is assumed that Reformation Christians went about the destruction of the Sheela na Gigs, but some have been found concealed by being built into the walls of churches, such as the find in Llandrindod in Wales. They remain evidence of the link between the new religion, Christianity, and folk beliefs before the collapse of Celtic Christianity. The practice of rubbing a Sheela's genitals with a stone continues today in parts of Ireland and Wales. It has to be noted that so-called folk practices which continued uninterrupted contain remnants of ancient rituals and meanings and so may not be viewed as entirely invented in the modern day. Is the Sheela na Gig a goddess? Some say so but what is known through the practice is that she is believed to be a healer and one who brings fertility.

As well as images and stories it should also be acknowledged that many of the festivals marking the seasons that were carried out by the older religions were co-opted into Christianity and became 'the history and ancient practice' of that religion! It is not unusual for Christianity to take the fabric of a society and impose its own ideas on it.

Coercion, torture, death and persecution were powerful tools for Christianity, and they almost eradicated pagan religions. It is logical that the aftermath of such a colonial religious enterprise would result in a thin connection to the roots of the contemporary pagan religions. Michael F. Strmiska states:

> Modern Pagans are reviving, reconstructing, and reimagining religious traditions of the past that were suppressed for a very long time, even to the point of being almost

Table 10.1 Pagan Festivities and Their Meaning

Festivity	Date	Meaning
Samhain	October 31st or November 1st (Northern hemisphere)/April 30th or May 1st (Southern hemisphere)	This festival, known as the Witches' New Year and celebrated as Halloween, marks the end of the harvest season and the beginning of winter, symbolising the transition between life and death. It is a time for sacred reflection and remembrance, honouring the dead
Yule	December 21st or 22nd (Northern hemisphere)/June 21st to 23rd (Southern hemisphere)	The Winter Solstice marks the longest night of the year and heralds the gradual return of longer days as the sun begins to 'reclaim' its strength. Yule originates from ancient Germanic and Norse traditions, where it was a time to honour the sun's rebirth and celebrate with feasting, fire and rituals. Many modern winter holiday customs—such as decorating with evergreens and lighting candles—trace their roots to Yule practices. It is also one of the eight Sabbats in the Pagan Wheel of the Year
Imbolc	February 1st or 2nd (Northern hemisphere)/ August 1st or 2nd (Southern hemisphere)	The Festival of Light is a day associated with the Celtic goddess Brighid—representing fertility, poetry, healing and fire—who was later incorporated as a Christian saint in Ireland and many other parts of Europe. Imbolc is also a time of purification, renewal and preparation for the growing season ahead
Ostara	March 20th or 21st (Northern hemisphere)/September 20th or 21st (Southern hemisphere)	The Vernal Equinox has retained much of its ancient significance in celebrating new life in spring. This festival—part of the Wheel of the Year in many Pagan and Wiccan traditions—is often associated with planting seeds, honouring nature's cycles and welcoming light and warmth
Beltane	May 1st (Northern hemisphere)/November 1st (Southern hemisphere)	A Day of Fire and Fertility signifies that the earth and all life upon it are fertile and ready to bloom. The occasion is often celebrated with rituals involving fire, dancing and the maypole, symbolising vitality and renewal. It is a time to honour the union of earth and sky while welcoming the abundance of the approaching summer
Litha	June 20th or 21th (Northern hemisphere)/December 20th or 21th (Southern hemisphere)	The Summer Solstice, sometimes called Midsummer, is the year's longest day. It is a time of celebration, vitality and abundance, honouring the fullness of life and the sun's energy. The occasion is often marked with bonfires, feasting and rituals that celebrate warmth, growth and the peak of the growing season
Lammas	August 1st (Northern hemisphere)/February 1st (Southern hemisphere)	It celebrates the First Harvest. In some traditions, this day is known as Lughnasadh, marked by honouring the Celtic god of craftsmanship, Lugh. The occasion is often celebrated with feasting, baking bread and honouring the cycle of life, along with rituals that express gratitude for the gifts of nature
Mabon	September 20th or 21st (Northern hemisphere). March 20th or 21st (Southern hemisphere)	The Autumn Equinox, or the Sabbat of Mabon, is a time of balance, with equal parts light and dark. In many Pagan communities, it is celebrated as a time of thanksgiving for the second harvest, particularly for fruits, vegetables and the abundance of the season

Source: Created by the authors.

totally obliterated in many cases. Thus, with only a few possible exceptions, today's Pagans cannot claim to be continuing religious traditions handed down in an unbroken line from ancient times to the present. They are modern people with a great reverence for the spirituality of the past, making a new religion—a modern Paganism—from the remnants of the past, which they interpret, adapt, and modify according to modern ways of thinking. Modern Paganism is, in this way, both old and new: an ancient/modern hybrid, like a tree with roots deep in the earth but branches reaching into the sky (2005: 10).

Both the United States and Europe have seen in the later twentieth and early twenty-first centuries a resurface of pagan religions, some of them linked to nationalistic/ethnocentric movements (Rountree, 2015). In fact, for some Pagan groups, ethnicity is central to their religion, and they often restrict membership to those who are of the same ethnic group as themselves (Strmiska, 2005: 17). According to Murphy Pizza and James R. Lewis:

> Contemporary Paganism—which consists of Wicca and Witchcraft, Druidry, Heathenry, Asatru, Goddess-worship, Ethnic Reconstructions, and many other traditions—is a movement that is still young and establishing its identity and place on the global religious landscape. The members of the movement confront a paradox of wanting to continue to grow and unify, and of also wishing to maintain its characteristic diversity of traditions, identities, and rituals. Not surprisingly, the modern Pagan movement has had a restless and schismatic formation period, most notably in the United States, but has also been the catalyst for some of the most innovative religious expressions, praxes, theologies, and communities (2009: 1).

Although some Pagan groups have a nationalist or ethnocentric agenda, not all Pagans share this spirit. Carol Barner-Barry states:

> Most contemporary Pagans concern themselves little or not at all with explicitly political ideas or activism. They are much more preoccupied with ritual and the personal practices of their tradition. Most, however, have some fear or uneasiness regarding the potential for the political and legal order to be used against them. They look back to the times when witches (or alleged witches) were tortured and executed in the name of Christianity and they wonder if what they call "The Burning Times" could return. They know that the names they call themselves, such as Pagan, Witch, Wiccan, or Druid, might be considered (at best) eccentric or (at worst) threatening by others. They fear for the safety of themselves, their families, and their fellow Pagans. Many choose to keep their religious beliefs secret—to stay in "the broom closet" (Chapin-Bishop, 1993, 35–37). Others are open about their beliefs in some situations and secretive in others (2005: 30).

Branches of Paganism

There is no universally agreed-upon method for organising the numerous branches of Paganism. Different authors and organisations use varying approaches to classify and map these diverse traditions. The complexity of Paganism reflects its rich variety of practices,

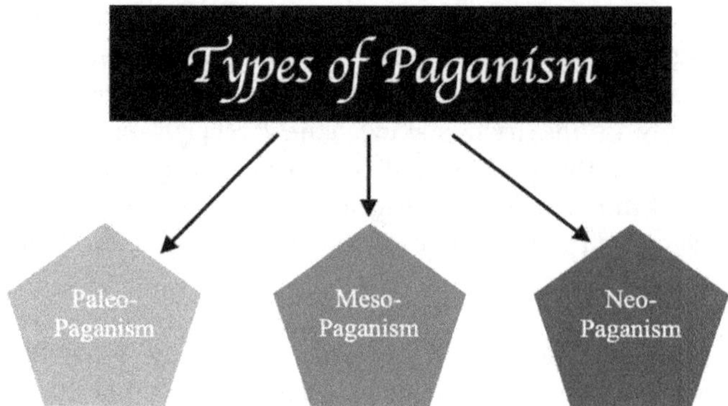

Graphic 10.1   Types of Paganism

beliefs and cultural influences. One common framework for understanding Paganism is the division into three broad categories: Paleopaganism, Mesopaganism and Neopaganism. This division helps to distinguish between ancient traditions, those influenced by external cultures, and modern revivals or reconstructions. These three categories are proposed by Druid scholar Isaac Bonewits (2006, 2007).

Paleopaganism

This category encompasses what are often described as 'original tribal' religions, cultural, polytheistic or animistic traditions practised without significant foreign influence. These traditions are found on every continent and include examples such as Shinto in Japan. However, Bonewits's characterisation of an 'original form' can be critiqued, as no religion exists in complete isolation. All religious traditions, at some point, have been influenced by interactions with other cultures or belief systems. This raises questions about the concept of 'originality' in religions and highlights the dynamic, interconnected nature of spiritual practices throughout history.

Mesopaganism

This category refers to forms of Paganism that have come into contact with other cultures and undergone significant influences as a result. Mesopagan cultural religions may operate independently or become integrated into another religious framework. While Mesopaganism retains elements of its original identity, its reconstruction has been shaped by external influences, particularly Judeo-Christian and Islamic thoughts. Despite this, Mesopagan practices often maintain an independent character, striving to recreate or revive aspects of earlier Paleopagan religions. Examples of Mesopaganism include Freemasonry, Rosicrucianism, Santería, Christo-paganism and Sikhism, each of which reflects a blending of cultural and spiritual traditions while preserving distinctive religious practices. This dynamic interplay illustrates the adaptive and evolving nature of Mesopaganism over time.

Neo-Paganism

This category encompasses Pagan traditions that emerged primarily in the twentieth century, particularly after the 1940s, although some trace their origins as far back as the mid-1800s. These modern forms of Paganism are often inspired by ancient sources and cultural practices but have been adapted to suit the lives and spiritual needs of contemporary people. Bonewits associates this form of Paganism with the ideals of the 'Aquarian Age', as described by Higginbotham and Higginbotham (2002), which emphasise personal spiritual growth, harmony and innovation. Additionally, Bonewits (2007: 5) notes that this modern Paganism often seeks to move away from traditional Western frameworks of monotheism and dualism, advocating instead for more inclusive and holistic approaches to spirituality.

Building on the distinction between Paleopaganism, Mesopaganism and Neopaganism, other scholars have further categorised Pagan organisations and traditions by considering regional variations and the ancestral roots of newer movements. This approach highlights the interplay between cultural heritage and contemporary adaptations, reflecting the global diversity within Paganism. Consequently, the landscape of Pagan traditions becomes increasingly complex, with overlapping influences and unique developments across different parts of the world. This complexity underscores the dynamic and evolving nature of Pagan spiritual practices.

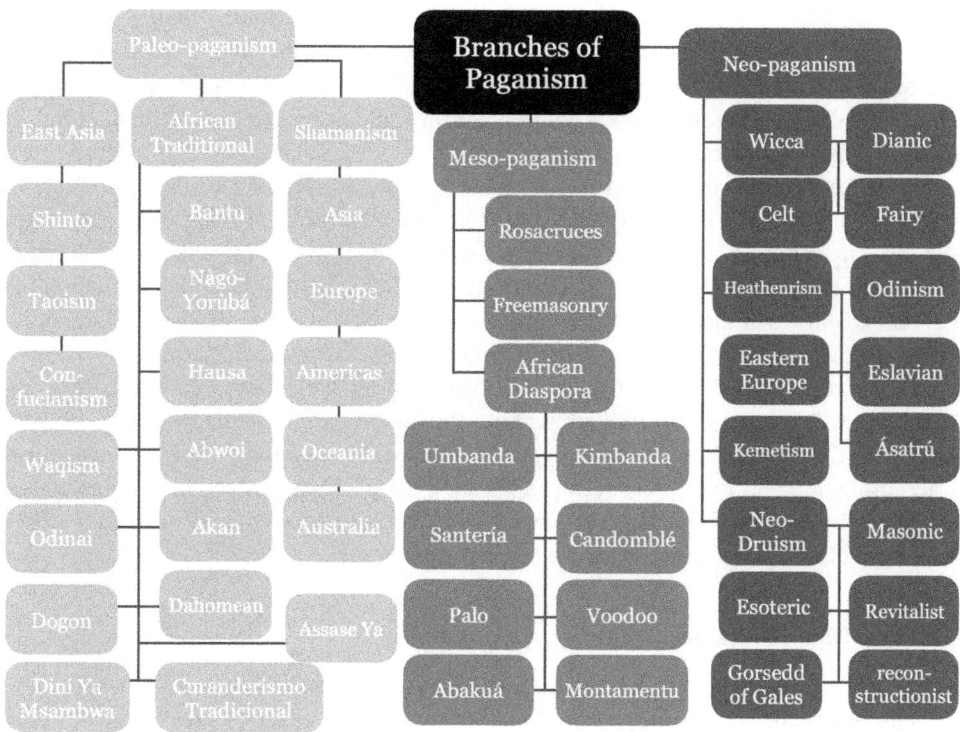

Graphic 10.2 Branches of Paganism

Pagan Queer Theologies

It may seem that no other religions can claim to be more accepting of queer believers than Paganism since it embraces the reality of all of its believers.

Pagan Celtic Culture and Sexuality

As oral cultures it must be acknowledged that much that we hear of the Celts came from their conquerors. The Romans and Greeks who did not wish to be seen in a similar light to those they considered barbarians and so report with dislike that the Celtic aristocracy preferred men over women and even had relationships with men of their own class, a practice frowned on by the Greeks. In Irish mythology we see that war-like men had special male friends who they fought beside and tenderly loved. This appears to give the view of an open society but for such a warlike society being called a 'bottom' was a huge insult. The Irish Brehon Laws refer to homosexuality as a legal reason women may divorce her husband, but scholars believe this is not as a punishment for the man but as a right for the woman to move on to have children. Its place in the Law seems to suggest that this was not an infrequent occurrence. Not much is said of women; however, the most prominent example refers to the warrior Queen Boudica who with the help of the Druids led a successful campaign against the Romans. After her husband was killed she was elected leader of a united Celtic resistance against the Romans. It was the custom that a Celtic leader should have a wife; of course up to then most leaders had been men but it is, some scholars suggest, possible that in order to appear a legitimate leader Boudica also took a wife (Williams, 2009). The only other mention of lesbian sexuality can be found in the twelfth century *Book of Leinster* (Best, 1954) which tells of two women having sex which is referred to as a playful mating with no disgust or condemnation. It appears then that in pre-Christian culture homosexuality was not frowned on and that even in Celtic Christian Ireland women were not condemned for playful mating.

Did the Celtic people have queer deities? Well, it seems Ireland did have one; Cu Chulainn had a relationship with his foster brother who he loved. However, this did not result in him refraining from killing his lover by thrusting a spear into his anus. A further example can be found with the Samodivi who are Eastern European Celtic deities described as nymph-like and bi-sexual. They attract men who become their servants, while the women who they attract become so jealous of their many lovers that they kill themselves (Aveela, 2015).

But can we talk about 'Pagan Queer Theologies'? Jo J. Green states that Paganism is 'for all self-identified queers who are looking for a spirituality that is open, accepting and sympathetic to the needs of the modern queer' (2016: 5). It is impossible to deny that Paganism is accepting of queer folks. However, the question about 'Pagan Queer Theologies' relates to (a) the (re)creation of practices that are all-inclusive as well as (b) theologising the beliefs from a queer perspective. This needs to be unpacked briefly.

Queering Pagan Practices

At the level of practices, Paganism does not exclude any believer, and this all-embracing acceptance of believers is beneficial for queer believers. They do have a part many times an important part in the many Pagan traditions. This does not imply that Paganism is free from discrimination. Christine Hoff Kraemer writes:

> Although contemporary Paganism is not without its own homegrown strains of homo- and transphobic theology, the movement as a whole has been welcoming of

sexual minorities. The notions that the body and sexuality are "sinful" or that the only divinely approved sexuality is heterosexual have driven many people out mainstream religions institutions and left them seeking a spiritual home. Paganism's openness to a variety of forms of sexuality has attracted significant numbers of LGBT people (2014: 21).

In his book *Walking with the Gods*, W. D. Wilkerson interviews a Pagan believer by the name of Lupus and informs us: 'the hetero-normativity of conventional Paganism, which tends to divide itself according to strongly pronounce masculine and feminine lines, drover Lupus to explore a more gender-fluid and queer religious sensibility' (2014: 323). This is important because the practices of any religious organisation affect the way that believers would relate to that organisation.

In truth, it could be very difficult to find any religion that is free from the influence of heteropatriarchalism. The difference in Paganism is that it has ventured, maybe due to its situation of being constantly under scrutiny from the Abrahamic religions, into deeper levels of acceptance of gender and sexual diversity.

Queering Divine Power(s)

Notwithstanding, at the level of theologising about the Divine Power(s) and the faith of the believers, things may not always be so acceptable in Paganism. The Goddess has re-emerged from ancient times, but it has been argued that it does not always change the power dynamics of heteropatriarchal binaries. That said it has been a huge benefit for women of all sexualities and genders as it gave them a sense of self and permission to claim power and authority. With such scholars as Carol Christ (1998, 2003) and Naomi Goldenberg (1979) leading the way 'thealogy' has become a respected academic discipline. Their work was aided by the monumental findings of Marija Gimbutas (1982, 2001), an archaeologist, who discovered and wrote on the goddesses of Old Europe. Her work uncovered societies with goddess worship at their heart which differed significantly from those societies around them.

These societies did not wage war, did not hold slaves and lived in harmony with nature; in other words they were peaceful and acknowledged the creative and procreative powers of human women and nature. Her work was challenged at first by male archaeologists who wished to keep prehistory in the hands of marauding men, but due to the careful and astute way on which she went about her work they eventually could not question her findings and this changed the face of European history. Her work meant that when speaking of contemporary Goddess religion we should do so with extreme caution since there is a history embedded in the deep past that many goddess groups know and claim in their practice. In short, worship of the goddess is not a purely made-up phenomenon; it has history throughout Old Europe and echoes remain in stories and landscapes.

Those following Gimbutas asked different questions of this research than she herself had asked, for example, are there queer gods and goddesses in this distant past? The answer of course is yes as is easily seen in Greek myth. In the poems of Sappho (2022) we hear that Aphrodite had guardianship over lesbians and that many of her priestesses were lesbian. Aphrodite herself also in the later stories took on largely male characteristics and was known as Aphroditus. In the cults of Artemis, Ishtar and Inanna there were queer priests and they were celebrated. It does appear that the historical goddess religions were inclusive and peaceful embracing all that nature, even in human form, gave birth to. The stories are far more nuanced in terms of gender identity than we have often been led to believe, and the celebration of a female deity does not exclude men or as we have seen queer folk.

Unsurprisingly after centuries of the divine being seen only as male and an academic system that supports such a theology we do find work that is uneasy with the notion of goddess religion.

Margaret McManus declares:

> My second objection to Goddess religion is what I see as a tendency toward glorification of the female and feminine qualities. Those engaged in Goddess religion seem not to make a distinction between valuing or cherishing women and glorifying women. It seems that glorification of the feminine serves to solidify the stereotyping of women, to affirm that 'biology is destiny,' to maintain a dualistic perception of humanity, and to exclude men from divinity in much the same way women have been excluded by ourselves and our history, need the Goddess for a time, a time of healing. Perhaps men, long glorified and over-valued, need to understand the experience of exclusion. Perhaps the presence of Goddess religion is prophetic – it reminds us of the tremendous understanding of itself. Nonetheless, I believe that exclusive concentration on the Goddess is quite inadequate to the depth of humanity's search for ultimate meaning (1984: 76–77).

McManus appears to be concerned about the extremes of the religion but does acknowledge that women may well need the goddess to overcome centuries of oppression within religion. Men also need to learn that their identification with a male god should not lead to societies in which they are glorified.

Kraemer has other concerns stating that sometimes the rigidity of understanding the God/dess may result in hurting the believers:

> Despite the fact that many Pagan communities are welcoming toward transgender people, transgender issues have been controversial in Paganism because of the strong influence of British Wiccan theology on the Pagan movement as a whole. British Traditional Wicca focuses on fertility and uses heterosexual sex (the union of the Goddess and the God) as a symbolic representation for the interaction of primal creative forces. Transgender people do not fit into binary gender roles, which has left some Pagans at a loss for how to include them in rituals that call for a priestess and a priest (2014: 23).

This seems a very narrow focussed criticism and does not hold water in the light of Gimbutas' work. The limitations referred to in this quotation lie with the contemporary believers involved not the entire system.

To counter some of those concerns we find Raven Brangwyn Kaldera (2010) clearly dealing with divinities who do not embrace a heteropatriarchal tone but a gender-fluid one. Kaldera says:

> The gender of Gods in relation to our own genders is also an exercise in diversity. Even the most male-preferring of Gods has a few female followers; the most woman-preferring of Goddesses has some men devoted to her (such as the men who were documented followers of Artemis). Most Gods and Goddesses tend to choose far more often on the basis of personality affinity rather than bodily configuration. This does not mean that specific bodily configuration cannot get you extra affinity points, especially if you are looking at a deity whose personal mysteries include the biological mysteries of a particular physical configuration (for example, Baphomet, who is deeply bound up with the bodily experience of mixed physical gender attributes in

any combination, and can be expected to respond to any intersex or transgendered person who has the courage to approach). However, it seems to be a guarantee that even those God/desses will accept someone who is not of that bodily configuration. Perhaps they are able to take on that configuration on an energy-body level—something which the Gods definitely recognize as much more significant than we do—or perhaps there is some other affinity of personality or life-sphere that we do not happen to see. Gods are not so monolithic of nature that they cannot make exceptions out of some version of divine love (2012: 107–108).

To queer the Deities appears to be no more than embracing the histories that have been uncovered of all-embracing communities. It is to continue developing an understanding that would translate in never-ending expandable boundaries for the believers in the many Pagan traditions.

Queering Gender and Sexuality

There is a source of great richness in Paganism at the intersection of gender and sexuality. Mary Jo Neitz (2000) is a feminist sociologist that has long researched on witches first from a gender frame to then moved on to a queer frame. The move seems clear when she starts talking about questions of power and their balance and equality. Her fieldwork has focused on Wicca organisations, basically Dianic, Neogarnerian and Neo-Pagan witches (2000: 373).

Her research centres on the Dragonfest, a Colorado festival, which according to their website is described as follows:

> Dragonfest is a large, regional, neopagan spiritual retreat held in the mountains of Colorado each August. People of all religions and spiritual traditions are welcome at Dragonfest, but workshops and rituals focus on various Neopagan, Wiccan, and other Earth-based spiritual practices (Dragonfest, 2017).

This festival is organised by the Front Range Pagans, who are named as such because they live 'along the front range of the Rocky Mountains in Colorado, ranging from Colorado Springs to Denver to Boulder to Fort Collins' (2000: 374).

Neitz is very clear in the way she defines and explains the many elements present in her research, for example, 'the Craft' is another term by which Wiccan believers are known, practitioners of the Craft. She also refers to 'the Great Rite' and informs the readers that sexual intercourse rarely happens in Wiccan public rituals. This is not to say that these rites have not been known in the history of nature religion. Oberon Zell-Ravenheart describes the Great Rite as follows:

> As a ritual of sex magic, the Great Rite is the hieros gamos,"sacred marriage', of the God and Goddess. Sex is a source of power, creative as well as procreative. This power rooted in polarity, a charged attraction of opposites. But that is only one of many ways that sexual energy flows. People of similar qualities or of the same sex may also generate pleasure and power together. The giving and receiving of sexual pleasure is an endlessly varied art (2006: 189).

One important aspect of this definition is that Zell-Ravenheart takes into account that same-sex couples also can participate in the rite. This clearly encourages queering the rite for same-sex couples. Christine Hoff Kraemer offers us an excellent overview of the intersection of gender, sexuality and Paganism. She affirms that 'Gender and sexuality are central theological issues for many contemporary Pagans; in fact, many Pagans came to the movement due to issues with gender or sexuality in the religions of their birth or in the wider culture' (2012: 391).

Kraemer (2012) contributes a clear map of contemporary Paganism and its intersection with gender and sexuality, she analyses and explains how the essentialist polarity masculine/feminine has been reinterpreted by queer Pagans to include them beyond biological determinism or gender essentialist identities. Kramer states:

> In the 2000s, queer-identified strands of Paganism began to make their voices heard more widely (Urban 2006, p. 189). The term "queer" was embraced as a blanket term for GLBT people and their allies, as well as sexual minorities of other kinds (for instance, BDSM practitioners, celibates, etc.) (Aburrow 2009). Queer Pagans also challenged the gender essentialism remaining in the sexual polarity still practiced (though less prescrip- tively than before) by some Wiccans (Neitz 2000, p. 382) and in feminist Paganism, which had a tendency to equate feminine divinity and its associated positive qualities solely with the bodies of biological women. Pagans began to explore the possibility of queer and transgender deity (Aburrow 2009, p. 151; Urban 2006, p. 189), and BDSM practices that had been present in mid-twentieth century Wicca, but had been discarded by many feminist Pagans, began to gain greater acceptance and visibility within the Pagan community (2012: 392).

Kraemer claims that feminist Pagans, despite their Goddess worship, do not actually have much analysis regarding sexuality. She bases this on reviewing a collection published in 2000. She says:

> Interestingly, however, in this collection there is little analysis of the role of sexuality in the Goddess movement, except to describe how Goddess worship celebrates sexuality (especially women's sexuality) as an integrated part of human life. Further, little to no attention is given to the differing experiences of heterosexual, bisexual, and lesbian women. Although Eller in particular argues that feminist spirituality can challenge gender essentialist attitudes and holds up Starhawk as one feminist Pagan writer who does so, several essays also speak of "women's mysteries," asserting a universality to women's experiences that transcends race, class, and sexual orientation (Kraemer, 2012: 393).

She does acknowledge that the over-generalisation of women's essentialism could be a '"strategic device" to create women-only groups' (Kraemer, 2012: 394), However, essentialism is not only an exclusive 'problem' of feminist Pagans but also of queer Pagans. This is a very intriguing aspect of Paganism. For this, Kraemer cites the example of the Radical Faeries (2012: 395–396) and the negative experiences of transgender Pagan women who were excluded from Dianic Wicca groups. Of course, not all Dianic Wiccans use derogatory comments about transgender individuals, and it has to be acknowledged that they have played a key role in empowering women in their gender and sexuality.

Neitz talking about Wicca states that believers 'argue that the prechristian (pagan) nature religions were also prepatriarchal and precapitalist, and that the Wiccan revival offers models for more egalitarian and ecologically sound ways to living today' (2000: 373). A fair statement in the light of the work of Marija Gimbutas which clearly showed that Old Europe in the days of goddess worship was egalitarian and communal.

Kaldera (2001) offers the important myth of Agdistis, daughter of the Great Mother Goddess Cybele. Kaldera is a Pagan shaman, educator, activist and priest, and his work has been important to 'uncover' gender-bending and gender-variant deities within Pagan traditions. The Deity that he focuses on, although present in mythology, is not well known.

Agdistis was a Greek deity. According to Pierre Grimal (1990), there are two different stories that narrate the fate of Agdistis. The first version was told by Pausanias, who was a Greek traveller and geographer of the second century CE and who lived in the time of Roman emperors Hadrian, Antoninus Pius and Marcus Aurelius. In this first version, Zeus spilt semen over the earth and from it, Agdistis was born as intersex. However, the Gods got angry at this and castrated Agdistis. From hir penis, an almond tree was born. Nana, daughter of Sangarius, took an almond, put it on her lap and got pregnant, later giving birth to Attis. As a teenager, Attis met Agistis, by now a woman, but he was already betrothed to marry the daughter of the king of Pessinus. Agdistis appeared at the wedding and Attis castrated himself, thus dying. Agdistis was granted that Attis body should not decay (Grimal, 1990: 27).

The second version Agdistis is the daughter of Zeus, who has left some semen on a nearby rock. Dionysus, seeing that Agdistis is intersex, castrated him. From the blood of the castration, a pomegranate tree grew and Nana inserted one of its fruits into her womb, thus getting pregnant and delivering Attis. King Midas of Pessinus decreed that Attis should marry one of his daughters. During an argument between Agdistis and Cybele, Attis and other guests got crazed and Attis castrated himself under a pine tree, thus dying. Cybele buried him and the daughter of King Midas, as she has also committed suicide. Violets grew from both tombs. Agdistis was granted by Zeus that Attis body should not decay. Therefore, Agdistis created a community of priests in Pessinus to do a festival in honour of Attis (Grimal, 1990: 27).

Agdistis should not be confused with Hermaphroditus, son of Hermes and Aphrodite, who was raised by Nymphs in the forest of Ida in Phrygia. Salmacis, Nymph of the lake in Caria, fell in love with him. Although rejecting the advances of Salmacis, Hermaphroditus entered the water naked and Salmacis prayed that their bodies would never be apart from each other. The Gods granted the prayer, and they joined into one body with a double personality/gender. (Grimal, 1990: 197).

The value of these myths present in ancient faiths is that they do not only defy the narrow binary conceptions of many religious beliefs, but also they are key elements for queer folks to identify with. However, the main point in recovering them is to particularly empower transgender Pagans, who are often made invisible by 'gay and lesbian' believers. Asked about his motives in writing a book like this Kaldera says:

> Because of the books that kept coming out on "gay" spirituality from the academic community. Many of them were well-researched and concisely written, but the authors lumped in a few "mysteries" that were clearly transgendered in with the "gay and lesbian" stuff. All right, there is some overlap, both in the community and spirituality. We are a continuum, not that little boys can be moved around as the lines are redrawn. But sexual preference is about just that, who you desire sexually—and what ramifications that has on your life and spirituality. Make no mistake, it does have ramifications; sexuality is one of the strongest forces in the universe. Being third gender is something else again. You can be third gender and desire men, women, other third gender people, all of the above, or nobody at all, and still be third gender. You can be third gender in a vacuum with no other human beings in existence. It's about who you are, not what you are or who you would be with. Both

should be respected, but one should not be confused with the other, especially by scholars who ought to know better (2001: 9–10).

Dealing with another hetero aspect in paganism, Chas S. Clifton focuses in detail on the creation of the Wiccan's Great Rite. As Clifton (2014) asserts, the Great Rite is not an ancient rite, an assertion that other scholars contest. They point to ancient agricultural cultures in the Middle East such as Mesopotamia and Phoenicia, although it has been suggested that the biblical Song of Songs may be a hierogamatic text. Nevertheless, Clifton asserts it does not trace its roots to ancient times in which nature religions existed. On the contrary, it is a creation by Wiccan founder, Gerald Gardner:

> The Great Rite, however, was found in Gardner's earliest draft of the B[ook] o[f] S[hadows], a handwritten folio entitled Ye Bok of Ye Art Magical, which included various borrowings from the Greater Key of Solomon and other grimoires plus his own drafts for ritual templates and which he assembled during the late 1940s, before Wicca's official launch in 1951, coincidental with his and Cecil Williamson's opening of their witchcraft and folklore museum on the Isle of Man (2014: 155).

Wicca then in the eyes of Gardner was a revival of fertility religions. This is one of the most primal rites that humanity has created. As Migene González-Wippler states: 'Fertility rites of primitive societies, both ancient and modern, embrace not only the fertility of the soul but that of the community as well. Thus the rites were and are used to increase both the crops and the race' (1978: 259). One of the most well-known fertility religions in Judeo-Christian cultures is that of Baal.

As fertility is related to the fertility of the soil, it makes sense that fertility rites emerged only when agriculture was birthed in the early Neolithic era in the Mediterranean. Emmanuel Anati says:

> The Epi-Palaeolithic cultures and other cultures usually developing in marginal areas showed concern about sexuality, the Mesolithic cultures, with the exception of the Natufians, seem to be little concerned with sexual representations. The Neolithic period develops a taste and an interest for this kind of depiction, revealing a new and much more sophisticated and "intellectualized" approach to the problems of human reproduction and of fertility of the fields (1985: 7).

The cleverness of Gardner was to connect his development of the Great Rite with that ancestral past. As Clifton (2014: 153) explains, it was the witches who developed the Book of Shadows that ended cementing the ideas and drafts of Gardner's rite into a stable central practice of the Wicca tradition.

David Green takes us back to Goddess worship and explores men who worship the Goddess. He carried out ethnographic work among the Male Goddess Movement (MGM) as he explains:

> Throughout my research into Paganisms I have become aware of, and increasingly interested in, a group of Pagan men who, following the dominant feminine spiritual idiom of many Neo-Pagan paths, rooted their magico-religious practices in veneration of goddesses, rather than in mythopoetic constructions of masculinity. Although they are by no means a unified community of practitioners I began to term them The Male Goddess Movement (MGM). The MGM appears to be a new and unresearched phenomenon within Contemporary Paganisms (Green, 2012: 306).

If it has been assumed that the essentialisation of the feminine tends to create a sense that only biological women can worship the Goddess, Green shows that this is not the case through his research of these men's experiences. Their positionality within Pagan traditions challenges long-seated beliefs, as Green indicates:

> traditional correspondences of women with nature and sexuality still remain at the heart of Goddess feminism. The Goddess, for example, is still identified with the primordial mother nature figure, the triple Goddess (of maiden, mother and crone), female sexuality, and the sacred landscape (2012: 313).

Green clearly indicates that the worshippers of the Goddess do not necessarily identify as queer in order to be devotees. On the contrary, many of these men are heterosexual men questioning, as well as, (re)elaborating a new sense of masculinity:

> The rise of this feminine – and indeed eco-feminist – spiritual idiom within Contemporary Paganisms clearly has implications for Pagan men. They see the feminization of Pagan spiritualities as mirroring broader societal dynamics which have been seen to marginalize certain constituencies of men, particularly masculinities traditionally associated with the working classes. This crisis of masculinity is driven both by the rise of second-wave feminism and the restructuring of work in the West, now rooted in a service-based knowledge economy rather than in traditional heavy industry. Just as Pagan women have sought to build thealogy upon feminist-friendly mythopoetic foundations, so some Pagan men, against the background of gender crises, have attempted to re-ground their spiritualities in eco-friendly archetypes of 'wild masculinity': a mythopoetic vision of man as wilderness which is congruent with the eco-feminist construction of women as sacred nature. These new androcentric spiritual dynamics are often termed Men's Mysteries (2012: 313).

In highlighting this phenomenon, Green shows that some Pagan traditions do resemble societal processes in postmodern societies, with the emergence of new masculinities, one may say queer masculinities when placed alongside longstanding models of maleness. The question that should be asked about these masculinities is: 'According to which culture?' as not only gender but also gender-role expectations and the sexual division of labour are based on cultural assumptions/mandates. The 'new masculinities' that Green points to are related to the Anglo-Saxon culture. Victor Jeleniewski Seidler refers to this when affirming:

> We cannot explore these diverse masculinities without seeing them through their relationship with imperial and colonial others. It is through these historical relations that masculinities have been defined. We cannot speak about 'new masculinities' until we have engaged with the complex histories which mark relations with our fathers and grandfathers. [...] In part this involves developing a critical relationship with different ways we have learnt to think about men and masculinities. It forces us to question an easy universalism and the temptation to cast masculinity abstractly as some kind of homogeneous entity that transcends history and culture. However, while there are resonances between different traditions and across diverse colonialisms, masculinities are always framed within particular histories of class, nation, religion, 'race' and ethnicities (2006: 34).

This is important to keep in mind as Paganism is not a unified movement and it has representatives in different contexts, many of which may not embrace the Anglo-Saxon cultural background. Nonetheless, the value of Green's work lies in the fact that there are men within some Pagan traditions seeking to destabilise the hegemony of essentialisation and biological determinisms.

Kraemer is part of a collection of essays that deal with embodiment in different religious traditions. The issue of embodiment is a key element when thinking about gender and sexuality as well as other issues pertaining to the daily-lived experiences of human beings. On this, Kramer, quoting Goodwin, states:

> In "Thinking Sex and American Religions" (2011), Goodwin emphasizes that the oversignification of sexuality is both typical of contemporary Westerners and relatively new. Our cultural obsession with sexual matters, including politicized aspects such as reproductive rights and same-sex marriage, often overshadow equally weighty issues of international relations, environment, and economics and are unique to our historical moment. As Goodwin states, scholars also perpetuate this trend by emphasizing sexuality over other aspects of embodiment, such as race, age, health, location, and the material conditions of life (2015: 144).

We agree with the author that the issue of race/ethnicity as well as able bodies and other aspects are often missed from the analysis of embodiment. It is a wonderful contribution that Kramer recovers this, especially since 'The majority of the communities that self-identify as contemporary Pagan (or, sometimes, neo-Pagan) are mostly English-speaking, white, middle-class, urban groups within the United States, Canada, United Kingdom, and Australia' (Kraemer, 2015: 144).

Kraemer refers to the work of Kaldera and says:

> 'Polytheist spirit worker Raven Kaldera (1966–) would agree that a body that transgresses social norms is a source of both pain and power. Kaldera is transgender and disabled, two conditions that put him on the boundaries of mainstream society. His writings suggest, however, that he feels his position gives him unique spiritual insights. Rather than seeing gender as a binary across which women and men can barely communicate, as many people do, transgender, genderqueer, and other queer-identified people stand outside these binaries and may more clearly see the harmful restrictions that rigid gender roles place on individuals. To live with a disabled body also sets one apart from the opportunities and obligations that consume most people's lives; it can place one outside of the flow of ordinary social life and allow space for spiritual work, as well as special opportunities to encounter others in marginalized or disadvantaged positions. Kaldera sees speaking for marginalized or disadvantaged groups, especially for queer people, to be a central part of being a spirit worker. Many of his books address the special concerns of these groups (2015: 158).

This chapter has covered some of the many traditions now contained under the umbrella term Paganism. It highlights how some may claim with good cause to have ancient lineage while others are modern or postmodern inventions and none the worse for that since religion must find relevance within time and place or die. The strength of paganism perhaps lies in its embrace of bodies and its potential for earth healing through practitioners' way of living, both aspects very much needed in the world of today.

For Further Discussion

1   In light of our recent studies, do you concur that this cultural context fosters a more inclusive environment for LGBTQ+ believers? If not, what specific concerns do you hold?

2   Have you interacted with practitioners of pagan traditions who embody the inclusive nature discussed? Could you elaborate on any personal experiences or stories you may have encountered?

3   How does the concept of gender and sexuality align within various pagan belief systems, and are there common threads that promote acceptance of diverse sexual orientations?

4   In your exploration of pagan practices, have you come across any historical or contemporary instances where homosexuality is celebrated or acknowledged within the context of rituals or ceremonies?

5   How do pagan communities address issues related to LGBTQ+ inclusion, and are there variations in their approaches across different pagan traditions or sects?

6   Considering the diverse nature of pagan beliefs, how do individuals within these communities navigate the intersectionality of their spiritual practices and their sexual identities?

References

Aitamurto, Kaarina (2016). *Paganism, Traditionalism, Nationalism: Narratives of Russian Rodnoverie*. London: Routledge.

Anati, Emmanuel (1985). "The Question of Fertility Cults." In: Archeology and Fertility Cult in the Ancient Mediterranean. Papers Presented at the First International Conference on Archaeology of the Ancient Mediterranean. The University of Malta, 2–5 September 1985, edited by Anthony Bonanno. Amsterdam: B. R. Grüner.

Aveela, Ronesa (2015). "Samodivi, Witches of Darkness or Thracian Goddesses?" *Mystical Emona,* June 22. Available at: <https://ronesaaveela.com/2015/05/22/samodivi-witches-of-darkness-or-thracian-goddesses>.

Barner-Barry, Carol (2005). *Contemporary Paganism: Minority Religions in a Majoritarian America*. New York, NY: Palgrave MacMillan.

Best, Richard I (1954). *The Book of Leinster: Formerly Lebur na Nuachongbala*. Dublin: Institute for Advanced Studies.

Blain, Jenny (2005). "Heathenry, the Past, and Sacred Sites in Today's Britain." In: *Modern Paganism in World Cultures*, edited by Michael F Strmiska. Santa Barbara, CA: ABC-CLIO, pp. 181–208.

Bonewits, Isaac (2006). *Bonewits's Essential Guide to Druidism*. New York, NY: Kensington Publishing Corporation.

Bonewits, Isaac (2007). *Neopagan Rites: A Guide to Creating Public Rituals that Work*. Woodbury, MN: Llewellyn Publications.

Brown, Peter (2000). "Pagan." In: *Late Antiquity: A Guide to the Postclassical World*, edited by Glen Warren Bowersock, Peter Brown and Oleg Grabar. Cambridge, MA: The Belknap Press of Harvard University Press, p. 625.

Butler, Jenny (2005). "Druidry in Contemporary Ireland." In: *Modern Paganism in World Cultures: Comparative Perspectives*, ABC-CLIO Religion in Contemporary Cultures Series, edited by Michael F Strmiska. Santa Barbara, CA: ABC-CLIO, pp. 87–126.

Cameron, Alan G (2011). *The Last Pagans of Rome*. New York, NY: Oxford University Press.

Campbell, Andrew (2000). *Old Stones, New Temples: Ancient Greek Paganism Reborn*. Bloomington, IN: Xlibris Corporation.

Carver, Martin, Alex Sanmark and Sarah Semple (editors) (2010). *Signals of Belief in Early England: Anglo-Saxon Paganism Revisited*. Oxford: Oxbow Books.

Clements, Jonathan (2005). *A Brief History of the Vikings: The Last Pagans or the First Modern Europeans?* London: Robinson Publishing.

Clifton, Chas S (2014). "Sex Magic or Sacred Marriage? Sexuality in Contemporary Wicca." In: *Sexuality and New Religious Movements*, edited by Henrik Bogdan and James R Lewis. New York, NY: Palgrave MacMillan, pp. 149–163.

Christ, Carol (1998). *Rebirth of the Goddess. Finding Meaning in Feminist Spirituality*. London: Routledge.

Christ, Carol (2003). *She Who Changes: Reimaging the Divine in the World*. London: Palgrave.

Dowden, Ken (2000). *European Paganism: The Realities of Cult from Antiquity to the Middle Ages*. London: Routledge.

Dragonfest (2017). "About Dragonfest." Available at: <http://dragonfest.org/about>.

Gimbutas, Marija (1982). *Goddesses and Gods of Old Europe, 6,500–3,500: Myths and Cult Images*. Berkeley, CA: University of California Press.

Gimbutas, Marija, with Marian Dexter (2001). *The Living Goddesses*. Berkeley, CA: University of California Press.

González-Wippler, Migene (1978). *The Complete Book of Spells, Ceremonies, and Magic*, Llewellyn's Sourcebook Series. St. Paul, MN: Publications.

Green, David (2012). "What Men Want? Initial Thoughts on the Male Goddess Movement." *Religion and Gender* 2, No. 2: pp. 305–327.

Green, Jo J (2016). *Queer Paganism: A Spirituality that Embraces all Identities*. CreateSpace Independent Publishing Platform.

Grimal, Pierre (1990) In: *A Concise Dictionary of Classical Mythology*, edited by Stephen Kershaw from a translation by A. R. Maxwell-Hyslop. Oxford: Basil Blackwell.

Goldenberg, Naomi (1979). *Changing of the Gods*. Boston, MA: Beacon Press.

Hehn, Georg (2000). "Paganismus." In: *Metzler Lexikon Religion: Gegenwart-Alltag-Medien, Volume 3: Paganismus-Zombie*, edited by Christoph Auffarth, Jutta Bernard and Hubert Mohr. Stuttgart: J. B. Metzler Verlag, p. 192.

Higginbotham, River and Joyce Higginbotham (2002). *Paganism: An Introduction to Earth-centered Religions*. Woodbury, MN: Llewellyn Publications.

Jones, Prudence and Nigel Pennick (1995). *A History of Pagan Europe*. London: Routledge.

Kaldera, Raven B (2010). *Hermaphrodeities: The Transgender Spirituality Workbook*. Bloomington, IN: Xlibris Corporation.

Kraemer, Christine H (2012). "Gender and Sexuality in Contemporary Paganism." *Religion Compass* 6, No. 8: pp. 390–401.

Kraemer, Christine H (2014). *Eros and Touch from a Pagan Perspective: Divided for Love's Sake*. New York, NY: Routledge.

Kraemer, Christine H (2015). "Pagan Traditions: Sacralizing the Body." In: *Religion: Embodied Religion*, edited by Kent L Brintnall. Farmington Hills. MI: Macmillan Reference USA, pp. 143–163.

Lesiv, Mariya (2013). *The Return of Ancestral Gods: Modern Ukrainian Paganism as an Alternative Vision for a Nation*, Mcgill-Queen's Studies in the History of Religion. Kingston, ON: McGill-Queen's University Press.

McKenna, Stephen (1938). *Paganism and Pagan Survivals in Spain: Up to the Fall of the Visigothic Kingdom*. Washington, DC: Catholic University of America Press.

McManus, Margaret (1984). "Women's Lives and Images of the Divine." Master's Thesis. Berkeley, CA: Graduate Theological Union.

Neitz, Mary J (2000). "Queering the Dragonfest: Changing Sexualities in a Post-Patriarchal Religion." *Sociology of Religion* 61, No. 4 (Winter): pp. 369–391.

North, John (1992). "The Development of Religious Pluralism." In: *The Jews among Pagans and Christians in the Roman Empire*, edited by Judith Lieu, John North and Tessa Rajak. London: Routledge, pp. 174–193.

Petts, David (2011). *Pagan and Christian: Religious Change in Early Medieval Europe*. London: Bristol Classical Press.

Pizza, Murphy and James R Lewis (2009). "Introduction." In: *Handbook of Contemporary Paganism*, edited by Murphy Pizza and James R Lewis. Brill: Leiden, pp. 1–9.

Rountree, Kathryn (2015). *Contemporary Pagan and Native Faith Movements in Europe: Colonialist and Nationalist Impulses*. New York, NY: Berghahn.

Rybakov, Boris A (1981). *Ancient Slavic Paganism*. Moscow: Izdatel'stvo "Nauka".

Sappho (2022). *Ode to Aphrodite, Poems and Fragments*, translated by John O'Hara. Bristol: Wine Dark Press.

Scott-Moncrieff, Philip D (1913). *Paganism and Christianity in Egypt*. Cambridge: Cambridge University Press.

Seidler, Victor J (2006). *Transforming Masculinities: Men, Cultures, Bodies, Power, Sex and Love*. London: Routledge.

Stanley, Eric G (2000). *Imagining the Anglo-Saxon Past: The Search for Anglo-Saxon Paganism and Anglo-Saxon Trial by Jury*. Woodbridge, Suffolk: D. S. Brewer.

Strmiska, Michael F (2005). "Modern Paganism in World Cultures: Comparative Perspectives." In: *Modern Paganism in World Cultures: Comparative Perspectives*, ABC-CLIO Religion in Contemporary Cultures Series, edited by Michael F Strmiska. Santa Barbara, CA: ABC-CLIO, pp. 1–54.

Urban, Hugh B. (2006). Tantra: Sex, Secrecy, Politics, and Power in the Study of Religion. Delhi: Motilal Banarsidass Publisher.

Wilkerson, W D (2014). *Walking with the Gods: Modern People Talk about Deities, Faith, and Recreating Ancient Traditions*. Tulsa, OK: Connaissance Sankofa Media.

Williams, Carolyn D (2009). *Boudica and Her Stories: Narrative Transformations of a Warrior Queen*. Newark, DE: University of Delaware Press.

Winterbourne, Anthony (2004). *When the Norns Have Spoken: Time and Fate in Germanic Paganism*. Madison, NJ: Fairleigh Dickinson University Press.

Zell-Ravenheart, Oberon (2006). "The Great Rite." In: *Creating Circles and Ceremonies: Rituals for All Seasons and Reasons*, edited by Oberon Zell-Ravenheart and Morning Glory Zell-Ravenheart. Franklin Lakes, NJ: The Career Press.

Part III

Queer Theologies, Spiritualities and Beliefs

A Brief Note About This Section

Within this section, our attention turns to the exploration of regional and global queer theologies, with a specific emphasis on reclaiming the contributions from ancestral spiritualities. The objective is to unearth and acknowledge the rich tapestry of diverse religious experiences that extend beyond the conventional understanding of 'religions' shaped by nineteenth-century perspectives. We aspire to showcase the intricate interactions of various spiritual paths outside these traditional frameworks. Moreover, our endeavour involves amplifying and bringing visibility to autochthonous voices in every region, recognising their unique perspectives and insights. By doing so, we aim not only to broaden the discourse on queer theologies but also to emphasise the significance of acknowledging and valuing the inherent diversity within religious landscapes. This approach seeks to foster a more inclusive narrative that encapsulates the multifaceted dimensions of global queer experiences and their intersection with diverse spiritualities, thereby enriching the understanding of the dynamic interplay between sexuality, gender and spirituality on both a regional and global scale.

In our exploration of queer theologies, it is imperative to recognise that religions and spiritualities are not static entities confined to specific geographical locales, they traverse borders and accompany individuals undergoing migration. This dynamic dimension contributes to the evolving tapestry of global queer experiences, reflecting the adaptability and transformative nature of religious and spiritual beliefs. We aim to delve into the complex interplay between migration and the dissemination of religious practices, shedding light on how these journeys impact and shape queer identities. Additionally, our examination extends to the burgeoning field of quantum/cosmic theologies, a contemporary discipline that introduces a distinctive and liberating perspective on life. This approach transcends conventional boundaries, exploring the intersection of spirituality and scientific inquiry. By incorporating quantum and cosmic dimensions, this discipline offers a unique lens through which to understand existence, presenting liberating aspects that transcend traditional religious frameworks. In the concluding chapter, we will underscore the trajectory towards global interaction, emphasising the translation of collaborations and voices at the cosmic level. This highlights a transformative shift, wherein the discourse extends beyond individual experiences and regional considerations to embrace a cosmic perspective, showcasing the potential for a unified and interconnected understanding of queer theologies on a global scale.

Glossary for Part III

Babalu-Aye	Deity of disease and healing in Santeria
Baron samedi	Sexually fluid patron of death
Candomblé	Dance in honour of the gods. An oral culture with no texts.
Cisgender	Gender identity matches what was assigned at birth.
Confucianism	A system that prioritises ritual as it acknowledges ancestral beings and says they need to be given respect.
Cultural colonisation	The way in which colonisers impose their ideas of civilisation on people they conquer; this includes ideas of gender and sexuality as well as language and customs.
Dao De Jing	Taoist texts speaking of aligning oneself with 'The Way'.
Femme	Term in LGBT culture used to describe someone who presents themselves in a traditionally feminine manner.
Ialorixa	Women who run Candomble temples.
Iweto	Marriage between women in the Akamba people.
K'ung Fu Tzu	Also known as Confucius, founder of Confucianism.
Kami	Important figures in Shinto, not divine so humans may become kami.
Kami no Michi	The way of the gods.
Kuan Yin	A transgender deity.
Kut	Shamanic ritual.
Lao Tzu	Thought to be writer of the Dao De Jing.
Machi	A Mapuche shaman who performs rituals for the community to heal and to ward off evil spirits. Also to control the weather for good harvests.
Mapuche Shamanism	Found in Chile and Argentina.
Mudang	Korean shamans.
Mugawe	Non-heterosexual priests in Kenya.
Ogan	Priest in Umbanda

Global Queer Theologies: Intercontextual and Interreligious Perspectives, First Edition. Lisa Isherwood and Hugo Córdova Quero.
© 2026 John Wiley & Sons Ltd. Published 2026 by John Wiley & Sons Ltd.

Olorun/Zambi	The supreme God in Umbanda.
Orixas	Spirits who possess people in Umbanda to give advice or to heal.
Religious colonisation	A practice by which Christianity wiped out indigenous religion in the name of "civilising" communities.
Santeria or Lucumi	A polytheistic religion that developed in Cuba between the sixteenth and nineteenth centuries. Santeria means worship of the saints.
Shaman	A healer.
Shamanism	Ancient and diverse practice.
Sinkyo	Meaning religion of spirits.
Taoism/Daoism	Began as a philosophy and later became a religion.
Torii gate	Marks the entrance to a Shinto shrine.
Two-spirit	A term used by Native North American/First Nations cultures to describe individuals who embody both masculine and feminine qualities, often encompassing spiritual roles within their communities.
Umbanda	African-rooted monotheistic religion.
Yin Yang or taijitu	Taoist symbol said to represent balance.

11

Ancestral Spiritualities in the Asian Context

We begin by examining how gender and sexuality have been constructed in the different regions of Asia. We pay attention to culture, language and colonial processes. How do Asian cultures deal with gender? What are the 'norms' expected in the different societies? How is the expression of sexuality allowed and controlled by societal expectations? We use the term 'spirituality' because some beliefs and practices either do not fit into the definition of 'religion' which is an eminently Western term, or do not want to be classified as such. Our goal is to recover the queer aspects already entrenched in those spiritualities. We see both religions and spiritualities.

Religions of East Asia

According to Ezekiel Musembe Kasiera, the study of religions tends to inquire into 'the study of the interpellations of various religious traditions and the manner in which religious themes and ideas are disseminated in those traditions' (2010: 10). Although each religion developed independently, there are common features that allow us to generalise hypotheses of relationship in the whole world (Kasiera, 2010: 5). This is exactly what happens when we talk about East Asian religions, which are Shintoism in Japan and Taoism and Confucianism in China.

Shintoism

The torii is a gate that marks the entrance to a Shinto shrine and passing through it symbolises entrance into the sacred. Many shrines and temples are red as this colour used to be viewed as scaring away evil spirits. Shinto priests also traditionally wore red.

Source: Luciano Mortula-LGM/Adobe Stock Photos.

Source: Jansambandhmedia / Pixabay.

Shintoism is the traditional religion of Japan that was made a 'state religion' from the early years of the Meiji period, or Restoration Period, in 1868 (Isomae, 2007a, 2007b, 2013). Essentially Shinto is the worship of nature and the ancestors, and the most important figures in Shinto are the kami. There is no supreme being in Shinto, but Amaterasu Okimaki, the sun goddess, is seen as the most important kami.

While she is seen as the most important, perhaps the most popular is Hotei, known as the laughing Buddha in the West.

He was originally based on a Chinese Chan monk and is now understood as the kami of contentment and abundance. As kami are not understood to be metaphysical beings it is possible for humans to become kami. It is quite common for dead humans to be seen as kami and as such to be seen as ancestral figures and protectors. There is no belief in Shinto that humans are born bad since they share the divine soul, but as life progresses people may do bad things but this can be corrected by purifying rituals.

Shintoism in Japanese is also called *Kami no Michi* [the way of the gods]. Ian Reader (1991: 24) states that the purpose of the Kami deities is in their relationship with humanity within the world for the benefit of those who live in it. *Kami* deities, as well as spirits within the Shinto religious worldview, permeate all that exists, so their naturalism is also animistic. Reader (1991) concludes:

> They are not just expressions of natural forces. The continuity between humanity and Kami means that human beings can also become Kami, retaining an influence in this world, usually through the continuation of the qualities that distinguished them in this life (1991: 25).

Reader (1991) also explains the belief that the *Kami* Izanami and Izanagi descended upon Japan to establish the imperial divine line from the *Kami* Amaterasu. In fact, the belief that the Emperor descended from the Sun must be put in context. The Sun is actually a Goddess, Amaterasu, the *kami* [God/Goddess] from whom not only the Emperor but by extension all the inhabitants of Japan are descended. Therefore, as a nation, there is no distinction between humanity and the Kami. In fact, the Emperor is the head of the *kazoku kokka*, Japanese 'nation-family,' which homogenises perceptions of nationhood, ethnic identity and social–political notions. Kosaku Yoshino states regarding these perceptions:

> The notion of Japan as an imagined racial community originated in the nationalist ideology of the late nineteenth century that conceived of it as a "family-nation" or "family-state" (*kazoku kokka*) of divine origin. In this nation-family, its members were perceived to be related "by blood" to each other and, ultimately, to the emperor.

Here we have an example of what Armstrong calls "the racialization of the imagined community." Kinship, race and religion merged to produce an intense collective sense of "oneness." Being this ideological backbone of prewar and wartime nationalism, the notion of nation-family came under heavy attack after the country's defeat in 1945 and has disappeared from the mainstream ideological scene. However, in the subconscious of the Japanese people, the nation as imagined kinship remains alive and kicking. This kinship-oriented group mentality is summed up in the racial metaphor of "Japanese blood." The fictional notion of "Japanese blood" reveals much about how the Japanese perceive their supposedly "immutable" difference (1992: 201).

On the other hand, the preeminence of the *Kami* Amaterasu has given women throughout Japanese history an important place in both spiritual and political spaces, especially as *Nyokan* [female officials]. They were prominent leaders in local villages where folk religions gave meaning to their inhabitants.

Japan's folk religions later evolved into what is known today as Shintoism, which is followed by approximately 80% of the Japanese population (Breen & Teeuwen, 2010: 1). Cleanliness is a central part of Shinto life, which is not only transmitted through the ritual (Ono, 2004) but also involves all daily life both personally, through physical cleanliness, and in the environment, through everything around us (Schadé, 2006). This can be observed, for example, on December 31 when the home is completely cleaned to welcome the New Year or in leaving street shoes at the door of the home. Shrines have a significant place in Shinto, being places for the veneration of the Kami (Markham & Ruparell, 2001). *Matsuri* or the summer festivals not only receive the spirits in the Obon season but also serve to socialise and honour the spirits associated with the festival (Schadé, 2006).

In traditional Japanese society, there existed a relatively fluid and accepting understanding of sexuality and gender identities, which was often integrated into various cultural practices, rituals and folklore. This acceptance of diverse expressions of sexuality and gender can be observed in historical accounts, literature and art, reflecting a society that was more tolerant and inclusive compared to many other cultures of its time. Shintoism, as the indigenous spiritual tradition of Japan, was part of this broader cultural milieu that embraced a more nuanced understanding of human sexuality.

Unlike some other religious traditions that have specific doctrines or scriptures addressing sexual ethics and morality, Shintoism does not provide explicit guidelines on homosexuality. As a result, Shintoism does not have a formalised stance on LGBTIQ+ issues, leaving room for individual interpretation and varying attitudes among practitioners. While Shintoism does not condemn or explicitly endorse homosexuality, it also does not have a history of stigmatising same-sex relationships. At most homosexuality was viewed as unnatural since children could not be conceived by members of the same sex, this was not to condemn such a lifestyle. Historically, diverse expressions of sexuality and gender were often integrated into Shinto rituals and folklore without judgement, reflecting a more inclusive cultural and spiritual landscape.

Shinto is actually full of stories of same-sex love and transgenderism. Tokugawa Era philosophers even wrote that the divine must logically be bisexual as the first three generations of the gods were all men. There is also a story regarding the origin of homosexuality which involves the male servants of the sun goddess who fell in love with each other. When one died the other fell into a depression and committed suicide, the goddess feeling their love ordered them to be buried together in a single grave. This story is understood to be the genesis of same-sex love with humans copying what these original divinities did. Sadly, conservative elements have added an ending to this story saying the sun was offended and refused to shine because of their love, so they were dug up and buried separately.

Some Shinto practitioners claim that there is a deity for the queer community; this is Shudo Daimyojin and in addition Inari-no-Okami is believed to be the protector of the transgender community. Homosexuality amongst the samurai was quite common and based on the Greek notion of an older male with a younger lover who he tutored in the ways of sex, manhood and gentlemanly conduct. Among the samurai this was understood as a sacred bond, and these relationships were monogamous.

Box 11.1

Samurai were originally an aristocratic warrior class but eventually came to mean any member of the warrior class who came to power in Japan in the twelfth century and dominated the Japanese government until the Meiji Restoration in 1868.

In contemporary Japan, some Shinto shrines and priests have shown openness to conducting same-sex marriage ceremonies, reflecting a growing acceptance and adaptation of Shinto practices to modern societal changes. However, attitudes towards LGBTIQ+ issues within the Shinto community can vary widely, influenced by individual beliefs, cultural norms and regional differences. Overall, the lack of explicit guidance on LGBTIQ+ issues in Shintoism allows for a range of interpretations and attitudes, with some practitioners embracing inclusivity and acceptance, while others may hold more conservative views.

Taoism or Daoism

Source: Natali2510/Adobe Stock Photos.

Taoism is also known as Daoism. The difference is linguistic, as Michael Carr (1990: 60) states when explaining that the 't' in the Chinese language is closer in its pronunciation to the 'd' than to the letter 't' itself. Hence the ways of writing the name of this spirituality in Latin characters.

In reality, Taoism originated as a philosophy and later became a religion. Jeffrey S. Siker explains:

> Taoism is a philosophical and later religious system derived largely from the Tao Te Ching, traditionally attributed to the Chinese philosopher Lao Tse, but probably not written down until the third century B.C. "Tao" is Chinese for "way" and refers to how the universe works in its natural, effortless order. To follow the Tao, human beings must learn to join this effortless flow of life and refrain from all effort and desire. This leads to true freedom and enlightenment. As China's main philosophy and system of religion, based on the teachings of Lao Tse in the 6th century BC and later revelations, it advocates preserving and restoring the Tao in the body and cosmos. As a religious system, Taoism borrowed several features from both Mahayana Buddhism and Confucianism (2007: 209–210).

We cannot do justice to any religion by saying 'This religion says' but 'some Taoists claim….' There are no homogeneous religious systems. Historically, Chinese society, deeply influenced by Daoist philosophy among other cultural and philosophical traditions, has exhibited a more fluid and nuanced understanding of sexuality and gender compared to some Western perspectives. Traditional Chinese literature, art and historical records often reflect this more inclusive and accepting approach to human sexuality and gender diversity.

Daoist texts, such as the *Dao De Jing* attributed to Lao Tzu and the writings of Zhuangzi, delve deeply into the natural order of the universe, stressing the significance of aligning oneself with the Dao, or the Way. These foundational texts often portray sexuality as an integral part of the cosmic order, seamlessly woven into the fabric of nature, rather than being confined by rigid moral or societal norms. While Daoism lacks explicit doctrines addressing homosexuality, its approach to sexuality resonates with a naturalistic and fluid understanding. Daoist teachings prioritise balance, harmony and the interconnectedness of all things, fostering a holistic view that encompasses relationships and sexuality as integral facets of human experience.

The Taoist symbol, the yin-yang or taijitu, is said to represent this balance and has been used in debate for and against queerness. The two sides represent the dichotomy of the universe and that fact that each side has something of the other in it. The yin is feminine, passive, emotional and creative, while the yang is masculine active, logical, hot and destructive, and together they bring balance to the world. This has led some people to say that same-sex relationships can therefore not bring balance to the world. A more spiritual understanding of the yin-yang says that the circles within the halves show that within couples a yang body may have an inner yin while an intersex person would be a self-completion of the yin–yang expressed towards others. Some even argue that the yin–yang symbol points to gender fluidity as it represents the non-static nature of all things. While others say it represents bisexuality as neither yin nor yang is completely pure in itself but possesses part of the other within the centre. Beyond the symbol the philosophy of Taoism admits that the true nature of the Tao is unknowable since it is limitless. Therefore, to place limits on the Tao through labels is unwise and as human sexuality is akin to the Tao it is acknowledged that it too is a limitless spectrum of possibilities.

In contemporary Chinese society, the topic of same-sex relationships remains a subject of ongoing discussion and debate. Daoism, with its emphasis on balance, harmony and acceptance, provides a philosophical framework that some interpret as supportive of LGBTQ+ rights and equality, despite the absence of explicit teachings on the subject. Modern Daoist practitioners and scholars, drawing upon the principles of Daoist philosophy, argue for a more inclusive and accepting approach towards diverse sexual orientations and gender identities. Siker (2007) aligns with this perspective, suggesting that the foundational principles of Daoism can be harmoniously integrated with contemporary understandings of LGBTQ+ rights, reflecting the evolving nature of cultural and philosophical discourse within Daoism:

> Some men (representing yang) have a very strong presence of yin (the feminine) within them, so homosexual relationships in principle are not a problem within the Taoist tradition. In practice, however, many Taoists are also strongly influenced by the Confucian tradition, which emphasizes the duty of sons to continue the family line through procreation. Thus, although homosexual acts in themselves are not wrong in the Taoist tradition, they are more acceptable if individuals also have children (2007: 210).

Within the rich tapestry of Daoist beliefs and practices, the perception of Kuan Yin as a transgender deity offers a profound exploration of fluidity, transformation and interconnectedness. In Daoist philosophy, the concept of gender is not rigidly fixed but rather seen as a dynamic aspect of existence, mirroring the constant flux and change inherent in the natural world and the cosmos. Kuan Yin, revered as a bodhisattva embodying compassion, mercy and wisdom, transcends earthly limitations and conventional gender categories. This transcendent quality of Kuan Yin resonates deeply with the Daoist emphasis on balance, harmony and acceptance, reflecting the overarching principles that guide Daoist thought.

Pauline Park (2013) highlights the significance of viewing Kuan Yin as a transgender deity, suggesting that this perspective offers a nuanced understanding of the complexities of gender identity within spiritual contexts. This interpretation not only enriches our understanding of Daoist and Buddhist traditions but also underscores their inclusive nature. These traditions have the capacity to embrace and honour diverse expressions of gender and sexuality, emphasising compassion, acceptance and the inherent dignity of all beings. By recognising Kuan Yin as a transgender deity, we are invited to explore deeper dimensions of spirituality that transcend binary categorisations and celebrate the multifaceted nature of human experience.

The previous paragraph implies that for LGBTIQ+ Daoist individuals, their faith offers a spiritual framework that can accommodate and validate their lived experiences and identities. By recognising Kuan Yin as a transgender deity, Daoism acknowledges the fluidity and diversity of gender expressions and sexual orientations, reflecting the intrinsic values of balance, harmony and acceptance within the tradition. This inclusive

Kuan Yin. *Source:* Haa900 / Wikimedia Commons / Public domain.

perspective can provide comfort, affirmation and a sense of belonging for LGBTIQ+ Daoist practitioners, affirming that their identities are not only accepted but also valued within the spiritual community. It suggests that the core principles of Daoism resonate with the complexities of human diversity, encouraging individuals to embrace their authentic selves while cultivating compassion, wisdom and spiritual growth.

Furthermore, the recognition of Kuan Yin as a transgender deity serves as a symbol of resilience, transformation and transcendence, offering hope and inspiration to LGBTIQ+ Daoist individuals navigating societal challenges and seeking spiritual guidance. Overall, Daoism's inclusive approach to gender and sexuality can empower LGBTIQ+ individuals to integrate their identities into their spiritual journey, fostering a deeper connection with the Dao and a sense of wholeness within themselves.

Confucianism

Confucius (551–479 BCE)
Source: dbossarte / Pixabay.

Kǒng Qiū, commonly known as Kǒngzǐ, meaning 'Master Kong', and recognised in the West as Confucius, was an educator, philosopher and politician during the Zhou dynasty (1046–771 BCE). His intention was to influence the society of his time, but this was only achieved by his followers after his death. Confucianism is a complex system of moral, social, political and religious thought. While it could be considered a system that emphasises the legal, the reality is that its major emphasis is ritualistic (Yao, 2000: 191). Understanding ritual according to the definition of Lee Dian Rainey (2010), as the 'mutual exchange of respect' (2010: 196). Its structure includes a complicated system governing duties and etiquette in all relationships. That becomes more evident as Confucian ethics focuses on family duty, loyalty and humanity (De Bary & Tu, 1998: 149). Thus, it proposes five types of relationships that are divided into two types: hierarchical (a) father–son affection, (b) lord–subject duty, (c) elder–youth order and horizontal, (d) faith/trust among friends and (e) husband–wife distinctions that shape life in society.

Confucianism did influence the societies where it spread and drastically changed various situations, such as gender issues. Over time, the only place where women were able to exert any influence until recently was in the religious sphere, apart from the domestic sphere.

From China, this religious philosophy spread to other regions of Asia. For example, in the eighth century, the Japanese introduced the Chinese Tang institutional model, thus basing society on a patriarchal family paradigm for gender relations. This was made concrete in the Ritsuryō Code. The term is the union in one word of two separate powers of authority: the penal [*Ritsu*] and the civil [*Ryō*] (Tonomura, 2009: 351). This set the tone for the gender imbalance that has influenced Japanese society to the present day.

Confucianism recognises the existence of ancestral spirits and deities and advocates giving them due respect (Sharot, 2001). However, Confucius did not acknowledge the existence of a creator God in the monotheistic sense (Gardner, 2014: 13). Its status as a spiritual or religious system cannot be defined according to Western standards, since it would not only mean colonisation of a system that was not created according to the rules of that region but also because it would prevent observing the elements that make the richness of Confucianism. Not all religious systems fit within the limited vision of 'religion' hegemonised by the West. Because of this, there is a growing consensus among scholars that Confucianism is indeed a religion and rather distinct, as understood, for example, by Hans Küng (Yao, 2000: 43). However, in Confucianism '[t]here is no priesthood, no central leader, no congregation (which might, for example, support the building and maintenance of a temple), no sacred texts, no God and no gods' (Rainey, 2010: 203), and yet it is a religion/philosophy that has survived for centuries.

Traditional Confucian teachings focus on familial relationships, hierarchical social structures and moral virtues that guide individual conduct and societal order. In the context of homosexuality, Confucianism generally adheres to traditional norms and values that prioritise heterosexual marriage and procreation as fundamental aspects of family and social continuity. Traditional Confucian texts, such as the *Analects* attributed to Confucius, emphasise the importance of adhering to conventional roles and responsibilities within the family and society, which often align with heterosexual norms.

Historically, Confucian societies have exhibited conservative attitudes towards homosexuality, viewing it as a deviation from societal norms and expectations. Same-sex relationships were often stigmatised and marginalised within Confucian cultures, reflecting broader cultural and social prejudices. Some scholars argue that Confucianism, as a primarily social and political philosophy, did not extensively address sexuality, whether homosexual or heterosexual, in its traditional teachings. Confucianism is fundamentally concerned with establishing social harmony, maintaining hierarchical relationships and fostering moral virtue through adherence to familial and societal roles.

In Confucian thought, the concept of filial piety (*xiao*) holds significant importance, emphasising respect, obedience and care towards parents and ancestors. Critics point out that under Confucian teachings, not having children was sometimes considered a failure to fulfil one's duty of filial piety, as it could be seen as neglecting the continuation of the family lineage and ancestral worship. This emphasis on procreation within the context of filial piety has been interpreted by some as potentially restrictive or judgemental towards individuals who do not conform to traditional family structures or reproductive norms. The focus on familial continuity and societal obligations could inadvertently marginalise those who identify as LGBTIQ+ or choose not to have children for personal reasons.

However, in contemporary Confucian discourse, there is a growing recognition of the need to adapt traditional teachings to address the complexities of modern society, including changing attitudes towards sexuality and gender (Li, 2020). While Confucianism historically emphasised adherence to societal norms and roles, some modern Confucian scholars and practitioners are reinterpreting Confucian principles to advocate for LGBTIQ+ rights and equality. For instance, William Theodore De Bary and Tu Weiming (1998) have discussed the importance of revisiting Confucian values in light of modern challenges, including issues related to gender and sexuality. They suggest that Confucian teachings on empathy, benevolence and humaneness (*ren*) can be extended to support the dignity and rights of LGBTIQ+ individuals.

In Taiwan, a Confucian-influenced society, there has been significant progress in LGBTIQ+ rights, including the legalisation of same-sex marriage in 2019. This societal shift reflects evolving interpretations of Confucian values, with many supporters framing LGBTIQ+ rights as consistent with Confucian principles of family harmony, love and respect for individual autonomy. Furthermore, organisations and advocacy groups throughout East Asia are actively engaging with Confucian teachings to promote LGBTIQ+ acceptance and inclusion. They highlight the inherent flexibility and adaptability of Confucian philosophy, emphasising the importance of interpreting Confucian values in ways that resonate with contemporary understandings of human rights and social justice.

Shamanism

Shamanism is a very ancient and diverse spiritual practice. People's encounters with shamanism, as well as anthropological and sociological studies of different shamanisms, have been varied.

For academics, the term shamanism can come from two possible sources. On the one hand, some scholars argue that it probably derives from the Manchu-Tungus language word šaman, part of the Tungusic language family, meaning 'one who knows' (Hutton, 2001).

Other scholars argue that the word may also have its origin in the Evenki language word *šaman*, most likely from the southwestern dialect spoken by the Sym Evenki people and meaning 'to know' or 'to warm up' (Pratt, 2007: xxi). In this regard Susan Greenwood states:

> The word 'shaman' comes from Evenki, a Siberian nomadic tribe from their term *šaman*, and was originally used by Russian scholars to refer to specific Siberian tribes. In the early 1650s, Avvakum, a dissident priest exiled by the Russian Orthodox Church, arrived in Evenki lands and began to describe šaman Evenki beliefs and practices. Avvakum was eventually executed for heresy in 1682, but his descriptions led to the study of what would become shamanism. Over the next 150 years, more stories emerged from travelers and missionaries about an 'animated world' in which everything was alive and filled with spirits. Almost every aspect of life could be related to these spirits: health, food, shelter, hunting success, and community welfare (2007: 70).

In the introduction to *An Encyclopedia of Shamanism*, Christina Pratt defines shamans as follows:

> A shaman is a healer who works in the invisible world through direct contact with "spirits." The invisible world contains all aspects of our world that affect us but are invisible to us, including the spiritual, emotional, psychological, mythical, archetypal and dream worlds. Shamans use an alternate state of consciousness to enter the invisible world and make changes in the energy found there in a way that directly affects specific changes needed here in the physical world. It is this direct contact with the "spirits" through the use of altered states of consciousness and the movement of energy between worlds that distinguishes the shaman from other practitioners (2007: viii).

However, one element is clear: shamanism is not a religion in the Western sense but a set of very diverse spiritualities, beliefs and practices. Since it is impossible to delve into the fascinating world of shamanism, we will now only focus on two examples.

Siberian Shamanism

In her work *Wayward Shamans: The Prehistory of an Idea* (2013), Silvia Tomášková focuses on Siberian shamanism. Historically, this shamanism greatly influenced shamanism in other Asian regions. Tomášková (2013) analyses the ethnographic records of cases of shamans among the 'Koryak, Chukchi, Yakut [Sakhá], Gilyak and Kamchadal of Eastern Siberia' (2013: 146).

One of the characteristics of many shamans of those nations is that today they would be labelled as 'transgender' people, as Tomášková states:

> One particular aspect of Siberian shamanism both fascinated and repelled early ethnographers: the apparent ability and willingness of males to transform into women to perform ritual functions. Descriptions of this phenomenon varied widely among sources, ranging from apprehensive denial to detailed accounts. Explanations, however, were harder to come by. Neither German nor Russian scientific backgrounds during the 18th or 19th centuries provided a conceptual framework that could accommodate such behavior. Early travelers found that Siberian connections between sexuality, religious ritual, performance, healing, and everyday existence were at best confusing and at worst completely incomprehensible (2013: 140).

Since then, the study of shamanism and the role shaman's play has followed a variety of paths. The authors and the populations that were their 'object' of study vary from one culture to another and across time and subcultures. Generalisation is impossible, and it would not be fair either! Graham Harvey and Robert J. Wallis conclude on this issue:

> Roberte Hamayon (1998) summarized Western interest in Siberian shamans into three broad periods, emblematically labeled diabolization, medicalization, and idealization. This is immensely useful and can be applied to some studies of shamanism, as well as to popular interest (however abhorrent or enthusiastic). But, in the end, it is too tidy. Just as shamans can be as ambiguous as tricksters, and just as shamanism can be too fluid to pin down, academic and popular interests and evaluations of shamans have generally been ambiguous (2007: 6).

Tomášková's work is important because it examines the archaeology behind the studies conducted with Siberian shamans. Other authors agree on the animistic character of their beliefs and the diversity of practices and understandings about that animate world (Greenwood, 2020). However, more progress is needed to understand sexuality and spirituality from the perspective of shamans, as the accounts that have come down to us suffer from the prejudices and stereotypes of those who observed these people's lives. One such prejudice was the indiscriminate use of the word 'shaman':

> In the early 20th century, Westerners began to use "shaman" to describe not only the specialists described above, but also and inaccurately healers, sorcerers, wizards, magicians, warlocks, and anyone who seemed to be in contact with spirits. This generalized use of the word "shaman" dilutes the meaning of the word, which arose to describe a group of specialists who continue to practice among us today (Pratt, 2007: xxi).

This suggests that Siberian shamanism is more widely recognised for its expertise than for a detailed study of its beliefs and practices (Tomášková, 2013). Silvia Tomášková explores this topic highlighting the historical influence of Siberian shamanism on the traditions of other Asian regions. She draws on ethnographic records of shamans among the 'Koryak, Chukchi, Yakut [Sakhá], Gilyak, and Kamchadal of Eastern Siberia' (2013: 146).

Amongst the Chukchi shamans the most powerful were queer individuals who were colloquially called 'soft men'. These were biological men who dressed their hair like women but did not adopt fully feminine ways. They even married cisgender men who were not viewed in any way as different from men married to women. Their tremendous power as shamans was believed to come from their gender fluidity. The idea of queerness and spiritual power seemed to go hand in hand in Siberia and children who showed queer tendencies were marked out as shaman early in life. Unlike people in other societies the people of the Chukchi did not force their children into patterns of behaviour viewed as male or female. Instead they were free to act as they wished in terms of gender. Not all queer shamans were born that way, some were directed by the spirit to break away from their traditional gender in order to further develop their powers. To help them in this process they married spiritual entities who could be male or female. If the spirit was a same-sex lover they would force the shaman into being more butch or effeminate depending on what they needed to learn and if an opposite-sex partner the teaching would be by example not domination.

The work of Tomášková is important because it examines the archaeology behind the studies conducted with Siberian Shamans. However, more must be done to understand sexuality and spirituality from the Shamans' perspectives.

Korean Shamanism

The origin of Korean shamanism is difficult to determine due to the diversity of its practices, which vary from one region to another. In addition, the influence of Taoism and Buddhism on Korean shamanism adds to its complexity. Therefore, there is no single, unified shamanism, but rather different connected variations. Traditional Korean shamanism is known as *Sinkyo* [Sinism], which literally means 'the religion of spirits' (Lee, 1981: 21).

Korean shamanism is also known as *Mukyo, Muism*, which literally means 'the religion of the shaman.' Korean shamanism is characterised by rituals performed by *Mudang*, the shamans. The role of the *Mudang* is to act as intermediaries between the spirits or gods and the human experience through *Kut*, chanting or dance rituals seeking to summon blessings and bring healing (Kim, 2010: 69; Pratt, 2007: 477). *Mudang* are predominantly women, also called *Munyeo*, while male Mudang are called *Baksu* (Yi, 2008: 78). Some *Baksu* have also been gender-diverse people (Pratt, 2007: 339). Although there is no systematic set of doctrines in Korean shamanism, its beliefs include nature spirits, ancestors and spirits that guide a person or region.

As mentioned, the *Kut* or *Gut* are the rites that include offerings and sacrifices to gods and ancestors (Lee, 1981: 27). These rites are intended to create well-being, promoting engagement between spirits and humanity (Lee, 1981: 27). Through song and dance, the *Mudang* pray to the gods to intervene in the daily lives of the people. Each *Mudang* wears a colourful costume, which is changed several times during a rite. Each time a *Mudang* speaks during the *Kut*, he or she does so in a state of ecstasy or trance. The rituals consist of several phases called *Gori* (Lee, 1981: 31). Ae-ju Yi (2014) states about the dance in the *Kut*:

> Given the nature of dance in which one touches one's body in various movements with a feeling of emotion, dance is based on emotion and, at the same time, emotion naturally arises while dancing. From the perspective of nature, dance has something in common with Gut (2014: 212).

Another important aspect of Korean shamanism is the purity of both body and mind, as this constitutes a necessary state to participate in rituals. This is because purification is considered necessary for effective communion between living beings and ancestral spirits. Before performing any *Kut*, the altar is always purified with fire and water as part of the first *Gori* of the ritual itself. The colour white is widely used in rituals and is considered a symbol of purity. The purification of the body is symbolically performed by burning white paper (Lee, 1981: 38).

For Further Discussion

1   How does Shintoism, as a traditional Japanese belief system, approach and interpret issues related to homosexuality, and are there any specific rituals, teachings, or historical perspectives within Shinto that shed light on the acceptance or rejection of diverse sexual orientations?

2   How does the relevance of Daoist principles contribute to understanding gender fluidity within contemporary discussions on LGBTQ+ rights and equality?

3   How has the emphasis on familial continuity within Confucianism been perceived as potentially restrictive towards individuals who do not conform to traditional family structures or reproductive norms?

4   How do authors summarise Western interest in Siberian shamans, and how does this classification differ from more recent perspectives on Siberian shamanism?

5   What are the main characteristics and roles of Mudang in Korean shamanism, and how do rituals like *Kut* reflect the beliefs and practices of this spiritual tradition?

References

Breen, John and Mark Teeuwen (2010). *A New History of Shinto*. Malden, MA: Blackwell.

Carr, Michael (1990). "Whence the Pronunciation of Taoism? *Dictionaries: Journal of the Dictionary Society of North America* 12: pp. 55–74.

De Bary, William T and Weiming Tu (1998). *Confucianism and Human Rights*. New York, NY: Columbia University Press.

Gardner, Daniel K (2014). *Confucianism: A Very Short Introduction*. Oxford: Oxford University Press.

Greenwood, Susan (2020). *Developing Magical Consciousness: A Theoretical and Practical Guide for the Expansion of Perception*. Abingdon: Routledge.

Harvey, Graham and Robert J Wallis (2007). *Historical Dictionary of Shamanism* (Historical Dictionaries of Religions, Philosophies, and Movements, No. 77). Lanham, MD: The Scarecrow Press.

Hutton, Ronald (2001). *Shamans: Siberian Spirituality and the Western Imagination*. London: Hambledon Continuum.

Isomae, Jun'ichi (2007a). "State Shinto within the Larger Process of Westernization." In: *Religion and the Secular: Historical and Colonial Formations*, edited by Timothy Fitzgerald. Oakville, CT: Equinox, p. 93.

Isomae, Jun'ichi (2007b). "The Formative Process of State Shintō in Relation to the Westernization of Japan: The Concept of 'Religion' and 'Shintō'," translated by Michael S. Wood." In: *Religion and the Secular: Historical and Colonial Formations*, edited by Timothy Fitzgerald. New York, NY: Routledge, pp. 93–102.

Isomae, Jun'ichi (2013). "Religion, Secularity, and the Articulation of the 'Indigenous' in Modernizing Japan." In: Kami Ways in Nationalist Territory: Shinto Studies in Prewar Japan and the West, edited by Bernhard Scheid and Kate Widman Nakai. Vienna: Austrian Academy of Sciences Press, pp. 23–50.

Kasiera, Ezekiel M.(2010). "The Scope of Comparative Religion." In: *A Comparative Study of Religions*, editado por J. N. K. Mugambi. Nairobi: University of Nairobi Press, pp. 3–13.

Kim, Mee-Jin (2010). *Korea-Knigge: der Türöffner für Auslandsreisende und Expatriates*. Munich: Oldenburg Wissenschaftverlag.

Lee, Jung Y (1981). *Korean Shamanistic Rituals*. Berlin: De Gruyter Mouton.

Li, Chenyang (2020). "Introduction: Can Confucianism Come to Terms with Feminism? In: *The Sage and the Second Sex: Confucianism, Ethics, and Gender*, edited by Chenyang Li. Chicago, IL: Open Court, pp. 1–21.

Markham, Ian S and Tinu Ruparell (editors) (2001). *Encountering Religion: An Introduction to the Religions of the World*. Hoboken, NJ: Wiley-Blackwell.

Oho, Sakyo (2004). *Shinto: The Kami Way*. Clarendon, VT: Tuttle Publishing.

Park, Pauline (2013). "Transgender Identities & Spiritual Traditions in Asia & the Pacific Lessons for LGBT/Queer APIs." Presentation at the Pacific School of Religion Chapel. Berkeley, California, April 2.

Pratt, Christina (2007). *An Encyclopedia of Shamanism*. New York, NY: The Rosen Publishing Group.

Rainey, Lee D (2010). *Confucius and Confucianism: The Essentials*. West Sussex: Wiley-Blackwell.

Reader, Ian (1991). *Religion in Contemporary Japan*. Honolulu, HI: University of Hawai'i Press.

Schadé, Johannes P (editor) (2006). *Encyclopedia of World Religions*. Cape Girardeau, MO: Concord Publishing House.

Sharot, Stephen (2001). *A Comparative Sociology of World Religions: Virtuosos, Priests, and Popular Religion*. New York, NY: New York University Press.

Siker, Jeffrey S (2007). "Taoism." In: *Homosexuality and Religion: An Encyclopedia*, edited by Jeffrey S Siker. Westport, CT: Greenwood Press, pp. 209–210.

Tomášková, Silvia (2013). *Wayward Shamans: The Prehistory of an Idea*. Berkeley, CA: University of California Press, pp. 140–161.

Tonomura, Hotomi (2009). "Women and Sexuality in Premodern Japan." In: *A Companion to Japanese History*, edited by William M Tsutsui. Malden, MA: Blackwell, pp. 351–371.

Yao, Xinzhong (2000). *An Introduction to Confucianism*. Cambridge: Cambridge University Press.

Yi, Pae-yong (2008). *Women in Korean History*. Seoul: Ewha Womans University Press.

Yi, Ae-ju (2014). "Shaman Ritual Dance: Understanding Korean Culture." In: *Dance of Korea*, edited by Ji-won Song (Korean Musicology Series N° 6). Seoul: National Gugak Center, pp. 211–222.

Yoshino, Kosaku (1992). *Cultural Nationalism in Contemporary Japan: A Sociological Enquiry*. London: Routledge.

12

Ancestral Spiritualities in the North/Central/South American Context

In this chapter, we explore the context of the Americas concerning queer/ethnic issues and ancestral spiritualities. Home to Latin America Liberation Theology, Central and South America have produced distinctive queer theologies that are contextual. However, ancestral spiritualities also play a role in the lives of queer believers, primarily through new religions such as the Afro-Brazilian and Afro-Caribbean influences and indigenous spiritualities. At the same time, the migration of Latinxs to the US and Canada has begun to produce new ways of dealing with queer issues.

Moreover, the presence of migrants also resulted in the expansion of literally every religion practised in other parts of the world. We will investigate some religious experiences of queer believers, with the disclaimer that it is impossible to explore every religion that compounds the mosaic of spiritual/ethnic/cultural/linguistic/sexual diversity of Latin America and the diasporic communities worldwide. We will examine the topic of embodiment, that is, the relation of bodies to sexuality, spirituality, desire and beliefs. We take into account how whiteness and colonialism has played a role in these cultures and affected the way those topics are seen. In other words, the way that theologians deal with bodies, sexuality, spirituality, desire and beliefs implies a de-colonisation from Western notions and the recovery of indigenous forms present before the arrival of Western colonisers.

The following materials reflect some of the variety of religions in Latin America and among Latinas/os in North America. Something noteworthy is that Christianity has greatly influenced Latin America. However, the increasing presence of every religion, some of them tracing roots even before the arrival of the Spanish and Portuguese conquistadors, means that much more work could be done if space allowed.

African-Based Religions

The African-based religions constitute a series of related religions that developed in several Latin American and Caribbean nations. They are heirs of traditional African religions that survived among the populations of African ancestry that were enslaved between the fifteenth and twentieth centuries CE. (Childs, 2023). Many of them were greatly influenced by Christianity, especially when they had to camouflage their religious practice in order to survive (Schmidt, 2006).

Global Queer Theologies: Intercontextual and Interreligious Perspectives, First Edition. Lisa Isherwood and Hugo Córdova Quero.

The African-based spiritual world emerged from its beginning with a transnational and multicultural character through the intertwining of local religions, European Roman Catholicism and imported faiths from Africa and Asia, brought by slaves and immigrants, respectively. For example, many people only appear in statistics as Roman Catholics, although in reality, more often, their only contact with that faith was during baptism when they were infants. Some of them are indeed Roman Catholics, but they have experienced multiple religious affiliations throughout their lives by mixing religious beliefs whose provenance is not rooted in Roman Catholic teachings. Yorùbá religions were among those imported traditions which needed to be hidden or camouflaged to survive the robust surveillance of Christianity. It is amongst those religions that appropriated much from Roman Catholic Church imagery. Evolving from a hybrid process of (re)appropriation of spiritual concepts from different religions, African matrix religions have flourished in the Americas and beyond. African matrix religions are many and varied, and so we offer just three examples below.

Candomblé

After centuries of oppression and segregation, a movement towards the strengthening of a more traditional African religion arose in the development of Afro-Brazilian religions. It was not until 1830 that some sisters of the *Irmandade da Nossa Senhora da Boa Morte* [Sisterhood of Our Lady of the Good Death] abandoned the sisterhood and established the first *Terreiro* [house of worship] in Salvador, Bahia, Brazil (Alonso, 2014: 52). This marked the restoration of the Yorùbá religion and soon paved the way for the emergence of Afro-Brazilian religions such as Candomblé and Umbanda.

Candomblé, which means dance in honour of the gods, combines elements of African religion and Christianity, especially from the Roman Catholic tradition. There is belief in one supreme God, Olodumare, but also a myriad of minor deities. Followers of Candomblé have their own personal minor deity who they believe protects and guides them. Worship consists in dance, African-inspired song, and practitioners becoming possessed by their particular deity. There may also be animal sacrifice involved in worship.

The restoration of the Nàgó-Yorùbá religion soon paved the way for the emergence of other Afro-Brazilian religions. Also known as *xangôs* [shango] or *batuques* [drums]depending on the region of the country it is mainly the result of the late forced migration of the Nàgó people from Africa to Brazil in the nineteenth century. The Nàgó people actually shaped the current profile of Candomblé, thus promoting its continued flourishing (Childs and Falola, 2004: 10). The religion is an amalgam of African religions intertwined with indigenous Latin American traditions and Catholicism.

Candomblé was practised widely in Africa and varied according to the region one lived in. This has had an effect on the type of worship found in Brazil, for example, the Bantu people focus on ancestor worship which is not unlike the indigenous Brazilian people. On the other hand the Yorùbá people practised polytheism which has had an influence on Candomblé. Most of the priestesses in Candomblé are descendants of Yorùbá slaves.

Many of the slaves brought to Brazil had been raised as Muslim, and this too had an influence on the development of Candomblé in certain areas. For example, worship happens on Fridays as in Islam. During slave revolts those with Muslim background were amongst the leading figures and adopted traditional Muslim dress, white garments and skull caps. While the slaves were meant to be Roman Catholic converts, many of course continued to practise their own beliefs. Thus, Roman Catholic saints and the Virgin Mary were used to hide indigenous gods and goddesses (Ogunnaike, 2020). For instance, for followers of Candomblé, Saint George was excellent cover for the brave warrior deity, Ogum.

Candomblé has no sacred texts and is entirely an oral culture. Unlike many other religions Candomblé does not have a set of good and evil behaviours, rather it advocates that people follow their own destiny to the full. It could mean they are people who are ethical or indeed unethical, and no unethical act carries negative consequences. That is because each individual determines their own destiny while possessed by their ancestor spirits. The purpose of life is to increase one's 'axe' which is the life force and is everywhere in nature. Candomblé does not focus on an after-life, but practitioners are buried not cremated so that their life force can continue to give life to other living beings.

Candomblé, as mentioned, has a number of deities, Obaluaie or Babalu-Aye as he is known in Santeria is the Òrìsà of disease and healing. While he is not necessarily understood as a queer deity himself he has become associated with AIDS/HIV and in that way has been adopted by the queer communities. In addition to his association with HIV/AIDS he is also known for his care of the outcasts of the world which is another reason the queer community have adopted him as their own. Baron Samedi is the patron of death and is depicted as wearing a frock coat and top hat mixed with feminine essentials such as a skirt. He is sometimes viewed as transgender and always depicted as having a preference for anal sex. His fluidability, beyond male female, straight gay, earth and underworld, life and death, make him popular in the queer community amongst those who do not wish to carry labels or be fixed into one identity.

Erzulie is a family of deities of which two members are associated with the queer community, Erzulie Freda and Erzulie Dantor. Erzulie Freda is thought of as the deity of beauty, dancing, luxury and male homosexuality. Gay men are under her protection, and many claim that their sexual orientation came about as a result of being possessed by her during rituals. Erzulie Dantor is the deity of women, children and specifically lesbians. She is often depicted as a black-skinned Virgin Mary who is well endowed and carries a black Jesus-like child and is the protector of lesbians.

In 1830 according to the report of Bahian researcher Edison Carneiro the first candomblé temple called *Ilê Iyá Nassó* was founded, which is commonly known as Engenho Velho [old wit] (Alonso, 2014: 56). This house of worship was also known as Casa Branca [white house] and focused exclusively on the praise of the Òrìsà, the Nàgó-Yorùbá nature spirits, a high point of the faith (Allen, 2008: 257) that had already begun its restoration. It was founded by three women: Adetá, Iyá Kala and Iyá Nassó (Alonso, 2014: 56).

Candomblé temples are usually run by women who are known as *ialorixa* meaning 'mother of saint'. These women go through a rigorous training once they have been approved by the oxiras deities. The training takes seven years starting with a seclusion period of several weeks. They learn songs, rituals and are tested to see what divination they are capable of, importantly they learn about Òrìsà food. The women are often supported in their ministry by men known as babalorixa or father of saint.

Around the 1960s, Candomblé, although it presented religious practices incompatible with Roman Catholic teachings, officially ceased to be persecuted. The same happened with the other Afro-Brazilian religions. Although the Roman Catholic Church ceased its attempts to demonise Candomblé, the neo-Pentecostal churches such as the Universal Church of the Kingdom of God (IURD) began their crusade against religions of African origin in the 1980s (Chesnut, 2003: 104). Despite this in the following decades, Candomblé along with other Afro-Brazilian religions gained a significant number of followers among the population in the growing urbanisations of Brazil and throughout South America.

Candomblé along with the other Afro-Brazilian religions also appealed to an ethno-racial component, which gave meaning to the oppressed sectors of society in neighbouring countries such as Argentina and Uruguay, where people of African descent have historically been made invisible by the dominant Europeanising society (Segato, 1991). Once a hidden religion, it is now practised widely in Argentina, Brazil, Venezuela, Paraguay and Uruguay.

Umbanda

On November 15, 1908, a group of Kardecistas met in a séance in the neighbourhood of Neves, city of São Gonçalo in the state of Rio de Janeiro, Brazil. Among them was Zélio Fernandino de Moraes, a 17-year-old boy studying to enter the Naval Academy. During the session, de Moraes incorporated a spirit who identified himself as the Caboclo das Sete Encruzilhadas [half-breed of the seven crossroads] and was the one who revealed that the religion should be called 'Umbanda' (Beraba, 2008). Subsequently, de Moraes incorporated another spirit who identified himself as Pai Antônio [Father Antonio], an old wise slave who had died after being savagely whipped by his master. De Moraes founded the *Centro Espírita Nossa Senhora da Piedade* [Spiritist Centre of Our Lady of Piety] in 1920, which served to orient umbandist *terreiros* throughout the country (Beraba, 2008).

Umbanda is a monotheistic religion that believes in one supreme creator God, Olorun, also referred to as Zambi. Followers of Umbanda, known as Umbandistas, believe in Òrìsà spirits that can possess the human body to facilitate communication. In Yorùbá religions and other Afro-based traditions, including Umbanda, Òrìsà are invoked to possess a person, enabling them to offer guidance for healing, counselling, or other spiritual matters (Engler, 2012).

Orixas have also been associated with Roman Catholic saints, a practice that historically served to mask their non-Christian origins. Such a hybridity arose as enslaved Africans, forced to adopt Christianity, continued to worship their own spirits, the Iwa. As in the case of Candomblé, to conceal this from their Roman Catholic enslavers, Umbanda followers linked their spirits to Roman Catholic saints (Hale, 2009). For example, Oxala is associated with a Jesus-like figure, while Yemaja, a water goddess, is often equated with the Virgin Mary.

Distinct figures in Umbanda include Preto Velho and Preta Velha, the Old Black Man and Old Black Woman who symbolise the countless individuals who perished under slavery. The Baianos represent spirits of the deceased, while the Malandros embody those marginalised by society (Engler, 2012), such as drug addicts, sex workers and queer individuals. The Pomba-Giras, meanwhile, are spirits of women who resisted oppression during their lifetimes. Many young practitioners regard Pomba-Giras as feminist spirits who continue to empower women today.

There is also a rainbow Òrìsà, Oxumare who has nothing to do with queer rights but rather the one who carries water from earth to the sky:

Source: phadoca / Pixabay.

During Umbanda rituals, practitioners wear white, a colour believed to represent a person's true character, and they do not wear shoes, as making a deep connection with the earth is considered essential. The priest known as the *Ogan* leads the rituals by drumming, singing and invoking the Òrìsà. The *Ogan* is also responsible for ensuring that no evil spirits enter the ritual space (Pinto, 2014). It is prohibited for anyone to stand between the priest and the altar or to sing or drum louder than the priest. Mediums participate by singing and dancing, hoping to be possessed by spirits so they can provide advice and guidance to the gathered community (Motta, 2020). Sacred symbols are drawn on the ground during the rituals, taking forms such as dots, lines, triangles, spears, waves, stars and suns (Lundell, 2016). These symbols serve to identify the Òrìsà and are reminiscent of the veve symbols used in Haitian Vodou.

Umbandism has a very complex cosmology rooted in spiritual evolution; it also has concepts such as reincarnation and karma from Spiritism which is a process some scholars call 'syncretism', 'hybridisation' or 'creolisation' (Capone, 2010: 75). Umbanda became a popular Afro-Brazilian religion reaching other countries in South America such as Argentina, Paraguay and Uruguay. Furthermore, the migration of Japanese Brazilians also spread the religion to Japan (Arakaki, 2008, 2009, 2014).

Umbandism is one of the religions that has welcomed people of gender diversity and empowered the active participation and leadership of women. Segato (2008) adds that issues such as 'the malleability of gender' and 'the flexibility and anti-essentialism of family arrangements' are factors that contributed to the dissemination of Nàgó-Yorùbá religious values among new converts in other parts of the world such as South America, as well as the development of other religions such as Kimbanda and Candomblé in Brazil, which also advocate this belief of gender and sexuality fluidity. Roman Catholicism is dominated by male power, but in the Nàgó-Yorùbá traditions women and men are indistinctly possessed by female or male spirits (Segato, 2008: 502).

Practices of possession and trance mediate the exchanges of offerings among believers and the sacred entities are embraced through detailed rituals presided equally by priests and priestesses. Rita Segato, who has extensively written about the Yorùbá religion, explains that even the deities could be transgender:

> Logunede, in Bahia, is said to be six months male and six months female, and Oya is said to have been male in the past and become female presently, though still exhibiting a rather virile personality. A continuum is traced along the range of orisas/personalities, resulting that some female saints are said to be more virile than others and the same for female. Regarding some particular trait of character, a female saint can be "more virile" or "more masculine" than a masculine saint (2008: 502).

This gender diversity within the religious symbolic world of the Yorùbá religion clearly has impacted the world-view of its followers within the broader Brazilian society. The Yorùbá, who worshiped the Òrìsà, are just a few examples of the intertwining of gender, sexuality and spirituality among the vast diversity in African cultures, which were suppressed by the power of both the Spanish and the Portuguese conquistadors.

Peter Fry (1995) explores the intersections of male homosexuality and religious practices within Afro-Brazilian possession cults, such as Candomblé and Umbanda. Fry is one of the few scholars to address same-sex desire within Afro-Brazilian religions. His research conducted among Umbanda followers in Brazil reveals how these religious practices provide a unique sociocultural context in which gender and sexual diversity can be negotiated, expressed and often valued. The roots of Afro-Brazilian religions trace back to the Yorùbá religion, practised among various African ethnic groups from Nigeria, Benin and Togo, who were forced into slavery in Brazil starting in 1549.

Fry (1995) observes, 'All the authors used the term "homosexual," but without ethnographic information about the classificatory scheme of the people concerned, it is difficult to assess the findings. [...] The term homosexual in Portuguese is, however, rarely used in the context of the cults' (1995: 201, 203). Such insight challenges conventional Western understandings of sexuality and highlights the complexity of translating terms like 'homosexuality' across cultures. Fry's work sheds light on how Afro-Brazilian religions particularly Umbanda often provide space for male homosexual practitioners to assume significant ritual roles. These roles are sometimes imbued with spiritual authority and cultural significance, defying dominant cis-heteronormative structures in Brazilian society.

This research offers valuable insights that can be linked to the development of queer theologies within the Umbanda worldview. Fry's exploration of how Afro-Brazilian religious spaces engage with non-heteronormative identities aligns with key themes in queer theology, such as the affirmation of marginalised identities and the deconstruction of oppressive gender and sexual norms. In Afro-Brazilian religions like Umbanda, individuals who identify as queer often hold respected ritual roles, such as mediums or spiritual leaders. That stands in stark contrast to mainstream Christian traditions, which have historically marginalised LGBTQ+ individuals. Queer theologies within Umbanda can draw on this inclusivity to argue that the integration of LGBTQ+ people into spiritual practice is not only possible but intrinsic to the divine purpose of the faith.

Fry also examines the concept of spirit possession, central to Umbanda, as a framework for exploring fluid identities. He discusses how spirit possession creates spaces where traditional boundaries of gender and sexuality can be transcended. This resonates with queer theology's focus on fluidity, embodiment and the dismantling of binaries, suggesting that queerness itself can be viewed as a sacred and transformative experience. Fry's observations emphasise that Umbanda rituals allow for expressions of sexuality and gender that challenge dominant societal norms. Queer theologies emerging from this context might highlight how these religious practices inherently resist colonial, patriarchal and heteronormative frameworks, creating sacred space for LGBTQ+ individuals.

Furthermore, the hybrid nature of Umbanda, blending African traditions, Roman Catholicism and indigenous practices, offers fertile ground for queer theological reflections. Fry notes how these traditions subvert rigid religious structures, creating inclusive spaces that challenge fixed dogmas. This aligns with queer theology's embrace of hybrid, intersectional and fluid religious identities. In particular, the role of spirits like the Pomba-Giras—who defy cis-heteropatriarchal norms and are often embraced by LGBTQ+ practitioners—provides powerful symbols for queer liberation. These figures resonate with Fry's analysis of how Afro-Brazilian cults empower marginalised identities.

The exploration of gender and sexuality in Umbanda reveals the potential for a 'queer Umbanda theology' that celebrates diversity, resists oppression and reimagines spirituality as inclusive. That exploration serves as a foundational text for theologians and practitioners seeking to articulate a queer theological perspective rooted in the Umbanda worldview.

Santería

Santería is also known as *Lucumí* or as the Regla de Ocha and developed in Cuba between the sixteenth and nineteenth centuries. Santería is polytheistic in that it worships Olodumaré as the supreme God and the Òrìsà as minor divinities. The term *Santería* means 'worship of the saints'. The names of the deities in Santería come from the Nàgó-Yorùbá religion: Eleggua, Orunmila, Obatalá, Oddudua, Chango, Oggun, San, Aganyu, Babalú-Ayé, Osain, Yemayá, Oshun, Oya, Orisha-Oko, Yewa, Dadá, Ibeyi, Oba, Inle and Osun.

Santeria dolls. *Source:* Mauro Didiero / Wikimedia Commons / Public domain.

Like its counterpart in Brazil, it also originated in the hybridisation of the Nàgó-Yorùbá religion and Christianity, especially the Roman Catholic church among slaves brought from Africa. According to Migene González-Wippler:

> In Cuba, where Santeria originated, the Yorùbá became known as Lucumí, a word meaning "friendship." [...] The Cuban Lucumís were deeply influenced by the Catholic iconolatry of their Spanish masters. In their efforts to hide their magical and religious practices from the eyes of the Spanish, they identified their deities with the saints of the [Roman] Catholic Church (2004: 3).

Some scholars claim that Santería is the fruit of hybridisation. Ernesto Pichardo (1998) states:

> Slavery in Cuba can be characterized as a process of dehumanization that sought to rehumanize Africans. In this colonial process, the [Roman] Catholic Church and the Spanish State united in common interest. Thus, the powers of formal and informal sanctions come together and affect the minority cultural group in a significant way. The formal interest of the State establishes the social and political norms, while religion in its official character establishes the new conversion and psychological conditioning of the minority cultural group.

The colonial period from the point of view of the African slaves can be defined as a time of perseverance as their world changed rapidly. Kings and tribal families, politicians, business and community leaders were enslaved in a foreign region of the world. Religious leaders, their descendants and the faithful were now slaves. Colonial laws criminalised their religion, and they were forced to be baptised and worship a new 'loving God' surrounded by a pantheon of saints. Early concerns during this period seem to indicate a need for individual survival and the ability to live in the harsh conditions of the plantation. Perhaps it is the context of slavery and the need to hide and disguise their religion that kept Santería believers from creating a proselytising attitude. Miguel A. De La Torre states:

> Santeria thus became the religion of an oppressed people. To truly understand the worldview of Santería, it is crucial that it be approached in these terms. We begin by recognizing that followers of Santería are not interested in proselytizing or justifying their beliefs to outsiders. Only those who are willing to take a step toward the orishas receive more detailed information. The closer one gets to the orishas, the more the mysteries of Santería are revealed (2004: 3).

Emerging in Cuba, Puerto Rico and the Dominican Republic, Santería has spread widely in the Caribbean and in the United States. As in the case of its Brazilian counterparts, one of the elements of its true diffusion was precisely the 'disguising' of the Òrìsà as 'Roman Catholic saints'. Some authors even affirm that it was the Cuban Revolution that provoked the expansion of Santería to the United States, since the great influx of immigrants in New York solidified the presence of the religion on US soil (Gregory, 1999: 27–28).

Salvador Vidal-Ortiz (2005) examines how Santería's rituals and cosmology create inclusive spaces for diverse expressions of gender and sexuality. He delves into the roles of Òrìsà, which often challenge binary gender norms, and highlights the ways practitioners reinterpret these figures to affirm LGBTQ+ identities. Vidal-Ortiz also discusses how spiritual practices and beliefs intersect with cultural dynamics, revealing both the affirming and contested spaces for Latinx LGBTIQ+ people within Santería communities. Vidal-Ortiz affirms: 'The discrimination that Latinos, as a radicalised ethnic group, experience in the U.S. context is highlighted in the milieu of Santería practice, itself a marginalized religion. Moreover, a marginalized religion's opening to marginalized sexuality is taking place' (2005: 135).

Source: Ji-Elle / Wikimedia Commons / CC BY-SA 4.0.

Salvador Vidal-Ortiz's research provides an essential lens for understanding the complex ways Afro-diasporic religious practices intersect with queer identity. His work examines how Santería, a religion with deep African roots, offers a spiritual framework where normative constructs of gender and sexuality are challenged and redefined. By exploring the lived experiences of LGBTQ+ practitioners, Vidal-Ortiz illustrates how these religious practices create spaces for self-affirmation and spiritual empowerment that diverge from the heteronormative traditions often dominant in other religious systems.

One of the critical contributions of Vidal-Ortiz's research lies in his analysis of the Òrìsà, who often embodies attributes that transcend rigid gender norms. For example, some Òrìsà are associated with fluidity and duality, offering theological symbols that resonate deeply with queer practitioners. These deities enable LGBTQ+ individuals to find sacred narratives that affirm their identities, highlighting the adaptability and inclusiveness of these spiritual traditions.

Furthermore, Vidal-Ortiz discusses how the ritual practices in Santería, such as spirit possession, provide opportunities to explore and express fluid gender and sexual identities. The act of possession allows individuals to embody the characteristics of the Òrìsà temporarily, transcending societal constraints and fostering a sense of liberation. This dynamic mirrors the broader objectives of queer theology, which seeks to dismantle oppressive structures and celebrate diverse embodiments of identity.

The intersection of Afro-diasporic spirituality with queer identity is not without its tensions. Vidal-Ortiz's research also addresses the challenges LGBTIQ+ practitioners face, such as reconciling traditional values with modern understandings of gender and sexuality. Nonetheless, his findings reveal the potential for these religions to act as sites of resistance against colonial, patriarchal and heteronormative frameworks. By situating queer identity within Afro-diasporic religious practices, Vidal-Ortiz's work expands the dialogue in both religious studies and queer theology. It underscores the need to consider spirituality as a vital component of LGBTIQ+ identity formation, particularly in communities historically marginalised by mainstream religions. His research, therefore, serves as a bridge between cultural anthropology, theology and queer studies, illuminating the transformative potential of Afro-diasporic spiritualities for queer empowerment.

Shamanism

Mapuche Shamanism

Among the Mapuche people of Argentina and Chile, the *Machi* is a person who serves the community by performing ceremonies to cure illness, ward off evil, influence the weather and harvest, and practice other forms of healing such as herbalism.

In Chile, the Mapuche nation is composed of the *Picunche* [people of the north], the *Huilliche* [people of the south] and the *Moluche* or *Nguluche* of Araucania. The latter are often referred to as Araucanians and are the ones who also extended into Argentinian Patagonia. The Mapuche nation inhabited the southern part of South America from 600 to 500 BCE (Bengoa, 1996: 14), long before the establishment of the Inca Empire.

In her essay 'The Mapuche male who became a female shaman: Personality, gender transgression and competing cultural norms' (2004), Ana Mariella Bacigalupo analyses the life of Marta, a transgender Mapuche shaman in Chile. Bacigalupo (2004) focuses especially on describing how Marta is able to inhabit the female heterosexual space within the symbolic religious world in Chile, deeply influenced by colonial stereotypes of the Virgin Mary, the basic Christian icon of women's cis-heteronormativity. Bacigalupo states that 'Marta demonstrates how religious motifs, personal struggles for identity, and contestable ideas about gender and sexuality are strategically drawn together in a process of self-making that one can understand as authentic self-expression' (2004: 451).

While Bacigalupo highlights several contextual and historical elements within Mapuche culture which need to be taken into account to understand their particular shamanism an unusual contribution for Latin America is her pointing out of the variations in the understanding of gender and sexuality based on colonialism. Mapuche is a collective term to designate the Native South Americans in the Chilean Patagonia which is different from the Argentinian Patagonia below the current capital of the country: Santiago. It means 'People of the Land' [*Mapu* = earth/*Che* = people].

To understand the spiritual context it is necessary to begin by saying that Mapuche is a collective term for the people of the original peoples in the Patagonian regions of Chile and Argentina. However, in the Mapuche cosmovision, Mapu not only defines the geographic space where people live but also the space where personal, family and community life takes place and also involves the supernatural world. Although they are interrelated, the 'natural' and 'supernatural' spaces have their own rules and modes of organisation. To say that a person is 'Mapuche' is to recognise the interrelationship of all these spaces at work in his or her life.

As for how the Mapuche cosmovision is organised, it is a complex and rich conceptualisation. The concept of *Wallmapu* defines the surrounding territory in which the Mapuche nation lives with all its resources: rivers, forests and minerals. The *Wenu mapu* space designates the land above. This is the upper part of the supernatural world and there the positive energies reside together with the spirits of the ancestors and the creator gods (Aldunate del Solar, 1986: 84–85). This plane is opposed to the *Miñche Mapu*, a concept that designates the land below. In the Mapuche worldview this is the lower space of the supernatural world, a dark and chaotic place. Negative energies reside there. In the middle of both planes is the *Ragiñ Wenu Mapu*, the Middle Earth. Finally, the *Pülli Mapu* is the land where human beings live, which contains the natural world. In this space coexist in a dynamic way the positive and negative energies are projected from the supernatural world (Cruz, 2010).

Carlos Aldunate del Solar offers a description of the interrelation between spirituality and daily life:

> [T]he Mapuche *ruka* generally has its entrance towards the East, the *ngillatué* or anthropomorphic wooden figures that preside over the *rogativa—ngillatún—*

> [prayers], are also oriented towards the mountain range, a site that must be kept clear for the duration of the ceremony. The *machi* installs his *rewe* towards this same point so that when he looks at it, he directs his prayers towards the East (1986: 86).

However, this delicate balance of forces and spaces was radically affected and continues to be so by the presence of colonialism. To understand the reality of the Mapuche nation, we need to focus not only on how it has impacted their belief systems but also on their culture and society, because these three aspects of their worldview are one and the same and give meaning to the concept of Mapu.

The spiritual leaders in native populations not only represent the embracing of the different understandings of gender and sexuality, but they are also accepted by their respective communities without prejudice. Of course, many understandings of this 'diversity' are based on heteropatriarchalism and, therefore, gender-fluid spiritual leaders are expected to respect the dicta of heteronormativity. This mirrors the situation in South America.

There are three aspects that we would like to point out in relation to the Mapuche nation in Chile that underline the article by Bacigalupo:

The Political Colonisation

Although Mapuche lived freely for centuries, the establishment of the Incan Empire threatened them with colonisation. It is well documented that the Incan Empire would colonise other nations in the region and annex them to their political structure. Chilean historian José Bengoa (1996: 37–38) reports that troops of the Inca Empire reached the Maule River and battled with the Mapuches between the Maule River and the Itata River. The Mapuche resisted the domination and kept the Incan Empire border at bay in that region.

However, with the arrival of the Spanish *conquistadores* the situation changed for the Mapuche. Slowly the Spaniards began conquering the territories and the peoples in the Chilean Patagonia. Bengoa affirms:

> Unlike the Incas and Mexicans, who possessed centralized governments and internal political divisions, the Mapuches possessed a non-hierarchical social structure. In the Mexican and Andean situation, the conquistador struck the centre of political power and, on conquering it, secured the rule of the Empire. In the Mapuche case this was not possible, since their submission entailed the domination of one of the thousands of independent families (1996: 37).

The domination of some Mapuche families did not reach the heart of the Mapuche nation. Thus, in January 5–6, 1641, the Mapuche Nation and the Spanish Empire signed the Quilín Treaty, which divided the territory of the Chilean Viceroyalty into two, taking the Bio Bio River as the limit. The north was Spanish territory, the south was Mapuche territory. This allowed Mapuches to live undisturbed for 240 years (Bengoa, 2007: 1). The situation began to change on July 2, 1852, when the Chilean government which became independent from Spain on September 18, 1810, created the Province of Arauco south of the Bio Bio river. This meant that the territory was no longer recognised as governed by Mapuches (Crow, 2013: 19). Ten years later, in 1862, the Chilean government began its military occupation campaigns that led to the complete colonisation of the Mapuche nation.

Since then, the Mapuche were viewed with suspicion due to their distinctive culture. This led to military dictator Augusto Pinochet enacting Law 18.314, also known as the 'Anti-terrorist Law'. Since its inception, this law gives harsher sentences for crimes involving fire, homicide and kidnapping, duplicating those established in the Penal Code. The law also allows for the use of 'faceless witnesses', restricts access to precautionary measures and extends the sentence periods for prison. It has been systematically used to imprison thousands of Mapuche people who resist expulsion from their lands. Once evicted their land is given by the government to transnational corporations from the Global North that mine the minerals and massively destroy the natural forest for wood exportation. The government also plans roads and freeways over the towns inhabited by the Mapuche people.

Some of the Mapuche political prisoners, who are mainly activists defending their right to inhabit their ancestral lands, have over the years begun hunger strikes that have jeopardised their lives. In 2001–2002, a large movement was raised against the Chilean government's application of the Anti-Terrorist Law, which resulted in the massive incarceration of the Mapuche people. The Inter-American Human Rights Court has ordered Chile to free these political prisoners (Latinamerica Press, 2014), something that Chile has not done yet. Even spiritual leaders such as Machi Francisca Linconao remain in prison. In 2013 Machi Linconao was jailed on arson charges along with 10 other Mapuche activists under the Anti-Terrorist Law. According to human rights organisations, the evidence against her is suspicious, and most of the witnesses have withdrawn their testimonies. Still, the government keeps Machi Linconao in prison, even when her life is at risk (Telesur, 2016).

The Religious Colonisation

Bacigalupo (2004) points out that Mapuche live in either Roman Catholic or Pentecostal communities. This is because the conversion of Mapuche to Christianity entails a territorial competence by these two branches of Christianity. Since the times of colonisation, Christianising the Mapuche nation was one of the 'civilising' goals of the Spanish Empire. The Mapuche spirituality was not considered to be of any value; indeed, it was demonised and there were attempts to erase Mapuche spirituality.

In the twentieth century, the development of Pentecostalism in Chile took the main responsibility for Christianising the Mapuche nation. The tone of Pentecostalism in Chile is aggressively conversionist, and it is not strange to see that their 'mission' extended to 'demonic religions that praise false gods'. Hence, here lies the impossibility for non-Pentecostal Mapuche to reside in the communities that have opted for Pentecostalism as their religion.

This, paired with the refusal of Roman Catholicism to acknowledge Mapuche spirituality as an equal religion, has paved the way for many Mapuche to be disconnected from their ancestral spiritual roots. Only in the second part of the twentieth century, many new generations have begun to embrace again their ancestral spiritual roots, especially the younger generation. Still, the 'religious wars' are a dividing factor amidst the Mapuche nation.

The Cultural Colonisation

One consequence of political colonisation is cultural colonisation. This can be related to language, cultural norms or gender/sexuality understanding. Bacigalupo (2004: 448–449) narrates how other Machi ostracised and critiqued Marta because of her self-affirmation as a woman. This is a consequence of the imported notions of cultural and religious notions brought by the European colonisers and their descendants. The effects of colonisation are not only visible in the economic hardships that the Mapuche nations suffer today, the lack of health services or education system, but also by the way that their lives are being policed and censored so that they can be 'normalised' into the already-conservative Chilean society.

At the same time, the hardships that the Mapuche suffer in society are paralleled by the discrimination that LGBT organisations in Chilean society display towards queer Mapuche. Roberto Fernández Droguett (2012) narrates his experience participating in the Gay Pride in Santiago. There, when Mapuche activists also appeared in the Parade, some attendees asked: 'Are these Mapuche gays?' The question is a significant one, as it presupposes untouchable spaces inhabited by 'gays' on one side and 'Mapuches' on the other, but never the recognition that the Mapuche inhabit different identities, including sexual diversity. This is a spirit that cuts across all LGBT movements in Latin America that have for the most part remained complicit in discrimination, outcasting and ostracism of Native Latin Americans. Droguett (2012) even questions whether 'the visibility of the (homo)sexuality of those Mapuche activists would have even granted them more legitimacy to their presence in the parade'.

There is an expectation not only that Mapuche have to comply with the dicta of the nuclear heterosexual monogamous nuclear family, but also with the stereotype that they are unable to understand sexual diversity. Such a construction of the Other/s as 'lesser than us' still legitimates the self-appointed right of Western descendants of the colonial regime to excerpt power over the Mapuche nation in their very same lands. Sadly, LGBTIQ+ movements in Latin America have some work to do to recognise other diversities.

North American Shamanism

Traditionally Native North American studies in religion have given priority to recover the spirituality of the different nations in that region. However, issues that pertain to body(ies), sexuality, gender, or sexual orientation have been simply put under the category of 'berdache', as this would be enough to cover the manifold experiences of sexual diversity among Native North American nations.

<table>
<tr><td>

Box 12.1

</td></tr>
<tr><td>

Berdache, a contested term, was often used to refer to a person who does not identify with their birth sex but rather with a variety of gender identities. They are now commonly referred to as transgender or two-spirit individuals. Two-spirit people are thought to be healers and prophets as in themselves they reflect the nature of the divine which was both male and female.

</td></tr>
</table>

That oversimplification entails a problem. The term 'berdache' is an imposition of the conquerors over Native (North)American queer individuals. It is in fact a French adaptation of the Arabic term for 'male prostitute'. This has given reasons to Native North/Meso/South Americans to reject it. On this, Qwo-Li Driskill, in his essay 'Doubleweaving Two-Spirit Critiques' (2010) states that the term Two-Spirit was chosen in an intertribal North American agreement to be used in English in order to communicate the different tribal traditions about queer individuals.

However, beyond the terminology, which is a very important topic, the phenomenon of the so-called Berdache and the allowing of transgender individuals to live their chosen display of gender among Native (North) Americans (Whitehead, 1981: 94) was not foreign to their counterparts in Meso and South America (Horswell, 2003; Trexler, 1995). However, all that was changed with the arrival of a new morality imposed by both Roman Catholicism and the Spaniard conquistadors (Garza Carvajal, 2003) which prosecuted and executed those who did not conform. Later, the Anglo-Saxon colonisation with its Protestant tone reinforced that prohibition.

Suzanne J. Crawford O'Brien affirms that,

> The experience of colonization is one of systematic cultural suppression and forced assimilation. A central tool of colonization is missionization: the imposition of the dominant religious tradition on a subordinate people, intended to suppress dissent, eliminate difference, and compel submission to the new colonial authority. [...] All of this matters when we are thinking about embodiment, gender, and sexuality in indigenous communities because it forces us to remember that there is no rarified "indigenous person" existing out of time and space with a pure and singular identity. Instead, there are indigenous people who live in complex intercultural contexts (2015: 165–166).

Nonetheless, Will Roscoe, in his essay 'We'wha and Klah: The American Indian Berdache as Artist and Priest' (1999) highlights the fact that Two-Spirit individuals not only invigorated the cultural traits of their people but also assumed spiritual leadership in order to produce communication between the spiritual forces and humans in terms of healing, counselling and ritual ceremonies performances.

Two examples of Two Spirit people are given below:

WE'wha of the Zuni
Source: John Karl Hillers (1843–1925) / The U.S. National Archives and Records Administration / Public domain.

WE'wha of the Zuni tribe was born in 1849 and became an ambassador for the tribe. Having learnt English We'wha was a contact point with the European colonisers and tried to educate them in Zuni ways. We'wha was a skilled potter and weaver. We'wha was taken to visit President Grover Cleveland and also donated an amount of Zuni art to the Smithsonian. We'wha was the most prominent llamana, who is a male bodied person who performs the ceremonial rituals associated with women. We'wha died in 1986.

Hosteen Klah
Source: John Karl Hillers / U.S. National Archives and Records Administration / Public domain.

Hosteen Klah (1987–1937) was a Navajo weaver who was considered to be intersexed. He was called Nadleehi which means one who changes. He was an artist, weaver and medicine man. Importantly he documented Navajo religion, ritual practices and ceremonies.

How Two Spirit people were recognised as leaders is an important question, as every nation has its own way to recognise this leadership. This is precisely what Crawford O'Brien aims to highlight. Her contribution to academic work is important because she offers a broad overview of different nations' practices and beliefs. By doing this, she upholds the diversity and variety of experiences and understandings that have governed Native North American nations for millennia. Thus, Crawford O'Brien concludes:

> Indigenous cultures are vastly diverse, and it is difficult to distill a list of common ideas. Yet, within this vast diversity, some common themes emerge. The embodied self in indigenous cultures challenges modern Euroamerican views of the finite, bounded individual. Instead, the self is a holistically interconnected self, where body, mind, and spirit are all intertwined (2015: 179).

Andrea Smith et al. deal basically with Christian Native North American theology. This is a fact that is clearly pointed out by Michelene Pesantubbe as follows:

> I should not have been surprised as the academy tends to equate theology with Christianity and, in some cases, assumes that the academic study of theologies of other groups, such as Buddhists or Hindus, is not rich enough (or for some religions nonexistent) to warrant intentional inclusion within the field of theological study. The same tendency applies to Native [North] American spirituality. Even when scholars address Native [North] American theology/theologies that are "inclusive of all Natives (traditional, Christian, neo-traditional, syncretic)," as stated in the book A Native American Theology, they are attending to Native [North] American Christian theologies. The intent is to facilitate a more inclusive, culturally relevant, Christian church by reinterpreting or revamping Christian symbols to express traditional Native [North] American ones. For many Native [North] Americans who are Christian such adaptations are welcome and reaffirming of their identities. For non-Christian Native people who practice traditional ways these adaptations are interpreted as appropriation by a colonizing institution and those Native [North] Americans participating in these adaptations as internalizing the colonizers' message and as serving the colonisers (Smith et al., 2006: 98).

We completely agree with her that there is Christian hegemony that tends to colonise other spiritualities/religions. At the same time, we would like to point out how entrenched one is in one's culture to the point of being unaware that terminology acts to colonise other experiences. For example, the appropriation of 'American' by people from the US continues to make invisible and to exclude other 'Americans' in the continent. It is not correct to say 'Native American' when one is referring only to a portion of the population in the Americas. This has been exactly the strategy of the colonisers by constructing the Other/s through terminology that differentiate them from the Other/s.

Duane Champagne does an excellent job in briefly interconnecting Native North American issues, religion and colonialism. This is a key aspect to keep in mind for an analysis that does not tend to spiritualise or diminish the seriousness of the situation of Native

North American nations. At the same time she agrees with other scholars about the fact that among Native North American nations:

> Alternative gender roles were respected and honoured, and believed to be part of the sacred web of life and society. If the Great Spirit chose to create alternative sexualities or gender roles, who was bold enough to oppose such power? (2011: xviii).

The author also notes the spiritual effects that traditional religion has in the inner lives of the believers, whether it be a Sun Dance or the interpretation of dreams. This is an important aspect because it invigorates the inner self of the believers against the many hardships that they still undergo due to US/Canadian internal colonialism.

William E. Baldridge is one of the first people to ask how to think Native North American Theologies. Still, Baldridge would acknowledge that this is a bit out of context:

> Doing theology, thinking theologically, is a decidedly non-Indian thing to do. When I talk about Native [North] American theology to many of my Indian friends, most of them just smile and act as if I had not said anything. And I am pretty sure that as far as they are concerned I truly had not said anything. [...] There is also a difference in Native [North] American theology and Native [North] Americans doing theology, as any Native [North] American student in theological training soon finds out (1989: 228).

It speaks about the colonial situation in which the West tends to push the many spiritualities already present in the continent to the margins and even to non-existence in the colonial mind. At the same time, this statement is important coming from an author such as Baldridge who is a mix-race Cherokee and a Christian. This piece is an important pilgrimage of someone like many other Native [North/Central/South] Americans who are the in-betweeners occupying a space created due to the material effects of a colonial past in their lives.

It is important and fair to recognise that for many of these 'hybrid' Native [North/Central/South] American believers, Christianity is also an option for their spiritual life. For many Christianity offered hope in their colonial situations. Yet, for these Christians, their own hybrid experiences led them to seek a hybrid experience of religion in a way of conversation and mutual enriching. Baldridge concludes after narrating a religious message from the Cherokee tradition:

> That Christ is Lord of all time, Lord of the living and dead, Lord of sacred time AND historical time; that message is what makes Native American theology "Christian" and not just Native American spirituality cast in theological language. What Native American Christians have to give to our Euro-American brothers and sisters is a more profound understanding of Christ as the eternal Logos. What Euro-American Christianity has to give to Native American spirituality is a more profound understanding of Christ in history: the redemption of history (1989: 237).

At the same time, we need to acknowledge that the personal pilgrimage of an individual can take her/him/them to different spiritual paths. This means that it should not be a problem for a Native [North/Central/South] American to change to another religion. In the same way, non-Native [North/Central/South] American people could also embrace any of these spiritualities as their own. This is a phenomenon that has cut across all history of humanity. People in their pilgrimage encounter different experiences. There is no 'right' or 'wrong', only ways that the divine power guides humanity and all elements in this universe in a dance that somehow makes full circle.

Our last point is extremely important. We believe that 'Native North American' or 'First Nations' are better terms to describe collectively the many communities in those countries without having recourse to odd terminology such as Indians. Of course, the most respectable way would be to use the particular name of every nation whenever possible.

For Further Discussion

1 In what ways has this chapter developed an understanding of cosmovisions and gender identity? Has it made you question your own world view?

2 How has this chapter informed/changed/(re)shaped your ideas about the intersection of religion, queer studies, race/ethnicity, (post)coloniality, gender and sexuality? Could you offer some examples?

3 We are also using a universalising term queer to define the sexual diversity present in every religion studied. Based on what we have already seen in the course, how could we approach this sexual diversity without being 'trapped' into co-opting terminology? What is your opinion on this issue?

4 In your own religious pilgrimage, have you encountered this 'solidarity' among marginalised groups, religious or nonreligious, that come together? Could you share your experiences?

References

Aldunate del Solar, Carlos (1986). *Cultura mapuche (Serie Patrimonio Cultural Chileno, Colección Cultura Aborígenes)*. Santiago de Chile: Departamento de Extensión Cultural, Ministerio de Educación de Chile.

Allen, Andrea (2008). "Candomblé." In: *Encyclopedia of the African Diaspora: Origins, Experiences, and Culture*, edited by Carole Boyce Davies, volume 1. Santa Barbara, CA: ABC-CLIO, pp. 256–257.

Alonso, Miguel C (2014). *The Development of Yoruba Candomble Communities in Salvador, Bahia, 1835–1986*. New York, NY: Palgrave MacMillan.

Arakaki, Ushi (2008). "Umbanda: Temporality and Identity in the Life of the Brazilian Nikkeijin Transnational Migrants." Paper presented at the Conference "Migration and Identities: Conflict and the New Horizon," Osaka, Nakanoshima Center, Osaka University and University of São Paulo, 24 October.

Arakaki, Ushi (2009). ""Toransunashonaru Jidai no Umbanda" [Umbanda in Transnational Times]." In: *Kokuritsu Minzoku Gakuhakubutsukan Chōsa Hōkoku [About the Regional and National Immigration Changes]*, Senri Ethnological Reports 83, edited by Hiroshi Shoji. Osaka: National Museum of Ethnology, pp. 89–104.

Arakaki, Ushi (2014). "Becoming Brazilian in Japan: Umbanda and Ethnocultural Identity in Transnational Times." In: *Transnational Faiths: Latin-American Immigrants and their Religions in Japan*, edited by Hugo Córdova Quero and Rafael Shoji. Farnham: Ashgate, pp. 171–188.

Bacigalupo, Ana M (2004). "The Mapuche Man Who Became a Woman Shaman: Selfhood, Gender Transgression, and Competing Cultural Norms." *American Ethnologist* 31, No. 3 (August): pp. 440–457.

Baldridge, William E (1989). "Toward a Native American Theology." *American Baptist Quarterly* 8, No. December: pp. 227–238.

Bengoa, José (1996). *Historia del pueblo Mapuche: Siglos XIX y XX.* Santiago de Chile: Ediciones Sur.

Bengoa, José (2007). *El tratado de Quilín: Documentos adicionales a la historia de los antiguos Mapuches del sur.* Santiago de Chile: Catalonia.

Beraba, Marcelo (2008). "O terreiro da contradição". *Folha de São Paulo,* March 30. Available at: <https://www1.folha.uol.com.br/fsp/mais/fs3003200804.htm>.

Capone, Stefania (2010). *Searching for Africa in Brazil: Power and Tradition in Candomblé.* Durham, NC: Duke University Press.

Champagne, Duane (2011). "Sharing the Gift of Sacred Being." In: *Two Spirit People: American Indian Lesbian Women and Gay Men*, edited by Lester B Brown. New York, NY: Routledge, pp. xvii–xxiv.

Chesnut, R Andrew (2003). *Competitive Spirits: Latin America's New Religious Economy.* Oxford: Oxford University Press.

Childs, Matt D (2023). "The Roots and Routes of African Religious Beliefs in the Atlantic World." *The William and Mary Quarterly* 80: pp. 325–354.

Childs, Matt D and Toyin Falola (2004). "The Yoruba Diaspora in the Atlantic World: Methodology and Research." In: *The Yoruba Diaspora in the Atlantic World*, edited by Toyin Falola and Matt D Childs. Bloomington, IN: Indiana University Press, pp. 1–14.

Crawford O'Brien, Suzanne J (2015). "Indigenous Traditions: Embodiment, Gender, and Sexuality." In: *Religion: Embodied Religion*, edited by Kent L Brintnall. Farmington Hills, MI: Macmillan Reference USA, pp. 165–181.

Crow, Joanna (2013). *The Mapuche in Modern Chile: A Cultural History.* Gainesville, FL: University Press of Florida.

Cruz, Eduardo A (2010). *The Grand Araucanian Wars (1541–1883) in the Kingdom of Chile.* Bloomington, IN: Xlibris Corporation.

La Torre, De and A Miguel (2004). *Santería: The Beliefs and Rituals of a Growing Religion in America.* Grand Rapids, MI: William B. Eerdmans.

Driskill, Qwo-Li (2010). "Doubleweaving Two-Spirit Critiques: Building Alliances between Native and Queer Studies." *GLQ* 16, No. 1–2: pp. 69–92.

Engler, Steven (2012). "Umbanda and Africa." *Nova Religio: The Journal of Alternative and Emergent Religions* 15, No. 4 (May): pp. 13–35.

Fernandez, Droguett (2012). "¿Y estos mapuches son gays? Una reflexión a propósito de las marchas por la diversidad sexual y por la dignidad mapuche." Blog de la Facultad de Ciencias Sociales, Universidad de Chile. Available at: <http://www.facso.uchile.cl/noticias/85891/y-estos-mapuches-son-gays-por-prof-roberto-fernandez-droguett>.

Fry, Peter (1995). "Male Homosexuality and Afro-Brazilian Possession Cults." In: *Latin American Male Homosexualities*, edited by Stephen O Murray. Albuquerque, NM: University of New Mexico Press, pp. 193–200.

Garza Carvajal, Federico (2003). *Butterflies Will Burn: Prosecuting Sodomites in Early Modern Spain and Mexico.* Austin, TX: University of Texas Press.

González-Wippler, Migene (2004). *Santería: The Religion. Faith-Rites-Magic.* St. Paul, MN: Llewellyn Publications.

Gregory, Steven (1999). *Santería in New York City: A Study in Cultural Resistance.* New York, NY: Garland Publishing.

Hale, Lindsay (2009). *Hearing the Mermaid's Song: The Umbanda Religion in Rio de Janeiro*. Albuquerque, NM: University of New Mexico Press.

Horswell, Michael J (2003). "Toward an Andean Theory of Ritual Same-Sex Sexuality and Third-Gender Subjectivity." In: *Infamous Desire: Male Homosexuality in Colonial Latin America*, edited by Pete Sigal. Chicago, IL: University Of Chicago Press, pp. 25–69.

Latinamerica Press (2014). "Inter-American Court of Human Rights Orders Chile to Annul Sentences Under Anti-Terrorist Law." *Intercontinental Cry*, August 31. Available at: <https://intercontinentalcry.org/inter-american-court-human-rights-orders-chile-annul-sentences-anti-terrorist-law-25431> [Accessed April 28, 2017].

Lundell, Eleonora (2016). "Exú's Work – The Agency of Ritual Objects in Southeast Brazilian Umbanda." *Journal of Ethnology and Folkloristics* 10, No. 1: pp. 43–69.

Motta, Roberto (2020). "Xangô, Jurema e Umbanda: anotações sobre três formas de religião popular na região do Recife." *Revista del CESLA: International Latin American Studies Review* 26: pp. 3–24.

Ogunnaike, Ayodeji (2020). "What's Really Behind the Mask: A Reexamination of Syncretism in Brazilian Candomblé." *Journal of Africana Religions* 8: pp. 146–171.

Pichardo, Ernesto (1998). "Santeria in Contemporary Cuba: The Individual Life and Condition of the Priesthood." Paper presented at the Third Annual So. Florida Symposium on Cuba "Faith and Power: Religion in Contemporary Cuba." James L. Knight Center, University of Miami, Coral Gables, Florida, September 12–13. Available at: <http://www.churchofthelukumi.com/santeria-in-contemporary-cuba.html>.

Pinto, Flávia (2014). *Umbanda religião brasileira: Guia para leigos e iniciantes*. Rio de Janeiro, RJ: Pallas Editora.

Roscoe, Will (1999). "We'wha and Klah: The American Indian Berdache as Artist and Priest." In: *Que(e)rying Religion: A Critical Anthology*, edited by Gary David Comstock and Susan E Henking. New York, NY: Continuum, pp. 89–106.

Schmidt, Bettina E (2006). "The Creation of Afro-Caribbean Religions and their Incorporation of Christian Elements." *Transformation: An International Journal of Holistic Mission Studies* 23: pp. 236–243.

Segato, Rita L (1991). "Uma Vocação de Minoria: A Expansão dos Cultos Afro-Brasileiros na Argentina como Processo de Re-etnização." *Dados-Revista de Ciências Sociais* 34, No. 2: pp. 249–278.

Segato, Rita L (2008). "Gender Politics, and Hybridism in the Transnationalization of Yorùbá Culture." In: *Òrìṣà Devotion as World Religion: The Globalisation of Yorùbá Religious Culture*, edited by Jacob Kẹhinde Olupona and Terry Rey. Madison, WI: University of Wisconsin Press, pp. 485–512.

Smith, Andrea, Michelene Pesantubbee, Dianne M Stewart, Michelle A Gonzalez, Sylvester Johnson and Tink Tinker (2006). "Roundtable Discussion: Native/First Nation Theology [with Response]." *Journal of Feminist Studies in Religion* 22, No. 2 (Fall): pp. 85–121.

Telesur (2016). "Movements Demand That Chile Free Mapuche Indigenous Leader." August 18. Available at: <http://www.telesurtv.net/english/news/Movements-Demand-That-Chile-Free-Mapuche-Indigenous-Leader-20160818-0006.html>.

Trexler, Richard C (1995). *Sex and Conquest: Gendered Violence, Political Order and the European Conquest of the Americas*. Ithaca, NY: Cornell University Press.

Vidal-Ortiz, Salvador (2005). "Sexuality and Gender in Santeria: LGBT Identities at the Crossroads of Santeria Religious Practices Beliefs." In: *Gay Religion*, edited by Scott Thumma and Edward R Gray. Walnut Creek, CA: Altamira Press, pp. 115–137.

Whitehead, Harriet (1981). "The Bow and the Burden Strap: A New Look at Institutionalized Homosexuality in Native North America." In: *Sexual Meanings: The Cultural Construction of Gender and Sexuality*, edited by Sherry B Ortner and Harriet Whitehead. Cambridge: Cambridge University Press, pp. 80–115.

13

Ancestral Spiritualities in the African Context

In this chapter, we will study Queer African Spiritualities. We explore the continent's historical, societal and cultural background, significantly how religions and colonialism have impacted this diverse region's many societies and cultures. While avoiding colonial impositions on African contexts, we must continue queering the notions of rigid heteronormativity already present in the continent due to that colonialism. How do gender and sexuality relate to the daily lives of people and communities? What are the situations that queer folks face while living their faith/spiritualities/beliefs? We will analyse how sexual theologies have been received and debated in Africa. Is there a correlation between the history of sexuality in Africa and how religions consider gender and sexuality? What role have both colonialism and right-wing Christian discourses from the West played in this context? What can we learn from the ancestral wisdom of spiritualities in this part of the world? The intermixing of Christianity, Islam and Traditional African Religions is a particular feature of Africa.

Traditional African Religions

The scholar Randy P. Conner helps us to reflect on the understanding of what we call 'traditional African religions'. He offers us some clues to understand from a geographical and cultural distance a phenomenon that those who practice these religions may not perceive in the same way. Conner states:

> Given the variety of indigenous traditions present on the African continent, it is impossible to make general statements about the beliefs and practices of African "religions" without doing an injustice to some or even most of them. Furthermore, practitioners of these "religions" often do not see their faith as such because they perceive religion as completely intertwined with the totality of their life experiences, rather than as a demarcated field of life experience (2003: 3).

This quote is important because it recognises how African spiritualities are perceived differently by those who participate in their practice and by those outsiders who seek to analyse those spiritualities.

A key aspect is the intertwining of faith and daily life. Although people have some systematisation of their beliefs, this does not mean that they follow the Western rationalist

Global Queer Theologies: Intercontextual and Interreligious Perspectives, First Edition. Lisa Isherwood and Hugo Córdova Quero.

model. This 'intelligent' way of relating to religion may be so alien to those who typify spiritualities around the world that it may even be exhaustive.

Add gender and sexual-gender diversity to the mix, and the result is something completely different from Western expectations. And rightly so, as these spiritualities in Africa have existed long before the established religions of the West set the tone for what is and is not 'religious'. Why is it important to bring these aspects to traditional African spiritualities? Because it is where beliefs manifest themselves in everyday life beyond ritual, that is, they are anchored in the everyday, and reveal aspects unexpected by those who only focus exclusively on the religious character of these spiritualities.

It would be impossible to detail the wonderful panoramic view that Conner presents in his chapter on the richness of 'traditional African religions'. The underlying question in this chapter is that of the perception of something we in the West call 'gender' and 'sexuality'. Conner states:

> In some African spiritual traditions, gender is not an indicator of identity, so the terms 'masculine' and 'feminine' are considered meaningless. In others, "masculinity" and "femininity" possess traditional designations that resonate remarkably with the yin-yang symbolism of Chinese Taoist cosmology (2003: 7).

This is important because it also raises the issue of what many authors label 'African sexuality' (Ahlberg, 1994; Caldwell et al., 1989). These authors do not always agree on this issue, and their positions may even be contrary to those of their colleagues. For example, John P. Caldwell et al. (1989) propose the thesis of denying the role that Christianity assumed in shaping the continent's perceptions of gender and sexuality. Indeed, despite the social and religious consequences of colonialism, for Caldwell et al. (1989: 188) this 'African system' is still 'largely intact'. These authors extensively summarise this system as follows:

> The following are typical characteristics of the African system: great emphasis on the importance of ancestry and descent, usually accompanied by a belief in the intervention of ancestral spirits in the affairs of the living; a related social system which, in its most complex form, lineage, gives greater importance to intergenerational over conjugal ties and which accords great respect and power to elders; a system of inheritance whereby property, which is generally communal, remains within the lineage or clan and normally passes between members of the same sex; agriculture characterized by rotation of plantations based on the use of the hoe, typically by women. In accordance with the goal of lineage perpetuation, fertility is emphasized: by society, ancestral spirits and even the high gods who otherwise have little importance in day-to-day life. Virtue is related more to reproductive success than to limiting waste; and in many societies, initiation ceremonies that allow the onset of sexual activity are ritually more important than the celebration of marriage (Caldwell et al., 1989: 188).

For some people, this long description actually fits, more or less, with other regions of the world where cis-heteropatriarchy has also forged such family/clan/caste systems. The authors continue their analysis around the institution of marriage:

> The marriage bond is typically weak, with spouses retaining strong lineage ties and with a marked conjugal separation of economic activities and responsibilities; marriage payment takes the form of bride wealth paid to the wife's family by the husband rather than to the couple themselves and never includes land; polygamy exists on a scale not found in the Eurasian system and, consequently, the basic family unit is the

mother and her children; husbands are usually much older than wives; divorce is fairly common among most ethnic groups; and women, at least in the past, abstained from sex after giving birth for a period that could extend to years (Caldwell et al., 1989: 188).

We should note that in Caldwell et al.'s (1989) description there is no single reference to the lives and activities of same-sex attracted individuals. By recognising this, we can better understand the fluidity as well as the rich diversity of understandings of gender and sexuality in the multiple African traditional religions.

Because it is not possible to analyse all the experiences of the immense African spiritual variety, we offer limited examples below.

Sub-Saharan Africa

In pre-colonial days there were two tribes in Kenya, the Kikuyu and the Meru, who were noted for queer inclusiveness. Their priests called *mugawe* were non-heterosexual males who dressed and wore their hair like women and publicly acted like women. A number of them were married to other men. Marriage between two women was also allowed and in the Akamba tribe the practice was called *iweto*. However, this was not necessarily to do with lesbianism but rather to do with fertility. If a woman was barren or widowed she could take a wife to act as a surrogate but had to court her, pay the bride price and if the husband was dead even decide who she should have sex with in order to become pregnant. If a child was born it was considered to be the child of the first wife and even her dead husband.

In Sudan a number of tribes, such as the Otoro, accepted transvestism as part of culture. This was nothing to do with religion or spirituality as in many other cultures but simply because individuals wished to live in this way. The Tira, Nyima and Moru tribes of Sudan also had pre-established transgender bride prices which the groom had to pay. The Mesakin and Korongo, who were studied by a British anthropologist in the 1903s, were noted to be reluctant to leave all male camps believing sex with women made them weak (Nadel, 1947). Nadel notes that such behaviour is seen most in tribes that are strongly matrilineal and where homosexuality and transvestism were practiced openly.

Modern-day Uganda, which is so anti-LGBTIQ+, has a history of queerness with cross dressing priests who were common amongst the Bunyoro tribe, while the Teso tribe recognised a third gender exclusively for men who dressed like women. The most famous of the queer tribes were the Langi who had a class of people known as the *mudoko dako* who were recognised from birth as being outside the norm. This was probably to do with some form of genital irregularity. It was legal for them to marry a male or a female and could dress and take on any work to do with either sex.

In Ethiopia the Maale tribe have queer ashtime people who are biologically male who dress and act as women. What makes them special is that the King of Maale extended special protection to them so could be argued to be the first in the world to extend specific protection for LGBTIQ+ folk. In other parts of Ethiopia the Harari people were noted for their liberal attitudes to sex where sex between men and between women was commonplace. They also recognised a third gender described as having the spirit of one gender and the body of another.

Western and Central Africa

In the modern region of Burkina Faso, a country in which homosexuality has never been criminalised, the Dagaaba tribe consider their queer folk to have unique talents which they use. They act as intermediaries in conflict resolution as well as acting between God and people. They also act as problem solvers between the genders either on the level of marriage or if the tribe is divided along gender lines on a particular issue. The Ashanti Kingdom in Ghana was well known for homosexuality amongst the nobility who took same sex slaves. While in the Dahomey Kingdom castrated males were often taken as royal wives and often held positions of great power.

In Gabon and Cameroon the Pangwe and Fang tribes used queer sex magic. Same-sex relations were used to pass spiritual 'medicine' to people, and interestingly it was not the top who passed it on but rather the bottom who passed the medicine onto the top. The Hausa people who make up the largest ethnic group in all of Africa have been very accepting of queer folk throughout their history. The term dan Daudu refers to a man who prefers to act like a woman and may live amongst women until they take a husband. If they marry a woman they are then thought of as lesbians, which is called kifi. They may also take a wife and father children while maintaining their status as women.

The Azande people of the Democratic Republic of Congo were a highly homosexual culture with the men practising a form of pederasty similar to the ancient Greeks. The women also had sex with other women, and the men were very respectful of lesbians believing they doubled their spiritual power by acting in this way making them more powerful than men. The Azande word for lesbian was adandara which is also the word for supernatural catlike magic beings believed to be the offspring of sex between women.

Nàgó-Yorùbá Tradition

To speak of the Nàgó-Yorùbá tradition is to cut into a much larger ethnic family. Yorùbá societies are in fact very diverse. For example, unlike their Bantú counterparts, which hold matrilineal societies, Yorùbá societies can be matrilineal or patrilineal depending on the organization of the clan. This variation stems from the fact that Yorùbá societies are based on the 'Ebi social theory' which understands the family unit which is extensive as the most sacred social feature. Therefore, expectations of gender roles, cis-heterosexual division of labour and gender equality vary according to two factors: (a) *social organization*, that is, whether the clan is matrilineal or patrilineal; and (b) *religion*, that is, whether the clan adheres to the traditional Yorùbá religion, Islam or different branches of Christianity: Roman Catholicism, Anglicanism or Protestantism.

The fact that a clan adheres to the traditional Nàgó-Yorùbá religion implies that its views on gender and sexuality will be very diverse and fluid. By Nàgó-Yorùbá we mean only the people living in the coastal areas of the present-day nations of Nigeria and Benin. Specifically, the term also designates the members of these people taken to the Caribbean or South America as slaves from the sixteenth century CE. onwards. It was especially in the nineteenth century CE. that the largest 'hunts' and 'sales' of Nàgó-Yorùbá people as slaves took place in the Americas and the Caribbean, especially Cuba and Brazil.

The Nàgó-Yorùbá religion is polytheistic, with the preeminence of a creator God called Olodumaré, also known as Olorun, the divine creator and source of all energy. This Supreme God is accompanied by intermediate gods called Òrìsà. Spirituality consists of belief in ritual practices such as singing, dancing and drumming while manifesting spiritual possession, ritual healing and respect for ancestors in divination. The Nàgó-Yorùbá religion is a ritual negotiation with the spirits. Each person is expected to eventually become one spirit with Olodumaré. Furthermore, the thoughts and actions of each person in Ayé [the physical realm] interact with all other living beings, including the Earth itself (Olabimtan, 1991).

On the other hand, in the Nàgó-Yorùbá religion, each believer has a special association with one of the deities, and it is not uncommon for males to often be possessed by female spirits and vice versa (Segato, 2008: 502). Possession and trance practices mediate exchanges of offerings between believers and sacred entities and are interrelated through detailed rituals presided over by priests and priestesses alike. Rita Laura Segato, who has written extensively on the Nàgó-Yorùbá religion, explains that even the deities could be transgender:

> *Logunede*, in Bahia, is said to be six months male and six months female, and Oya is said to have been male in the past and become female in the present, although she still exhibits a rather virile personality. A continuum is traced along the range of orisas/personalities, resulting in some *Santas* being said to be more virile than others and the same for females. With respect to some particular character trait, a female saint may be "more virile" or "more masculine" than a male saint (2008: 502).

This gender diversity within the religious symbolic world of the Nàgó-Yorùbá religion has clearly impacted the worldview of its followers. In this sense, for example, the marriage of heterosexual persons in the Nàgó-Yorùbá context includes respect for women who can choose whom to marry before asking for family permission. Once the prospective bride and groom agree that their relationship can progress to marriage, the groom's family arranges a meeting with the bride's family.

Both families must agree for the marriage to take place and, once done, the groom's family pays a dowry for this ceremony. Only after all these steps, the bride and groom can get married. Marriage is not only considered a union of husband and wife, it is also seen among the Nàgó-Yorùbá as the union of the families on both sides because the family unit is the most sacred aspect of society.

African Queer Deities

In Yoruba mythology Erinle is the spiritual deity of hunting, who enjoys fine clothes, often with animal plumage and he is extremely wealthy.

He is associated with queer people because of his ability to switch gender, in his male form he is the hunter but as female he is flexible and understood as the flowing of the life-giving rivers. He is known for having two relationships, one with a woman and one with a man. With his wife he has many children, but the story goes his wife left him for long periods of time to be a single father to their children. Single fathers view him as having magical patronage in their lives.

The Rain Queen, who is known as Madjadji, is a hereditary position of royal and spiritual authority among the Balobedu of South Africa. Although born a mortal she is believed to be divine in nature and have power to influence and control weather. She is understood to be non-heterosexual, while in other areas of the country she is understood to be lesbian and is surrounded by women who are recognised as her wives.

Traditional African Healing

African traditional healers have existed for many centuries in the south of the continent. Their function is to practise traditional African medicine. They fulfil different social and political roles in the community, including divination, healing physical, emotional and spiritual illnesses, conducting birth or death rituals, searching for lost livestock, protecting warriors, fighting witchcraft and teaching the history, cosmology and myths of their spiritual tradition. Although they do not fall within the Western religious scheme, this does not mean that they lack concepts about the divine or the different aspects of spirituality. Traditional healers remember their ancestors and serve the divine forces in their mission to bless humanity and its environment. In fact, their whole function is to channel the healing power of the ancestors whom they incarnate for rituals.

Ruth Morgan and Graeme Reid have conducted extensive research and analysis among the *sangomas*, Zulu traditional healers of Soweto, South Africa. Theirs is an ethnographic work that chronicles the religious experiences of these healers in intersection with their sexuality and activism. To people in the West, it is very surprising that *sangomas* can flourish in an ancestral religion when the political and social environment is so adversarial against same-sex-oriented individuals and communities. This is something Morgan and Reid point out when analysing the discourses of politicians in the region:

> These comments have two things in common: first, an appeal to traditional African values and customs and, second, a rejection of homosexuality as a "perversion" imported from the West. The context in which these comments occurred is revealing. In both cases, the statements were made in a political environment in which there were far more pressing social and economic concerns. The sentiments were intended to, and evidently did, generate popular support against the former colonial masters and perceived domination by Western powers (2003: 377).

Given this context, *sangomas* have chosen different paths to relate to the term 'lesbian' and its place in African traditional religion. Morgan and Reid report that:

> All of the sangomas interviewed used the term "lesbian" to identify themselves, although two also identified as bisexual. However, the exact meaning of the term "lesbian" in this context is elusive, and most sangomas shy away from formal lesbian and gay political activism and avoid social venues (2003: 383).

At the same time, their relationship to religion and activism carries a generational characteristic:

> Younger women had a more hybrid sexual identity as sangomas and lesbians. They first came out as lesbians before becoming sangomas, and they had to accommodate the primary male ancestors who play an important role in their lives as healers and in the construction of their sexual and gender identity (Morgan & Reid, 2003: 385).

However, they need to negotiate multiple aspects to make a place for themselves in the midst of South African society. Their role as spiritual leaders can facilitate this:

> The social position of *sangoma* allows them to mediate between the living and the dead, between the individual and the collective. [By affirming the agency of the ancestors, they establish a dialogue between the often conflicting pressures of individual desire and the social good. In a social context where there is enormous pressure to procreate, which is directly linked to the perpetuation of the ancestral line, an exclusive same-sex relationship is unlikely to gain social credibility (Morgana & Reid, 2003: 386).

This may not please the gay and lesbian movements in the West, but this is the way *sangomas* have found not only to survive in societies that are adverse against same-sex desire but also to flourish as religious leaders with a different sexual orientation than expected by society. In this sense, the agency and creativity in negotiating liberating spaces in which to live their lives give much credit to the work that *sangomas* have done in South African society.

It must be said that having legislation that is favourable to same-sex desire such as the South African constitution is no direct guarantee that social understanding and acceptance of same-sex desire will follow the legislation immediately. It takes longer for society to change its ideology than it does to change its laws. This is something we must take into account in recognising and valuing the distinctive situations faced by sex-gender diverse individuals and communities in different cultures.

Finally, we must recognise that the fact that Morgan & Reid (2003) have studied women who are *sangomas* does not exclude the fact that men can also be *sangomas*. At the same time, we must even acknowledge that not all *sangomas* are exclusively of African descent. Since colonialism has permeated all of Africa, many Caucasian people have been born in different countries and African cultures. White *sangomas* [*sangomas mlungu*] also exist and can also be people of gender diversity.

Morgan and Reid state: "The sangomas view their same-sex desire through the authoritative power of the male ancestors. Thus rather than claiming a marginal status, the very basis of marginality—same-sex desire—assumes social status and becomes the source of power" (2003: 388).

At the same time, we need to acknowledge that when African leaders speak about 'homosexuality' not being an 'African feature', they are right from a linguistic point of view. As the term 'homosexuality' is a creation in the Western world in the nineteenth century (Foucault, 1990). We recall the work of renowned scholar Deborah P. Amory who in her work "'Homosexuality' in Africa: Issues and Debates" (1997) briefly states the emergence of a subfield of studies: Gays and Lesbians in African Studies (GALS). Amory is an important scholar in the study of sexualities in Africa, and she has co-authored entries on homosexuality in Africa in several encyclopaedias (2005) as well as written numerous academic works. She makes two important points that need to be considered for our studies.

On the one hand, the fact that the terms 'homosexuality', 'gay', or 'lesbian' is recent and may not be suitable for the long cultural and traditional customs in the continent, as Amory affirms:

> (...) I occasionally bracket the term "homosexuality" in order to highlight the fact that same-sex erotics, practiced by many people in many different historical contexts, do not always necessarily lead to the emergence of homosexual identities. This bracketing of the term emphasizes the fact that homosexuality as a social identity is a fairly recent phenomenon, as Michel Foucault and others have demonstrated and theorized. Interesting debates revolve around the use of terms like "homosexuality," "lesbian," and "gay" in African contexts (2005: 5).

We believe that it is unavoidable nowadays to dismiss those terms as they are part of our language. Still, we do need to keep in mind that while we use them as tools to communicate ideas, that same process of communication may be conditioning our understanding of the topics. Language is a very unstable terrain.

On the other hand, the second aspect that Amory (1997) brings to our attention is the bias and agendas that Western scholars and researchers may have, as she states:

The institutionalized racism, sexism, and homophobia of professional organizations are also reflected in debates within lesbian and gay studies about research on and representations of same-sex sexualities. Cross-cultural lesbian and gay studies has been accused more than once of cultural imperialism. For example, anthropologists and others have been criticized for roaming the world in search of cross-cultural evidence of the universality of "homosexuality," in much the same way that Euro-American feminists have been criticized for collapsing all women into a single monolithic category of "woman," one that ultimately serves the interests of western feminism (1997: 8).

However, she does recognise that organizations drawing on human rights discourses are taking those same concepts to establish their grounds in the African context (Amory, 1997: 8). The question remains whether this is the right path or if this represents a new stage in Western colonialism in the continent. This is a recurrent topic that allows us to see the clash of Western and native conceptions of gender and sexuality, or as Morgan & Reid (2003) state "It is in the context of this interplay between the 'traditional' and 'modern' that we situate this study of same-sex sexuality" (2003: 381).

Given this context, sangomas have chosen different paths to relate to the term 'lesbian' and their place in an African Traditional Religion. However, they need to negotiate multiple aspects to carve a niche amidst South African society but their role as spiritual leaders may help this situation.

Randy P. Conner seeks to offer an overview of what we call 'Traditional African Religions' something that the practitioners of those religions may not perceive in the same way. Conner writes:

> Given the variety of indigenous traditions present on the continent of Africa, it is impossible to make general statements about beliefs and practices of African "religions" without doing an injustice to some or even most. Moreover, practitioners of these "religions" frequently do not look upon their faiths as such because they perceive religion as completely interwoven with the entirety of their life experiences rather than as a demarcated arena of life experience (2003: 3).

This quotation is important because it acknowledges the way that spiritualities are perceived by those involved in their practice and by the outsiders seeking to analyse those spiritualities. One key aspect is the interlacing of faith and daily life. Although people have some systematisation of their beliefs, this does not mean that they follow through with the rationalist model of the West. This 'brainy' way of relating to religion may be so foreign to partitioners of spiritualities around the world that it may turn out to be even incomprehensive. Add sexuality to the mix, and the result is completely different from Western expectations. And rightly so, these spiritualities in Africa have been practised long before the established religions in the West set the tone of what is and is not 'religious'.

Beyond the wonderful overview that Conner lays out in his chapter, the underlying question is about the perception of something that in the West we call 'gender' and 'sexuality'. Conner states:

> In some African spiritual traditions, gender is not a marker of identity, so the terms "masculine" and "feminine" are viewed as meaningless. In others, "masculinity" and "femininity" possess traditional designations resonating rather remarkably with the yin-yang symbolism of Chinese Daoist cosmology (2003: 7).

This is important because it also raises the topic that many authors label as 'African sexuality' (Ahlberg, 1994; Caldwell et al., 1989). These authors do not always agree on this topic, for example, Caldwell et al. (1989) propose denying Christianity's role in (re)shaping the continent's perceptions of gender and sexuality. In fact, despite the fact that colonialism has consequences at the social and religious level, for Caldwell et al. (1989: 188) this 'African system' is still 'largely intact'. They summarise at length this system as follows:

> The following are the typical characteristics of the African system: great emphasis on the importance of ancestry and descent, usually accompanied by a belief in ancestral spirit intervention in the affairs of the living; a related social system that, in its most complex form, the lineage, places greater importance of intergenerational links on conjugal ones and that gives great respect and power to the old; an inheritance system whereby property, which is usually communal, remains within the lineage or clan and normally passes between members of the same sex; agriculture characterized by shifting cultivation based on the use of the hoe, typically by women. In keeping with the aim of lineage perpetuation, emphasis is places on fertility: by society, the ancestral spirits, and even the high gods who are otherwise of little day-to-day importance. Virtue is related more to success in reproduction than to limiting profligacy; and in many societies the initiation ceremonies allowing sexual activity to commence are ritually more important than the celebration of marriage. The marriage bond is typical weak, with spouses retaining strong lineage links, and with a marked spousal separation of economic activities and responsibilities; the marriage payment takes the form of bride wealth paid to the wife's family from the husband's rather than to the couple themselves and never includes land; polygyny exists on a scale not found in the Eurasian system, and consequently the basic family unit is a mother and her children; husbands are usually much older than wives; divorce is fairly common among most ethnic groups; and women, at least in the past, abstained from sexual relations after giving birth for a period that might extend to years (Caldwell et al., 1989: 188).

To some, this long description really matches, more or less, other regions of the world where heteropatriarchalism has also forged these types of family/clan/caste systems. Note that in the description of Caldwell et al. there is no single reference to the lives and activities of same-sex attracted individuals. In a postcolonial tone, Conner affirms:

> Although Christianity has been practiced in Africa since the era of Roman occupation and Islam has been a significant presence since the ninth century C.E., African indigenous religions were not threatened with extinction until the eighteenth and nineteenth centuries, which saw massive and tremendously violent efforts to convert Africans to these faiths (2003: 28).

Beth Maina Ahlberg (1994) has an interesting analysis from her studies about the Kikuyu in Kenya. Her findings not only affirm a particular understanding of sexuality in Africa but also the influence that colonialism, both political and religious, have played in every African society. The result of this situation is that people in Africa debate between two moral systems, that inherited by their ancestors, on the one hand, and that imposed by the external colonial and religious powers, on the other hand. Caught in between, individuals and communities struggle to make sense of their gender and sexuality. One tangible consequence is the HIV/AIDS pandemic that has decimated the population of the continent.

The question about a 'distinct African sexuality' has material consequences in the daily lives of millions of individuals. This is why, beyond this discussion, authors seek to make visible the consequences of colonialism as well as the ingrained cis-heteropatriarchalism present in the continent, especially when this translated into persecution of those who do not comply with the hegemonic notions of gender and sexuality(Oloruntoba-Oju, Taiwo, 2011). Amory also states:

> Our analyses need to be informed by an awareness of the multiple causes of political persecution and oppression: gender, race, ethnicity, class, religion, as well as sexuality. We need to work to form alliances with other scholars and groups who share these goals (1997: 9).

By acknowledging this, we can better understand the fluidity as well as the rich diversity of understandings of gender and sexuality in the manifold African Traditional Religions.

For Further Discussion

1   Drawing on the concept of agency, this technology empowers *sangomas* to navigate South African society without compromising their same-sex desires. In light of the materials covered in this chapter, can you identify and elaborate on other instances of agency technologies found in the analysis of different cases? Please provide examples for clarity.

2   Having examined similar colonial scenarios in previous weeks across various regions, what steps do you believe major religions can take to facilitate decolonization and address the historical harm inflicted upon other religious traditions?

3   How do African Traditional Religions traditionally view and incorporate diverse sexual orientations, and are there instances within these belief systems that challenge or affirm contemporary understandings of homosexuality?

4   In the context of African Traditional Religions, how have modern interpretations and adaptations influenced attitudes towards LGBTIQ+ individuals, and are there examples of acceptance or resistance within these communities?

5   Exploring the intersectionality of sexuality and spirituality within African Traditional Religions, can you identify rituals, practices or narratives that either embrace or stigmatise individuals based on their sexual orientation?

6   Considering the impact of colonial history on African Traditional Religions, how have these belief systems evolved in their perspectives on homosexuality, and are there ongoing efforts within these communities to reclaim pre-colonial attitudes and practices?

References

Ahlberg, Beth M (1994). "Is There a Distinct African Sexuality? A Critical Response to Caldwell." *Africa: Journal of the International African Institute* 64, No. 2: pp. 220–242.

Amory, Deborah P (1997). "'Homosexuality' in Africa: Issues and Debates." *Issue: A Journal of Opinion* 25, No. 1: pp. 5–10.

Amory, Deborah P and Mark Gevisser (2005). "Homosexuality in Africa." In: *Africana: The Encyclopedia of the African and African American Experience, Volume 2*, edited by Anthony Appiah and Henry Louis Gates. Oxford: Oxford University Press, pp. 227–231.

Caldwell, John C, Pat Caldwell and Pat Quiggin (1989). "The Social Context of AIDS in Sub-Saharan Africa." *Population and Development Review* 15, No. 2: pp. 185–233.

Conner, Randy P (2003). "Sexuality and Gender in African Spiritual Traditions." In: *Sexuality and the World's Religions*, edited by David W Machacek and Melissa M Wilcox. Santa Barbara, CA: ABC-CLIO, pp. 3–30.

Foucault, Michael (1990). *The History of Sexuality, Vol. 1: An Introduction*. London: Allen Lane.

Morgan, Ruth and Graeme Reid (2003). "'I've Got Two Men and One Woman': Ancestors, Sexuality and Identity among Same-Sex Identified Women Traditional Healers in South Africa." *Culture, Health & Sexuality* 5, No. 5 (September–October): pp. 375–391.

Nadel, Siegfried F (1947). *The Nuba: An Anthropological Study of the Hill Tribes in Kordofan.* London: University of Oxford Press.

Ọlabimtan, Afọlabi (1991). *Yoruba Religion and Medicine in Ibadan*, translated by George E. Simpson. Ibadan: Ibadan University Press.

Oloruntoba-Oju, Taiwo (2011). "A Name My Mother Did Not Call Me: Queer Contestations in African Sexualities." Paper presented at the 4th European Conference on African Studies (ECAS). The Nordic Africa Institute (Nordiska Afrikainstitutet),Uppsala, Sweden, June 15–18, 2011. Available at: <http://www.nai.uu.se/ecas-4/panels/141-156/panel-151/Taiwo-O-Oju-edited-version.pdf>.

Segato, Rita L (2008). "Gender Politics, and Hybridism in the Transnationalization of Yorùbá Culture." In: *Òrìṣà Devotion as World Religion: The Globalization of Yorùbá Religious Culture*, edited by Jacob Kẹhinde Olupona and Terry Rey. Madison, WI: University of Wisconsin Press, pp. 485–512.

Further Reading

Kaoma, Kapya J (2009). *Globalizing the Culture Wars: U.S. Conservatives, African Churches, & Homophobia*. Somerville, MA: Political Research Associates.

Kaoma, Kapya J (2012). *Colonizing African Values: How the U.S. Christian Right Is Transforming Sexual Politics in Africa*. Somerville, MA: Political Research Associates.

Manigault-Bryant, Le Rhonda S (2015). "African and African Diaspora Traditions: Religious Syncretism, Erotic Encounter, and Sacred Transformation." In: *Religion: Embodied Religion*, edited by Kent L Brintnall. Farmington Hills, MI: Macmillan Reference USA, pp. 183–201.

O'Hear, Ann (2004). "The Enslavement of Yoruba." In: *The Yoruba Diaspora in the Atlantic World*, edited by Toyin Falola and Matt D Childs. Bloomington, IN: Indiana University Press, pp. 56–73.

Part IV

Pathways of Transformation: Queerness Across Earth and Cosmos

A Brief Note About This Section

This section delves into the transformative dimensions of queerness, examining how it traverses and reshapes physical, cultural and cosmic landscapes. It explores the ways queer identities and theologies are profoundly impacted by movement, both literal, such as migratory processes, and metaphorical, such as spiritual or ideological journeys. By focusing on the intersections of displacement, belonging and transcendence, it highlights how queerness operates as a fluid and transformative force across borders, whether geographical, social or metaphysical.

Migration, in its many forms, is central to this exploration. It reflects the movement of queer bodies and identities across spaces that are often hostile or unwelcoming, yet also full of potential for the creation of new communities and forms of kinship. These journeys are both challenges and opportunities for transformation, as queer individuals navigate systems of exclusion while simultaneously carving out spaces of belonging and resistance. In this way, migration becomes a metaphor for the broader queer experience—a constant negotiation of boundaries and possibilities.

At the same time, the section extends beyond the earthly realm to consider the cosmic dimensions of queerness. It invites readers to imagine queerness not just as a social or cultural construct but as a cosmic principle that redefines our understanding of relationality and existence on a universal scale. The cosmic framework provides a space to question traditional binaries and hierarchies, envisioning queerness as a force that disrupts fixed notions of identity and belonging. By doing so, it opens up infinite possibilities for being and becoming, where queerness is not bound by earthly constraints but is instead expansive and transformative on a cosmic level.

Through this lens, queerness emerges as a powerful and dynamic force that reimagines our relationship with space, identity and community. It challenges static understandings of existence and offers new ways of thinking about interconnectedness, resilience and creativity. These pathways of transformation compel us to reflect on the profound ways queerness reshapes our understanding of belonging, not only on Earth but also within the broader cosmos. Ultimately, this section invites readers to see queerness as a vital, expansive and evolving aspect of life that transcends borders, systems and even the limits of imagination.

Global Queer Theologies: Intercontextual and Interreligious Perspectives, First Edition. Lisa Isherwood and Hugo Córdova Quero.
© 2026 John Wiley & Sons Ltd. Published 2026 by John Wiley & Sons Ltd.

Glossary for Part IV

Apophasis	Apophatic theology is also called negative theology as it only says what may not be said about the divine.
BDSM	Bondage, discipline, sadism and masochism—but consensually.
Closet devotions	Reading of Christian worship with a queer eye.
Cosmology	A branch of physics and metaphysics dealing with the nature of the universe with which theology is engaging positively.
Creation ex nihilio	Creation out of nothing.
Diaspora	Communities living away from their place of origin.
Eco-centric	Focussing on the earth as starting point for theology.
Ignatian spirituality	A spirituality of action finding God in all things. St Ignatius Loyola developed this form of spirituality.
Incarnation	The notion that the divine takes flesh.
Margery Kempe	Lived 1373–1438 and was a Christian mystic who had sex with God.
Migration	The movement of people across continents
Omnigender	A theory proposed that suggest Jesus was intersexed due to the nature of virgin birth.
Polyamorous relationships	A form of ethical non-monogamy involving the consent of all.
Queer eye	Looking beyond the heteronormative gaze.
Radical incarnation	The expansion of human and non-human life due to this human/divine embrace.
Rainbow theology	A theology of diversity via multiplicity.
Tohu vabohu	The depth cloaked in darkness referred to in Genesis.
Trans God	One who transgresses all the boundaries we place on God.
Trickster figures	Enactments that subvert accepted norms such as gender.

14

Queer Theologies in Europe, UK and US Contexts

This chapter will present the context, history and critical figures of queer theologies in the UK, Europe and the US regions. To say that someone does queer theology in our times explicitly implies acknowledging that there are multiple ways in which sexuality is expressed beyond the cis-heteropatriarchal 'hetero/homo' dichotomy so rigid in the Anglo-Saxon context. We must recognise that the concerns of both queer movements and queer theologies transcend, the struggle for recognition of same-sex marriage, so prominent in the Global North, to address other issues that are also crucial. Therefore, we will trace the work of different LGBTIQ+ theologians and body/sexual theologians as forerunners of current queer theologies in the Global North.

United Kingdom

Lisa Isherwood and Marcella Althaus Reid were perhaps the first in the United Kingdom to put together a theological text on transgender theology. *Trans/Formations* (SCM, 2009) brought together the voices of trans folk in order that they could speak for themselves. Their backgrounds and theological contexts were diverse, and their voices spoke clearly and loudly about their lived experience. As Isherwood says on the back cover of this groundbreaking book 'It is a book that wishes to shake not shock, it seeks to shake us out of the contented narrowness of a cosy Christianity and into one that seeks always to expand the incarnational tent that is our home' (2009). Edited at a time when trans issues were coming to the fore in society we were mystified that churches were slow to recognise the lives and contributions of trans folk. We believed that an incarnational religion had to take the enfleshed stories of people as part of a redemption history and no better place than in enfleshed trans/liminal spaces.

BK Hipsher (2009: 92–104) calls her chapter in the above book, God is a many gendered thing and argues that we need a trans God precisely because it is so unsettling to people. A trans God transgresses all the ideas we have about God and allows us to move into unknown, or at least unexplored areas of both divinity and humanity. Hipsher does say that even a trans God may not be big enough given the vastness of the cosmos, but it is a start. Is this an outrageous idea within a religion that starts from the notion that God took human flesh, which is surely a trans identity writ large? In the introduction to this work the editors point out that in their view such a destabilising event for both human flesh and the divine nature should not lead to stable categories in gender and sexuality, the very fundamentals of human life. The introduction outlines ways in which the Christian tradition is about unstable categories of transformation. The author of John's Gospel shows how God pitched a tent amongst us not a solid unchanging structure but rather one that could move with the winds of change and from this flexible foundation the man Jesus ascends to hell, rising again and is present on the altars of the world in the form of bread and wine. These various manifestations through a range of material substances all proclaim the nature of God. Despite this very transforming essence of Christianity many still believe that stable categories are the heart of Christianity and further that trans identities are a new phenomenon. A brief glance at Christian history shows how untrue this is, it is littered with cross dressing women the reasons for which have been much debated by scholars, but perhaps they were in some way embodying the Galatian declaration that in Christ there is neither male nor female. Certainly, this gave them more space in which to function, but we argued also gave them a fuller understanding of the flesh in which God was manifest, theirs and they could embrace their bodies beyond strict gender codes of the day.

Isherwood and Althaus Reid also edited a book entitled, *The Sexual Theologian: Essays on Sex, God and Politics* (T&T Clark, 2004). In this work they lay out how queer theory works with theology in order to produce a new approach called queer theology. This approach is more than simply a reflection on God and the world; it is a praxis that aims to create radical ways of transformation in our present world. Traditional theology is organised around a givenness, held in place by a monotheistic belief system, and the exercise of the authority of the metanarratives of heteronormativity. Queer theology allows for the irruption of new knowledge from the margins of this heterosexual discourse. Different ways of loving produce different ways of befriending, compassion and creating relationships all of which give space for different ways of imagining God.

The essays collected in this book demonstrate how queer theory impacts theology and show how all areas of theology can be transformed by this approach. Theology has become self-referential and afraid to look outside itself in case it should become irrelevant. The authors in this book show that it is still relevant if only it has the courage to embrace all lives and loves. In this book Marie Cartier (2004: 16–25) is bold in proclaiming that if history is not looked at with a queer eye then it is not historically accurate, while Hugo Cordova Quero (2004: 26–46) argues that queer readings allow different questions to be asked of the past allowing us to plot different courses for the future, a lesson churches desperately need to learn. Isherwood shows how Margery Kempe actually queers the divine through her physically intimate relations with God the Father and the son, she does not leave Mary out of that physical intimacy either. Graham Ward reminds readers that knowledge is never stable as it changes over place and time or at least should do. Marcella Althaus Reid lifts the skirts of God in order to be truly intimate and transform the divine and the human in that encounter, an encounter beyond heteronormativity. Ken Stone demonstrates how biblical texts may be queered and in so doing how inclusion is the outcome. He argues that demands for inclusion usually simply strengthen the boundaries between in and out; he suggests turning the boundaries inside out through presence on the margins, a long-term strategy as margins can often change.

Lisa Isherwood underpins all her theology from the notion of radical incarnation by which she means an incarnation that is erotic, sensuous and powerful, one that urges us forward to relationality and flourishing, to life in abundance. It is the glorious abandonment of the divine into flesh and the passionate dance of the human/divine that ensues. Incarnation tells us that our bodies are our homes, that is to say our divine/human dwelling places; therefore, our Christological journey is home, to the fullness of our incarnation, to the co-creative reality of our fleshy heaven. The Christology that this assumes is not one of denial and narrow boundaries; it is one of embrace and expansion that takes as read that politics is not an added extra to an internal relationship with an ethereal Christ but rather radical, countercultural politics is the skin we put on, the Christ we incarnate.

Incarnation is about the flesh and blood reality of people's lives, so it follows that all manner of embodiment and embodied experience is a further unfolding of the divine/human reality that we live. It declares that God takes human experience seriously and demands that we take our divine natures just as seriously. Heyward says:

> We are left alone untouched until, we choose to take ourselves, our humanity, more seriously than we have taken our God. (Heyward, 1982)

This is a queer move in a religion that has always insisted on fallen human flesh and distance between the divine and the created world. It is a move that has enabled Isherwood as a body theologian to have a radically different starting point when asking questions of lived experience. Isherwood's work on the English woman Margery Kempe (1373–1438) who, when her book was discovered, was declared queer even in a queer age, demonstrates that queer moves in religious enfleshed experience are not uncommon. Margery marries the godhead and in this way inserts herself into it, like all healthy marriages there is a healthy sex life. Margery has sex with Jesus who she refers to as her son and with God who she says was a good lover and is understood as female, as is the spirit. Margery also understands herself to be father, son and spirit and in this way her understanding of herself as a true subject is expanded. She becomes a nomadic subject, this divine human subjectivity has no edges, it is boundaryless which has new meaning, yet as we see nothing is fixed as it is in traditional understanding of the godhead. Reflecting on her life Isherwood speculates that while we continue to allow the enactment of fixed binary opposites, stable and unequal categories on our bodies through sexual stereotyping or sexual intimacy we fail to open to the diverse/surprising wonder of radical incarnation.

Turning her attention to Christian worship and particularly the Eucharist Isherwood (2023: 55–68) asks how it may be more inclusive starting from a radical incarnation starting point. She states that Christian theologians will have to think again about their naïve division of the deeply human, deeply divine elements of humanity, and how to represent this in the central Christian sacrament, the Eucharist. Elizabeth Stuart argues that this central sacrament of the Christian church stands as an embodied practice suggesting erasure of gender and sex. It takes both to a symbolic level and displaces them (2009: 127–138). The symbolic world, which for Stuart is metaphysical, is the world in which Lacan says that women, and even queers, have no place, since the symbolic is wholly and purely male and is conveyed through language and culture which necessarily excludes all but heterosexual males. This highlights a dilemma, in that symbolic world there can be no subjectivity until women find a place in this constructed male culture, since this belonging gives psychic leverage to our personhood. This dilemma is equally true for queers, perhaps historically even more so in both a church and a world that has not offered a sense of their belonging as whole persons. Bodies can be radically subverting of culture when they find their voice beyond the fixed language and meaning of the master's discourses. However, we do need those bodies and cannot have them erased in a symbolic realm which many queer people would say has been their experience within churches. We have to find new ways of being by thinking through the body. The connection of body and being is crucial for those who have suffered under the dualistic metaphysics of church doctrine.

A Roman Catholic theologian Gerard Loughlin sees things very differently from Stuart and states,

The body of the Church which is most clearly visible in the Eucharist is startling. It is composed of many diverse bodies and is yet also one body which is both human and divine, being the body of Christ. At the same time it is a maternal body with enough substance for everyone; while also a nuptial body where each is brought together through desire of the other, attracted by the beauty and allure of Christ's body. As bride and mother the Church is properly sexed as female but as composed of many bodies she is also multi-sexed, as male and female, gay and straight and as all other variations and dispositions. Thus part of what it is for the Church to speak her sex is to say, for example, that she is a woman or that she is a lesbian (2009: 86–98).

There is no call here for erasure but rather for an embrace of the multi-sexed possibilities based on the words and ways the church has and does understand itself. The celebration of the Eucharist then becomes a celebration of this extraordinary body of Christ. It becomes possible to argue that the presiders should also display this remarkable kaleidoscope of being in and through their physical representation and through the objects on the altar, which could reflect the queer lives of those gathered to worship. There is also a change in emphasis from ingesting Christ for remission of sin and a path to heaven to party time, allowing Eucharist to become a vibrant celebration of the diversity of life within all creation.

University of Exeter–based Susannah Cornwall (2009) outlines how medical and social essentialist models are driven by a desire to make people 'normal'.

She also suggests queer theory itself does not always allow for diversity beyond already stabilised categories. As Marcella Althaus Reid pointed out, the formation of gay and lesbian identities has often been created against what heterosexual identity is meant to be and so embody the opposite against which it is defined and judged. In this way queer identities remain linked to heterosexuality. Cornwall feels that this is even true for trans identities as it is difficult to think outside all that has been in place for centuries in relation to gender. Cornwall argues that sexual identity is not the only way to differentiate from heteronormativity. She engages in a reflection on apopahtic theology and says that as God is never fully known then becoming like God involves giving up what we think we have known about ourselves as human. For Cornwall this is a positive step rather than a tragic abandonment of a search for self. She writes:

> that apophatically-influenced theologies, those which resist a finality of understanding and are grounded instead in a proactive unknowing about God might, in fact, be important sites of solidarity for transgender. In this way, transgender need not be unproblematically aligned with either heteronormative or homonormative modes of discourse, but might stand in tension with both, inherently neither fully like or fully unlike either (2009: 16).

This gives way to a broader and more creative picture of God as the narrowness of human metaphors is set aside. It sets before us a God who is ever changing and of course challenges us to not hold on to set ideas of gender even within ourselves; these too Cornwall tells us are only penultimate. She says that in clinging to a particular human gender believing it is important in relation to the image of God is in her view idolatrous. In clinging to what we already know we shut off what it is possible to know. It can be said that in this way queer theologies hold within them tensions between the fulfilled and the partial, the completed and the ever incomplete (2009: 34). Cornwall concludes her argument but saying that homonormativity can never be the answer to heteronormativity since apophasis means never arriving at the limits of perfection or understanding. So no gender or identity can be said to be the final word on being human made in the image of a not-yet-knowable God (2009: 35).

As we will see in Chapter 16 a queer understanding of incarnation lends itself to embracing the new cosmologies in theology. It is there that we find that chaos, and ever-changing and expanding life is the norm for all of creation of which we are part and it is therefore argued also for the divine itself.

United States

Virginia Mollenkott (2001) who writes from a background in Christianity although not a theologian argues that Matthew 1:23–25 is read literally by many Christians and so the Virgin Birth of Jesus was a parthenogenetic birth. In that case, 'he' was chromosomally female, yet according to Gospel accounts he was phenotypically male.

She suggest that anyone who takes the Virgin Birth literally must acknowledge that Jesus was intersexual and thus a perfect incarnation of the entire sex/gender continuum. Accordingly, an early baptismal formula, Galatians 3:28, testifies that in Christ 'there is no longer male and female' and the Christian Scriptures contain many transsexual images, for example, women are called brothers, men are called the brides of Christ while Jesus and Paul are depicted as mothers (John 16:21, 17:1: Galatians 4:19). Further she argues Jesus is depicted as Holy Sophia (Wisdom) and the church is described as a female body with a male head (Ephesians 5:23–33) which, she notes is a rather worrying aspect as the female body of Christ is urged to grow up and become the male head (Ephesians 4:15). Mollenkott's point being that we do not have to read texts strangely in order to see that they carry some interesting twists on gender and the nature of the human. On the biblical theme Lewis Reay (2009: 148–168) points out that the earth creature Adam was not male or female but full of the potentiality of possible in God and this included gender potential. Trans and intersexed people then mirror the very complexities of this original earth creature in their own imaging of the divine. Further they can present a challenge to all to move away from the binary oppositions of gender that had no part in the original blessing of God's creation. Transgender theology is inclusive as it inhabits the liminal space which is God's territory and the realm in which co-creation and co-redemption are worked through.

Another North American theologian Richard Rambuss has undertaken some interesting research in the area of erotic desire and the sacred within Christian history and what he has uncovered is the way in which the sacred erotic transgresses the boundaries of vanilla heterosexuality (Rambuss, 1998). Rambuss quotes Michael Warner who says 'religion makes available a language of ecstasy, a horizon of significance within which transgressions against the normal order of the world and the boundaries of self can be seen as good things' (Rambuss, 1998: 4). Rambuss shows how throughout Christian history the iconised body of Christ is very changeable and does not hold fast to or fix sex, gender or sexuality either in itself or in those who adore it. For example, Catherine of Sienna marries Christ who crosses genders for Catherine who eventually becomes engaged passionately with, sinking into the flesh of, a female Christ. Catherine is but one example of many littered throughout Christian history who engaged with the body of Christ only to experience a crossing of gender either for Christ or for themselves.

In the sonnets of John Donne he implores God to ravish him, to batter his heart, to take him, break him, imprison him. These may appear to be rape fantasies, but one must also not forget they are homosexual rape fantasies. Rambuss wonders whether in the work of

Donne we see that redemption is sodomised or that sodomy has a place in redemption. Either way this religious and pious outpouring moves us beyond the edges of conventional morality. This theme of divine rape is carried on in the work of the metaphysical poet and Anglican clergyman Thomas Traherne (1637–1674) who in a poem entitled 'Love' imagines himself drenched in and impregnated by Christ's 'sweet stream'. He goes on to say that he offers himself to Christ as 'His Ganymede! His Life! His joy!' whereupon Christ comes down to get him and takes him up that he may be 'his boy' (2002). Rambuss insists that closet devotion is to be found throughout Christian history and is a way by which the soul becomes a subject; it allows a space in which the sacred may touch the transgressive and even the profane. It seems then that Christianity has queer moves at its very heart

Mark D. Jordan (2007), a North-American theologian, addresses a very important topic in Christianity from a queer perspective which is the issue of corporality and sexuality in the body of Jesus. For centuries Christianity has invested energy in affirming the Incarnation while denying the gender and sexuality of Jesus. The topic is very important because queer folks have been denied the means of salvation by using Jesus as a celibate heterosexual moralising tool. Jordan states that the genitals of Jesus are typically and normatively excluded from speech. To talk about them is indecent or provocative or blasphemous. To meditate on them would be obscene. We are urged to meditate on Jesus' acts and sufferings 'but if our meditation should drift downward towards his pelvis, we are immediately rebuked and then condemned as perverted or pornographic' (2007: 283).

Jordan is correct in what he says but what a long way we have come from the closet devotions mentioned by Rambuss; it does seem that earlier generations of Christians were not as prudish as we appear to be today. We could laugh at this except that the prudish attitude around the body of Jesus has profound implications for the bodies of believers who do not fit that tight pattern of embodiment that theology has imposed on Jesus. The fact of the Incarnation of Christ is difficult to assume if we tie the whole process of salvation to Jesus' heterosexual, celibate, maleness. The categories of gender, sexuality, power and order are intrinsically related to the Incarnation, and conditioned by culture, political environment, economic relations, historical events and social processes. Feminist theologians addressed the issue of gender and some took on the issue of sexuality also and now queer theologians have begun to take into account Jesus' sexuality. If Jesus was indeed human then these are two aspects fundamental to humanity and can no longer be overlooked in a world that acknowledges a wide range of gender performance and sexual activity.

Bob Shore-Goss (2018) introduces us to the emerging debates around Christian theology and Bondage, Domination, Sado Masochism (BDSM) reminding us that Christian religious practice had many objects with which to mortify the body. Shore-Goss, who holds a positive view of incarnational theology and thus of the human body, spent time trying to remove himself from the negative images that accompanied a more traditional view of theology and the body.

The breakthrough for him came when he met the leather community in Los Angeles, CA, and found that many of the Christian ascetic practices he had been encouraged to adopt during a period of Jesuit priestly training were quite similar in the leather community. Further, he noted that they were both understood as spiritual practices and in the case of the leather community led to ethical community actions. Both Christian asceticism and BDSM use pain to transcend the self and create a new understanding of the self. Some 'bottoms' told him they align themselves with Christ's voluntary suffering, while some masters have set up their leather families along the lines of religious orders. Shore-Goss suggests that BDSM lies very close to Christian asceticism and that for some people it fulfils the role of religious groups. Shore-Goss notes that those who practise BDSM report that they achieve ecstasy through pain when the self is stripped of all external trappings. Shore-Goss believes he sees connection between leathermen and Ignatian spirituality expressed by a leather master who says that the goal is to experience ecstasy, grasp the meaning of a higher state and become more like the higher state experienced in ecstasy (2018: 228).

Shore-Goss refers to what he calls sacred pain and reflects on conversations he had with tops who told him they have to be attentive to the physical pain the bottom is in and can endure. They spoke of being mindful of the emotions and mental state of bottoms which Shore-Goss understood as a kind of meditative attentiveness to the sacred pain and flesh of the bottom. Shore-Goss addresses what might be feminist and womanist concerns with master slave scenarios saying that he agreed with Judith Butler that queer gender performances are repetition with a critical difference; hence, it is often true as the leather community asserts that the bottom is in charge. Shore-Goss, in his ministry to leather communities, also notes that there is a great deal of parody and ritual. Shore-Goss was taken aback when he was presented with a clergy leather slave collar with an eye hook as he realised that to his parishioners as a Christian clergyman he projected an archetypical submissive (2018: 233).

Shore-Goss notes that BDSM does disrupt the status quo and subvert social privilege and power at the same time reimagining possible relationships. Pointing out that practitioners often refer to what they do as play he speaks of the exchange of power that can be within the play and notes that practitioners find this liberating and even healing if they have been in abusive relationships where power just goes one way. However, Shore-Goss wishes to offer a means of judging and evaluating these encounters based in the Ignatian spirituality with which he is familiar. He asked questions he would ask of those following a prayer life, how do they treat others, how do they serve their community, is there always consent and what guidelines are there for safety. He found that with the community he knew best all aspects were not simply thought of, but the community treated each other tenderly and with care and were involved in community activities. Shore-Goss mentions the fetish theology of Marcella Althaus-Reid with God as master and Jesus as submissive and concludes that a Christology from the bottom is dangerous as it opens a theology of loving power and humble reverence and becomes a powerful symbol of the preferential option for the poor (2018: 242).

Hugo Córdova Quero is Argentinian and works at Starr King in the United States and so deserves a mention here especially as the work he and Joseph Goh did on queering the Trinity is an important addition to the queer canon. They frame their argument in terms of friendship and polyamory (2018). Acknowledging the work of feminist theologians in the area of friendship they take the argument further by broadening friendship qualities and understanding it as a radical relational dialogue between those involved in numerous forms of relationality (2018: 304). They note that Trinitarian theology begins with the number three thus disrupting the binaries so often in place. They also wish to assert that all friendship is sexual as it involves human bodies, but they resist narrow definitions of sexuality rather viewing it as relationality on diverse levels. They take this step because they understand that God created humankind in the divine image and wishes to be known through human lives in all their diversity. The divine Trinity they claim can only function because of deep love and a sense of justice which does not wish to make each separate part take on the attributes of the other. They argue that it is with this understanding that human relations such as polyamory should be built. They do not see the Trinity as a once and for all situation but rather argue that it is constantly growing as each part invites the other into more intimacy and unity.

Those who criticise polyamorous relationships usually do so from the point of view of questioning the commitment and the ethics of such relationships. However, research shows that polyamorous friends work on inclusiveness, community and freedom. Cordova

Quero and Goh state that this way of relating enfleshed resistance not only to compulsory heterosexual coupling but to neocolonial and globalising discourses (2018: 305). The authors argue that this image of relationality based in Trinitarian thinking destroys exclusivist images of both God and humanity. The three persons of God underpin the intra-relationality of people and point to the need for these relationships to be committed and long lasting just as the internal dynamics of the Trinity suggests. This is not to argue for sameness but rather for distinction and difference held in honesty and equality (2018: 307). 'Such queer arrangements of relationality become avenues for incarnating the divine in actual queer lives' (2018: 309). This approach makes queer lives visible and at the same time makes a rather abstract doctrine comprehensible and dynamic. The relevance and importance of queer theology is exactly that, it is connecting theory to real lives and in so doing expanding the understanding of both.

The Rev. Dr Patrick S. Cheng is one of the most prominent Asian North-American religious scholars who is at the forefront of the development of Queer Asian-North-American Theologies as well as Queer Asian Theologies. In the case of Asian North-American communities, queer theologians have assumed the task of challenging not only the more Anglo-oriented queer theologies but also the cis-heteronormative tones of Asian North-American theologies, since Asian-American queer people are doubly oppressed both by the American racial formation with its feature of white supremacy and by the gender-role expectations and the sexual division of labour among Asian communities. When talking about Asian-American communities we are placing under one term very diverse and sometimes very distinctive communities with particular cultures and linguistic legacies.

Cheng's book *Rainbow Theology* (2013) represents a solid contribution towards understanding the different ethnic queer theologies in the United States as well as to developing a theology that counters a monochromatic theology, that is, oriented to one particular understanding of queerness, vis-à-vis a rainbow theology characterised by diversity through the themes of multiplicity, middle spaces and mediation.

Therefore, Cheng envisions a 'rainbow theology' in order to show how diversity intersects faith, sexuality and ethnicity in the lives of Asian American queer believers. Queer Asian American theologies seek to represent the experience of queer people who wish to embrace their faith, sexuality and ethnicity in a harmonious and meaningful way. Cheng notes how this multiplicity is also at the heart of God who is represented as Trinity (2013: 107). This book demonstrates how race and sex are intimately linked and adversely affected by white hetero supremacy. Despite the weight of society Cheng declares the rainbow theology of multiplicity to be a gift from God.

In his book *From Sin to Amazing Grace. Discovering the Queer Christ* (2012) Cheng writes of the grace of coming out. He agrees with white writers who have viewed coming out as aiding spiritual growth of the LGBTIQ+ person or as representing the constant coming out of God/Christ. However, he argues that for Asian LGBTIQ+ folk coming out has an added dimension, referring to the experience of a bisexual woman who came out to her mother, he says that it helped her mother understand the connection between homophobia and race as oppressions that support each other (2012: 88).

Filipino-American theologian Michael Sepidoza Campos makes an interesting contribution in his piece 'The Baklá: Gendered Religious Performance in Filipino Cultural Spaces' (2012) which takes a contextual performance of queer: the Baklá, or the effeminate gay men in the Philippines, as a Christic trickster figure who simultaneously (re)defines and challenges not only heteronormative spiritual assumptions but also the very construction of gender and gender-role expectations.

Kwok Pui-Lan, born in Hong Kong but working in the United States, exposes the consequences of Christianity over cultures and religions through the colonialism it brought with it. Kwok (2007) clearly summarises:

> When Christian missionaries arrived in Asia they were surprised to find in some cultures a wide range of expression of sexual intimacy and relationships. Because of their cultural imperialistic attitudes, missionaries regarded some of the sexual practices of the natives as symptomatic of the inferior status of 'heathen' cultures and propagated monogamous heterosexual marriage as the norm. Such attitudes were reinforced by British colonial rule, which treated male homosexuality as a criminal offense, forcing gay men to hide further in the closets. At the same time, colonial fantasy portrayed Asian men as soft and effeminate, and less masculine when compared to the colonizers. The consolidation of white heterosexual masculinity as normative reflects the deployment of gender and homophobia in the construction of empire and racist projections in the narratives of colonialism (2007: 59).

Colonialism has left consequences in all the Global South, some of them at the point of no return in relation to recovering aspects of the distant past in relation to the understandings of gender and sexuality.

Pamela R. Lightsey (2015), a womanist queer theologian, makes connections between race, slavery and sexuality. Pointing out that black bodies have been spoken about rather than to she notes the constructions of sexuality that have been placed upon them. In her work she sets out a healthy view of sex and black bodies and includes within this the sexuality of LGBTIQ+ folk aiming to show that God is alive in all forms of sexuality. She does not look at black churches through a rosy glow; she is aware that they have not always recognised heterosexism and homophobia as forms of oppression, and it is this that she wishes to transform. Focussing on the creation story she comments that God never simply made one form of human or insisted that only one type of human was acceptable, what comes through the story is how we inhabit the earth. Lightsey argues that relationality and loving kindness not genitals and how we express ourselves sexually is the most important. For black women too grasping and holding on to the Imago Dei is of ultimate importance since their bodies have borne the brunt of hatred and oppression over centuries. This has for many led to a self-deprecation and lack of self-love perhaps doubled if that body is queer and black. Lightsey calls for queer black women to love their bodies in the raw since God stood back from creation and saw it was good. She calls for churches to honour all forms of human love.

Europe

Montse Escribano-Carcel from Spain addresses the tension between religion as 'sacred canopy', which provides order and normativity, and religion as 'prophetic critique' as a transgressive force has always been at the heart of Christian theological endeavours. Sex happens every day. Yet, sexual activity is not simply a biological imperative, as the evolutionary theorists have made foundational to their understanding of human life, but also one of the most culturally regulated aspects of life there is. It is within this tension between the scientific understanding of sexuality as integral to life and the historicist understanding that culture in large part determines what even counts as sex that we can see the beginnings of recurring confusions between normalcy, normativity and transgression in thinking about sex. The fact that neither science nor religion can be abstracted from their contexts and reified as a coherent framework for normative positions is a crucial starting point for thinking through theological options for transgressivity.

In recent years, moreover, some LGBTQ+ voices have started to wonder if norms and normalcy are all bad, after all. Hardly an advocate of the status quo, Janet Jakobsen published some musings on norms, noting that feminists have shied away from reflections on norms, 'because they are frequently read as constituting prescriptive codes of action' (Jakobsen, 1997: 120). Generally sympathetic to this critique, and somewhat sceptical of the need for norms, she nevertheless refuses to let go of the question, 'do norms have any role to play in lesbian and feminist ethics?' (Jakobsen, 1997: 120). She turns to the work of philosopher Seyla Benhabib as an example of a feminist attempt to reclaim norms for ethical reflection. Benhabib advances a commonly heard argument that norms are necessary to sustain critique of unjust societies. Through her close reading of Benhabib's argument that norms mediate critique and community, Jakobsen finds that Benhabib slips back into the imperialist mode of constructing a 'we' of Western rationality that allows for discussion and debate over against 'other' communities that are united through the non-rational forces of ethnicity or religion (Jakobsen, 1997: 120–126). Jakobsen proposes as her solution the replacement of normative frameworks with norm-making networks, an active, relational understanding of norm-making, rather than norm-accepting (Jakobsen, 1997: 136). This active, relational work of making norms avoids the imposition of rigid rules on complex lives but still holds out the possibility of setting parameters by which one can judge the injustice of a situation.

Renato Lings was born in Denmark and lived for many years in Spain. He works on biblical translation and claims that much has been lost in translation when it comes to how LGBTIQ+ people were understood and how the churches should approach the issues of sexuality and gender.

Working for many years as a translator it was natural that his theological work would involve examining how the texts in the Bible have been translated over many centuries and in many languages. His seminal work '*Love Lost in Translation*' (2013) is an extensive examination of these issues in which he applies linguistic and literary criteria to the task of translation.

He reexamines texts that have been used against homosexuals and convincingly shows how due to mistranslation from Greek to Latin and then to multiple languages that serious errors in translation occurred early and continue to occur today. The book examines passages usually thought to condemn homosexuality such as Sodom and Gomorrah, Judges 19, Romans 1:26–27 and 1 Corinthians. His analysis demonstrates the psychological insights and spiritual depth of the bible and shows how open to different interpretations the texts are. For example, Lings shows how the Jewish interpretation of the Sodom story is nothing to do with sexuality at all but rather to do with hospitality or indeed lack of it. Hospitality being of the utmost importance in the biblical world. He argues that a problem arises in understanding this text as it has been linked to the so-called prohibition of homosexuality in Leviticus 18:22. So-called as he points out that the passage may be understood as ambiguous. He demonstrates how English translators have added words to the Hebrew to make it flow in English, these words are 'as' and 'with'. Without them the rather straightforward 'thou shalt not lie with a man as with a woman' becomes something quite different and difficult to understand; hence, the English translators attempt to make it easier. It would read directly from the Hebrew as 'and with a male you shall not lie down a wife's bed or with a male you shall not lie down the lyings of a woman' (2013: 2005–2006). Lings, the translator, notes that there is nothing wrong with using a hypothesis when attempting to translate a difficult passage. However, as this is a biblical text this hypothesis has been understood as absolute truth, and so the wording has not been examined leading to a prohibition and indeed exclusion of a group of people when it may not have meant that at all. Lings points out that actually what is being condemned is equally opaque but never questioned.

Deryn Guest from the University of Birmingham works in the field of biblical hermeneutics and has shed light on issues to do with same sex love in the bible. She applies gender theory, queer theory and psychological theory to her work of interpretation. Her work examines texts through the lenses of queer theory and she gives particular mention to transgender understandings. She is anxious to show how biblical texts do not have strict gender codes in the way that many contemporary readers believe them to have.

In *When Deborah met Jael (2005)* Guest defines what she considers to be elements in lesbian reading of scripture. She evaluates strategies that have been used for lesbian readings and considers if any are useful moving forward. In addition she also examines the label lesbian and considers what, if anything, might be thought of as lesbian sensibilities. She does not overlook the social situation of many lesbians which is bound to affect the way in which they read texts. She is alive to the social, economic and religious othering of lesbians and hopes to provide a method by which lesbians may read with empowerment. This of course means reading from experience and thereby ensuring that all lesbians regardless of social, political and economic circumstances may have a voice. She alerts us to the fact that a hermeneutic of suspicion looks different under a lesbian gaze and she gives tools for achieving this. Given the history of biblical readings and the comments about lesbians that have sprung from them, Guest also examines the knotty question of biblical authority.

In the work *Transgender, Intersex and Biblical Interpretation (2016)* which Guest wrote with Teresa J. Hornsby the authors call for 'trans literacy' which they believe to be necessary if the violence towards trans folk is to be reduced and halted. They show how translation is everything, and they highlight how biblical translation has tended towards making heterosexuality and a two-gender system not simply normal but in fact divinely ordained. Through their own work they show how this is indeed a bias and one that under their skilful interpretation does not hold up in terms of various biblical passages. They claim that the Bible always treated sex and gender as fluid and dynamic categories. They are clear why this book was necessary and of course as mentioned it is hoped that violence will decrease with further understanding. However, they also mention how homosexuality has in some ways become more acceptable as it copies heterosexuality and in this way trans folk are othered even further, they are the queer bodies that do not fit.

Guest takes us on a trans reading of Genesis via the abyss or the deep of Genesis 1:1–3. Her aim she says is to make it difficult for non-critical readers to use the text against trans folk. In her hands we delve into the fluidity suggested by the text, a fluidity with no boundaries. This tehom, as the Hebrew may be translated, is also very disturbing; it troubles the waters. For Guest this is exactly what it should do (2016: 23). For her the chaotic does not simply test boundaries but actually dissolves them and at the same time allows us to think about the harmful implications of what she calls boundary anxiety. Of course when applied to matters of gender and sexuality we see how her textual analysis opens the way not simply for different readings but for different ways of life in terms of how we embrace others rather than discard them. As we will see in the final chapter of this book Catherine Keller examines tehom and chaos in order to give us a wider sense of who we are and the multiplicity of embodiment.

For Further Discussion

1   What is your opinion of Stuart's suggestion that the Christian Eucharist erases identity? Is this helpful for queer folk?

2   To what degree is Cornwall correct that queer identities often remain within the heterosexual matrix?

3   In what way do you understand Cordova and Goh's contention that polyamory is at the heart of the Trinity and should it be at the heart of a Christian life?

4   What might it mean to say that God comes out in the person of Jesus and in your life?

5   In what ways do you understand the connection between race and sexuality?

6   How might trans and intersex biblical interpretation help the churches?

References

Campos, Michael S (2012). "The Bakla: Gendered Religious Performance in Filipino Cultural Spaces." In: *Queer Religion: Homosexuality in Modern Religious History*, edited by Donald L Boisvert and Jay Emerson Johnson. Santa Barbara, CA: Praeger, pp. 167–192.

Cheng, Patrick S (2012). *From Sin to Amazing Grace: Discovering the Queer Christ*. New York, NY: Seabury Press.

Cheng, Patrick S (2013). *Rainbow Theology: Bridging Race, Sexuality and Spirit*. New York, NY: Seabury Press.

Cordova Quero, Hugo and Joseph Goh (2018). "More than a Menage a Trois. Friendship, Polyamory and the Doctrine of the Trinity." In: *Contemporary Theological Approaches to Sexuality*, edited by Lisa Isherwood and Dirk Von Der Horst. London: Routledge, pp. 289–312.

Cornwall, Susannah (2009). "Apophais and Ambiguity: The Unknowingness of Transgender." In: *Trans/Formations*, edited by Lisa Isherwood and Marcella Althaus. Reid. London: SCM Press, pp. 13–40.

Guest, Deryn (2005). *When Deborah Met Jael. Lesbian Biblical Hermeneutics*. London: SCM Press.

Heyward, Carter (1982). *The Redemption of God*. Lanham, MD: University of America Press.

Hornsby, J Teresa and Deryn Guest (2016). *Transgender, Intersex and Biblical Interpretation*. Atlanta, GA: SBL Press.

Isherwood, Lisa (2023). "Worshiping the Queer Jesus." In: *Queering Christian Worship: Reconstructing Liturgical Theology*, edited by Bryan Cones, Sharon R Fennema, W Scoot Haldeman and Stephen Burns. New York, NY: Seabury Press.

Isherwood, Lisa and Marcella Althaus Reid (editors) (2004). *The Sexual Theologian: Essays on Sex, God and Politics*. London: T&T Clark.

Isherwood, Lisa and Marcella Althaus Reid (editors) (2009). *Trans/Formations*. London: SCM Press.

Jakobsen, J. (1997). Working alliances and the politics of difference: Diversity and feminist ethics. Indiana University Press.

Jordan, Mark D (2007). "God's Body." In: *Queer Theology: Rethinking the Western Body*, edited by Gerard Loughlin. Malden, MA: Blackwell, pp. 281–292.

Kwok, Pui-Lan (2007). "Asian and Asian American Churches." In: *Homosexuality and Religion: An Encyclopedia*, edited by Jeffrey S Siker. Westport, CT: Greenwood Press, pp. 59–62.

Lightsey, Pamela R (2015). *Our Lives Matter: A Womanist Queer Theology*. Eugene, OR: Pickwick Publications.

Lings, Renato (2013). *Love Lost in Translation: Homosexuality and the Bible*. Bloomington, MN: Trafford Publishers.

Mollenkott, Virginia (2001). *Omnigender: A Trans Religious Approach*. Cleveland, OH: Pilgrim Press.

Rambuss, Richard (1998). *Closet Devotions*. Durham, NC: Duke University Press.

Reay, Lewis (2009). "Toward a Transgender Theology: Que(e)rying the Eunuchs." In: *Trans/Formations*, edited by Lisa Isherwood and Marcella Althaus Reid. London: SCM Press, pp. 148–168.

Shore-Goss, Robert (2018). "Queer Incarnational Bedfellows: Christian Theology and BDSM Practices." In: *Contemporary Theological Approaches to Sexuality*, edited by Lisa Isherwood and Dirk Von Der Horst. London: Routledge, pp. 222–244.

Stuart, Elizabeth (2009). "The Priest at the Altar: The Eucharistic Erasure of Sex." In: *Trans/Formations*, edited by Lisa Isherwood and Marcella Althaus-Reid. London: SCM Press.

Treharne, Thomas (2002). *Poetry and Prose*. London: SPCK.

Further Reading

Cheng, Patrick S (2011). "The Rainbow Connection: Bridging Asian American and Queer Theologies." *Theology and Sexuality* 17, No. 3 (September): pp. 235–264.

Escribano-Carcel, Montserrat (2018). "Neurotheologies and Sexualities." In: *Contemporary Theological Approaches to Sexuality*, edited by Lisa Isherwood and Dirk Von Der Horst. London: Routledge, pp. 71–89.

Lacan, Jacques (2001). *Ecrits: A Selection*. London: Routledge.

Loughlin, Gerard (2004). "Sex After Natural Law." In: *The Sexual Theologian: Essays on Sex, God and Politics*, edited by Marcella Althaus-Reid and Lisa Isherwood. London: T&T Clark, pp. 86–98.

Puar, Jasbir K (2007). *Terrorist Assemblages: Homonationalism in Queer Times*. Durham, NC: Duke University Press.

Shore-Goss, Robert (1993). *Jesus Acted Up: A Gay and Lesbian Manifesto*. San Francisco, CA: Harper San Francisco.

15

Peripatetic Roads: Queer Theologies and Migratory Processes

Religions and spiritualities undergo a dynamic evolution as they accompany individuals and communities in diaspora. How does a religious or spiritual expression navigate its evolution within novel cultural and societal contexts? Does linguistic adaptation influence this process? Moreover, how do adherents engage in the adaptation, negotiation and cultivation of their faith in unfamiliar territories in relation to their gender and sexuality? These questions prompt an exploration of the multifaceted ways in which religious traditions interact with and transform within diverse diasporic landscapes. Through the examination of migratory process, we aim to shed light on this burgeoning phenomenon of our era, offering insights into the intricate interplay between gender and sexuality and religious identity, cultural adaptation and societal change.

Towards the Promised Land?

Migration is a crucial phenomenon for understanding the movement of people and products within the modern world-system. Terms referring to migration are common in our daily lives. *Migration* refers to the displacement of people, which can be transitory or permanent, voluntary or forced (Arango, 1985; Micolta León, 2005). In the latter case, we speak of exile, i.e., taking refuge in another place due to political, ideological, religious, gender, sexual orientation reasons, also known as sexile (Guzmán, 1997), among others. These different types of displacement occur at the national or international level. On a daily basis, these terms confront us with real stories of people who leave their place of origin and also with state policies that enable, restrict or deny the possibility of in/migration (Sutcliff, 1998). Roberto S. Aruj (2008) summarises it this way:

> The migratory decision, then, would be based on a complex combination of internal and external factors; among the most significant external factors, we highlight the following:
>
> 1) Lack of alternatives for occupational attainment.
> 2) Social uncertainty about the economic future.
> 3) General insecurity in the face of growing violence.
> 4) Unsatisfied basic needs.

Global Queer Theologies: Intercontextual and Interreligious Perspectives, First Edition. Lisa Isherwood and Hugo Córdova Quero.

Among the internal factors we highlight:

1) Frustration in life expectations.
2) Frustration in personal fulfilment.
3) Generational mandate linked to the community of the family migratory chain.
4) Access to information about options abroad.
5) Conviction of the impossibility of ethical-value fulfilment in the society of origin (2008: 98–99).

Migrations are complex and never easy as they involve a series of multiple and sometimes dissimilar situations. However, the question always remains: Why does someone migrate? There are several explanations, although, contrary to popular belief, migration is not only the result of a personal decision. On the contrary, they also include a set of factors, social, historical, geographical, cultural and legal, that are ideologically constructed and depend on political will and economic fluctuations that transcend the power of the individuals in/migrating. In the words of Saskia Sassen:

> Migrations do not just happen; they are produced. And migrations do not involve any possible combination of countries: they are shaped. Moreover, the employment of immigrants is also shaped; immigrants rarely have the same labor and industrial distribution as citizens in the receiving countries (1998: 56).

Although there is a point at which people make the decision to immigrate, this decision cannot be carried out without a framework to support it. In other words, if there are no legal and political decisions already made in the receiving country, economic and social factors that allow the migration to take place, for example, the funds to purchase tickets and favourable consideration for receiving the im/migrants, the movement cannot occur or will be affected negatively. In addition, im/migrants who successfully arrive at their destination still have to face the reality of the host country. Very often, upon arrival at their destination, in/migrants discover that they are 'declassed' to be incorporated into that new society. That is, they experience a downward social mobility whereby, for example, a person who practised medicine in their country of origin may end up cleaning floors and toilets in the host country.

Migration and Religion

When we review the history of religions we discover that almost all of them are connected to migration. Their expansion throughout the world is due, in most cases, to the in/migration of their followers (Córdova Quero & Shoji, 2014). At the same time, religion plays an important role in modern societies, for example Christianity in the Western world, Islam in West Asia and North Africa, or Buddhism and Hinduism in Asian countries, among other examples. This is particularly visible when connected to migration experiences. For example, in the process of adapting to the new society, the role of faith communities has been remarkable in offering support, facilitating various integrative forms of belonging and establishing networks for the protection of the rights of in/migrants. This is an experience shared by almost all in/migrants in the contemporary world. Charles Hirschman notes that in/migrants tend to be more religious in the host society:

> Customary religious practices, such as attending weekly services, lighting candles, burning incense in front of a family altar, and reciting prayers, are examples of communal and family rituals that were brought from the old country to the new. However, these activities often take on new meanings after migration. The normal sense of loss experienced by immigrants means that familiar religious rituals learned in childhood, such as listening to prayers in the mother tongue, provide an emotional connection, especially when shared with others. These feelings are heightened from time to time by the death of a family member or some other tragedy. (...) beliefs and related [rituals] have stronger roots after immigration than before (2004: 1211).

Faith and gender are intricately intertwined with the cultural and social context of migrants' places of origin. Both are deeply entrenched in cultural frameworks, shaping individuals' identities and experiences. To practice faith or affirm gender identity is inherently bound to this cultural milieu. As elucidated by Hirschman (2004), faith practices are profoundly influenced by cultural settings, underscoring the inseparable relationship between belief systems and cultural norms. Therefore, understanding the intersection of faith and gender within migrant communities necessitates a comprehensive appreciation of the cultural backgrounds from which these practices emerge and evolve:

> Immigrants, (...) have spiritual needs, which are most meaningful when packaged in a familiar linguistic and cultural context. In particular, immigrants are drawn to the ethnic church and temple community, where primary relationships among congregants are reinforced by traditional foods and customs. Immigrants also have many economic and social needs, and (...) churches, temples and synagogues have a long tradition of service to the community, especially directed to those most in need of assistance. The combination of spiritual comfort and material assistance in a culturally attuned manner increases the attraction of new immigrants to church membership and participation (...) (Hirschman, 2004: 1207–1208).

This underscores the essential role of social networks in facilitating the adaptation and survival of migrants in their new societal contexts. The cohesion of these networks relies on the intersection of culture, language, ethnicity and gender. As observed by Melville Jean Herskovitz (1948), these elements form the bedrock of migrant communities, fostering solidarity and support systems crucial for navigating the challenges of integration and belonging in unfamiliar environments:

> Culture is essentially a construct that describes the total body of beliefs, behaviors, knowledge, sanctions, values and objectives that mark people's way of life (...) In the final analysis it comprises the things people have, the things people do and what they think (1948: 625).

Culture accompanies migrants on their journey, remaining integral to their identity and resilience in the receiving country. As Tanner (1997: 25–29) shows, culture is not discarded or replaceable, rather, it remains a fundamental aspect of migrants' lives, essential for their survival and adaptation in new environments. This recognition underscores the significance of preserving cultural heritage and traditions amidst the challenges of migration, as they serve as anchors of familiarity and belonging in unfamiliar territories.

Migration and Gender

Typically, when considering migration, our focus gravitates towards legal frameworks, often associating migrants with male identities, given their prominence in visible sectors such as construction, landscaping, restoration and cleaning. Historically, scholarly analyses of immigration have revolved around the archetype of the 'male immigrant', with female immigrants and their children seldom integrated into discussions except within the context of family reunification. This tendency to prioritise male perspectives has persisted for years, overshadowing the nuanced experiences of female migrants and their families in migration studies.

However, since the 1980s–1990s the situation started to change. The complex and diverse realities of migrations led some scholars to pay attention to the issues pertaining to 'gender' (Harzig, 2001; Lee, 1996). In fact, many scholars began to seriously consider that, in the words of Pierrette Hondagneu-Sotelo, '... gender permeates a variety of practices, identities, and institutions implicated in immigration' (2003: 9). Although the struggles of in/migrant women most often related to sustaining their homes in the country of origin they were not very visible in the twentieth century, but in the second decade of the twenty-first century it is almost impossible to keep track of every piece published. These works fill the gap in theories of migration which usually do not take gender as a key aspect of their theoretical frameworks (Oishi, 2002).

It should be noted that the jobs migrant women secure in their host countries often come with exploitative elements, including sexual connotations such as the sexual harassment of foreign domestic workers by local employers. This dynamic highlights the systemic disadvantages in/migrant women face compared to their male counterparts. In her book *Engendering Forced Migration*, Doreen Indra argues that in most migration and ethnic studies, gender is frequently treated as a peripheral issue rather than as a primary lens for analysis (2004: 4). She further emphasises that gender should not be conflated with 'women' but understood as a 'key relational' concept (Indra, 2004: 2). Drawing on Michel Foucault's theories of power relations (1990) and evolving approaches to gender, Indra concludes that '(...) there is a growing consensus that cultural, race, class, ethnic, national, and sexual orientation differences between women and men should matter more' (2004: 8).

In essence, gender serves as a unifying framework for analysing the daily realities of migrants and immigrants. Gender emerges as a pivotal factor, particularly evident in labour market dynamics and wage disparities. It underscores distinctions between national and migrant women, as well as national and migrant men. Moreover, gender influences various aspects of labour markets, including differential integration systems, racial and ethnic hierarchies and social expectations shaped by cis-heteronormative labour divisions. When examined through the lens of gender studies within migration and ethnic studies, these intersections reveal a complex yet essential terrain for exploration. When we refer to 'immigration and gender', we delve into how displacement dynamics affect both women and men concurrently, albeit potentially in different ways. For a specific focus on women's migration experiences, the term 'female immigration' accurately delineates that particular case.

Migration and Sexuality

In migration studies, the assumption often prevails that immigrants primarily adhere to heterosexual norms. However, the presence of queer immigrants not only disrupts conventional understandings of gender and sexuality but also unveils the disparate impacts of migration policies on them. The term 'queer immigrants' encompasses a broad spectrum of individuals, each navigating unique circumstances, including gays, lesbians, bisexuals, transgender and intersex persons, among others. Each label corresponds to distinct challenges within migration policy frameworks. Transgender and intersex individuals, in particular, grapple with the most severe repercussions of both internal and transnational migrations, as migration is an inherently embodied process. Originally derogatory, the term 'queer' has been reclaimed since the 1990s as an act of resistance, countering traditional cis-heteropatriarchal norms (Jagose, 1996). Queer theory underscores the multiplicity and fluidity of gender identities, reflecting the diverse realities encountered by individuals and communities in our constantly evolving global landscape, encompassing facets of sexual orientation, embodiment, self-identification and identity politics.

Although queer individuals can migrate when having the appropriate documentation for many of them the 'uncertainty' of being able to stay in the host country remains. Failing to renew the proper visa, unemployment, economic status and the like are situations that could change immigrants' situations overnight. Furthermore, while countries with long experience of immigrations have 'family reunion' programmes to bring heterosexual families together, queer couples or families often live separately because of visa-related issues. All these situations may be a cause for the lack of commitment or the stability of some relationships as well as the painful experience of separation from and longing for beloved ones. Gay and lesbian individuals are banned from entering some countries, and in other countries this ban was lifted only recently such as the United States in 1990 (Luihéid, 2005). The reality is that the set of rights traditionally entitled to marriage are not extended to non-legally recognised queer couples.

The plight of queer immigrants has been exacerbated by the climate of fear engendered by the 'war on terrorism', leading to heightened surveillance and restricted immigration avenues, particularly affecting transgender and intersex individuals. In the aftermath of 9/11, the landscape for transgender and intersex immigrants has drastically shifted, especially when discrepancies arise between their outward gender presentation and the information on their passports. This disparity exacerbates the challenges faced by transgender and intersex immigrants, highlighting the urgent need for inclusive and equitable immigration policies:

> Even without discrimination as a result of bias on the part of the immigration officer, it may be that the specific criteria for immigration will present barriers for trans people. Barriers may result in part from the effect of the sex/gender distinction, and the male/female, man/woman dichotomies.... The post-9/11 climate of fear of terrorism, and increasingly rigid identity-fraud procedures, combined with suspicion and discrimination resulting from inconsistencies in a trans person's presentation and their birth certificate and/or passport, may result in difficulties for trans people wanting to immigrate (Seuffert, 2009: 444–445).

The assorted experiences of transgender and intersex individuals may remain occluded in daily life, although being invisible crumbles when queer migrants' passports are requested at customs or at immigration detention centres. For example, Avery Edison was detained in Canada in February 2014 over an issue of overstaying a visa. Despite the fact that she was listed as female in her passport, she was sent to a male correctional facility in Milton, Ontario, because she '(...) has male genitalia' (CBC News, 2014). Not many countries have 'gender identity laws' in order to honour the displayed gender of transgender and intersex individuals. These types of laws basically give the right for individuals to obtain birth certificates and IDs that would match their displayed gender. The following countries have these type of laws: 'South Africa, Japan, Turkey, Belgium, Finland, Germany, Italy, Netherlands, Portugal, Romania, Spain, Sweden, United Kingdom, Mexico, Panama, Uruguay, Canada (most provinces), the United States, Australia and New Zealand' (Global Commission on HIV and the Law, 2012: 52–53), Argentina and India. Concurrently, countries that culturally and sometimes legally recognise a 'third sex' include Australia, India, Nepal, New Zealand, Pakistan, Thailand, Oman, Indonesia, the Philippines, Ethiopia, Kenya, Democratic Republic of Congo, Mexico and Germany.

Even when they do exist in one country by being territorially based these laws may not be recognised as such in another country. In many cases, queer immigrants are able to seek asylum due to persecution in the home country. Many of these individuals fall under the category 'sexile', coined by Puerto Rican sociologist Manuel Guzman, who defines it as '(...) the exile of those who have had to leave their nations of origin on account of their sexual orientation' (1997: 227, note 2). Sexiles pursue a new start in the host country through relinquishing the situation they left behind.

Religious Dynamics in Migration: Unpacking Gender and Sexuality

Religious narratives are deeply intertwined with cultural and social paradigms, exerting profound influence on perceptions of gender, bodies and sexuality. Within immigrant communities, religious institutions can serve as both pillars of support and sources of challenge regarding gender and sexuality dynamics. Immigrants navigate the intersection of host society gender norms and those dictated by their religious affiliations, often adhering to the latter. While this alignment may be advantageous in certain contexts, it can also perpetuate hetero-patriarchal norms, potentially restricting gender and sexual expression.

Moreover, individuals may not always recognise the cultural mediation through which religion and gender intersect. Religious beliefs frequently validate and perpetuate prevailing cultural constructions of gender, reinforcing societal norms surrounding sexuality. Consequently, immigrant experiences are shaped by the interplay of religious teachings, cultural expectations and host society dynamics, influencing how gender and sexuality are perceived, negotiated and practised within these communities. Understanding these complexities is essential for developing nuanced approaches to addressing gender and sexual diversity within immigrant populations while respecting religious beliefs and cultural identities.

Contemporary understandings of gender roles, the cis-heterosexual division of labour and norms surrounding decency and morality are products of complex social, historical and cultural processes. These constructs evolve over time within specific societal contexts and are heavily influenced by dominant religious teachings. For instance, in societies where a particular religion holds hegemonic sway, its doctrines inevitably shape prevailing gender norms. While Christianity has historically exerted significant influence in Western societies, similar dynamics exist in regions dominated by other faiths such as Confucianism in China, Hinduism in India, Buddhism in Japan and Islam in the Middle East, among others. Notably, the contemporary concept of the cis-heterosexual monogamous nuclear family prevalent in the West owes its origins to the teachings of the Protestant Reformation (Nussbaum, 1997). This underscores the profound impact of religious doctrines on shaping societal structures and norms, including those related to gender and family dynamics.

Understanding these intersections is crucial for comprehending the complexities of gender dynamics and family structures across diverse cultural and religious contexts.

Moreover, religious doctrines have historically reinforced hetero-patriarchal structures by portraying the Divine in masculine terms, a paradigm challenged by the emergence of Feminist Theology (Radford Ruether, 1993; Schüssler Fiorenza, 1994). The entrenchment of hetero-patriarchalism within cultural and religious frameworks (Hirschman, 2004) underscores the complex interplay between migration, religion, gender and sexuality. Migration experiences often serve as arenas for resistance, renegotiation and reconstruction of traditional gender roles and norms within host societies. As globalisation accelerates transnational and transcultural interactions through migration, religious institutions play pivotal roles in individuals' lives, families and communities. Consequently, it is imperative to scrutinise the various roles assumed by religious organisations in migrant contexts. In the subsequent analysis, we will examine three key roles played by religious institutions in shaping the experiences and identities of transnational migrants.

First, religious organisations often offer '(…) newcomers a space where their language is spoken, their culture reproduced and their situations understood' (Córdova Quero, 2008). These organisations provide immigrants with a familiar linguistic and cultural milieu, offering a sense of belonging and understanding in an otherwise unfamiliar environment. For migrants who have recently departed their homeland, leaving behind familiar customs, kinship networks and social ties, religious communities offer invaluable social and emotional support. They mitigate feelings of disorientation, loneliness and estrangement in a foreign land by fostering connections and facilitating the process of assimilation into the diaspora community. Through religious practices and communal rituals, migrants find comfort, camaraderie and a semblance of home in their newfound surroundings. As such, religious organisations play a pivotal role in easing the transition for immigrants, providing a sense of continuity and stability amidst the uncertainties of migration.

Second, religious institutions serve as crucial conduits for immigrants to connect with wider social networks, extending beyond the confines of their immediate community. These organisations, encompassing physical spaces and congregational communities, act as bridges to facilitate interactions with broader societal structures such as city- or town-level international programmes, legal services, counselling and healthcare facilities. Such linkages represent pivotal steps in the acculturation process for immigrants, enabling them to navigate the complexities of life in the host country more effectively. Providing these connections necessitates religious organisations to navigate multifaceted legal, cultural, societal and group dynamics to adequately support immigrants in their adaptation journey. Moreover, some of these initiatives may be spearheaded by immigrants themselves, who discover newfound purpose and agency in their post-migration lives. By serving as gateways to essential services and resources, religious institutions play an indispensable role in empowering immigrants and facilitating their integration into the host society.

Third, religious communities play a crucial role in nurturing the faith of immigrants by attending to their inner and existential dimensions, thereby sustaining their spiritual well-being. While religious organisations initially serve as vital hubs for newcomers to connect with fellow co-nationals and expatriates upon arrival, they transition into enduring focal points for immigrants even after they have adjusted and settled into the host society. These communities serve as anchors for immigrants' spiritual lives, providing spaces to impart religious values and rituals to their children and to perpetuate cultural traditions linked to their homeland. Thus, religious institutions serve as more than mere places of worship; they become integral to immigrants' ongoing religious practices and cultural heritage preservation. By providing a sense of continuity and connection to their roots, religious communities offer immigrants a source of solace and identity in their new environment, facilitating a sense of belonging and continuity across generations.

Cis-heterosexual Immigrants Connecting with Religion(s)

Will Herberg, Hirschmann (2004) has pointed out that immigrants tend to become more religious in the host society, a statement endorsed by Glenda Tibe Bonifacio and Vivienne SM. Angeles:

> Migration (...) is a continuing process that intersects with the ways in which we view the world as shaped by our belief systems and our place in it. Often when immigrants are faced with a hostile environment and myriad challenges of settlement, religion fosters the building of social networks and sense of community belonging (2010: 1).

Notwithstanding, religion could also become a place which reinforces the gender-role expectations and the cis-heterosexual division of labour of either the home country, the host country or both simultaneously.

Thus, religious discourses in general tend to conflate migration, gender and sexuality within the hetero-patriarchal framework. This statement reflects how many parents who attend the Roman Catholic Church consider faith to be an important factor in their lives and in the lives of their families while enforcing within their religious expectations not only the cultural elements of their faith but also the notion of the nuclear family.

On the other hand, it is important to note that sermons and bulletins ignore that there are cultures which support polygamy as the 'natural' family construction. Those 'other' family constructions are required to fight for their right to co-exist in contexts where the 'heterosexual monogamous nuclear family' is hegemonic. If in the immigrants' home countries this is 'normal', when they migrate, they face conflict with the Western notion of 'heterosexual nuclear monogamous family'. Immigrants, who carry these notions along with other cultural and social behaviours learned in their home country, confront censorship in the host country. The same is true of individuals from matrilineal societies or societies where the cis-heterosexual division of labour differs from the prevalent in the West, as for example the Mosuo people in China.

Notwithstanding, the intersection among migration, religion, gender and sexuality does not always imply negative views, and sometimes it could take unexpected turns.

Queer Immigrants Connecting with Religion(s)

Being queer and at the same time a person of faith is not easy. Many queer immigrants view religions with suspicious eyes. In fact, many have even been hurt by the discourse or the attitudes of a religious organisation. It is even puzzling for some queer immigrants to understand a fellow queer immigrant who would like to be part of an organisation that rejects queer individuals.

Traditionally, Christianity in the West has not welcomed queer individuals, although a shift has been notable since the 1960s; however, many organisations still remain unwelcoming. If this is true for nationals, it is truer for queer immigrants and their descendants.

To talk about sexuality from a religious point of view entails interrogating how gender-role expectations, the cis-heterosexual division of labour, the formation of couples and families, the concept of marriage and the performativity of affection, intimacy and eroticism are produced within the context of each culture and often determined by hetero-patriarchal hegemonic religious discourses. On the other hand, migration further challenges religions to re-think those issues within the global context by (re)considering how diversity and transnational movements additionally complicate those elements in the life of queer immigrants. This is a task that many theologians are starting to address.

Religion, gender and sexuality are important lens for an emerging and necessary area in the study of migration. Immigrants embody and live out gender, sexuality and religious experiences in different and meaningful ways. For immigrants, their religious experiences do not constitute 'extra baggage' in the migration process. On the contrary, religious experiences give meaning, sustain and condition their lives in the host society. Every religion adds abounding aspects that diversify even more the composite of migrations experiences.

This chapter sought to provide glimpses at the complex issues underlying the manifold experiences of heterosexual and queer immigrants. Particularly, females and males whether heterosexual, gay, lesbian, bisexual, transgender, intersex and the like bring lavishly diversity to the study of migrations, a richness that is often missed when the intersection of migration, gender and sexuality is absent. Future research would benefit from examining how families and couples which do not confine to the 'heterosexual monogamous nuclear family' such as polygamous, polyamorous, as well as diverse sexual practices and communities such as swingers, bears, S/M, divergently relate to the migration experiences.

As an emerging area in the study of migrations, the importance of gender, sexuality and religion as lenses of analysis challenge us to explore new terrains. In the second decade of the twenty-first century it is more and more crucial to pay attention to this challenge.

For Further Discussion

1   According to the authors studied, what internal and external factors influence the decision to migrate?

2   How do faith communities support immigrants in adapting to new societies, and why do religious practices often become more significant for immigrants after migration?

3   How has the historical focus on male immigrants overshadowed the experiences of female migrants, and how has the study of gender and sexuality changed in migration research?

4   How do religious discourses and practices among immigrants reinforce traditional gender roles and hetero-patriarchal frameworks, and what challenges do immigrants from non-heteronormative or polygamous cultures face in host societies?

5   How do queer immigrants navigate their religious experiences within the context of migration, particularly when faced with religious organisations that may reject or marginalise their identities?

References

Arango, Joaquín (1985). "Las leyes de las migraciones de E. G. Ravenstein, cien años después." *REIS—Revista Española de Investigaciones Sociales* 32: pp. 7–26.

Aruj, Roberto S (2008). "Causas, consecuencias, efectos e impacto de las migraciones en Latinoamérica." *Papeles de Población* 14, No. 55: pp. 95–116.

Bonifacio, Glenda T and Vivienne S M Angeles (2010). "Introduction." In: *Gender, Religion and Migration: Pathways of Integration*, edited by Glenda Tibe Bonifacio and Vivienne S M Angeles. Lanham, MD: Lexington Books, pp. 1–16.

CBC News (2014). "Transgender Woman Avery Edison to Fly Home After Stay in Ontario Jails: Avery Edison Moved to Facility for Women After Public Outcry." *CBC News* [Toronto], February 12. Available at: <http://www.cbc.ca/news/canada/toronto/transgender-woman-avery-edison-to-fly-home-after-stay-in-ontario-jails-1.2534743>.

Cordova-Quero, Hugo (2008). "The Role of Religion in the Process of Adaptation of Brazilians of Japanese Ancestry To Japanese Society: The Case of the Roman Catholic Church." In: *Sociedade Japonesa e Migrantes Brasieros: Novos Camninhos na Formacaode uma Rede de Pesquisadores*, edited by Chiyoko Mito. Hugo Corova Queroa, Aaron Litvin and Sumiko Haino, Tokyo: Center for Lusophone Studies, Sophia University, pp. 79–90.

Córdova Quero, Hugo and Rafael Shoji (2014). "Introduction: On Transnational Faiths and Their Faithfuls." In: *Transnational Faiths: Latin-American Immigrants and Their Religions in Japan*, edited by Hugo Córdova Quero and Rafael Shoji. Aldershot: Ashgate, pp. 1–31.

Foucault, Michell (1990). *The History of Sexuality, Volume 1*. London: Allen Lane.

Global Commission on HIV and the Law (2012). *Risks, Rights, and Health*. New York, NY: United Nations Development Program.

Guzmán, Manuel (1997). "'Pa' La Escuelita con Mucho Cuida'o y por la Orillita': A Journey through the Contested Terrains of the Nation and Sexual Orientation." In: *Puerto Rican Jam: Rethinking Colonialism and Nationalism*, edited by Frances Negron-Muntaner and Ramón Grosfoguel. Minneapolis, MN: University of Minnesota Press, pp. 209–228.

Harzig, Christiane (2001). "Women Migrants as Global and Local Agents: New Research Strategies on Gender and Migration." In: *Women, Gender and Labour Migration. Historical and Global Perspectives*, edited by Pamela Sharpe. London: Routledge, pp. 15–28.

Herskovitz, Melville J (1948). *Man and His Works: The Science of Cultural Anthropology*. New York, NY: Alfred A. Knopf.

Hirschman, Charles (2004). "The Role of Religion in the Origins and Adaptations of Immigrant Groups." *The International Migration Review* 38: pp. 1206–1233.

Hondagneu-Sotelo, Pierrette (2003). "Gender and immigration: A retrospective and introduction." In: *Gender and U.S. Immigration: Contemporary Trends*, edited by Pierrette Hondagneu-Sotelo. Berkeley, CA: University of California Press, pp. 3–19.

Indra, Doreen (2004). "Not a Room of One's Own." In: *Engendering Forced Migration: Theory and Practice*, edited by Doreen Indra. New York: Berghahn Books, pp. 1–22.

Jagose, Annamarie (1996). *Queer Theory: An Introduction*. Washington Square, NY: New York University Press.

Lee, Sharon M (1996). "Issues in Research on Women, International Migration and Labor." *Asian and Pacific Migration Journal* 5, No. 1: pp. 5–26.

Luihéid, Eithne (2005). "Introduction: Queering Migration and Citizenship." In: *Queer Migrations: Sexuality, U.S. Citizenship, and Border Crossings*, edited by Eithne Luihéid and Lionel Cantú Jr. Minneapolis, MN: University of Minnesota Press, pp. ix–xlvi.

Micolta León, Amparo (2005). "Teorías y conceptos asociados al estudio de las migraciones internacionales." *Trabajo Social* 7: pp. 59–76.

Nussbaum, Martha. C. (1997). "Constructing love, desire and care." In: *Sex, Preference and Family: Essays on Law and Nature*, edited by David M Estlund and Martha Nussbaum. Oxford: Oxford University Press, pp. 17–43.

Oishi, Nana (2002). "Gender and Migration: An Integrative Approach." CCIS Working paper No. 49. San Diego, CA: Center for Comparative Immigration Studies/University of California-San Diego.

Radford Ruether, Rosemary (1993). *Sexism and God-Talk: Toward a Feminist Theology*. Boston, MA: Beacon Press.

Sassen, Saskia (1998). *Globalization and its Discontents: Essays on the New Mobility of People and Money*. New York, NY: The New Press.

Schüssler Fiorenza, Elizabeth (1994). *In Memory of Her: A Feminist Theological Reconstruction of Christian Origins*. New York, NY: Crossroads.

Seuffert, Nan (2009). "Reflections on Trangender Immigration." *Griffith Law Review* 18, No. 2: pp. 428–452.

Sutcliffe, Bob (1998). *Nacido en otra parte: Un ensayo sobre la migración internacional, el desarrollo y la equidad*. Bilbao: Hegoa.

Tanner, Kathryn (1997). *Theories of Culture: A New Agenda for Theology*. Minneapolis, MN: Fortress Press.

16

Queerly Cosmic

We consider this the next step in the queer dance. Therefore, this chapter will ground the analysis in all human and non-human beings and the whole universe. All religions embrace a standpoint related to the cosmos. How does this translate into our daily lives in a globalised, diversified world like the one we are moving into in the third decade of the twenty-first century? How does this new perspective give space and new concepts to theologians who wish to expand queer theologies? For example, this cosmic vista demonstrates how diversity and repetition with transgressions at each repetition is the nature of the cosmos. It is the basis of life itself.[1]

Queerly Cosmic

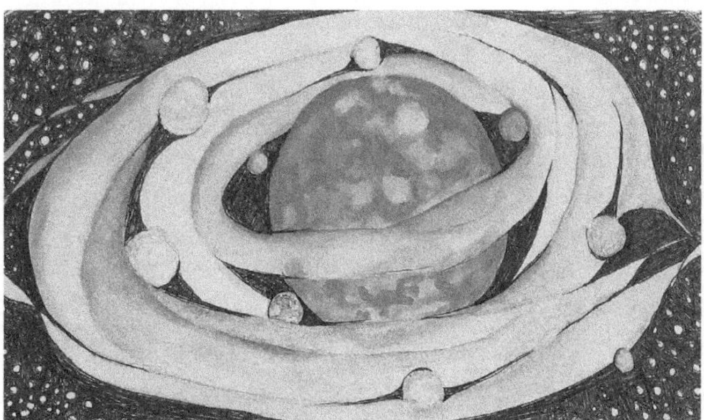

Source: Megan Clay.

---

1 Images in this chapter are by Dr. Megan Clay, University of Wales, Trinity St David.

Global Queer Theologies: Intercontextual and Interreligious Perspectives, First Edition. Lisa Isherwood and Hugo Córdova Quero.
© 2026 John Wiley & Sons Ltd. Published 2026 by John Wiley & Sons Ltd.

<table><tr><td>

Box 16.1

</td></tr><tr><td>

Cosmology brings together the natural sciences to examine how the universe works. In itself it does not deal with questions to do with god.

</td></tr></table>

It may seem quite strange to move into the cosmos to deal with queer theologies but it can be demonstrated that this is the most logical step for theologies that speak of multiplicity. It needs to be made explicit at the beginning however that by making this move there is no regression to dualistic metaphysics and otherworld theology. Quite the contrary, what is suggested in this chapter is enfleshment and embeddedness in a vast array of multiplicity. The cosmos is after all our home, we are made of the very stuff of the universe and so we may argue that our flesh is by nature multiple and transgressive as the cosmos itself is. Perhaps the biggest challenge in this chapter is the suggestion that the creative divine, that is the energy with which we are all born, is the very essence of the cosmos itself. This is the way in which all life, including our own came into being. This is of course a large shift away from a divine being who sits apart from even the cosmos itself directing all events in heaven and earth. We do need to remember that this view within theology is a very late invention in the history of religions and for centuries the divine was understood to be more embedded in all that lives. There is also a challenge to the notion that God is male once again this is not how centuries of people understood the divine and religious stories are full of the creative power of women as well as men. Further, of course the divine was understood as multiple as many different incarnations of the divine energy.

Most creation stories acknowledge that creation came from darkness, or nothing as Christianity prefers, perhaps wrongly, to call it. Today scientists call it dark matter. In the darkness creativity waited as the energy of the universe took its course. Our foremothers told a powerful story about how in this darkness the galaxies came to birth. They spoke of Eurynome, the goddess of chaos, who lived in the darkness of the uninterrupted night. She was lonely and to ease her solitude and pass the time, she danced. Her dance created a following wind and this wind impregnated her and she, the great goddess of chaos, gave birth to all that is. Light flowed from her as she filled the darkness with stars. The cosmos danced and all came into being through these mystical movements composed of darkness. So unlike the Christian story chaos did not need to be subdued but rather her creativity is understood as powerful and creative.

Source: Megan Clay.

One star, Tiamat, is particularly important to us as it is from her atoms that our bodies are created. In her fiery womb she knit the wonder that we are. With the violent collapse of stars there is an interesting twist called the supernova as not everything gets collapsed into the nothingness. The outside edges which contain carbon, oxygen and nitrogen get released from the gravitational pull of the dying star and journey out into the night sky and are eventually drawn together in other elements. Under their own attraction they form other stars, planets or life forms. Our birth required dramatic disruption of a well-ordered system, but as she died Tiamat's creativity went out into the future unfolding of the universe, she let loose tungsten, copper, magnesium, rhodium, silver, silicone and started our adventure. In her story we witness a burst of glory and a dangerous and joyful release of power (Swimme & Berry, 1992: 61). She had forged within her calcium which one day would support hummingbirds on our earth and phosphorus which would enable photosynthesis to appear. She invented the cosmic novelties of carbon and nitrogen which would one day sparkle as life, as consciousness that would be laced into our genetic coding. Her story is one of the majestic intensification of the journey of the universe. Tiamat is named after the Babylonian goddess whose dismembered body formed the earth and the skies, whose body became the source of all that is.

The cosmology of most contemporary Christian theology is based on the archaic world of a three-tiered universe with earth as the central point and humans as the pinnacle of creation, God and heaven are 'up' and everything is neatly in its place without much disturbance, let alone chaos. This is out of step with what we now know about the universe and also with the essential purpose of theology which is to orientate believers to their place, relationships and meaning within the world. The first step has to be to bring God down and amongst creation, and the larger theological task is to challenge and unpack centuries of dualistic thinking. A God who is distant, abstract and dividing the world through dualistic understandings has been no friend to queer folk, women and creation itself. Indeed, the authors would like to suggest that this image of God is precisely what has created such difficult situations for queer folk who are not made in the image of this abstract being.

It has to be acknowledged that Christian theology has moved a long way in the last 200 years, and while challenging the existence of God was once largely the task of atheists this has now moved within the theological realm itself. To be more precise some theologians are questioning the notion of a mono-God. Interestingly, this questioning comes more from ethical concerns than from metaphysical doubts. Marcella Althaus-Reid (2003) was amongst the first to point out that the power of the Mono-God has quite significant impact on how we arrange the world. The 'One' white, male, straight, disembodied God easily relegates to secondary, and below, those who do not mirror him. We see the attempt at disembodiment within Christianity initially in the martyr cults where death was the answer, followed by extreme aestheticism and latterly by doctrines that encourage the view that our reality does not lie in our flesh but in our soul. It is easy to see how the Mono-God, the white, straight male has contributed to a sexist, racist and homophobic set of societies down the ages. This then is a dangerous model and one not in keeping with the world we inhabit, created by the divine itself.

Further, Christian monotheism also exerts a devastating hold over human desire viewing it as the cause of sin and the downfall of the human race. It was the woman who desired knowledge that led to the downfall and her more fleshy/earthy existence that still leads to misdirected desire. Christian desire is still understood to be something that should only find true satisfaction in God and so should be controlled in order to desire things in this life that are seen to be pleasing to that one God. We will always be uneasy, unfulfilled until we are in God, which of course can only happen after death and not in this world which is holding us slave to false desire. Human desire is dangerous therefore as it may indeed not always be so directed and so controlled. This approach has, according to Heyward (1989), disempowered us as humans and made us impotent since we are afraid to harness the power of desire in service of the world for fear of doing it wrong. Heyward refers to Keller who says 'The divine is always becoming flesh what else does Eros desire?' (1986: 250) and this is the basis of Heyward's theology and Keller's search for intercarnational possibilities. It could also be added that it has made us slaves within our own skins as we have doubt and uncertainty placed at the heart of what actually makes us human, that is the capacity to desire and in that way reach out to others and the world. It is this attitude amongst others that queer theology has attempted to address and correct since it is queer desire that has been used by the churches to oppress and even kill queers. By speaking of desire in theological terms theologians have opened the way to move from damnation to celebration within bodies. Bodies that one may argue are formed from the desire of an emerging cosmos.

Returning to monotheism, Althaus-Reid (2003) gives illuminating examples of how the mono-relational pattern works. Firstly the hetero-Christ even defines sexual relations that are not cis-heterosexual, the gay man is seen as effeminate and the lesbian as either butch or femme. These are heteronormative categories that prohibit naming the diverse range of sexual identities that are actually operational within people's lives. Cis-heteronormativity stabilises categories and colonises experience in order to keep some control, if only through ostracising what is deemed not to fit. We have seen this in action in recent years when some churches have been open to gay people attending. However, we have noticed that the 'straighter' the gay person or couple then the more accepting the churches seem to be. We doubt that a leather couple in full regalia or a dominatrix let alone people into puppy play, with the puppy on a leash, would be welcome in even the most accepting church. That form of diversity would not be welcome in churches other than Metropolitan Community Churches (MCC).

The second example Althaus Reid gives is of how mono-relations lead to economic oppression. Using the colonisation of Africa as an example, she points out that the relationship under one [mono] heavenly Father could never be equal—that divine father was not flexible enough. The exclusion of 'otherness' meant that needs and desires of the other do not enter the equation and exploitation not only steps in but is understood as the natural order of things. As we have already seen in an earlier chapter Althaus-Reid argued that her development of the Bi-Christ dismantles the mono-relations of naming, organising, exploiting and owning that underpin economic, racial and sexual exclusions and the worlds this leads to. For Marcella the Bi-Christ, a figure who is not bi in the sense of sexual preference but rather in terms of thought and life, is one who is fluid and full of contradictions and therefore enables the destabilisation which she saw as crucial. The Bi-Christ allows other ways to think and it is queer because in examining real lives, categories will just not do, boxes are just too small and all kinds of crossing over becomes necessary in order to grasp something of the reality we experience within and between us. It has to be noted that in terms of the complexity of the cosmos that birthed us even a bi ideology is not flexible enough - for theology it was seen as too far.

Lesbian theologian Laurel Schneider (2007) examines the mono model closely concluding that it is also incompatible with an incarnational religion. Schneider believes that within the logic of the 'One' there can be no room for multiplicity or even diversity. For her the choice is clear: do we settle for the world of categories and abstractions that the 'One' presents us with or do we embrace what she calls the multiplicity which is the diverse nature of embodiment. An embodiment that refuses categories as bodies do not tend to come as one rigid category with one set of identity marks and ways of being in the world—this is just not how the cosmos birthed human beings. Schneider points out that a fundamental goal of love and peace cannot be satisfied under the regime of the 'One'.

In accordance with other feminist theologians she suggests that love needs another; it cannot be without encounter and it cannot be ethical unless it recognises the presence of others as they are. Heyward spoke powerfully of this saying that it was the desire to love and be loved that drew the divine from the heavens and into relation through incarnation. She says that God, the source of all that is, moaned and yearned, laboured and rejoiced, she held the earth tenderly in her arms and yearned for relationship, knowing that what is good is shared she embraced the earth and from this yearning humanity was born (1984: 49–50). No mention here of creating in her own image but rather a free-flowing love and tenderness, a desire for relationship with all that comes from her desire. Although she wrote many years before, perhaps Heyward anticipated the move in theology known as quantum or cosmotheology since the movement of the divine within the early stirrings of the universe does not set patterns but rather explodes with energy and possibility. The explosion of multiplicity is the very nature of things.

Heyward would say that it was God's desire to love and be loved that brought about this outpouring, and it is the continued desire that means the divine will never retreat to the heavens and the place of Absolute Oneness, in such a move all relation is lost, all possibility of loving and being loved. While Heyward and others refer to God in this move towards relationality we know that scientists also acknowledge that relationality is central to the unfolding of all that lives and even to the continuation of all that lives. Different language, yes of course, but shared ideas that theology does need to embrace.

For Schneider this way of seeing things signals a notion of the divine so based in love that it is willing to show up and fully risk, nothing less will do (2007: 206), it is this and this alone that changes things. Schneider speaks plainly when she says, 'to follow God who became flesh is to make room for more than One it is a posture of openness to the world as it comes to us, of loving the discordant, plentipotential worlds more than the desire to over-come, to colonise or even to 'same' them' (2007: 207) Schneider is not alone in her desire to derail the 'One'.

Maaike de Haardt (2010) from the Netherlands is amongst those that argue monotheism itself is the root cause of many of our ways of thinking and being and as such is a threat to our global relationality. There is no space for development only repetition and the spread of one ideology, so de Haardt argues that it is the singularity of the creator and creation that has set in place very destructive mono-thinking in the Western world. We become locked into what she sees as a unilateral relationality where the power is all on one side and does not reside in us as subjects. For de Haardt this is clearly demonstrated in the story of the sacrifice of Isaac which has become foundational for western culture through the Judeo-Christian heritage.

It is a story that in itself is damaging enough in terms of societal underpinnings but when we realise that it is still within theology referred to as prefiguring the 'ultimate' sacrifice of Christ we begin to understand where de Haardt's objections lie. For her the core problem is this unconditional absolute obedience to God as the only authentic way to express faith which sets in place a psychology of abuse. A psychology that does not question the hierarchy of obedience and suffering, one that can live with the historical and contemporary abuse and rejection of queer people in church and society and encourages the self-doubt and shame that many queer youth suffer as they grow. The hierarchy of obedience to and suffering for that is inherent in Christianity has been pointed out many times in the history of feminist theology but as already stated has not always led to questioning the ethical implications of continuing with monotheism itself.

What has been more usual when addressing the issue of monotheism has been the notion of co-creation and co-creativity within a process model of the relation between the divine and humans. However, for de Haardt this also falls short as it is she claims a largely male-centred model which fails to move from the inherent problems of a mono-generativity. She believes there remains an unequal notion at the heart of even the process model that leads to at least a devaluing of the female and we would add queers and at worst a system that actually takes for granted that hierarchy and therefore service and suffering are inevitable.

It is in the work of Catherine Keller that de Haardt sees some way ahead from the mono-generativity of Western monotheism through an engagement with the Deep or the multiplicity of difference in relation that God is thought to be. However de Haardt still remains uncomfortable as she feels even these theologies that she admires are attempting to find models that fit at the same time as attempting to overcome models that have dominance and power at their heart. It is here that she makes her main point, which is that perhaps we need new practices that change the still dominant imperialistic abusive unilateral relations, language and reality under which we live. Practices because she is not sure to what extent ideas, concepts and theologies impact on social reality, but of course she acknowledges that they do. The challenge to monotheism that she offers is to a way of living that stems from deeply rooted notions that are so deep that they have largely been forgotten but still impact on the way society and international relations and economics are shaped. Of course Christians will reflect and think, but it seems then that for de Haardt the way ahead is to 'live' ourselves to a new space a new shape of being that challenges the violence to women, queers, children and the planet of mono-thinking, and offers more relational ways of being together in all our diversity.

Box 16.2

Monotheism

Monotheism is a set of beliefs that just allows the worship of one God. It is the system in Christianity, Islam and Judaism. In terms of the development of world religions monotheism came late to the party and is as noted not held to be the case by all religions.

Mayra Rivera (2015) brings a postcolonial understanding to the question of the One God when she demonstrates how the dominant imperial theology of the West has never acknowledged anything beyond itself, as indeed according to Schneider and others it cannot. While using the disembodied nature of the 'One' God to set in place the Western masculinist symbolic, it at the same time stops the world, both physical and symbolic, at its own narrow vistas. Rivera of course is also aware that falling into the untouchable, vertical transcendence that usually follows on is no place to go for those who sit beyond the vista of the western mind, those who have not been seen or acknowledged as inhabiting land and ways of life that fall beyond. It is precisely because of this that she sees the need for a form of transcendent theology that breaks down the western stranglehold.

For Rivera there is nothing abstract about transcendence as in the hands of the powerful it even controls the creation of time and our spatial perceptions. Her argument is that Western industrialism needed to move beyond the rhythms of natural time and impose a universal time in order to maximise the profits it wished to extract and to disconnect people from their land and their natural ways of being. This also separated the public and private sphere with the private time being seen as feminised and trivial while public time was of the greatest importance, the masculinised time of uninhibited production and detached transcendence (Rivera 2015: 8). She argues that horizontal transcendence has divided space itself with what is north as being understood as closer to God, while the south is nearer the depths of stagnation and even depravity. She believes that such overarching systems of knowledge produce rather than discover all-encompassing foundations, they create the illusion of totality and suppress anything that is at odds or as Rivera sees it anything that is beyond. They create a tightly bounded world view.

It is this view of the world she wishes to challenge and she states her hope in 'the ineffable affinity that links all creatures in open relations of mutual transformation which may help us to envision the beyond in the world without losing sight of the transcending character of all creation. This world is indeed more than it appears, calling us to apophatic alertness. God, the creatures and even we exceed all our representations' (Rivera 2015: 38). While Rivera does not directly address gender and sexuality we can see how her criticism of monotheism and her insistence that all creatures exceed all representations lends itself to an embrace of the reality of all living beings, including humans, once again without expectation of conformity. Rivera is happy to declare that the profane no longer exists but, contrary to how this has been understood, it is not an elimination of transcendence but rather a refusal to understand it as identifying God with the status quo.

Transcendence is understood to be in history, because if we see God as external, then the liberation claim that salvation lies in a re-making of history, undoing injustice and replacing it with inclusive and just systems in the here and now, is a false hope and an empty theology. It is the possibilities lying in the living of history in the material body that allows for the great hope of humankind, things may happen that have never happened before, 'newness is not just discovered as being already present in nature, nor is it externally imposed upon reality. Genuinely new things come into existence from the actualisation of possibilities through collective choice' (Rivera 2015: 43). Rivera claims that this notion of historical transcendence is dynamic, allowing for contextual structural difference without implying dualism, and for intrinsic unity without strict identity categories imposed. Her work is extremely important for queer theology embracing as it does postcolonial understandings and holding out the hope for a new way of living, for the remaking of history and the inclusion of all that inhabit the planet.

Kristeva sums the situation up well when she said: 'One betrays ones naiveté if one considers our modern societies to be simply patrilinear...or capitalist...monopolist and ignores the fact that they are at the same time governed by monotheism' (1974: 22). Can queer theologians remain that naïve or must we shift this concept of monotheism which seems so essential to Christianity without abandoning the core of faith? What can be the next steps in the queer theological journey?

The central theological task to engage with if God is to come down from 'up there' is to re-think how Christians have understood the person of Jesus and the event called incarnation. For an earth facing/cosmological understanding and the creative chaos and plurality this involves it is best to start with incarnation telling us that our bodies are our homes, that is to say our divine/human dwelling places. Therefore our journey is home, to the fullness of our incarnation pitched as it is in diverse bodies both human and non-human. This is no individualistic 'pitching' but rather the multiple sites draw our attention to each of them as we need to engage with the ruptures that this multiplicity by its existence creates in what we otherwise have thought of as mono-reality or monotheism. Our attention is drawn, since this multiplicity is what we understand as the divine within and around us, to the places of our becoming. We are drawn into the conversation that is the way of our discursive matter, but we are drawn to listen intently not simply to speak and certainly not to hear dictation from beyond corporeality. Incarnation allows for the questioning of who 'I/we' are, its free-flowing desire makes it difficult to speak of edges and ultimate 'me-ness', we are entangled. The work of Catherine Keller points further towards the queering of incarnation. While Keller herself does not deal with queer theology, her work proposes a larger vista with implications for queer bodies and Christian queer theology.

Catherine Keller (2003) introduces us to cosmic beginnings, to void and chaos, and we are asked to make our theology from that ground, that is, to understand who we are and who we might be from *tohu vabohu*, the depth veiled in darkness. Keller's use of beginnings here is important because beginnings are always relative, contested and historical, whereas origins are absolute and power-laden. The absolute and the power it bestows are two concepts that have contributed to the narrow theology we now encounter in all areas of life and love. However, beginnings give theologians the chance to decolonize the space of origins in creation and the inevitable creator who sits apart. They allow us to challenge, as Keller, puts it 'the great supernatural surge of father power, a world appearing zap out of the void and mankind ruling the world in our manly creator's image' (2003: 6).

Once we give agency to void and chaos there can be no creation out of nothing as our power-laden dualistic origin. Creation ceases to be a unilateral act, and the divine speech in the pages of Genesis is no longer understood as a command uttered by the Lord and warrior King who rules over creation. On the contrary, as Keller tells us, 'let there be' is a whisper of desire, and what comes forth emanates from all there is, rather than appearing from above and beyond. In this shift we also see the possibility for incarnation to be understood as the rule of creation rather than its exception because the whisper desires enfleshment. This moves us so far from the once and for all incarnation of the Son of God who has in history dictated that perfection is white, male, straight—despite the fact that Jesus was certainly not white and possibly not straight!

Keller enables us to move from a bounded and narrow monotheism through an investigation of the Deep, which is the very ground of who we are but has no fixed identity relying on the One. It is a Deep situated in the cosmos itself that gives the lie to *creatio ex nihilio* and opens before us the God who is of intimate/infinite entanglements. This is the God who is the 'all in all' of First Corinthians, not beyond, not distant, but entangled. Keller visits Paul's writings in First Corinthians on the body of Christ, noting the use of *energeia* in 12:4–6 when Paul describes human differences but asserts it is the same God who is in all. For Keller this disables any theology of distance and separation: God is not above, nor is the divine simply androcentric. Rather the scripture itself declares God to be eco-centric, 'all in all'.

Energy then is not something we have but something we are, and it is the same energy that gives life to all. It is the stuff of entanglement. Keller writes, 'feeling the pulsations of our bodies in our planet and the pulsations of the planet in its universe our earthly interactions are rendered simultaneously intimate and virtually infinite' (2012: 13). This is the energy of incarnation which comes from the free flow of these energies uninhibited by repression, exploitation and denial. Just as Heyward accused theology of making us less than we are by dampening and denying desire within us, so Keller suggests that exploitation and denial of entanglement blocks energy, which leads to depression and lack of meaning. As Keller puts it, 'God in heaven who we create without a body to do work for us and who in the name of religion represses the rhythms of the human body and pulsations of desire' (2012: 15) leaves us adrift. We would argue it is this God without a real body that we find represented in theology, doctrine and on altars. The God who dictates how real bodies may conduct themselves, and it is this God that needs to be replaced by the diverse incarnational realities in which we live, which we enflesh.

Importantly, Keller argues the cosmos did not emerge from Platonic forms but rather from tehomic chaos. There was no set-in-stone blueprint but rather a glorious outpourings of surprise and novelty. This unformed future is made up of repetition but from very early in cosmic development, this repetition always adds something new. In every repetition is a transgression: Our bodies and that of the cosmos are in constant flux and as they regenerate they change. They are then in essence transgressive, so our earthly home is a place where stable identities and categories cannot find an eternal home. Keller allows us to take a large step forward in terms of destabilising notions of identity while remaining within God's creation, namely the cosmos. The very ground beneath our feet and the universe above are ever changing, this is the nature of things, the divine nature of things. Therefore, to fix identity through rules and regulations, notions of sin and so forth are against the very nature of the divine itself. Keller certainly moves us significantly from creation out of nothing to a place where the divine is grounded in the ever-changing chaos at the heart of the cosmos.

So questioning the harm the 'One' God has done and continues to do in the lives of queer people and indeed the planet has crystallised the core of the issue for the future of queer theology—what to do with the ultimate edge, the end point, the unchanging all powerful God within a form of theology that is always moving beyond, expanding, displacing and unsettling? Schneider is quite clear that we have to get rid of 'monotheistic eschatologies that fantasise the end of all difference in the truth of God' (2007: 12). And she is quite right we cannot fantasise or have the end of all difference, all transgression, if for no other reason than this is the very nature of the ground that made us and forms part of our bodies, the cosmos itself. It seems that if we wish to move from queering theology to having a truly queer theology then tackling the mono divine in our traditions is the next step and surprisingly moving in the direction of the new cosmologies appears to enable some of that task. It has been a way of destabilising the mono-God with the mono-ethics, identities and world views that go with it which have caused so much harm to people and the planet, yet not actually writing the divine out of the picture.

A further issue that enters theology when we view it through a cosmic vista is that of how we view time and space. Rivera alerted us to how time was used to industrialise the world and set time boundaries and exclude the movements of nature. However, this linear notion of time has also influenced eschatology and thus theology that speaks of ultimate ends and recipes for climbing the ladder to that end in a successful manner. While there is a theology of the afterlife this is still in a rather linear manner and theology speaks of the end of time in an alarming way. Embracing the natural cycles of nature removes us from this tight linear pattern that is quite false in terms of the cosmos from which we emanate and also changes the theological world. Perhaps we can stop thinking in terms of individual salvation and the right and wrongs that accompany such a view and understand our lives as part of a bigger whole and one that connects through time and space with others before and after us, human and non-human. There is then no end of time but rather a continuous cycle. No doubt such a view would make us understand nature in a different way, but it may also allow us to think more expansively in terms of human nature.

If we are to take incarnation seriously then we have to lessen our grip on absolute monotheism and give space for bodies and lives to be narrative realities in the creation of theologies. We must allow ourselves to be more uncertain than we have ever been in Christian theology, to embrace creative chaos as the very ground of our being; it is here that the movement of the divine lies in the change and challenge that incarnation embodies. The language used for the divine is now much wider and deeper than we perhaps ever thought; yet, it is rooted in bodies here and now. These bodies are also more inclusive than we ever imagined, queer bodies most certainly but let us not make the mistake of making narrow boundaries even when we speak of queer. The entanglement we are encouraged to experience is with human bodies, non-human bodies and the body of the cosmos itself, to feel the life energy in all and to be open to the endless possibilities such an engagement offers.

For Further Discussion

1 Does Christianity require a God who is 'up there'? How does this sit with an incarnate religion?

2 Is monotheism essential for Christianity? What are the implications of this in terms of sexuality, gender and race?

3 What are the implications for queer folk of engaging with Keller's theology?

4 How important is it that Christian theology embraces contemporary understandings of cosmology?

5 In your understanding how might horizontal transcendence help the development of a more inclusive and expansive theology?

References

Althaus Reid, Marcella (2003). *The Queer God*. London: Routledge.

De Haardt, Maike (2010). "Monotheism as a Threat to Relationality." In: *Through us, with us, in us: Relational Theologies in the 21st Century*, edited by Lisa Isherwood and Elaine Bellchambers. London: SCM Press, pp. 181–196.

Heyward, Carter (1984). *Our Passion for Justice*. Cleveland, OH: Pilgrim Press.

Heyward, Carter (1989). *Touching Our Strength. The Erotic and the Love of God*. New York, NY: Harper Collins.

Keller, Catherine (1986). *From a Broken Web: Separation, Sexism and Self*. Boston, MA: Beacon Press.

Keller, Catherine (2003). *Face of the Deep: A Theology of Becoming*. London: Routledge.

Keller, Catherine (2012). "The Energy We Are: A Meditation in Seven Pulsations." In: *Cosmology, Ecology and the Energy of God*, edited by Donna Bowman and Clayton Crockett. New York, NY: Fordham University Press, pp. 11–25.

Kristeva, Julia (1974). *About Chinese Women*, translated by A. Barrows. New York, NY: Boyars.

Rivera, Mayra (2015). *Poetics of the Flesh*. Durham, NC: Duke University Press.

Schneider, Laurel (2007). *Beyond Monotheism: A Theology of Multiplicity*. New York, NY: Routledge.

Swimme, Brian and Thomas Berry (1992). *The Universe Story: From the Primordial Flaring Forth to the Ecozoic Era. A Celebration of the Unfolding of the Cosmos*. New York, NY: Harper Collins.

Further Reading

Alaimo, Stacey (2010). *Bodily Natures: Science, Environment and the Material Self*. Bloomington, IN: Indiana University Press.

Barad, Karen (2007). *Meeting the Universe Halfway: Quantum Physics and the Entanglement of Matter and Meaning*. Durham, NC: Duke University Press.

Roughgarden, Joan (2013). *Evolution's Rainbow: Diversity, Gender and Sexuality in Nature and People*. Berkeley, CA: University of California Press.

Index